Ma
Te

Hamburg

Liverpool
London
Southampton Rotterdam
Cherbourg Le Havre
•Paris

Queenstown

Genoa

Steamer Routes on the
NORTH ATLANTIC

Summer Tracks   Winter Tracks
- - - - - - - -   - - - - - - - -

D1465464

The Only Way to Cross

The Only

John Maxtone-Graham

Way to Cross

With a Foreword by Walter Lord

Patrick Stephens, Cambridge

ACKNOWLEDGMENTS

CHAPTER 3: Permission to use extracts from Frederick A. Hamilton's diary was given by A. W. H. Pearsall, Assistant Keeper of the Department of Manuscripts at the National Maritime Museum, Greenwich, England.

CHAPTER 4: Arthur J. Davis's remarks in the *Journal of the Royal Institute of British Architects* of 1922 are reprinted by kind permission of Mr. David Dean, librarian of the R. I. B. A.

CHAPTER 6: Two passages quoted are from *The Amateur Emigrant* by Robert Louis Stevenson, Charles Scribner's Sons, New York, 1913. The epigraph, as well as two excerpts, are taken from R. A. Fletcher's *Travelling Palaces*, Sir Isaac Pitman & Sons, London, 1913.

CHAPTER 7: New York Harbor's description is taken from Rupert Brooke's *Letters from America*, Charles Scribner's Sons, 1916. The quotation about the *Queen Mary*'s whistle is found on page 14 of *Here Is New York* by E. B. White, copyright 1949 by E. B. White, Harper & Brothers, 1949. The excerpt of Christopher Morley's is reprinted with the kind permission of the editors of the *Saturday Review of Literature*, the issue of October 3, 1925. The extract about the *Berengaria*'s cabin comes from *Siegfried's Journey* by Siegfried Sassoon, published by the Viking Press, 1946.

CHAPTER 10: The quotation about the *Normandie* gala is from Edmond Lanier's *Compagnie Générale Transatlantique*, published by Plon, 1962. The final quotation in this chapter, as well as additional excerpts in Chapter 11, are reprinted from *I Love You, I Love You, I Love You* by Ludwig Bemelmans, copyright 1942 by Ludwig Bemelmans, copyright renewed 1970 by Mrs. Madeleine Bemelmans and Mrs. Barbara Bemelmans Marciane. Reprinted by permission of the Viking Press.

CHAPTER 11: The captain's diatribe comes from *The Wonder Book of Ships* by Harry Golding, editor, published by Ward Lock & Company. Harold Nicolson's letters are quoted with the kind permission of Nigel Nicolson.

CHAPTER 14: The passage about Gibbs' death is reprinted from *By Their Works Ye Shall Know Them* by Frank Braynard, published by Gibbs & Cox, 1968.

Originally published in the United States of America by The Macmillan Company, New York. First published in Great Britain in 1972 by Cassell & Company Ltd under the title *The North Atlantic Run*.

This edition published in 1983

ISBN 0-85059-672-6

Printed in Great Britain on 120 gsm Sicilian Bulky cartridge, and bound, by The Garden City Press, Letchworth, Herts, for the publishers, Patrick Stephens Limited, Bar Hill, Cambridge, CB3 8EL, England.

For Katrina,

FELLOW PASSENGER,

BELOVED SHIPMATE

Contents

Foreword

It's hard to believe they are gone. The piers are still there. The bon voyage baskets, piled high with impractical fruits and jellies, still line the shelves of the gourmet shops. In midtown Manhattan there's even a post card still for sale, showing the *Queen Elizabeth,* the *Mauretania,* a *Sylvania*-class Cunarder, the *America* and the *Independence* lying side by side at their berths, just as though they were sailing tomorrow.

But there is no tomorrow. Every one of these fine transatlantic liners —and nearly all the others too—have vanished from service. They are gone as completely as the dirigible, and almost as fast. If the river boats quietly faded away like a genteel lady in polite decline—if the railroads sagged into shameless decay like a Bowery bum—the Atlantic liner was taken from us like a good friend hit by a truck: swiftly, mercilessly and leaving a sudden emptiness that is only beginning to be felt.

It was the jet, of course, that did it. While plane travel steadily increased after World War II, ships continued to hold their own until the late 1950s. In fact, 1957 saw sea travel reach a new postwar peak, as 1,036,000 people sailed on some seventy steamers. In 1958 air passed sea for the first time, but the ships continued strong, with more than a dozen liners sailing from New York during a typical summer week.

Then, on October 26, 1958, the first American commercial jet took off for Paris, and a whole new era was born. With flight time cut from twelve to less than seven hours, the lure was irresistible. By 1960 the jets had seventy percent of the business, and by the end of the decade only four of every hundred travelers still went to Europe by sea. White elephants almost overnight, the great liners were quickly taken out of service, or shifted to the bland pursuit of cruising.

Perhaps it's better that way. At least the ocean traveler has been spared the pain of a slow decline. He will never feel the pang of the train buff, who must suffer through that long twilight of boarded-up stations, leaky plumbing, broken seats, peeling paint and lavatories awash with dirty towels and crumpled cups.

On the Atlantic liner the stewards' jackets were starched to the end, and all the memories are pleasant: the creaking woodwork . . . the noon whistle . . . the morning bouillon . . . the hum of the rigging . . ."Boots" . . . the clack of shuffleboard disks on the boat deck. Of course, there were less pleasing moments too—cramped cabins in tourist, an occasional lost appetite—but these details are magically erased by the euphoria of something so generally good, clean and happy.

Or so it would seem, if the current boom in ocean liner nostalgia is any measure. Finding the ships so suddenly gone, the public has turned to any reminder in sight. Deck chairs from the *Queen Mary* are selling for $97.50 apiece; a souvenir plate from the old *Cedric* recently brought $25; even post cards go for one or two dollars apiece. Items like baggage labels, menus and swizzle sticks—once regarded as mere throwaways—have achieved instant status as sacred relics.

And along with the memorabilia have come books. There have recently been several good ones, but of them all none recaptures the *feeling* of going by sea the way this book does. John Maxtone-Graham has a superb instinct for detail, encompassing not only the sights but the sounds and smells of ocean travel. Any Cunard passenger will recognize immediately that bouquet which Mr. Maxtone-Graham calls "an evocative blend of tea, flowers, floor wax and whatever stern British antiseptic had survived the war intact."

Not that his book is pure nostalgia. It is full of history, sometimes controversial, as it covers the great years of the ocean giants that dominated the Atlantic from the turn of the century till after World War II. Nothing could make more dramatic reading than the account here of the launching of the first *Mauretania,* or the heart-breaking fire that swept the *Normandie* in that dark year of 1942.

This is an extremely personal book—Mr. Maxtone-Graham has his own opinions, make no mistake about that—but there is not a dull moment in it. He is like that intriguing conversationalist one used to find in the smoke room late at night. Certainly he is never that other traditional character, the ship's bore, resplendent in plus-fours and snap-brim cap.

Enough. The whistle is blowing; the stewards are calling, "All visitors ashore"; and the sailing hour is at hand. Relax, enjoy the trip, and discover or rediscover the bracing delights of "the only way to cross."

WALTER LORD

Introduction

In September of 1819, a kinsman of mine, Thomas Graham, Lord Lyne-doch, took passage from Stockholm to St. Petersburg on an elegant American vessel called the *Savannah*. She had just crossed the Atlantic from her home port of the same name to Liverpool with empty cabins and holds. Lynedoch thus had the distinction of being the first passenger to board the first transatlantic steamer. He so admired the little steam frigate that he presented her captain with a silver teakettle, suitably inscribed.

Perhaps there is some connection between this bit of family history and my perpetual fascination with steamships. Of course, there are other reasons as well: I have a Scots father and an American mother and was raised and have roots on both sides of the Atlantic. I crossed it before I was a year old and a dozen times before I was ten. In the peculiar national twilight that is dual citizenship, my allegiance was divided between America and Great Britain, so much so that I have not been shaped by either culture exclusively. Rather, I share them quite happily. Transatlantic links of this kind are common enough, particularly between a nation of immigrants and the continent from which so many of them originated. Americans and Europeans have good reason for preoccupation with the ocean that both joins and divides them.

Steamers designed for the Atlantic service have always been the most ambitious in the world. They were floating superlatives—sumptuous interiors contained in record-breaking hulls. One of the problems faced by the historian is where to begin, where to interrupt the close sequential development, from one class, one company or one country to the next. To go back to the brave little *Savannah* and treat the major vessels that sailed in her wake makes for a compendium of ships, dates and facts that assumes bewildering proportions even prior to 1900. I have chosen to take up the story just after the turn of the century and continue to the present. The *Lusitania* and *Mauretania* of 1907 represented a significant tonnage increase as well as the initial application of steam turbines driving quadruple screws. Furthermore, beginning within our century puts the book in reach of living memory.

I may have neglected certain favorites. Passengers are notoriously partisan about ships they have enjoyed. However, my choices have usually been dictated either by a vessel's historical significance or the need for clarity. Then again, certain ships have a compelling appeal to which I have occasionally succumbed.

There are two passages in the book where some readers may suffer technological fatigue. Chapter 2 details the *Mauretania*'s construction, and the tragic demise of the *Normandie* occupies the bulk of Chapter 13. I have done my best to make the material palatable and sympathize with those perplexed by things mechanical. However, to ignore the functioning and vulnerability of these miraculous vessels is to tell only half their story: what gives the Atlantic express liner its unique flavor is the combination of dispatch and *de luxe,* the reassuring steel beneath those polished veneers.

Much material for this book has been assembled from firsthand accounts—either contemporary records or, whenever possible, interviews with participants. Captains, crew, shore staff, pilots and steamship enthusiasts have been overwhelmingly cooperative. Former passengers were also helpful but curiously divided: habitual Atlantic travelers tended to recall little of interest while those whose shipboard experience was limited to one or two voyages cherished the memory and were generally articulate on the most specific detail.

It seems axiomatic that an ailing industry turns its back on former glories. The regrettable decline of passenger revenues within recent decades, followed by consolidation and retrenchment to less spacious quarters, has meant the loss or destruction of company records. The French Line has happily retained its sense of history and numbers among its Paris staff M. René Bouvard, whose zeal as *propagandiste* combines with the dedication of an *archiviste*. But Cunard's vaults in London house only a fraction of the original Liverpool and Southampton accumulations.

Further erosion of sources has occurred outside the companies. The Hoboken Public Library in New Jersey stands on a quiet square only a stone's throw from piers that once accommodated the world's greatest liners. I arrived there too late, several years after thousands of photographs and clippings, for which no room remained, had been discarded. On the other side of the Atlantic, the great Channel and Baltic ports suffered cruelly during World War II. Large portions of Rotterdam, Hamburg, Plymouth, Le Havre, Cherbourg and Southampton were reduced to rubble. Also, in the rebuilding since 1945, the disappearance of historical environs has destroyed the intangible riches of harbor atmosphere.

Maritime museums both here and abroad have survived as repositories of documents, brochures, models, plans and memorabilia. One of the most ambitious, the South Street Seaport Museum, grows visibly here in Manhattan. In all these museums, sailing lore understandably predominates; obsolescence and extinction stimulate the urge to preserve. No such anxiety colors our attitude toward passenger steamers, thereby paralleling a curious phenomenon about our past in general: between the contemporary and the historical, there has always been a peculiar limbo of wrong distance, neither far enough away nor close enough. We tend to equate age with importance, revering the antique and neglecting the recent. It is still somewhat of a shock for the middle-aged to realize that 1920 was over a half a century ago, fifty years during which incalculable losses of source material have been sustained through lack of proper care.

Acknowledgments are very much in order. Above all, I am indebted to my wife, Katrina, for her patience and encouragement, as well as her understanding in allowing research and writing requirements to disrupt three successive summers. Writers with four children who work at home can do so only with the protective insulation that a sympathetic wife can provide; for this, I am eternally grateful.

Robert Markel, formerly editor-in-chief at Macmillan, must take credit for initiating the idea of this book. Subsequently, Adolf K. Placzek, Librarian of the Avery Architectural Library at Columbia University, deserves special thanks for vetting the final manuscript; his enthusiasm seemed never-ending. I am grateful to Mrs. Neville Thompson, Avery's Reference Librarian, for her courtesy in putting the Library's resources at my disposal. I should also acknowledge the invaluable contribution made by my mother, who crossed the Atlantic dozens of times before I was born and remembers extraordinarily well. Ann Novotny and Susan Hartung, partners in Research Reports here in New York, handled portions of the American research with their accustomed thoroughness.

I am further indebted to a host of maritime experts: Frank Braynard, author/collector *extraordinaire,* for abundant use of his clippings, photographs and memorabilia; Norman Morse, whose instant recall of North Atlantic deck plans made him an invaluable ally; Malcolm Dick, the naval architect with Gibbs & Cox who served so cheerfully as technical adviser; Walter Lord, for the use of his excellent library and the wisdom of his advice, to say nothing of his kindness in writing a foreword; Edward Kamuda and John Eaton of the Titanic Enthusiasts of America, for supplying details of the great White Star liners available nowhere else; the staffs of the Peabody Museum of Salem and the Steamship Historical Society of America; and Captain George Seeth of the Sandy Hook Pilots Association.

Research in Washington was made immeasurably more profitable by the kind assistance of Melvin Jackson, Curator of Marine Transportation at the Smithsonian Institution, Jerry Kearns of the Prints and Photographs Division of the Library of Congress and Mary Raitt, who pointed the way so helpfully in the stacks of the Library of Congress. Further south, in Newport News, I thank John Lochhead and his staff at The Mariners Museum as well as Robert Terrell of the Newport News Shipbuilding and Drydock Company.

In France, I am grateful to Edmond Lanier, head of the Compagnie Générale Transatlantique, Albert Brenet, who painted the cover for the U.S. edition, Georgette Mewès, for supplying valuable details about her father's life and Michel Eloy, of Le Havre's Porte Autonome, whose encyclopedic knowledge of French liners was enormously helpful.

Across the Channel, my activities centered around the excellent National Maritime Museum at Greenwich. Pat Hodgson's contribution in the way of research, as well as ferreting out British picture sources, proved invaluable. Maps and endpapers are the inspired work of an old friend, Peter J. L. Strachan. I am indebted to Lord Mancroft, formerly a director at Cunard, for putting the Company Archives at my disposal. Jack Pierce of Trinity House was immensely kind in supplying details of pilotage in Southampton Water.

Enshrined in glass at the United States Merchant Marine Academy at Kings Point on Long Island is an improbable-looking maritime prize called the Hales Trophy. On temporary loan from the United States Lines, this pretentious gilt and silver confection was the mid-thirties brainchild of a Member of Parliament for Sheffield called Henry Keates Hales; he had it made as a physical incarnation of the mythic Blue Ribband. Awarded belatedly to the *Rex* in June of 1935, the prize passed almost at once to the *Normandie*. When the *Queen Mary* took the record in 1936, Cunard refused the garish memento and it dropped from sight until the early fifties. The *United States*'s record-shattering crossing in July of 1952 ensures the near-permanent tenure of the Hales Trophy, like the America's Cup, on this side of the Atlantic; it seems unlikely that we shall ever relinquish it. In the jet age there is little impetus to build express liners that perpetuate the archaic competition.

As I complete this book, there is every indication that the airplane rather than the ship will shortly be the only way to cross. Liners still in service will presumably confine their activities to the Caribbean. Like so many other civilized delights, the elegance and enjoyment, the comfort and convenience of that legendary passenger service on the North Atlantic will pass into history.

Spring, 1972   JOHN MAXTONE-GRAHAM
New York City

Introduction to new edition

The Only Way to Cross was originally published over a decade ago and I am as delighted by its gratifying success as by the re-issue of this hardback edition in time to celebrate the book's eleventh birthday. The jacket's Ship Chart is a decade wider, incorporating the 'seventies now, re-drawn and updated beautifully by my friend and fellow-author, Bård Kolltveit.

The Only Way to Cross has changed my life dramatically. It was my first book and the fact that it flourished—strong-seller rather than best-seller—initiated a new career of writing and lecturing—largely about ships—all over the world, afloat and ashore. It gave me a hobby as well: generous readers sent souvenirs of their crossings and I count myself now amongst a host of collectors of ocean liner memorabilia.

The book was the first of a projected trilogy: the second, *Crossing to Cruising*, is in my typewriter now. It will explore the current passenger-ship boom, the transformation of liners into cruise ships, the reprieve of some Atlantic stalwarts as well as the launch of new vessels to meet the incredible and, it seems, insatiable demand for new cabin space.

In the process, new generations of passengers are becoming addicted to shipboard life, just as their grandparents and parents were, sparking a resurgent interest in the immortal Atlantic Ferry that started it all. Recently, I joined with a group of historians, collectors and enthusiasts to found an Ocean Liner Museum, the only one of its kind in the world devoted exclusively to ocean liners. It will be located, fittingly, in New York City, great western terminus of the Western Ocean.

June, 1983   JOHN MAXTONE-GRAHAM
New York City

If there was ever a kill or cure, it was a
Western Ocean mailboat in wintertime.

—CHARLES LIGHTOLLER,
THE TITANIC'S SECOND OFFICER

1.

Atlantic Overture

The North Atlantic is the most dangerous ocean in the world. It is also
the most heavily traveled; the sea lanes connecting Europe and North America carry more people and goods than all other oceans of the world combined.

The natural hazards to be met on this ocean defy invention and read
like a seasonal catalogue from hell. Hulls of all oceangoing vessels carry a
painted symbol called a load line, indicating permissible displacements for
various seasons and types of water. The lowest level bears the terse abbrevi-
ation "WNA"—Winter North Atlantic. No other ocean has this specific
billing.

In the spring, terminal fragments from the northern glaciers thunder into the sea and drift south as icebergs. For the summer and early fall, there is a jingle that warns of tropical hurricanes spawned in the Caribbean:

> July, stand by—
> August, you must—
> September, remember—
> October, all over.

Most of them don't get far north but those that do are remembered.

All year round, there is fog. The North Atlantic is famous for it. Off the Grand Banks, where the Labrador Current chills the vapor-laden air above the Gulf Stream, it is almost perpetual, an opaque mist that can shroud the sea for days on end. Ship captains hate it more than any other single danger they face.

So frightful was this Western Ocean that for hundreds of years, sailors never ventured onto it. There was no reason to do so and a very good reason not to: legend had it that the known world ended just over the horizon and any ship unfortunate enough to sail in that direction risked toppling into an abyss. The Vikings were the first to ignore this. Four centuries before Columbus, they reached the northern tip of Newfoundland, navigating with a remarkably accurate sun compass.

Well into the nineteenth century, fear of this most terrible of oceans persisted. By then, it was not only a superstition but a statistic: one out of six sailing packets, or coffin brigs, as they were called, failed to reach its destination. Passengers embarking for the New World quite simply risked their lives. In 1877, Katherine Ledoux published a slim volume called *Ocean Notes for Ladies*. Readers were advised to dress sensibly and respectably:

> Accidents, too, and loss of life are possible at sea, and I have always felt that a body washed ashore in good clothes, would receive more respect and kinder care than if dressed in those only fit for the rag bag.

The traditional bon voyage party that exists to the present had its origins in lugubrious pier-side gatherings when friends and relatives gathered on board to pay respects that might well prove their last. Mrs. Ledoux's recommended decorum for those affairs betrays her anxiety:

> Say aurevoir [*sic*] as cheerfully and as bravely as if you were only going for a short journey. Do not sadden others who are trying hard to be brave too. Leave yourself and them in God's hands, for he will be with you and them, though the trackless deep lies between.

THE ONLY WAY TO CROSS

"Going to sea," remarked Dr. Johnson, "is like going to prison with the chance of being drowned." Landfalls were particularly hazardous and the shores of both continents were littered with wrecks. Sailors christened the ocean the Graveyard of Ships.

But graveyard or no, the profits were enormous and trade grew. The earliest bulk passengers were slaves, the most profitable cargo in the ocean's history. It has been estimated that, in all, thirty million wretched blacks were carried from Africa in chains. Despite the care with which they were packed into the holds, a pitifully small proportion survived the crossing.

In the early eighteen hundreds, American sailing ships had a distinct edge over their European competitors. Not the least of their advantages was their adherence to fixed schedules. The term "liner" was used to describe a vessel that left port on a specific date and made directly for its destination. Elementary as this innovation may seem to us, it was the custom prior to that for mail, goods and passengers to wait until the holds were filled; a delay of several weeks was not uncommon.

Although the steam engine was a reality before the end of the eighteenth century, application of this new power to marine use was slow. An enterprising American, John Fitch, raised capital enough in 1787 to construct a steam-powered rowing mechanism that drove a boat on the Delaware at three knots. His investors were assured that it "would be the mode of crossing the Atlantic in time, for packets and armed vessels." He was only half right in his prediction: steam was the answer but the mechanical oar was not, and although he experimented briefly with a crude propeller, the wooden hulls of his time were better suited to a more ancient device, the paddle wheel.

A late Roman bas-relief from the sixth century A.D. shows a ship equipped with three paddle wheels, each driven by a pair of yoked oxen. What speed was produced by six ox-power is not recorded but a similar idea was used by Moses Rogers for powering an East River ferry in 1814; horses operated a treadmill that drove paddle wheels, complete with a patented gear that enabled the ferry to reverse without having the animals about-face. It was a huge success and its duplication on other American rivers earned more money for its inventor than he ever realized from his first love, steam.

Rogers was the first to take a steamboat to sea: in 1809, he had nursed the *Phoenix* from Hoboken to Philadelphia. She was a river steamer with a temperamental engine, fragile paddle wheels and a hull that could hardly be called seaworthy. So Rogers steamed cautiously, hugging the coast, and took two weeks to reach his destination. But he learned a great deal from the passage and eleven years and four ships later, he was in command of the *Savannah* which crossed, from its home port of the same name, to Liverpool in just under thirty days.

Marine historians, like baseball addicts, thrive on statistics. They have never fully agreed where credit belongs for the first steam crossing of the Atlantic, and division on this matter falls predictably along national lines. American claims for the *Savannah* are dismissed by the British who point out tartly that she was a mere auxiliary whose engines were in use for only ten percent of the time; they argue that their *Sirius* steamed for the first time, continuously, in 1838. However, she was equipped with sails too, and the fact that the American effort preceded the British by nearly two decades deserves more than passing acknowledgment. The *Savannah* was, in point of fact, a hybrid, launched as a sailing packet but with the addition of steam in mind. Holes were left in her decks and sides for the installation of engines and paddle-wheel shaft. As a result of damage sustained by paddlewheels at sea, those on the *Savannah* were made collapsible and could be shipped inboard during rough weather. The ninety horsepower engine delivered steam at a pressure of one pound per square inch, turning the shaft eighteen times a minute.

The crossing was without incident and a complete success, although the *Savannah* carried neither cargo nor passengers. She turned down more than one offer of help to put out the smoky fire that seemed to rage amid ships; off the south coast of Ireland, Rogers raced away from H.M. Revenue Cutter *Kite,* bent on unwanted assistance, confounding his pursuer by out-distancing him under bare poles. His entry into Liverpool was triumphant, but following the sensation, there were no offers for employment of the rev-olutionary craft. The *Savannah* was, in fact, years ahead of her time, and after a fruitless trip to Russia, she returned to America under sail, had her engines removed and ended her days as a sailing packet.

In 1833, the Canadian *Royal William* steamed eastbound from Halifax but, every day, had her engines stopped while scale was chipped from the boilers. Copper boilers, despite their superiority over iron ones, were still prey to salt accumulation, and it was Samuel Hall's invention of the first practical marine surface condensers the following year that opened the way for the *Sirius*. Originally designed as a steamer for the Irish service, she was small; too small, according to her mutinous crew, who had no confidence in the overloaded vessel or her engines. Yet despite a succession of headwinds, she cut a third off the *Savannah*'s time. Her forty passengers disembarked in New York, which sent her back to England after a week of giddy celebra-tion with a seventeen-gun salute.

Shortly thereafter, Samuel Cunard, one of the *Royal William*'s owners, crossed from his native Halifax in pursuit of a lucrative mail contract. The British Admiralty was concerned about American sailing superiority and had invited offers for a monthly steamship service between Liverpool and North America. Cunard's drive was such that he secured the contract, the ships and a maiden voyage all within the incredibly short space of sixteen months. Investors were impressed by his direct approach: "We have no tunnels to drive, no cuttings to make, no roadbeds to prepare. We need only build our ships and start them to work." His instructions to the Scottish yard that built his ships were equally blunt: "I want a plain and comfortable boat, not the least unnecessary expense for show." He got the first one, the *Britannia,* on schedule and it sailed for Halifax and Boston on Independence Day of 1840. Upon their arrival in America, the passengers presented Captain Woodruff with a large silver cup, a company relic that has a place of honor today in the *Queen Elizabeth 2*'s Columbia dining room.

The success of the British and North American Royal Mail Steam-Packet Company, happily shortened to Cunard Company, was guaranteed from the first by an astonishing concern for safety. The company motto was "Speed, Comfort and Safety," and the founder had a particular mania for the third of these offerings. During the first thirty-five years of operation, there was not a single fatality; at a time of high risk on the Atlantic, this was an enviable and incredible record. Cunard's standing orders to his masters forbade racing, rivalry or risk-taking, three taboo R's of Atlantic service, and he concluded: "Your ship is loaded, take her; speed is nothing, follow your own road, deliver her safe, bring her back safe—safety is all that is required." He was convinced that standards of uncompromising reliability would bring fortune in their wake and he was quite right. Before he died in 1878, he had not only fortune but a knighthood as well, and had established the most famous company name in Atlantic history.

The *Britannia* has been immortalized by her most famous passenger, Charles Dickens, who crossed on her in January of 1842, two years after her maiden voyage. He and his wife were seen off in Liverpool by a party of friends who shared his horror at the size of his cabin: "an utterly impractical, thoroughly hopeless and profoundly preposterous box" he described it later in his *American Notes.* On sailing day, the decks were impassable, stacked with passengers' luggage and a squalid assortment of perishable food; in her padded pen amidships, the ship's cow bellowed moodily into the fog. The master, speaking trumpet in hand, paced back and forth on the paddle box, waiting for the mails, the last item to come on board. He had good reason to fume, since the Company's contract with the Admiralty spelled out stiff penalties for delayed sailings. The tender arrived, two hours late, by which time the passengers, Dickens included, were below, struggling to find room for their trunks. The *Britannia*'s lone stewardess chattered incessantly, detailing for all within hearing the pleasures of a January crossing; there were almost none, Dickens was to find out.

The weather held for the first two days, and he spent much time on deck, entranced with the spectacle of ship and sea. On the third, however, having cleared the Irish coast, the full strength of the winter Atlantic drove all passengers below. Distinctly unwell, Dickens retired to his cabin and "read in bed (but to this hour I don't know what) a good deal; and reeled on deck a little; drank cold brandy and water with unspeakable disgust and ate hard biscuits perseveringly: not ill, but going to be." The weather deteriorated as the *Britannia* thudded into a series of westerly gales. His cabin floor awash, Dickens lay in a coma of nausea. The ship slammed violently from side to side, terminating each roll with a tintinnabulation of smashed crockery from the saloon. Overhead, he could hear the thunder of feet in ominous haste. When he was well enough to investigate, he found the decks in wild disorder, one lifeboat reduced to matchwood in its davits. Part of the starboard paddle box had been carried away, and the naked paddles churned up a fountain of spray that hissed onto the hot iron funnel, streaking it white with salt.

When he was able to face food, there was little to tempt him. Passengers ate in a "hearse with windows," and for lunch there might be a dismal spread of "pig's face, cold ham, salt beef" or "perhaps a smoking mess of hot collops." Dinner, scarcely an improvement, was dished up three hours later: "More potatoes and meat," climaxed by a "rather mouldy dessert of apples, grapes and oranges." And so it went for fifteen days. Dickens and the ship's doctor played endless games of whist, collecting tricks in their pockets rather than have them pitched onto the floor from the table. Despite the precaution of carrying the Halifax pilot from England, the crossing ended with the *Britannia* temporarily aground outside the harbor.

Dickens' account is penned with obvious relish, but allowing license for his caustic wit, it does not differ greatly from others'. Passage on those early steamers was hideously uncomfortable and often slower than that obtainable on fast sailing vessels, where there was less noise and far more room. Yet unique on the Cunard ships was a strict schedule of departure, an advantage that attracted passengers, even though their comfort was a secondary consideration for many years. First and foremost, the very raison d'être of the *Britannia* and her sister ships was the swift and regular passage of the mails.

When the ocean behaved, preoccupation with food, despite its monotony, seemed a common affliction. The saloon was converted for dining by the addition of an oilcloth over the green baize of the central table. Leather-covered benches ran along each side, positioned far enough from the table's edge to facilitate both late arrivals and hasty departures. If the ship rolled suddenly, full plates tended to slip into the lap, and children whose feet could not reach the floor disappeared under the table. Food was prepared in a separate galley, carried across a stretch of open deck and down a steep companionway into the saloon. It was usually cold and sometimes wet. Pea soup was almost a tradition for first course, followed by fish that was fresh the first day out but, together with the beef, salt thereafter. A stand-by common to all ship's cooks was sea pie, a mysterious amalgam concealed beneath a layer of mashed potatoes. The captain ate with his saloon passengers, seated at the head of the table and more often than not serving the food.

Passages off the saloon led to sleeping cabins. Less expensive accommodations were within the saloon itself; upholstered benches that lined the walls were curtained off at night for conversion to bunks. Occupants of these Pullmanlike beds could count on an early call when the stewards set up the saloon for breakfast. Summoning a steward from cabin or berth was a matter of shouting anonymously, to which the time-honored reply was: "What number, sir or madam?" Plumbing was almost nonexistent, there was no hot water, and sanitary facilities were primitive. The walls dividing the cabins had a glass-sided compartment near the ceiling which housed a candle, one for each pair of cabins: it was extinguished by the night steward promptly at midnight.

It is not surprising that, by 1850, there was serious competition from America. Edward Collins obtained a mail subsidy from Congress and planned a four-ship service. The *Atlantic,* the first to appear, was not only as fast as Cunard's ships but infinitely more comfortable, with larger cabins, improved ventilation and, even then an American predilection, steam heating. The elegance of their interiors was deceptive, however. In port, there was a profusion of rich carpets and brocades, window dressing for those who inspected the ship before booking passage. Once the Narrows were cleared, away went the finery to be replaced by coconut matting and canvas hangings; salt water and seasick passengers were more than a match for too refined a decor.

Yet, having displaced Cunard on the first two counts of their motto, Speed and Comfort, Collins was unfortunate enough to founder, quite literally, on the third, Safety: in 1854, the *Arctic* sank following a collision off

Newfoundland's Cape Race and shortly thereafter her sister ship, the *Pacific,* disappeared without a trace. Public confidence was lost and it was a convenient excuse for a Southern-dominated Congress to drop the subsidy. By 1860, on the eve of the Civil War, the United States lost interest in Atlantic shipping, a detachment that continued for several postwar decades. Americans were preoccupied with Westward expansion and their engineering priorities centered about the railway. What ships they did build were for inland waterways rather than the ocean; even then, American crews demanded and got higher wages, an economic hardship that has gone hand in hand with American registry ever since.

America's greatest contribution to Atlantic steamers during the nineteenth century was, in point of fact, the vital business of regulating their lanes. Matthew Maury, a U.S. Navy lieutenant assigned to Washington's Hydrographic Bureau, proposed a series of routing recommendations as early as 1855, designed to create high-speed lanes specifically for the new express liners. If they were slightly longer than a more direct route, the rationale of their existence was brought home to shipowners in the wake of each midocean collision, and the universal adoption of Maury's tracks exists to this day.

Although American competition proved ineffectual, there was no lack of it from the Continent. The six years from 1856 to 1862 saw the establishment of three new companies, Germany's Hamburg-Amerika Line and North German Lloyd and the Compagnie Générale Transatlantique of France. Yet so advanced was Britain's technical skill that all rival services built their ships in British yards. Britain's nautical preeminence was hardly surprising; in fact, it was a tradition. Nelson's victory over the French at Trafalgar was no more than naval confirmation of her proclivity for things maritime, to be expected from an island in which it is impossible to be more than seventy miles from the sea. Political stability, coal and iron in abundance, superb internal communications and an empire hungry for goods— all the benefits that had spawned Britain's Industrial Revolution before anyone else's—worked to further advantage in the era of peace that followed the Congress of Vienna.

Historians called it the Pax Britannica. It was an age when capable Britons would administer the world's largest empire with the same enthusiasm their grandfathers had displayed in conquering it. An unwritten rule seemingly equates Nordic temperament with successful colonization. Britain and Holland fashioned empires based on trade rather than greed, whereas their more southern rivals, France and Spain, tended to squander their overseas wealth. There was severe economic crisis in Madrid, for in-

THE ONLY WAY TO CROSS

stance, long before Drake dispatched the Armada. The Crystal Palace and the wonders it housed may have lacked the artistic sensibilities of the Escorial or Versailles, but the principle embodied in its conception proved exceptionally more resilient. The very structure itself, all iron and glass, was representative of the new age, aping the cathedral of the past yet glorifying the limitless possibilities of the future. Consistent with Napoleon's scornful sobriquet, Britons happily solidified their image as a nation of shopkeepers, shops that were not only retail but machine shops as well. Engineers were the new prophets who, with a rapidly expanding technology at their command, wrought miracles of railways, bridges, tunnels and ships.

In terms of the new ships, the riches of the American traffic made innovation a realistic economic risk. The largest, the fastest and the grandest were built and launched exclusively for the Atlantic service. As a result, perfection of hulls and propulsion was accelerated. The paddle wheel disappeared, superseded by the screw propeller. Dubious Admiralty officials were convinced of its advantage only after witnessing a tug of war between two vessels, one equipped with the new device, the other with conventional paddles. Almost simultaneously, their Lordships refused to endorse an iron ship; they had it on no less an authority than the Duke of Wellington that an iron hull would not float and they were also convinced that it offered less protection against gunfire than wood. But having agreed to the propeller, they were ultimately forced to accept it in an iron hull, for wood could not withstand the underwater thrust of the screws.

By the turn of the century, the world's greatest merchant ships sailed the Atlantic, flying the colors of half a dozen energetic companies. Whether these companies chose to acknowledge it or not, each class of vessel they built was designed in specific response to a rival's challenge. This was the hallmark of Atlantic competition and the vigor with which it was pursued compressed a quite remarkable evolution within the brief span of six decades. But despite the bewildering escalation of tonnage and speed prior to 1900, ship specifications to follow were even more astonishing.

. . . You can start this very evening if you choose
And take the Western Ocean in the stride
Of thirty thousand horses and some screws
The boat-express is waiting your command!
You will find the Mauretania *at the quay,*
Till her captain turns the lever 'neath his hand,
And the monstrous nine-decked city goes to sea.

—"THE SONG OF THE MACHINES," BY RUDYARD KIPLING

2.
Building the Mauretania

The *Mauretania* was, if not quite the first, certainly the most famous of a new breed of liner built at the start of the twentieth century. Her name has always been surrounded with a particular aura of success and prestige. Her sister ship, the *Lusitania,* was less fortunate, sunk by a German submarine in 1915 after only eight years in service. These two almost identical ships, launched three months apart, achieved contradicting celebrity: *Lusitania* is synonymous with tragedy while *Mauretania* became an Atlantic legend, Cunard's golden ship.

It is appropriate, I think, to examine her origins, design and construction as archetypal of the creation of an Atlantic express liner. Shipbuilding has developed surprisingly little since her time with only one exception: the plates that form the outer skin are welded now rather than riveted. In terms of assembly, very little else has changed. Refreshingly enough, there are aspects of shipbuilding that cannot and never will be executed by machine. There is today a factory in Sweden that mass-produces seventy-thousand-ton tankers on an assembly-line basis; but the traditionally complex task of gauging the exact curve of a steel plate is still a craftsman's job that has resisted automation.

In 1901, J. P. Morgan, turning his attention from America's railroads, decided to apply the same ruthless financial leverage to Atlantic shipping. A ruinous rate war was in process at that time and Morgan swiftly gained control of several lines, including the Dominion, Atlantic Transport, National, Shaw Savill and Albion, Red Star and twenty-five percent of Holland-America; to the British, his most alarming purchase was the White Star Line, Cunard's rival. Those lines that didn't join under the corporate banner of the International Mercantile Marine, as Morgan aptly named his company, were quick to make peace with it. The only holdouts were Cunard and the French Line.

Although backed by a seemingly inexhaustible supply of capital, this formidable assembly of tonnage was an enterprise that would ultimately founder. But in the early years of its formation, it gave rise to considerable unrest in Britain. It was rumored that loss of ownership of the White Star Line might deprive the Admiralty of valuable armed merchant cruisers in the event of war, and an empire with no means of moving regiments across the seas would be sadly vulnerable. So Lord Inverclyde, Cunard's chairman, approached the Balfour government and requested a subsidy for the construction of two express liners with a speed capability of at least twenty-four-and-one-half knots. There were other specifics in the proposal of particular interest to the Royal Navy: a double hull, comprehensive watertight subdivision, deck strengthening for the installation of guns and positioning of coal bunkers to protect the engine spaces from raking fire. Never mentioned but implicit was the recapture of the Blue Ribband from North German Lloyd. In 1903, Germany had the four fastest ships on the Atlantic, a state of affairs hardly compatible with British maritime pride.

Parliament voted the subsidy and contracts were let to two yards: Messrs. John Brown Company on the river Clyde was to build the *Lusitania* and the Tyneside firm of Swan, Hunter and Wigham Richardson Limited the *Mauretania*. Swan Hunter felt that the hull tests completed in the Admiralty tanks at Haslar were not conclusive enough, so their carpenters made an electrically driven model to one-sixteenth scale. This meant a hull forty-seven-and-a-half feet long. It had room for four passengers and was tested exhaustively on a quiet stretch of the Tyne near the Northumberland Dock. After two years of trials, the patient engineers were satisfied that they had the perfect hull for the job. It would have four propellers, each of which could transmit at least twenty thousand horsepower.

The *Mauretania*'s proposed length exceeded the width of the river into which she was to be launched. But by taking advantage of a fortunate bend in the Tyne, engineers managed a launch run, on paper, of twelve hundred feet. This was considered just adequate and a berth was prepared. Sixteen thousand piles were driven into the riverbank. On top of these went a grid of pitch-pine balks, decked over with six inches of oak. On the cleared floor of the berth went three rows of blocks. The longest one in the center would support the keel for most of its land-based existence, while shorter rows on either side would take the weight of the bilges. The ways, or banister down which the ship would slide into the water, would not be built until the hull neared completion. Overhead, there was an iron and glass roof, sound investment against the rigors of a Northumbrian winter. The underside of the roof was dotted with arc lamps and tracked with cranes that could, singly or in pairs, shift the enormous masses of steel already assembling in the yard. The *Mauretania* would be built, if not indoors, certainly under cover.

The launch of a ship is usually the most perilous journey she undertakes. Once released, she travels at a brisk pace, slow enough to be checked before ramming the opposite bank but fast enough to pass nimbly through the dangers en route. For the launched hull, in its forty-second race down the ways, would be prey to a familiar compendium of stresses, exactly the same range of pressures to which she would be exposed later in a heavy sea. The moving stern, before getting wet enough to float, hangs ponderously over the water with no support, precipitating a hull stress called hogging. Seconds later, when flotation does occur, the stresses reverse dramatically, and now it is the unsupported midships that tends to sag. At the same time, only partially waterborne, in the dangerous no man's land between wet and dry, the hull has only a portion of its stability; there is, concurrently, an unpleasant tendency to capsize. Thus, during the period of her launch, the *Mauretania* would experience a condensed preview of all the battering she would ultimately take. These problems were not unique to the new vessel, but the dimensions were. The builders would contend with previously unknown risks. There was no comfort, additionally, in the knowledge that once begun, a launch cannot be stopped until the vessel is entirely afloat.

There followed the first ceremonial moment in the life of a ship, the laying of the keel. This was the start of assembly, the visible beginning of

The Hamburg-Amerika's *Deutschland*,
which won the Blue Ribband in 1900.
Although ultimately impractical, she was
typical of the stiff German competition
that had Britain in second place by the
turn of the century. (*The Peabody
Museum of Salem*)

the hull. The keel was the ship's spine, unseen but essential. It did not project below the hull, yet it was the single most important structural element. From it, all else would grow; without it, or with any damage to it, the ship could not survive. Its height marked the distance between the two skins, inner and outer, which the Admiralty, in its cautious wisdom, had decreed as part of the design.

On the blackboardlike floor of the moulding loft, the plans of the *Mauretania* were enlarged to actual size. In the frame-bender's furnace, lengths of U-shaped steel were brought to white heat, withdrawn, and wrought into the exact shape dictated by the full-scale plans. One of the many talents of the frame-bender was judging how much the cooling frame would straighten itself; by that exact amount was the frame *over*bent. Port and starboard pairs of the same frame were made consecutively and laid one on top of the other to ensure absolute duplication. Then they were taken to the berth and attached to the double bottoms, exactly thirty-two inches apart. They were numbered from the stern and became coordinates in the geography of the ship.

Steel plates more than an inch thick formed the skin, or shell plating, of the ship. Some were fifty feet long and weighed five tons. They had arrived from the mill in rough oversize and were reduced to their final dimension by means of wooden duplicates which were taken to the hull, put in place on the frames and fitted exactly to size. Back in the plate shop, rivet marks were transferred onto the steel, and each plate, suspended on chain hoists, was maneuvered into the jaws of a battery of machines that stamped, bent and tortured it into the required shape. The edges were shaved to dimension by a steam plane that peeled off spirals of silver metal like so much cold butter. Stamping machines punched out rivet holes in the clean edge, ten at a time. Finally, passed by the critical eye of the shop foreman, the plate was delivered back to the berth for hanging up.

It would require four million rivets to assemble the hull and superstructure of the *Mauretania*. Soft iron ones were used, and the yard designed oil-fired wheeled furnaces that cooked up scores of them at a time. They were pulled from the hot box and flung to the catcher boy, who grabbed them in midair with a thick leather mitt. Transfered to tongs, the rivet was held in place above the aligned rivet holes and driven home by the holder-up. Then, yelling to his partner on the other side of the plate, he would brace against the head; and the riveter, inside the hull, would attack the glowing shank with a pneumatic tool, flattening and spreading the point into a rough duplicate of the rounded head. As it cooled, the rivet would contract and draw the plates tightly together. Unlike the wooden planks they supplanted, steel plates needed no caulking material. There were many places on the hull where there was enough space to employ heavy gap riveters. These were pneumatically operated riveting machines, six feet of giant lobster claw that hung from overhead booms. They could, in one convulsive shuddering hiss, flatten a rivet point with a fifty-ton squeeze. In fact, much of the shell plating had been specifically designed with this construction shortcut in mind. But in tight quarters, where the frames closed up, hand riveting prevailed.

Both the *Lusitania* and *Mauretania* were to be driven by a new kind of prime mover only recently installed, experimentally, on a few smaller vessels. The momentous decision to use it came at such a late date that construction on the after part of each vessel was delayed in favor of the forward sections. The new engine was the steam turbine, and its perfection and application to marine use was the singular accomplishment of a man called Parsons.

The Honorable Charles Parsons was a product of the late Victorian era, a gentleman engineer. He was one of the children of Lord Rosse, an astronomer and a Fellow of the Royal Society. In the large and comfortable houses in which he grew up, there was an atmosphere of scientific curiosity and achievement. There is an early sepia photograph of Charles as a boy, standing proudly beside a homemade model of a helicopter. This early mechanical aptitude was responsible, in later engineering pursuits, for his engaging habit of wading in and getting his hands dirty, sharing with his staff the grapple with a piece of recalcitrant machinery. He bridged the gulf between drawing room and shop, and was immensely liked in both.

After leaving Cambridge, he embarked upon a brilliant career. His preoccupation with turbines reflected an obsession with thermal and mechanical efficiency, and he was convinced that a well-designed turbine might be a formidable rival to the reciprocating steam engine. (A subsequent generation of engineers would repeat this process by replacing piston with jet engines on aircraft.) The turbine was in existence long before his time, but no one had put its potential to use. The principle was ageless—in its simplest form, a windmill. A jet of high-pressure steam is brought to bear against a wheel rimmed with steel vanes. Parsons built his first rough model out of one of his wife's cotton reels and some pieces of cardboard; he was to progress rapidly from there.

By 1844, he made a turbine that whizzed around eighteen thousand times a minute. Parsons realized, however, that the steam, having turned the wheel, was still loaded with energy. So he extended the turbine shaft, adding a series of wheels along its length. Because the steam was losing pressure as it passed from one wheel to the next, the diameter of each subsequent

Above, first in service of Cunard's contenders was the Clyde-built *Lusitania,*
shown tying up for the first time at
Cunard's 14th Street pier in Manhattan in
September of 1907. (*Prints and Photographs Division, Library of Congress*)

Below, the *Mauretania*'s hull takes shape. Note the yard-built furnaces for heating rivets and the massive claws of the pneumatic riveter marked "5–6" at lower right. Further forward rises the protective inner skin of the coal bunkers. (*Engineering*)

wheel was gradually increased. This meant that as the steam lost its vigor, its task was made easier by a larger vane area and greater turning moment.

Parsons was utilizing here a principle of energy conservation long implemented in steam engines: the term "triple-expansion engine" means quite simply that steam from the first cylinder has been reused twice, at lower pressures in larger cylinders. However, the beauty of his application was the relative simplicity of his engine. It had, in effect, only one moving part, as well as muscle, speed and efficiency. There was no vibration and no familiar noise; the thunderous clatter of the steam engine was replaced by an alien whine. Two years later, the Chief Constable at Gateshead was pleased to use one of Parsons' turbo-generators to provide night illumination for a skating pond. The apparatus was delivered pulled by a horse.

In 1894, Parsons formed his own company, the Marine Steam Turbine Company, with the express purpose of building the world's first turbine vessel. What emerged after months of drenching labor, was really a floating testbed: a pencil-slim craft, one hundred by nine feet with a gross weight of forty-four tons. It was driven by a formidable assembly of nine propellers, distributed among three shafts, each connected to a turbine. To prevent excessive trim at high speeds, the underwater surfaces aft were flat, a major innovation in its day. Parsons christened his creation *Turbinia* and tested her both on the Tyne and off the Northumberland coast.

His trials were completed by the summer of 1897. Coincidentally, there was to be a naval review at Spithead, a maritime extravaganza in honor of Queen Victoria's Diamond Jubilee. The entire British Home Fleet, together with overseas squadrons that could be safely recalled, would be drawn up in two imposing lines, to be inspected by the Prince and Princess of Wales from the quarterdeck of the royal yacht *Victoria and Albert*. It was a unique assemblage of the world's naval powers.

In June of that Jubilee year, the *Turbinia* was nursed secretly down the coast from Newcastle, a perilous journey for a craft whose effective freeboard was a matter of inches. There is no record extant of the trip south, around the bulge of East Anglia, across the mouth of the Thames and along the coast to Portsmouth. But secrecy was maintained and Parsons and his crew were ready at exactly the right moment. He wrote later: "If you believe in a principle, never damage it with poor expression. You must go the whole way. I had to startle people." "Startle" was the right word.

It was a flawless summer's day. Spithead was packed with small craft, jockeying for position to see the royal procession. The lines of dreadnoughts faced each other, dressed with signal flags, the casemates and rigging thronged with sailors in Number One dress. Out of Portsmouth steamed the

THE ONLY WAY TO CROSS

With Parsons at the helm,
Turbinia slices through the
North Sea at top speed.
(*Science Museum*) Below,
portrait of an interloper. The
world's first turbine-driven
vessel racing through the Fleet
at Spithead in the summer of
1897. (*The Mariners
Museum, Newport News,
Virginia*)

royal yacht with the Prince, dressed as Admiral of the Fleet, standing on her quarterdeck. As she entered the gauntlet, each ship's band in turn struck up the national anthem and the crew gave three cheers. Prince Edward returned the salute and continued past, down the line toward the next battleship. Naval pickets patrolled behind, chasing out intruders; all, that is, but one which defied interception.

From under the counter of a French warship, *Turbinia* streaked into the road, racing along in the very wake of the ponderous *Victoria and Albert*. Parsons called for full throttle and, with a roar of steam and smoke, trailing a twenty-foot flame from the stack, the tiny vessel leaped past the astonished royal party. Nothing could keep up with her, let alone stop her; one picket that tried had her ensign staff snapped off, panicking her commanding officer; he was seen by a delighted member of Parsons' crew divesting himself of sword and belt preparatory to abandoning ship. After one evasive move, the *Turbinia*'s towed launch broke loose and caromed like a torpedo into the flank of a French yacht. It is fortunate that the resulting Anglo-French exchange did not carry as far as the terrace of Osborne House on the Isle of Wight, where the Sovereign could see the whole outrageous performance through a telescope.

The *Times* for the following Monday remarked that "her lawlessness may be excused by the novelty and importance of the invention that she embodies." The *Daily Mail* prophesied that "if that shrimp of a turbinet comes to anything, all these black and yellow leviathans are done for." "The *Turbinia*," reported the *Graphic*, "the fastest vessel in the world, advertised itself in the most audacious manner by darting, or rather flashing, hither and thither after the Royal procession."

Parsons completed his run and made for the companionway of the liner *Teutonic*, to give Thomas and Bruce Ismay a trial run. The father and son who controlled the destiny of the White Star Line were thrilled at the speed of the *Turbinia*, if not a little nervous. Moving over water at a speed approaching forty miles per hour was a novel experience in those days. Later in the day, the Kaiser's brother, Prince Henry of Prussia, signaled from the battleship *König Wilhelm* that he would like a chat with Parsons. It was an incredible triumph, an audacious feat of public relations that established the unquestionable superiority of his invention.

Within a short time, the Royal Navy had built two experimental destroyers driven by Parsons' engines. Two Allan liners, *Victorian* and *Virginian*, were the first turbine-driven merchantmen on the Atlantic. Cunard, cautious as always, put into service two ships which were to be nicknamed "the pretty sisters": the *Caronia* and *Carmania*. They were identical except

for their engines; *Carmania* had the new turbines while her sister was pow-
ered with conventional steam engines. After a carefully logged season, it
was discovered that the *Carmania* had averaged a full knot faster with an
identical consumption of coal.

Thus, the risk of installing essentially experimental power plants in the
Lusitania and *Mauretania* was economically justified. However, considering
the unprecedented size of the ships, it was a gamble with potentially disastrous results. If for some reason the engines failed in service, the necessary
refit would be a staggering blow to public confidence. As it was, the specially appointed commission that advised Cunard's Board of Directors to
proceed was prompted by the knowledge that there was no alternative: the
very size and requirements of the new giants, together with their projected
service, made the adoption of turbines all but mandatory.

News of the decision was welcomed at the Swan Hunter yard and work
on the after part could proceed. The sense of a ship gradually emerged.
From the clutter of pneumatic hose, steel plates and wheeled furnaces rose
a monstrous skeleton, spine down, thrusting a forest of ribs into the smoky
air. Workers bound for the upper decks rode in electric elevators, past the
tumblehome, that most picturesque of terms in naval architecture, the in-
ward slope of the midships hull above the water line. As each strake or row
of plating was hung up, scaffolding followed, along which rolled a wheeled
pneumatic tool like a giant cookie cutter on edge, whose revolving steel bit
would scribe and cut the portholes.

Elsewhere in Britain, components were completed. Giant steel castings
of those after frames to support the tail shafts were poured in Darlington
and tested for soundness by being dropped onto a concrete floor. Delivering
them the forty-odd miles to Wallsend was almost as difficult as making
them. They traveled early on a Sunday morning, projecting awkwardly over
the edge of flatcars, at five miles an hour. By late afternoon, they finally
arrived at the London-North-Eastern Railways' spur adjacent to the berth.
The Welsh works of Brown Lenox Company produced yards of the largest
anchor cable ever made. Three links were later "tested to destruction" in
Lloyds' proving house: destruction proved elusive although under a three-
hundred-fifty-ton pull, the two-foot links did stretch an additional inch. The
propellers were assembled, quite literally: shipbuilders in those days favored
blades bolted onto a central boss. Propellers were surprisingly fragile and
blades were forever being chipped or sheared off; it was cheaper and easier
to replace a blade rather than the entire assembly.

Between the triple row of blocks beneath the hull, joiners began construction of the cradle and ways. They worked in uncomfortable quarters; it

Above, an overhead look at the *Queen Elizabeth 2*'s entry into the River Clyde on September 20, 1967. On the right are the twin white lines of the fixed ways, the same berth from which the *Aquitania* and both *Queen*s were also launched. To either side lie piles of drag chains, jerked into lozenge shape by the downward rush of the hull. The new ship is afloat in waters still turbulent from the launch. River launchings create identical hazards and the *Mauretania*'s builders shared the same concern for the proximity of the opposite bank exactly sixty-one years earlier on the Tyne. (*British Ministry of Defence photograph, Crown Copyright Reserved*)

Right, massive application of Parsons' invention. Members of the launch party pause before the rotor of one of the *Mauretania*'s low-pressure turbines. The chauffeur has been relegated to the back seat. (*Swan Hunter Shipbuilders Ltd.*)

was impossible to stand up straight, and the din of the steelworkers reverberated from the plates overhead. By the time they had finished, the noisy cave had been filled with a complex of timber. Part of this sloping structure, the fixed ways, would remain anchored to the floor of the berth; everything above it, the moving ways, would slide down into the River Tyne with the *Mauretania*. The bearing surface between fixed and moving ways was coated with a slippery mix of hot tallow and soft black soap. (Launches of large liners in northern Europe were invariably scheduled in warm months so that this lubricant retained maximum effectiveness.) Although thrust up tightly against the hull, the cradle had incorporated into the structure a horizontal seam filled with a series of oak wedges. On the day of the launch, these wedges would be driven in, expanding the entire cradle vertically—not very much, just a matter of inches, but enough to jack up sixteen thousand tons of hull free from the keel blocks.

Each end of the cradle reared up into poppets: the fore-poppet, a compact mass of timber balks bunched together with steel tie rods, extended its grasp high up under the curve of the bow. Nothing less than this massive grip would serve to bear the weight of the hull in midlaunch as well as discourage its capsizing. The after-poppets rose under the stern, cupping the shell plating where it was pierced by the two inboard propeller shafts. The entire cradle was a miracle of vast cabinetry.

It was imperative to arrest the progress of the ship once she was in the water, before she rammed the opposite bank. So on each side of the berth, five U-shaped piles of chain were laid, the open end of the U facing the water. Each eighty-ton stack was composed of links of old anchor cable, garlanded in massive bunches. A free end was shackled to a wire rope which was led up, in a series of triced loops, to padeyes temporarily riveted to the hull's sides. Only after the *Mauretania* entered the water would the action of these chain drags start: the tricing lines would snap, as designed, in sequence, cushioning the initial shock. Similarly, the free end of chain, reaving through itself, would further absorb the initial tug, before the entire bulk of each stack was pulled along the berth.

In addition, the *Mauretania*'s stern anchor, newly arrived on a flatcar, would be dropped down river of the berth and buoyed. On launch day, a cable ran from this anchor to the stern, thus adding another considerable braking pull. It is symptomatic of the fine degree of engineering involved that this anchor was dragged, in point of fact, exactly the predicted number of feet through the Tyne bottom mud.

The day of the launch, September 20, 1906, was marred at the outset by rain, as are most outdoor ceremonies in the north of England. A platform

　　　　　　　　　　　THE ONLY WAY TO CROSS

had been erected under the bows, at the center of which was a toy capstan which would activate release of the hydraulic launching triggers. From the masthead on the bow hung a line tied securely around the neck of a bottle of champagne. This was concealed gracefully in a bower of beribboned flowers. The Dowager Duchess of Roxburghe had consented to christen the ship. Unlike some later Cunarders, the name was no surprise and was already emblazoned across the white painted stern, together with Liverpool, the port of registry. (All Cunard's ships were given names ending in -*ia*. During that particular period, the Board of Directors favored names of Roman Provinces: Mauretania, comprising portions of Morocco, and Lusitania, which we now call Portugal. Later would come the Gallic Aquitania.) Under the graceful sweep of the counter, the four propellers were in place, their delicate edges concealed by a protective wrapping. The rudder was locked amidships.

Although it was Thursday, every Tyneside firm had dismissed its employees for the day and a carnival air prevailed. Hawkers did a brisk trade in souvenir cards and booklets among the crowds that gathered early for a good position from which to see the launch. The giant shed was now an obstruction. Thousands waited for hours on the pilings on either side of the ways, content with a tantalizing glimpse of the stern. Across the river, the Ballast Hills were black with tourists, picnicking in defiance of the rain. Crossing the Tyne was no easy matter, for one set of ferry terminals had been demolished for the occasion. Furthermore, every enterprising boat captain had chartered his vessel for the day. Although closed to normal traffic, the river was cluttered with dangerously overladen steamers, their decks thronged with the curious.

There was no holiday for the men of Swan Hunter. High tide would be at four-thirty in the afternoon, and a series of irrevocable mechanical steps was already in progress. From under the *Mauretania* came the *thunk* of sledge against oak as the wedges all along the line of the cradle were driven home. This was the process of "setting up," shifting the weight of the hull from block to cradle. Suddenly, after supporting the *Mauretania* for nearly two years, the keel blocks were redundant and were left in place only as a safety precaution. During the day, stress gauges were examined for any premature movement. A trip switch had been rigged, so that those on the launching platform could be alerted by the ringing of an electric bell the instant the vessel began to move. A waterborne team of workmen inspected the dredged-out portion of river between the ways. The ends of the ways that projected from under the stern had been covered with planks to protect them from the weather.

Those who had been invited as guests of the builders began their day with a tour of the Wallsend Slipway and Engineering Works, adjacent to the Yard. One of the six turbines had been opened, and they could gape at the thousands of gleaming steel blades. Parsons was there, and Andrew Laing, manager of the Works, who would be memorialized, as would the ship, in the stained glass of Newcastle's St. Nicholas' Cathedral. An elaborate luncheon was given in the temporary splendor of the pattern shop, after which there were speeches and toasts, full of ponderous Edwardian jocularities. Cunard's chairman reminded his listeners roguishly that the turbines still weren't paid for (laughter), assured them that Great Britain would recapture the speed title of the Atlantic (Hear, Hear!) and that the Company's reputation was safe (cheers). Then the Duchess was toasted and presented with a large silver box bearing an engraved likeness of the *Mauretania*.

Mr. Hunter, one eye on the sky and the other on his watch, hurried the guests from the table. They assembled outside in a fleet of open cars for the drive to the hull. Miraculously, the rain had stopped and a pale sun cheered the party. And so the convoy began, chairmen, managers, mayors and mayoresses, foreign consuls (the American was named Nixon) and a sprinkling of northern gentry, waving and chattering. The way led through a gauntlet of giant boilers, past the works building with roofloads of cheering workmen and, just before they swept into the berth itself, an astonishing novelty: three of the *Mauretania*'s four funnels lay on their sides, end to end, large enough to receive the caravan of motors two abreast. With squeals of delight from the ladies, the tourers puffed up the planked incline and passed through the three immense caverns. As the lead cars emerged into the daylight, the chauffeurs drew up as cameras immortalized the moment.

At the head of the berth, the party descended from the vehicles as the band of the 1st Newcastle Artillery thumped and fussed into a medley of patriotic airs. From beneath the hull came a raucous musical counterpoint as gangs of workers, wielding immense battering rams, attacked the rows of supporting shores. They sang rhythmic chanties as one length of timber after another fell under their blows. As soon as one was down, workers pulled it aside; others, with giant mauls, knocked away the keel blocks.

There was just time for an eye-popping promenade down to the water's edge and back before yard foremen prodded the gentry onto the sloping launch platform. High water was at hand and would remain thus for nearly an hour. The crowd grew quiet, the band stopped in the middle of "Hearts

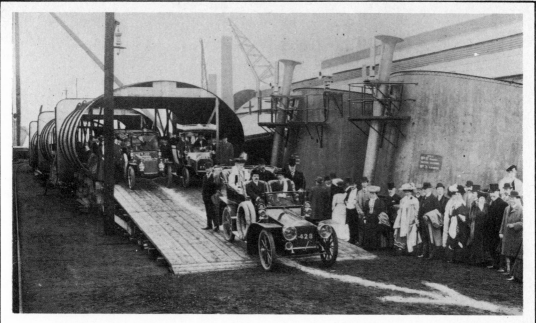

It all started in 1906. Later steamship publicists who sought to amaze with representations of vehicles passing through funnels owe their inspiration to Swan Hunter. Having passed through portions of three of the *Mauretania*'s funnels, the Duchess of Roxburghe sits for a unique portrait. (*Shipping World and Shipbuilder*)

Within the confines of the *Mauretania*'s launch platform, the delay has been tedious. Early excitement gives way to ennui as yard officials wait for the tide. (*Swan Hunter Shipbuilders Ltd.*)

of Oak" and Her Grace fidgeted with the bottle of champagne. Nothing happened.

Stephenson, the yard manager, had opted for a further wait. The river would rise another inch or two before starting the ebb, still leaving enough time for maneuvering the launched hull to the fitting-out berth. So the band crashed into life again, the postcard vendors reworked the crowd. Over the river, thousands chafed at the delay; the local papers had said three-thirty sharp and ribald jests at the expense of the shipyard echoed across the hills. But the sun was warmer now and they had a capital view. Finally, they heard the warning bray of the yard's klaxon.

The *Mauretania* was poised, ready for her majestic entry into the Tyne. There were still men under the bilges and the thump and clatter of their hammers continued right up to the last. The entire timbered substructure, taking the full weight of sixteen thousand tons of steel hull, creaked and groaned alarmingly. Then the Duchess was asked to turn the miniature capstan. There was an appalling crash as the giant steel triggers dropped from their retaining slots on the moving ways. For an instant, nothing gave. Swan was seen to raise his hand, as though to signal the engineers standing by hydraulic rams to assist with a nudge. But he was caught in mid-gesture as the electric bell shrilled joyously and the immense rivet-studded wall began to move. The Duchess christened her hastily *"Mauretania!"* and flung the bottle of champagne at the receding stem, where it splintered and foamed. The only injury of the afternoon was sustained by a workman below, struck on the head by a piece of broken glass.

Down she went, the ways cracking and squealing. Now the rivercraft saluted with a deafening chorus of whistles and sirens. First the rudder, then the propellers and finally the graceful counter thrust into the Tyne, sending up twin sheets of water, the naissance of a tidal wave that soaked watchers lining the opposite shore. As she entered her natural element, the first buoyant lift raised up the midships hull and the fore-poppet under the bows took on the added weight. Exactly as designed, portions of it crumbled into a splintery cushion. Pine screamed against oak in dreadful conflict on ways already stripped clean of their lubricants.

As she passed down the ways, opposing banks of spectators suddenly were revealed to each other. They joined their cheers with those of the workers who rose from between the ways over which the *Mauretania* had just traveled, caps off and cheering "as only hearty British Workmen know how to cheer," a local paper exulted the following day. The band, music forgotten, shook their instruments in schoolboy glee. Over the launch platform rippled a sea of glistening, waving toppers.

Moving at fourteen knots, the bows dropped from the land. The union jack at the masthead dipped in frantic salute and the riding crews clutched the rail as the stem plunged down. Another wave lashed back up the berth. The hull recovered and then the tricing lines took up the vital business of arresting that backward rush. In successive pairs, the piles of drag chain leapt into life, snaking and roaring along the edge of the berth in pursuit of their charge, driving up monstrous divots and clouds of dust. The stern cable tautened on cue and a fleet of six tugs left off their salutes long enough to harry their giant sister to a stop. From across the Tyne, even high on the hills, it was the steam from the tugs and ferries that finally obscured the glistening white hull as she floated, unnaturally light, riding higher out of the water than she ever would again. But the sense of particular ceremony that is a launch, the combination of engineering miracle, opening night and stupendous passage, was complete; in the roiled muddy Tyne, cluttered with chain and timbers, the *Mauretania* was afloat at last.

While high water remained, the tugs took charge, maneuvering carefully through waters still littered with the paraphernalia of the launch. The fore-poppet, now debris floating at either end of a length of chain, was retrieved by yard craft. The *Mauretania* was nudged against two dolphins, clusters of stout piles bolted and lashed together. They had been built one hundred feet from shore and the ship's port side rested against them, her bow pointing down river. She could have been moored closer to the bank but her working draft by trial time would prohibit it. A system of booms was suspended over the after railings to protect the four screws and rudder.

A monstrous floating crane called the Titan was tied up against the offshore starboard side. German-built, it was the world's largest, capable of a hundred-and-seventy-ton lift. Nothing less would suffice to install the *Mauretania*'s engine components. The Titan's first task was simple, merely a matter of leaning over the ship and swinging one end of a girdered bridge into place on C-deck. The next day, hundreds of feet of timber that had strengthened the interior of the hull during the launch were dismantled and lifted ashore. It was the last of the off-loading—for the next year, during the process of fitting out, the traffic on both crane and bridge would be one way, from shore to ship. As each pound of fittings, each ton of machinery came on board, as the superstructure climbed, as the funnels were set in place, as each element of the working ship left the shore and assumed its rightful place on board, the boot topping, that painted prediction of the water line, crept down towards the waters of the Tyne.

For six months of that year of fitting out, there was little appreciable change in the silhouette that had emerged from the glass-roofed shed. The brutal job of transferring boilers, turbines and condensers from the machine sheds ashore into the engine-room spaces had first priority. Vertical shafts had been left open to the skies and the bottom half of the turbine casings were first lowered down through seven decks. The rotors themselves, the real test of the floating crane, were inched out of the heavy machinery shops on flatcars, pulled by steam rollers. The actual lift of these enormous steel masses was done only on windless days to minimize any possible movement, no matter how gentle, of either the *Mauretania* or the barge on which rested the crane. If the rotors had been made of glass, they could not have been treated with more care; the thousands of delicate steel vanes needed only the slightest nudge to be damaged. Slings were placed under each end of the shaft, the crane's machinery clattered and hissed and up went the first one in a graceful lift seventy feet high, followed by an arc across the water to a position over the top of the vessel. Here, a long pause as riggers on guide lines let the swing dissipate before the descent began. Then down the open shaft, down through seven decks to the tank tops, down with agonized precision into the U-shaped bearing that lay directly beneath them. Six enormous rotors were lowered in this fashion, followed by the tops of the casings which were bolted home. The turbines were in place and would remain there for thirty years, to be removed only when the *Mauretania* was scrapped.

Only then could the fiddley gratings be closed up and the funnels lifted into place on the boat deck. The original design had been amended from three to four at the last moment; there are still some Cunard posters today with an artist's rendering of the new express liner *Mauretania* sporting three stacks. There was also a move by the designers to pair the funnels, two and two, in the manner of the German ships they were trying to beat. But the final choice was for four, evenly spaced and parallel, with a graceful yacht-like rake. The *Mauretania* and *Lusitania* were the first British four-stackers, a popular silhouette that Cunard would repeat with the *Aquitania*. Similarly, three White Star ships were to follow suit: *Olympic, Titanic* and *Britannic* would all have the same distinctive quartet.

Although it was functional on the *Mauretania,* the number 4 stack was often a dummy. Involved here was a question of popular esthetics. In cold fact, a funnel had two purposes: to provide a good draft for the furnaces and to dispel soot and fumes from the open decks in the most efficient manner possible. Anything else was icing on the cake. Furthermore, of all the elements of ship design, funnels are the most readily identifiable—they bear the company colors and are easily recognized either in port or at sea. It was not lost on steamship companies anxious to attract immigrants that their

THE ONLY WAY TO CROSS

clients attached considerable significance to the matter of funnels, the number of them in particular. Somehow, to their minds, this was directly related to the power and reliability of the ship. Two stacks were better than one, three stacks even more attractive and four the very acme of marine dependability. The following recorded incident was not unusual: the Hamburg-Amerika Line had the utmost difficulty in persuading a Serbian immigrant to accept passage on the brand-new three-stacker *Imperator*. He refused to be mollified and kept waving a grimy Company brochure bearing a likeness of the *Deutschland,* older and smaller, but with four funnels.

It was a myth that naval architects perpetuated until the early twenties, when Congress choked off the flood of immigrants. Then, companies wooed the new mass passenger with a new brand of funnelmanship only slightly more sophisticated than before: fewer and fatter. Four funnels, comforting for immigrants, were passé for tourists. So the numbers game was reversed and it was the Germans who led the way even before the war. The Hamburg-Amerika Line laid down a trio of enormous liners with three funnels only. The first went into service in 1913. Fifteen years later, the *Bremen* was the first of the superliners with two. (There were some embarrassing adjustments to both experiments: the *Imperator*'s funnels were shortened to improve stability while the *Bremen*'s were lengthened to keep cinders off the decks.) The Compagnie Générale Transatlantique, France's premier steamship company, followed suit with their two ships in the twenties, the *Paris* and *Ile de France*—the *Ile*'s three stacks being reduced to two in the course of a post-World War II face lifting.

As funnels lost their height and gained weight, the need for guy wires was obviated. These massive sculptured *objets* were free standing, often pearshaped in plan. More recent designs have embraced sampan tops, ailerons, latticed walls and ultimately, the nonfunnels of the *Rotterdam* and *Queen Elizabeth 2*. This latter is particularly significant. Cunard has eschewed the traditional. The stack is aft and of a radical design: a pencil-slim pipe with a clever windscoop arrangement in its base that bends the thirty-knot slip stream upwards to help carry away the stack gas.

Efficient and functional as this may be, I feel it has somehow hurt the image of the new ship; perhaps I am merely susceptible to the potent mystique of the conventional funnel. For my own taste, the *Mauretania*'s silhouette had a quality that was unique. There was something honest and workmanlike about those four riveted funnels, a dashing rake their only concession to style. Reflecting a sturdy Edwardian functionalism, they were reminiscent of early steam engines. For generations of schoolchildren and illustrators, that four-stack silhouette was synonymous with ocean travel, a symbol combining grace and function to perfect proportion. The *Mauretania* had a no-nonsense attitude happily characteristic of the ship's later performance. More than just the funnels, it was also the impenetrable clutter of the upper decks, dense with skylights, ventilators, guy wires and blowers. This look predated the tendency to conceal the working parts of the vessel, to tidy things up and create expanses of open deck. The *Mauretania* showed her sinews, presenting a surface profile of excitement and vigor equal to the promise of the revolutionary turbines installed below.

Once in place, the funnels were painted in Cunard's company colors: black tops and banding, the intervening expanse an indescribable orange-red. This color dated from the *Britannia*'s single stack in 1840, a practical solution to the inadequacies of mid-nineteenth-century paint that blistered from the heat of the furnaces. Samuel Cunard borrowed a trick from the coastal steamers and daubed the stack with a reeking soup of buttermilk and ochre. The distinctive vermillion that resulted successfully defied the heat. The furnaces of later and larger vessels were insulated from the funnels by so many intervening decks that blistering ceased, but the color remains a cherished Company trademark. The current flagship carries it on her windscoop and the lettering on her side. It also appears on the cover of the Company's annual report.

The cabins and public rooms for the *Mauretania*'s first-class passengers were located in the center of the ship, a sensible innovation dating from the first White Star liner, the *Oceanic* of 1871. Ismay had sensibly broken with the quarterdeck tradition of Royal Navy vessels by moving his choicest passengers forward to midships. Several factors dictated the move. The stern was now for business rather than pleasure and no longer the tranquil haven it had been under sail or even with paddle wheels. Early propellers set up vibrations noticeable amidships but appalling in the stern. Furthermore, pitching, the longitudinal rocking of the ship in a heavy sea, was minimal at the pivot point or center of the ship. Finally, hulls had become sufficiently deep for cabins to be built over the engine spaces. So the move made genuine sense for all except those who had only recently been charged with the architectural design of the interior. The funnels, however reassuring ranged against the sky, topped casings which were a frightful nuisance between decks. Like unwanted relatives, they lodged immovably on every level; and although they were boxed in, upholstered, used as bench backs or disguised in scores of ingenious ways, funnel casings were inescapable frustrations. The traditional Versailles concept of a series of large rooms leading one from another to create vistas was an impossibility. Grandiose schemes of this kind foundered on these large stumbling blocks, situated annoyingly in the prime spaces of the ship, necessitating compromises in the form of split entrances and circumventing corridors.

So the *Mauretania*'s promenade deck followed the tradition of the day. The public rooms were dovetailed with the stacks, progressing aft in an arrangement more or less consistent with all passenger vessels of the world. Forward, a library, writing room and drawing room—this latter a sop to the ladies, who would find neither solace nor welcome in the smoking room —then a grand staircase which led down to the embarkation hall and dining room; aft of this, the main lounge, the smoking room and finally, an innovation for Cunard, a veranda café.

This was a concession to the possibility, however remote, of fine weather on the New York run. Rush matting was laid directly on deck, treillage, potted palms and wicker furniture completing the illusion that one could sit outdoors. This would be a rare pleasure, even in summer. I can count on the fingers of one hand the number of crossings I have made when it was possible to sit comfortably outdoors on an express liner. In the Caribbean or Mediterranean, yes, but on the North Atlantic, no. Outdoors on the *Mauretania* was a brisk walk on the promenade deck, a sheltered deck chair shrouded in rugs or, near the American side, deck tennis on the boat deck. Cruising, or the marketing of shipboard life in warm waters, was a promising novelty, but Cunard had no interest in it; theirs was the business of carrying rich, impatient landlubbers across a treacherous sea. The emphasis was on the indoors, a cozy civilized refuge from midocean misery.

By our standards, the interior of those public rooms on the *Mauretania* would be considered restrained beyond belief. The grand salon gave to the correspondent of *Engineering* "a wonderful impression of quiet grandeur, with its panels of beautifully grained mahogany, dully polished a rich brown, each lit by its surrounding moulding of gold, and relieved by slender pilasters of *fleur de pêche* marble of a lilac hue with caps and plinths of sombre ormulu." He went on to marvel that it seemed "a room unequalled in any steamship and rarely surpassed even in a palace." Paneling was used lavishly throughout the first-class quarters: mahogany in the lounge, stairs and passages, maple in the drawing room, walnut in the smoking room and weathered oak in the triple-decked dining room. In all cases, the carving was extensive and meticulous, of a degree of workmanship rare today. Three hundred craftsmen, imported from Palestine, had labored for months in the joinery shop and produced cords of stunning boiserie. Some were so proud of their work that they initialed the tops of the columns, a fact that came to light only when the ship was scrapped. The paneling was installed with infinite care, layers of felt insulating the wood from the steel members of the ship that it concealed, to minimize creaking. The movement of a ship at sea influences countless decisions of design: the prisms on the chandeliers, for instance, of normal appearance, were hung rigidly so that they would remain "suspended" no matter what the vessel's motion. Cabin cupboard doors were equipped with patented hooks to hold them in any open position. Most stairs on liners have a direction of climb parallel to the fore and aft axis of the vessel, rendering them less dangerous in rough weather.

Shipbuilders were still preoccupied with skylights and the grand salon was capped with a ground-glass, bronze-filigreed ellipse. Years before, passengers on the Atlantic craved two comforts—light and ventilation. On sailing vessels, the builders' response was limited to little greenhouse roofs set between the masts. These modest structures admitted daylight and fresh air to the central saloons without hampering the working of the sails. As steam supplanted canvas and rigging diminished, the greenhouse roofs grew into deckhouses; when sail disappeared completely, the deckhouses blossomed into superstructure. Yet no matter how many layers of deck arose, far enough above the water line for the inclusion of substantial fenestration, the skylights remained. Naval architects refused to abandon them, perhaps in an attempt to convince passengers that fresh air and light were still being provided from above. In actual fact, the admission of air was systematically defied by double glazing and the light that did penetrate this barrier was a cold, shadowless wash, as though from a permanently overcast sky. All the skylit public rooms of the ship, snug by night, approximated the chilly gloom of an aquarium by day. There were two other distressing side effects, one esthetic, the other practical: skylights turn into oppressive black panels at night and in cold weather there is an annoying tendency to condensation.

It should be pointed out that the *Mauretania,* despite her ultimate fame, was not a particularly luxurious ship. Acceptance of a government subsidy with its attendant specifications predicated an economy of frills, and she boasted none of the more recent extravagances of her competitors either already in service or on the drawing boards. Her basic decoration was perfectly adequate, indeed handsome, and it could be argued justifiably that her speed more than compensated for omissions of luxe. Express liners on the North Atlantic were designed either for speed or comfort, qualities equally desirable but seldom compatible. Cunard had always chosen the former and it was a choice quite consistent with its founder's original mission, the fast dependable passage of mails and passengers. Sixty years of Atlantic preeminence offered overwhelming proof that it was a profitable policy, and it was axiomatic that a record-breaking ship carried an aura of prestige and success guaranteed to attract passengers.

Fitting out on the north bank of the Tyne. The *Mauretania*'s superstructure has been painted white but the decks have yet to be machine-sanded smooth. All sixteen lifeboats are on board and only the scarred hull lacks its black paint. (*Engineering*)

Below, her last day at Wallsend. The *Turbinia* comes alongside for a historic photograph; she was to have accompanied the *Mauretania* down river but the last-minute failure of a valve prevented it. (*Science Museum, South Kensington, London*)

But commitment to speed is a relentless proposition. It predicates an entire design philosophy, including a rigid list of hull specifications that cannot be violated. The only constant is a fixed service speed and the higher it is set, the more the related factors must adapt to it. Manpower, income, machinery spaces, capacity and horsepower have to be juggled and it is inevitable that frivolities will be restricted to maintain a twenty-five knot speed. Furthermore, it is hideously expensive: it has been estimated that, at speeds over twenty knots, each additional knot costs as much as the original twenty.

Incongruously, then, in the splendor of a François I dining saloon of such uncompromising authenticity that each panel was carved differently from its neighbor, the world's richest travelers would find that they were sharing tables democratically with their fellow passengers. Admittedly, it was not the communal board of the sailing packets, but the essential privacy of individual tables was ignored. Clubmen weary of toasting themselves by the smoking-room fire were to be denied athletic alternatives. Diversions of that kind were left to Cunard's competitors who, conceding the issue of speed, built slower and roomier ships. Having eschewed the struggle for the Blue Ribband, they were spared an enormous technological preoccupation.

They were spared, too, the complacency peculiar to a defending champion. In the rarified air of Atlantic supremacy, there was little urge to innovate. Turbines, consistent with the quest for speed, were, after exhaustive tests, acceptable; but simple creature comforts or passenger-pleasing items that intruded on the running of a fast ship were not. I have always felt that Cunard, despite their disclaimer for speed, were quite able to supply at least some of the frills their competitors were only too happy to provide. Whether or not they were essential is not important; what is important was that their competitors, in opting for comfort in favor of speed, made the provision of these very things their business, and the passenger revenues that resulted could not be ignored.

So the company brochures, already issued as the *Mauretania* completed her fitting out, could be faulted for a dearth of compelling statistics. What they did list was characteristic of seagoing luxury of that era: the provision of facilities commonplace ashore yet somehow remarkable afloat. Passengers, for instance, could be coiffed in the first hydraulically operated barber chair ever placed on board a ship—scarcely valid recommendation for booking immediate passage but the kind of smug trivia so dear to publicists. Many cabins boasted telephones, hooked into a switchboard vastly superior to those previously encountered. More cabins than usual had private bathrooms (unfortunately, not enough, since this critical shortage would ultimately doom the ship).

The year previous, Harland & Wolff had installed an electric elevator on the *Amerika,* an astonishing novelty that soon became a feature of every first-class liner. Early critics of this convenience had predicted gloomily that the car would jam in its vertical tracks whenever the ship rolled; happily, this was proven nonsense. The *Mauretania* had a brace of elevators suspended in the well of the grand staircase. The facsimile of fifteenth-century grillwork surrounding them was wrought anachronistically in aluminum, the first marine application of a metal currently popular for most superstructure; hundreds of pounds of topside weight was eliminated. It was a fortunate economy since Edwardian tastes favored inordinate amounts of marble to sheath the walls and plumbing fixtures in all the bathrooms. Every gentleman's urinal throughout the vessel boasted marble dividers, of a quality that improved "according to class." The engineers gave equal attention to the matter of reducing the shuddering of the water pipes; it is unfortunate that they were unable to cope as efficiently with the vibration subsequently produced by the quadruple screws.

By late summer of 1907, the paneling which was to become as famous as the ship itself was complete. The lavish plaster ceilings, from the groined vault over the well of the dining room to the encrusted mullions of the Italian Renaissance smoking room, were dry and painted. Hundreds of swivel chairs, the inescapable seating for dining, were anchored to the deck, a motif repeated diminuendo in the children's playroom under a mural of the four-and-twenty blackbirds. The staircase and lounges were carpeted in a soft green while halls and passages were surfaced with traditional patterned rubber tiling, supplied by a firm with the improbable name of the India Rubber, Gutta-Percha and Telegraph Works Company of Silvertown. Over the latticed gangway connected with the shore came the final loads, the ultimate dressing for passenger use: linen, blankets, crystal, cutlery, napery and stores. Coal barges tied up to the hull and the first full load of coal rattled down the ports into the bunkers. Watchers on both shores who took note of such things saw clouds of smoke pour from the funnels. For the first time since they left the machine shops ashore, the turbines were turned over cautiously for a static test. Sixteen lifeboats, the Board of Trade's standard number in those days, were hung in the freshly painted davits, eight to a side. The *Mauretania* was ready for her preliminary trials.

Parsons brought the *Turbinia* alongside for a historic photograph, mute testimony to the giant application afforded his invention since the Naval

Review a decade earlier. On September 17, the *Mauretania* was taken down to the sea for five days of secret builder's tests. By the trial's end, those on board were faced with the sobering fact that the problem of vibration was critical. Although the engines were not pressed to full power, near twenty knots the *Mauretania* shuddered badly, so much so that those on the bridge, at least five hundred feet away from the nearest propeller, were shaken quite uncomfortably.

It should be pointed out that the turbines were not at fault. The vibration in question was not the subdued throb of the engines; that sensation had been reduced in the switch from reciprocating engine to turbine. The jarring, ship-shaking rattle that turned eight hundred feet of steel hull into an expensive tuning fork came from the four screws. There was nothing defective about them and they represented the last word in propeller design in 1906. But it was an infant science and, coincidentally, a field in which the ubiquitous Parsons had done pioneering work; quite naturally, since anyone concerned with the business of fast hull speeds must inevitably encounter propeller problems. *Turbinia* had ended up with nine propellers on three shafts. Parsons had arrived at that solution following a series of tests conducted in a glass-walled tank that enclosed an electrically driven single screw. By using intense illumination and high-speed photography, he was able to study and photograph the phenomenon of cavitation: a rapidly revolving propeller creates such a thrust and resulting suction that the water behind it is literally vaporized. The vapor appears at the trailing edge of each blade in the form of an elongated spiral bubble. Water, rushing to fill the vacuum created, hammers at the blade surface and can, in a short space of time, pit and weaken the material.

The little electric launch that was the *Mauretania*'s prototype, equipped with scale propellers, had been invaluable for determining the relative placement of the screws; however, it could give little evidence of the intense vibration that first plagued the ultimate ship. Apart from the sizes involved, wooden and steel hulls do not resonate at the same frequency, and the complex nature of the turbulence that roared about the after end of the *Mauretania* as she raced through the North Sea that September of 1907 could not be duplicated in a laboratory tank. Just as frustrating, short of passing a plucky diver at high speed, there was no method of observing propeller performance while under way. Those in the shaft tunnel near the tail could hear the thunder of the blades thrashing the water and the water boiling against the shell plating. But when this same hideous racket was both felt and heard in the comfortable sanctity of the passenger spaces amidships, then something had to be done about it.

Back at Wallsend, in the month remaining before the scheduled departure for the west coast and acceptance trials, strengthening members were introduced discreetly into the after sections of the vessel. There was talk of a new set of propellers but this would wait until a year hence, when one of the originals was lost at sea. The replacement set put immediately into work at that time were vastly superior and vibration was happily reduced. It is indicative of the *Mauretania*'s superb design that she made eight voyages on three screws while waiting for the new ones.

On the afternoon of October 22, 1907, a select company of visitors embarked for passage around the north coast of Scotland. Thousands lined the river as she made her cautious way downstream. Their affection for the ship was based not on her size or speed, but a very special pride of creation. That Wallsend's grimy sprawl could produce such a glistening marvel was a kind of industrial miracle in itself; that she was on her way to service in the Atlantic was less important than her making a brave show for their rivals on the Clyde. The competition between those two northern ship-building centers was intensely emotional. Tyneside stokers in the boiler rooms spat on their blackened hands. "We'll lick the Lucy," one of them remarked, "even if we bust the Mary to do it!"

At Tynemouth, the tugs left her and Mary, Lady Inverclyde, wife of Cunard's chairman, was given the honor of transmitting the first command from the bridge that would send the *Mauretania* on her way north. The shrilling gong of the telegraph echoed down on the starting platform in the engine room. Duty engineers spun the four wheels that admitted steam through sluice valves to the turbine casings. The revolution counters began to climb and the great ship stood away into the autumn dusk.

It was a pleasant two-day cruise to Liverpool. The weather was fine and the *Mauretania* steamed along at a brisk twenty-two knots. The afternoon of the second day, grouped about a semicircle of wicker chairs borrowed from the veranda café for the occasion, the assembled brass of Cunard and Swan Hunter were photographed on the boat deck, squinting happily into the watery northern sun. They reached the Mersey at dawn on the twenty-fourth and by day's end, the ship was safely ensconced in the Canada dry dock. She was by then double her launch weight and the wooden blocks interspersed on the dry-dock floor were purposely an inch higher than their cast-iron neighbors; as the water was pumped out of the dock, the *Mauretania*'s vast deadweight settled down, crushing the oak to a uniform height.

The Canada dock was but one of a series of renovations the Mersey Docks and the Harbor Board had put into effect in anticipation of the two new ships. Nearly a quarter of a million tons of mud had been dredged from the Sloyne, the body of water that gave sheltered anchorage awaiting pier space. Two enormous new buoys, Cunard North and South, had been provided for *Lusitania* and *Mauretania*. On the Princess Dock, the floating pier where passengers would board, there was a new train shed.

Across the Atlantic, Army Engineers had begun dredging a new channel into New York Harbor. It was a familiar pattern to harbor authorities in all Western Ocean ports who were forced to keep pace with the new giants. For the hundred years prior to World War II, length, tonnage and displacement of Atlantic passenger liners grew with staggering rapidity. It would seem never ending: Hudson piers long enough for the *Mauretania* would be unable to accommodate the *Olympic* four years later. And if New York dragged its feet, port officials needed only the specter of a Boston or Montauk terminal to goad them into action.

In early November, fully coaled again, the *Mauretania* sailed from Liverpool for acceptance trials. Company officials were joined by a deputation from the Admiralty. These latter had set a stern test, the length of England, north to south through the Irish Sea, a distance of three hundred and four miles. To discount the possibility of assistance from a following wind, it was laid down that the course must be run twice in both directions. When the ship crossed the finish line at the Corswall Point Light, after two complete voyages, the resulting figures were heartening: *Mauretania*'s average of twenty-five-and-a-half knots not only exceeded Admiralty requirements by a comfortable margin but had beaten the *Lusitania*'s time over the same course. The Royal Navy was satisfied, Cunard delighted and Swan Hunter ecstatic.

Following the long-distance trials, the ship turned into the Firth of Clyde for tests off the Skelmorlie Mile. Large ocean vessels require a section of shoreline of deep draft, so that exact tests over a measured mile can be made between two onshore markers. All British ships, up to and including the second *Queen Elizabeth,* used the Skelmorlie Mile. (American shipbuilders have their choice of three measured miles: off the coast of Maine, Delaware or in Cuba's Guantanamo Bay. However, speed trials for the *United States* took advantage of a radar buoy that pinpointed, with extreme accuracy, the speed at which the ship departed a fixed point.)

The *Mauretania*'s performance over the Skelmorlie was the occasion for additional rejoicing on the bridge: twenty-six knots was topped. Finally, the ship was put through a series of jarring, shuddering tests for maneuverability. They are known succinctly as crash ahead, crash astern and crash turns and are all that the names imply, subjecting vessels and their machinery to stresses seldom if ever experienced again. Scarcely a decade later, the *Mauretania* did make a crash turn to port in the Mediterranean, avoiding by a matter of feet a German torpedo across her stern. The trials were again successful and the day's only excitement was the near swamping of a coastal steamer unfortunate enough to be passing by; the wash from a high-speed turn nearly engulfed her.

Back at her home port, the ship was handed over officially to Cunard. Her maiden voyage came a week later. It was in a sense anticlimactic, in that the press had expended their superlatives on the *Lusitania*'s three months earlier. Yet a crowd of fifty thousand braved a cold misty rain to watch the new ship leave her buoy in the Sloyne and tie up at the landing stage. First on board was a record shipment of gold bullion, twelve tons in all. The boat train from London was an hour late so that it was nearly dark by the time first-class passengers and their luggage were hurried on board by the marine superintendent. Occupying the two regal suites, complete with statuary marble mantelpieces over their electric fires, were a Drexel and a princess respectively; this symbolic combination of wealth and royalty was happily symptomatic of future passenger lists when aristocrats of birth and wealth graced the ship.

At seven-thirty, the lines were cast off and tugs pulled her clear of the land. Her maiden voyage had begun; to the whistled greetings from Mersey craft was added a firework salute as she passed the New Brighton pier. At eight o'clock, as Liverpool's lights dropped astern, the bugle summoned passengers for the first time down to the dining saloon. The next morning, in Queenstown, she took on mail and more passengers, deluging the post office ashore with a record number of cables and letters. That evening, the eighteenth of November, Company headquarters in Liverpool had a message: MAURETANIA, 207 MILES WEST OF FASTNET AT 10 P.M. SUNDAY. ALL WELL.

In truth, all was not well for very long. Maiden voyages are seldom scheduled for November and the *Mauretania* ran into three days of very dirty weather, a fitting baptism into the grim realities of the North Atlantic winter. The spare anchor on the fo'c's'le broke loose and there ensued a desperate three-hour grapple to secure it, all the while hove to against mountainous seas. Several promenade deck windows were shattered and were patched with wooden plugs. The teak rails of the monkey island, high above the sea on top of the bridge, were twisted and battered by green water. Rivulets of sea water could be seen inside the ship and the catering department had a backlog of unconsumed stores, traditionally a concomitance of rough weather. There was, in point of fact, one single memorable statistic of

R.M.S. *Mauretania* sails on her maiden
voyage. Liverpudlians scurry for a last
look as Cunard's second turbine-driven
monster joins her sister in service on the
North Atlantic. (*Radio Times Hulton
Picture Library*)

that ghastly crossing: on the last full day at sea, with good weather, the *Mauretania* made a record run of six hundred twenty-four miles.

Her arrival off Sandy Hook on the twenty-second of November was masked by an impenetrable blanket of fog. The ship crept up to Quarantine and dropped anchor at noon. Captain Pritchard was quite resigned to waiting there until the following morning, but his passengers were not. It was inevitable that they should feel bilked; having weathered the discomforts of the passage, racing across the Atlantic in the world's newest liner, it was galling to think of spending another night on board within sound, if not sight, of their destination. But New York Harbor fogs are as notorious as they are commonplace. The master was quite right in resisting the entreaties of outraged passengers who approached him on the bridge, demanding that they be put ashore. Fortunately, the fog lifted quixotically near dusk and at six-fifteen, the *Mauretania* tied up at Cunard's 14th Street pier.

She sailed for Liverpool at the end of the month, completing the second half of her maiden voyage. The *Lusitania* and *Mauretania* were finally in service and it was apparent at once that Lord Inverclyde's enthusiasm for their construction was amply justified. The patient research that produced the hulls, their rugged construction at the hand of Britain's shipbuilders, and the efficiency of Parsons' magnificent turbines were to pay dividends both financial and national over the next decade. Cunard swept the seas and called the bluff of the American threat. The German racer *Kaiser Wilhelm II* was hopelessly outclassed and the *Mauretania* was to hold the Blue Ribband for twenty-two of her twenty-eight years' service.

*In the case of the Titanic, the unlikely
happened.*
> —THE SHIPBUILDER

3.
Olympic-Titanic

When Samuel Cunard won the mail contract in 1840, his zeal to formalize Atlantic sailings prompted adherence to a regular weekly service. He realized that passengers as well as government would be attracted by a company advertising departures from Liverpool to America on the same day, week in and week out. His assumption was correct and it is a pattern that exists to the present. Weekly sailings became a constant in the schedules of all transatlantic competitors. Given this established criterion, naval architects and shipbuilders then worked to reduce the number of ships required to maintain it.

For more than sixty years, it took four. But the successful debut of the *Lusitania* and *Mauretania* initiated a reduction to three. The *Aquitania* didn't arrive until 1914, and for several years prior to that time the company compromised with the two new turbine ships and their slower sister of a previous generation, the *Campania*. In the stormy winter months, the short-comings of this mismatched trio illustrate an inescapable maxim of Atlantic competition: ships in the same service should have the same service capa-bilities. Among the many disadvantages faced by the United States Lines in running the *Leviathan* in the twenties was that she had no adequate run-ning mates. Her superior size and speed alone were not enough, for what counts in the long run is the ability of a company's ships to sustain a bal-anced express service.

By the summer of 1914, following the maiden voyage of the *Aquitania,* third and largest of the trio, Cunard was the first to have its three-ship service in operation. On any given Saturday, one of the three would sail from Liverpool, not completing the voyage for seventeen days. (It should be un-derstood here that "voyage" is defined as a round trip, out and back to the home port.) The time was divided as follows: six days to New York, five days turnaround and another six back. The remaining time, from Tuesday to Saturday, the ship was coaled, cleaned and victualed, ready to start the cycle again. With minor variations, this tempo was maintained by all Atlan-tic liners for the next three decades, until the advent of a two-ship service inaugurated by the *Queens* after World War II.

But for the First World War, Cunard's monopoly would not have lasted very long. Energetic competitors at home and overseas were of the same mind. The Oceanic Steam Navigation Company or White Star Line planned an ambitious trio of their own. There had existed a long and special rela-tionship between this company and Harland & Wolff, the Belfast shipbuild-ers. Every White Star liner from the *Oceanic* had been launched there. Thomas Ismay, founder of the Line, had made other innovations on that famous ship besides placing the first-class passengers amidships. Skylights and deckhouses were joined and the roofed-over perimeter served as the Atlantic's first promenade deck. Wooden bulkheads were replaced with the familiar teak and iron railings; this was primarily a safety factor, allow-ing swifter drainage of decks in rough weather. The *Oceanic*'s passengers used bathrooms equipped with fresh and salt water taps that could be reached without crossing the open deck. They could summon a steward by ringing an electric bell rather than yelling, they could dine seated on a chair instead of a bench, and gentlemen were provided with a room specifically designed for smoking, so that after-dinner cigars could be enjoyed in cir-cumstances inestimably more cheerful than the leeward fiddley grating. Ladies could pass the time in a carpeted lounge, complete with a piano

Cunard's final entrant for the North Atlantic's first three-ship service. The *Aquitania* sails from Liverpool on her maiden voyage in late May of 1914, joining the *Mauretania* and *Lusitania* on the run to New York. (*Cunard*)

Below, midocean on the *Mauretania*'s starboard boat deck. The expanse of rail free from lifeboats dates the picture pre-*Titanic*. After April of 1912, additional boats were installed on all North Atlantic liners. (*National Maritime Museum, Greenwich*)

chained to the wall. Eight years after her maiden voyage, a system of electric lighting was installed on the *Oceanic,* assuring brightly lit interiors on board a ship for the first time. An earlier experiment with gas illumination had been rejected when it was discovered that the working of the ship tended to rupture seams in the piping.

One night in 1907, J. Bruce Ismay, son of the line's founder, dined at the Belgravia house of Lord Pirrie, chairman of Harland & Wolff. It was midsummer; the *Lusitania* was already in service and the *Mauretania* nearing completion. Conversation between the two men and their wives turned to the ship that should be built to counter Cunard's lead. From this informal discussion came a proposal to build a giant triple threat, a class of liners so vast that both men knew as they spoke, that there did not exist a berth, a dry dock or even a pier that would accommodate them. The ships would make the crossing in under a week but the emphasis was to be on safety and comfort, comfort on a scale so magnificent that the few additional hours at sea would pass unnoticed. The sumptuous elegance that Ismay envisioned was, quite logically, an extension of his father's original pursuit of elementary convenience.

That two of the three ships would never see New York Harbor was in no way attributable to the extravagance of their accommodations. The loss of the *Titanic* gave birth to a romantic notion in some quarters that shipbuilders were being punished by some seagoing providence, that such *embarras de richesses* violated the rules of nautical dependability; absurd as this was, it is no coincidence that at about this time, the expression "floating palace" came into popular usage.

The first of the three to be launched was the *Olympic,* in October of 1910. All White Star names ended with *ic,* part of a ship identification system paralleling Cunard's *-ia* suffix. Unlike the rival company, however, White Star did not by custom make the launch much of an occasion. A string of signal flags spelling out SUCCESS draped across the *Olympic*'s bow was practically the only concession to celebration: there was no bunting, no speech, not even a bottle of champagne. A signal rocket soared into the air over the yard, the triggers fell and twenty-seven thousand tons of steel hull, nearly nine hundred feet long, slid into the river Lagan. Her bulk alone was ceremony enough. Although only four short years had passed since the appearance of the *Mauretania,* the increase in size was remarkable. Even more astonishing, Harland & Wolff had assembled enough industrial muscle to build both *Olympic* and *Titanic* in near tandem on specially constructed adjoining berths. It was both the first and last time that two ships of this size would take shape as neighbors. On May 31, 1911, the same day that the *Titanic* was launched, her sister ship sailed to Liverpool.

However, the Mersey port was only an intermediate stop. To the despair of Liverpudlians, the White Star Company had moved its base of operations to Southampton and the *Olympic* was the first of the giant ships to start her maiden voyage from that port. The move south brought the Company's terminus not only much closer to London but, more important, into direct competition with those continental ships that made England's south coast a regular stopping point en route to America. The southern port had a harbor vastly superior to Liverpool's. The same Isle of Wight that affords a sheltered anchorage to Southampton water is responsible also for a unique local phenomenon, the double tide. As the tide ebbs down the Channel toward the Western Ocean, enough water is diverted by the projecting spur of the Ryde peninsula to partially reflood the entire estuary. Before the present harbor channel was dredged, this extended availability of deep water gave the port an advantage over its neighbors that it had enjoyed since Roman times. Cunard, whose *Mauretania* had twice broken loose from her moorings in the Sloyne during storms, was to follow suit and move its first string of ships south after World War I.

Both the visitors who, in return for a charitable donation, thronged the *Olympic* in Liverpool and passengers who later boarded her at Southampton were overwhelmed with the ship's scale. Not since the *Great Eastern,* that mid-nineteenth-century freak built fifty years before her time, had the seagoing public been assigned such vast acreage. Less than a hundred feet longer and only four feet broader than the *Mauretania,* the *Olympic* was half again as great in gross tonnage. By eschewing the fine hull lines demanded by a Blue Riband candidate, her builders had achieved a spatial opulence nothing short of miraculous. Almost seven of a total of ten decks were devoted exclusively to the accommodation of over twenty-four hundred passengers.

For the more than seven hundred traveling first class, the dominant sensation was one of apparently limitless space. Adequate elbowroom was and still is the primary characteristic of "first-class" accommodation of any kind, be it the Daimler's back seat or the splendid isolation of a private Pullman. On board ship, it is a consideration that outweighs all the caviar, high-servant ratio and sumptuous decoration: room enough for trunks in the cabin, room enough for a table for two in the smoking room to become a table for ten, room enough for a private conversation in a public room. There should never be a need to get anywhere first or, God forbid, to line up. This awareness that one is never crowded contributes heavily to the

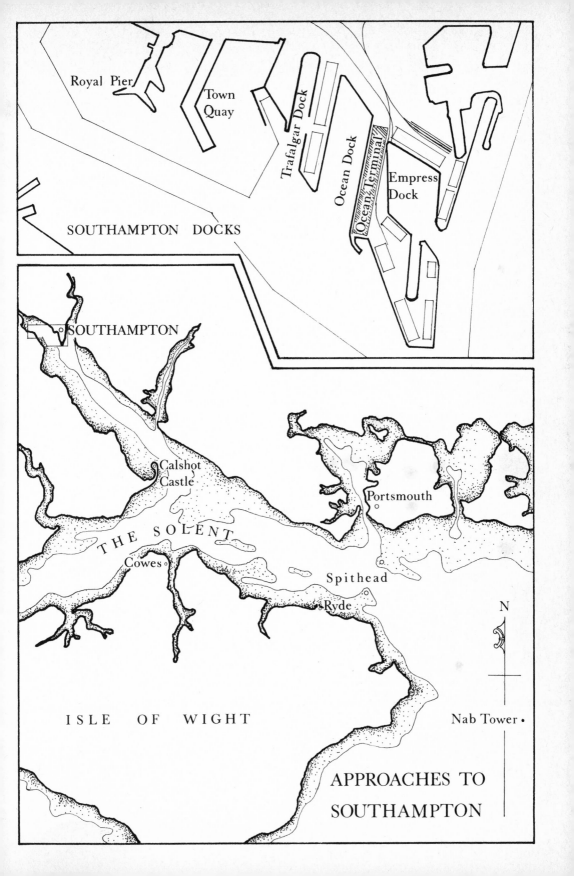

Royal Pier

Town
Quay

Trafalgar Dock

Ocean Dock

Ocean Terminal

Empress
Dock

SOUTHAMPTON DOCKS

SOUTHAMPTON

Calshot
Castle

Portsmouth

THE SOLENT

Cowes

Spithead

Ryde

ISLE OF WIGHT

N

Nab Tower •

APPROACHES TO
SOUTHAMPTON

special euphoria of a good crossing and is without question the most precious return on investment in a first-class ticket. It had been exploited to the full in the new ship.

The *Olympic*'s boat deck was as clean swept as the *Mauretania*'s had been crowded. The ventilating systems, clustered about a quartet of buff, black-topped funnels, were confined to a supplementary deck a few feet higher, the upthrust roofs of the public rooms on A-deck. These rooms were less remarkable for their size than the entrances that led into them. Vestibules of grandiose pretension, with lavish provision of space devoted to casual or intermittent use, were a spectacular novelty throughout the ship. The main staircase descended successively through four foyers, each ample enough to have concealed in its forward end a triple bank of elevators. Aft of the lounge was yet another staircase, surely as grand as the first, merely a prelude to the Georgian smoking room. Outside the dining saloon on D-deck was a reception hall fully half as large as the vast chamber it anticipated. With seemingly endless reserves at their disposal, the builders' largesse was unique.

The design miracle that they had wrought was that those extravagant interiors could be housed in such a graceful hull. The *Olympic* only just preceded a period in the evolution of the Atlantic express liner when increased tonnage would prohibit adherence to traditional hull forms. Forty-five thousand gross tons was a ceiling beyond which it was inadvisable to venture without a severe reassessment of stability factors. It was a limit that Harland & Wolff sensibly observed and that the Kaiser did not: the *Imperator* class tended toward a lumbering grotesquery that the British ship neatly avoided. The *Olympic* was, in the same breathtaking instance, the last of the lean, yachtlike racers and the first "floating palace."

Combatting the enforced idleness of previous crossings was a profusion of time-killing diversions. Within the mahogany walls of the boat-deck gymnasium was a traditional selection of foils, Indian clubs, and dumbbells. The instructor had additionally at his command a battery of motorized exercisers imported from Wiesbaden, *body-kultur* capital of the world: electric horses and camels, rowing machines, vibrators, counterweighted pulley devices and punching bags. Six decks below was a modest yet novel swimming pool, tucked above the number five boiler casing on the starboard side. There was also a squash court, complete with spectator's gallery, as well as a complex of Turkish and electric baths. These latter were nothing more than horizontal iron maidens whose spikes had been replaced with electric bulbs; what benefits were sought by Edwardian health faddists

THE ONLY WAY TO CROSS

other than heat was not advertised and I suspect that "electric bath" was a euphemism sufficiently delicate for "sweatbox."

The Company's preoccupation with exercise was perhaps in compensation for the indulgencies possible on D-deck, courtesy of the catering department. The dining room, happily for White Star publicists, was the largest afloat. It could accommodate over five hundred at one sitting, all but those first-class passengers who chose the restaurant two decks above. Gone was the infamous swivel chair, bolted to the deck; passengers luxuriated in handsome Jacobean reproductions upholstered in green leather, set at a selection of tables that seated from two to twelve. For the first time in Atlantic history, passengers in a dining saloon could dine à deux if they so desired. Privacy was further augmented by partitions creating six dining areas, with passengers removed from but within sight of the central oval where Captain Smith entertained a select dozen of their fellows. The sides of the saloon coincided with those of the ship and daylight that passed successively through grouped portholes and handsome mullioned windows was electrically reinforced to provide the illusion of perpetual sunlight.

Deck plans of early twentieth-century steamers define contemporary sociosexual prejudices far more effectively than reams of women's liberation tracts. Although the smoking room as a shipboard fixture was only forty years old in 1911, it was nevertheless the largest of the Olympic's public rooms on A-deck; "public," that is, to gentlemen, but not to their wives. Ladies were provided with two alternative strongholds: the reading and writing room forward and two verandas and palm courts aft. When surfeited with the pleasure of their own company in either purdah, they had available as rendezvous with their husbands a lounge of surprisingly modest proportions. This arena of bisexual activity, unlike the airplane hangars in today's ships, could seat no more than one sixth of the entire first-class complement. Thus, it appears that male and female passengers on the Olympic were neither encouraged nor expected to mingle in the hours between dining and retiring.

After-dinner relief from feminine chatter was a male prerogative ashore and there was evidently no reason to amend it at sea. The provision of a handsome, totally masculine haven was symptomatic of, quite literally, a gentlemen's agreement between builder and those of his clients who paid the bills; it guaranteed segregation of the sexes in the evening and for a portion of the day as well. Women who yearned for something more rewarding than the triple role of sweetheart, wife and mother (in that order) could find scant solace in the bursts of jocular good fellowship that seeped, with good cigar smoke, between the brass-studded leather doors of the

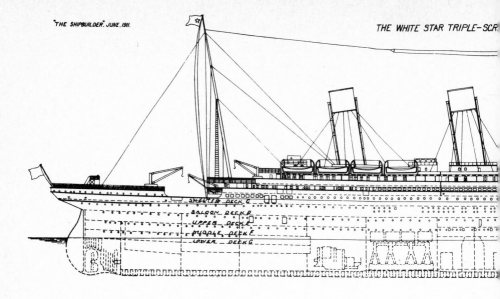

SHELTER DECK C
SALOON DECK D
UPPER DECK E
MIDDLE DECK F
LOWER DECK G

Harland & Wolff's masterpiece: The
clean, balanced line of the *Olympic* had a
unique grace never since equalled. Shown
here are the builder's elevation and plans
for the top two decks. (*Shipping World
and Shipbuilder*)

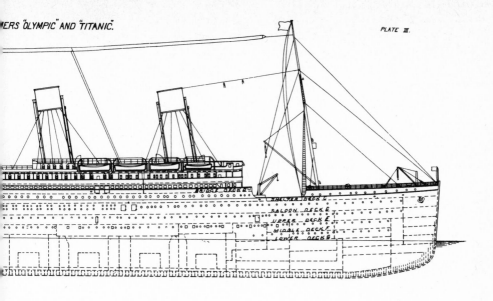

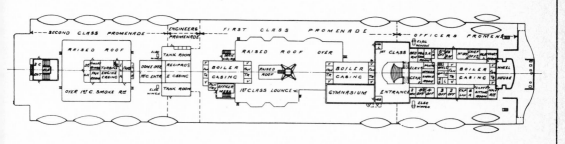

BOAT DECK.

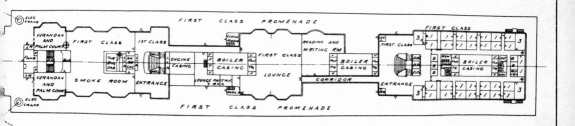

PROMENADE DECK A.

smoking room. An aunt of mine who still refers disparagingly to dirty stories as "smoking-room stories" articulates not only a rankling objection cherished since childhood but unconsciously, I think, a keen sense of deprivation. Very little of interest occurred in the clubs and rooms from which she was barred; what distressed her most was the unquestioned dogma that dictated her exclusion.

Fortunately, the *Olympic*'s maiden voyage in 1911 coincided with the coronation of George V, whose accession to the throne terminated the apotheosis of Anglo-Saxon *machismo* perpetuated by his father. Edward VII gave more than a name to his reign: he brought to stifling perfection the Victorian myth of male dominance, personifying in his corpulent self the invulnerable majesty of an attitude that had somehow survived for sixty years of a woman's reign. Changes were in the offing that were reflected almost immediately in ships' interiors: the following year, the *Titanic*'s B-deck promenade had carved out of its starboard side a Café Parisien as an additional focus for mixed recreation. The *Imperator,* the Kaiser's answer to the *Olympic,* would boast a lounge large enough for enormous numbers of couples to dance in the evening. And even on the *Olympic* herself, it would not be too many years before women, voting, smoking and trousered, often as not, would invade the hallowed sanctum, access to which they were traditionally denied.

Passengers on the maiden voyage who mastered enough of the *Olympic*'s geography to explore the ship remarked on the relatively handsome surroundings of their shipmates in second class. Venturing lower in both the hull and social scale, they would have found less to marvel at. It is a popular Atlantic cliché that a new ship's cheapest quarters rival the best accommodation of earlier vessels. *The Shipbuilder* concluded in its souvenir issue devoted entirely to the new class of ship: "Third class passengers today have greater comforts provided than had first class passengers before the great modern developments in passenger carrying, for which the White Star Line has been largely responsible."

It is doubtful whether the occupants of a cramped little stateroom somewhere just above the *Olympic*'s propellers would have been entirely in sympathy with this cavalier pronouncement. Indeed, it is comparable to the flatulent admonishment parents have used on generations of homesick schoolboys: "If you think this is bad, you should have been here when I was a lad. . . ." No matter how well intentioned, this is more a rebuke than a comfort. It is impossible to equate the utilitarian dreariness of immigrant quarters with the polished splendor of the first class from any decade. One might as well assume that the mechanical conveniences of a villa in Levit-

Lord Pirrie, her builder, and Captain E. J. Smith, her master, confer on the *Olympic*'s boat deck. It is June 6, 1911, sailing day for the maiden voyage; paint crews are aloft, touching up the buff on number one funnel. (*Radio Times Hulton Picture Library*)

town can approach the proportioned luxe of a Georgian country house. Apart from the perquisites of taste and style, the two are simply not in the same league.

A fuller discussion of immigrant conditions follows in a later chapter. Suffice to say for the *Olympic* that, given the small number of open berths, constructed of galvanized iron rather than vermin-prone wood, given the availability, at a price, of some double cabins, given adequate light, ventilation and sanitary arrangements, life in the third class was only the faintest carbon copy of first. Moreover, it is an incredible fact that the cooling room of the Turkish bath was half again as large as the third-class galley; in other words, food for a thousand was prepared in a space less commodious than the Byzantine grandeur allotted for the use of a dozen first-class passengers. On the opposite side of the ship, no less than forty-two third-class stewards were housed in a room of comparable size.

Rather than lining the sides of the hull, the bunkers lay athwartship so that each boiler room was separated from its neighbor by a transverse barrier of coal and watertight bulkhead. A ready supply of fuel was thus convenient to each furnace and a smaller work force was adequate to manhandle coal to the stokers. In the full hull width resulting from this bunkering arrangement, four of the six boiler rooms had a quintet of enormous boilers packed into them; that this left the *Olympic*'s flanks unprotected assumed tragic significance for her sister ship the following year. The center of the three propellers was driven by a low-pressure turbine, Harland & Wolff having decided that a combination of reciprocating and turbine engines was the most economical arrangement for the new class.

The maiden voyage, traditionally in June, attracted great interest on both sides of the Atlantic. The ship was only half full yet so popular was the squash court that players were restricted to half-hour sessions. There was labor unrest among the Southampton coal passers and five of the ship's boilers remained unlit. Nevertheless, she made a respectable crossing, having sailed on Wednesday the fourteenth and arriving the following Wednesday. Captain Smith assured reporters who swarmed on board at Quarantine that the *Olympic* would require a full week to make its crossing and would not arrive on Tuesday. As if to buttress the reporters' point, the *Lusitania,* which *was* a "Tuesday ship," passed downstream en route for the coronation as tugs edged the White Star vessel to her berth; inexplicably, the Cunard skipper did not join in the noisy salute to his new rival. Pier 59 had been extended into the river by ninety feet to protect the stern of the *Olympic*. It was at best a Rube Goldberg effort, rendered even more fragile by the *Celtic* which had rammed it the week previous. Permission to extend

The White Star Line's *Olympic* anchors off Quarantine for the first time. Three tugs have already arrived to escort her up to the pier. (*Prints and Photographs Division, Library of Congress*)

Below, the *Olympic* at her western terminal. New York harbor authorities were understandably reluctant to extend the pier to accommodate the White Star's new giant. (*Edwin Levick Collection, The Mariners Museum, Newport News, Virginia*)

Divers examine the *Olympic*'s shell plating directly below the point where H.M.S. *Hawke*'s ram sliced open a bank of second-class cabins. (*Frank Braynard Collection*)

the pier had finally been given after the International Mercantile Marine had appealed to Washington over the heads of a reluctant harbor board.

On the return leg of the maiden voyage, one of the ship's American passengers "forgot" his spectacles; I can only assume that it was a staged lapse of memory, since Wanamaker's supposedly dispatched a replacement pair to a young British aviator in Garden City, whose Howard Wright biplane was airborne as the *Olympic* was passing through the Narrows. Although provided with the largest floating target in the world, the mission was a failure and the pilot, whose name was Sopwith, saw the parcel hit the side of the vessel and fall into the water. He went on to become one of Britain's most successful aircraft designers, responsible for the immortal Sopwith Camel of World War I. Astonishingly enough, his failure to "bomb" the *Olympic* successfully was used as reassuring evidence that airplanes would never pose a threat to ships. That they would, both tactically and economically, was evidently a possibility so remote as to be ludicrous in 1911.

In September of that same year, the *Olympic* was involved in a freak accident, the first of three notable collisions in her long career. This one was with the Royal Navy cruiser H.M.S. *Hawke* and occurred in the Solent at the start of her fifth voyage. It was one of those incredible convergences, in full daylight on a calm sea within sight of land, where two normally operated vessels steamed blithely to a point of impact as though mesmerized. A court of inquiry later decided against the White Star Line, completely absolving the cruiser's commander. I personally find it strange that a vessel whose bow has pierced the flank of another can retire from the scene of the collision totally free of guilt; however, Royal Navy experts put the blame on powerful forces of suction exerted by the larger ship and chose to ignore the admission that the *Hawke*'s steering gear was jammed seconds before the accident.

It was a miracle that there were no casualties. The second-class cabins sliced open were empty, their occupants lunching in the dining saloon one deck higher. Fortunately, the bow of the naval ship was equipped with a ram which absorbed the shock of impact above the water level; there was relatively little damage below. Thomas Magee, an American anxious to get home to San Francisco and his three-year-old child, dropped through the hole after the ship had anchored in Osborne Bay, pressed three sovereigns into the hand of a boatman and reached Cowes after a fierce row against wind and tide. Once there, he informed company officials that the *Olympic* would not sail and booked passage on the *Adriatic* sailing the following day from Liverpool. Quite understandably, the White Star office in the Isle of

Wight didn't believe him, since this was the first news of the accident they had received. Their shock can be equated with the distress experienced by Mrs. Magee on board the *Olympic,* who was hysterical at finding no trace of her husband. The ship was out of service for six weeks while plating was replaced in the Belfast drydock.

The *Titanic* entered service the following year and sank after colliding with an iceberg in the most notorious maiden voyage in history. The disaster has been the subject of countless books and articles, films, plays and the shock climax of Noel Coward's *Cavalcade.* It continues to engender a grim fascination that shows little sign of abatement even now, sixty years after that frightful April night in 1912. Bookshops and museums specializing in maritime affairs report that requests for information about the ship outnumber all others. The Smithsonian's Department of Marine Transportation has mimeographed a form reply to *Titanic* inquiries. Harland & Wolff have long ceased to acknowledge correspondence on the subject. There is a society founded as recently as 1963, called the Titanic Enthusiasts of America, to perpetuate the memory of the *Titanic* and her two sister ships. Membership is composed of those survivors still alive and a group of surprisingly young enthusiasts, some of whose parents were not even born when the ship was lost.

The circumstances surrounding the sinking made irresistible copy: the first crossing of the world's largest and most luxurious ship, initially neglected because it seemed only a repeat of the *Olympic*'s maiden voyage the year previous; a passenger list larded with names from America's moneyed aristocracy; the appalling lack of lifeboats and a death toll that was kindest to the first class; and overall, an aura of extraordinary gallantry typified by Benjamin Guggenheim's "We are dressed in our best and prepared to go down like gentlemen."

But all this was to appear later. For four days, in the absence of hard news, the world's press had a field day concocting elaborate accounts barely distinguishable from wishful thinking. From the moment when the first ghastly rumors swept New York and Southampton, the public was insatiable in its demand for news of the ship, practically all of which was the inventive product of editors desperate to fill their front pages. Marconi's wireless, then in its infancy and largely responsible for those lives that were saved, inadvertently triggered a monstrous falsehood: the unfortunate juxtaposition of two isolated sentences picked up by the *Olympic*'s wireless had the *Titanic* still afloat and being towed to Halifax. A gala boat train, packed with American relatives, was halfway to the Canadian port before telegraphed instructions from White Star headquarters in New York flagged it down in the Maine woods.

When the truth finally did emerge, it was subject to a curious, almost supernatural embellishment consistent with those initial inaccuracies. It appears that the starker the tragedy, the more outrageous fantasies it proliferates. The assassination of President Kennedy in our own generation is a fair case in point: the most incredible elaborations have clouded those events in Dallas, as though the impact of a particularly horrifying reality can be minimized with a garnish of fanciful trivia. Similarly, the *Titanic* disaster produced its own blend of fact, superstition and wishful thinking, imparting significance to even the most ordinary occurrences.

A surviving steward remembered that his White Star badge had disintegrated in his wife's hands when she transferred it to a new cap. At another Southampton house, a picture fell from the wall suddenly—according to local superstition, evidence of a lost ship. A host of visionaries, spiritual Monday morning quarterbacks, confessed to pier-side forebodings after the ship went down. Their premonitions seemed immediately validated when the *Titanic*'s propellers dislodged the liner *New York* from her Southampton moorings. A coal fire smoldered in bunker number 5 for the entire aborted voyage, ironically extinguished by the fatal inundation of sea water. (Most of the *Titanic*'s coal was a scratch lot, much of it coming from New York in the bunkers and public rooms of the *Olympic;* Southampton was in the grip of a coal strike again.) At Queenstown, a stoker poked his blackened face over the rim of the dummy fourth funnel, prompting a susceptible passenger to recall an angel of death. As the ship passed the Old Head of Kinsale, the signal halyard carrying acknowledgment of a bon-voyage message from the lighthouse parted, necessitating a complete turn about to retrieve the loose end flying to leeward. At sea, the day prior to the fateful Sunday, a fireman saw half a dozen rats, rare on a new ship, scurrying aft, away from the point of eventual collision.

Long after the *Titanic* was gone, the myths persisted. In England, it was rumored with some conviction that hundreds of Belfast steelworkers had perished in the wreck, their existence suppressed by the Board of Trade. Despite authentic reports that he went down with his ship, Captain Smith exhibited a durable capacity to pop up in the most unlikely places: a fellow sea captain "saw" him on a Baltimore street a week after the tragedy and, years later, newspapers reported the passing of a penniless derelict in Columbus, Ohio, nicknamed Whispering Smith, who confessed on his deathbed that he was the master of the *Titanic*. There is still, making the rounds of auction rooms in England, a violin touted as one that serenaded passengers on the doomed ship.

It was on page 26 of *The Shipbuilder*'s souvenir issue mentioned above that the word "unsinkable" had first appeared. (In all fairness to that scrupulously honest periodical, it was preceded by a qualifying "practically.") Nevertheless, the word stuck and filtered without discouragement into the popular gossip that surrounds any new ship on the Atlantic. It was a piece of gratuitous publicity that the White Star Line came ultimately to regret. Naval architects will discredit an unsinkable ship just as surely as will firemen a fireproof building; both are impossible. The *Titanic* sank because of reckless seamanship and a scheme of design inadequate for the particular accident that befell her.

The Arctic winter of 1911–1912 was exceptionally mild, a phenomenon tied to a cycle of eight-year frequency. Break-offs from glaciers jutting into the sea along Greenland's west coast were accelerated, proliferating bergs of abnormally large size; this meant survival for a longer period as they drifted down toward the waters off Newfoundland. The fishing ground there owes its formation to a confluence of the ice-bearing Labrador current with a northbound spur of the Gulf Stream. Thousands of years of this thermal interaction have deposited layer upon layer of Greenland stone and debris on the sea bottom, detritus liberated from melting icebergs. In the early spring of 1912, then, there was not only more ice but more ice farther south.

The *Titanic* was traveling in lanes specifically routed to avoid ice for that season, lanes that were moved even further south following the disaster. She was steaming at a brisk pace through waters that no fewer than six wireless reports had indicated to be filled with ice. Her two forward lookouts, stationed traditionally in the crow's-nest, might have been better posted on the forepeak: for on a calm moonless night, no matter how bright the stars, icebergs are not easy to spot from above. The telltale line of white breakers around the base is not there and the advantage of height is nullified by lack of a silhouette against the sky. Compounding the visibility problem that bitterly cold night was a suggestion of fog, a deceptive wraithlike mist lying close to the water. One of the lookouts, Frederick Fleet, later had a sketch drawn of his first sight of the berg; it shows the peak looming over the horizon, obviously miles away. Neither lookout was able to see that far ahead and it was critically close before the bridge was notified.

Although Murdoch, the *Titanic*'s first officer, died in the sinking, his quartermaster testified that he was ordered to put the helm hard over, the engines were stopped and the watertight doors closed. Those in the crow's-

Second of the White Star's new class, the *Titanic* leaves Harland & Wolff for acceptance trials ten days before her maiden voyage. The forward half of the promenade deck has been glassed in at Ismay's request, providing immediate visual distinction from the *Olympic*. (*Compagnie Générale Transatlantique*)

nest, party to the emergency, felt that the turn to port was agonizingly slow in coming. This delay can be traced to one of three factors: first, tests on the *Olympic* revealed that it took thirty-seven seconds for the ship to respond to the helm at full speed. If in addition the engines were reversed at the beginning of that time period, it would take even longer. Murdoch might have done better to leave the engines full ahead and make a sharper turn. Second, there was discussion later that the surface area of the rudder on both *Olympic* and *Titanic* was smaller than it might have been. On a triple-screw ship, central placement of the third propeller obviates employment of a balanced rudder. The latter is not more efficient but, turning more easily, it could have been larger and given a better helm response.

Finally, if there was a delay in giving orders to the helmsman, Murdoch might have been waiting to see the iceberg himself or was weighing the possibility of remaining on course. No officer of a Western Ocean mailboat was ignorant of the fact that ramming an iceberg is infinitely preferable to sideswiping it. In 1879, the *Arizona* had inadvertently done so in almost exactly the same spot; her bow crushed, she proceeded stern first to Newfoundland. It is more than probable that Captain Landy of the Canadian Pacific liner *Montrose* profited by Murdoch's mistake sixteen years later. Turning to avoid an iceberg, he came upon another behind it and rammed it head on rather than attempt passage between the two. Again, the forepeak crumpled like tinfoil and her forward hold flooded, but she remained afloat and made Liverpool under her own steam.

Yet if the *Titanic*'s first officer lost valuable seconds in making a decision that proved ultimately fatal, one cannot fault him for it. If there seemed a chance to avoid the iceberg completely, he must and did take it. The necessity for that nightmarish choice, thrust upon him with scant notice, is one of the dreadful obligations of command.

It is not surprising that almost all who survived the sinking of the *Titanic* recall in vivid detail the sensation of that impact. Those below, whether crew or third class, felt it more strongly than passengers higher up in the ship; the lookouts didn't feel it at all. What is extraordinary to me is that no one mentioned any prior swing or sheering off of the ship. A helm that is put hard over at any point near full speed produces a reactionary roll away from the turn. This abrupt sag to starboard would be especially pronounced on a calm sea. But universal silence on this point suggests that Murdoch did not, in point of fact, initiate the kind of crash emergency reaction that the situation warranted.

For whatever reason, then, whether the late sighting of imprudently placed lookouts, the faulty reaction of their superior officer or the inadequacies of her rudder, the *Titanic* turned too slowly to avoid a scrape along her starboard flank. The side of the berg that struck the ship had an odd overhung conformation. Tons of ice fell into the forward well deck, shaved off by the starboard rigging and railing. The absence of damage to shell plating above the water line suggests that the wall of ice curved away from the hull, shelving out under water in a spur that delivered the *coup de grâce*. Although only a narrow slice in places, no more than inches wide, it extended a hundred yards aft from the bow. With no lateral bunkers, that design convenience that made coal passing so much simpler, there was nothing to impede the inrush of cold green sea; a fatal proportion of the *Titanic*'s lower decks filled rapidly.

It was eleven-forty at night. The ship stopped and lay dead in the water at the eastern margin of an enormous ice field, superfluous steam venting furiously from her first three funnels. Violet Jessop, a stewardess, had once nearly capsized on the *Adriatic* and so bored her shipmates with the telling of it that she suspected a leg-pull when informed that the *Titanic* was in trouble. She was not alone in her disbelief that this massive ship was endangered. On the bridge, Captain Smith found it equally hard to accept, even though assured of it by the man who knew more about her design than anyone in the world. Thomas Andrews, Lord Pirrie's nephew and Managing Director of Harland & Wolff, was on board as troubleshooter for the maiden voyage. After he and Smith had inspected the forward compartments, they returned to the bridge. There Andrews informed the Captain, in company with White Star's Managing Director Bruce Ismay, that there was not the remotest chance that the ship could remain afloat.

Of the three who initially shared this bleak intelligence, it was Smith, oddly enough, whose subsequent behavior belied its urgency. Having dispatched a radio distress call and ordered out the lifeboats, he exhibited a curious capacity for nonleadership. Throughout the *Titanic*'s final ordeal, there was a vacuum at the top, a paralysis of command. Paramount in her captain's mind seemed the need to avert panic; given the appalling shortage of lifeboats, this was a valid consideration. Yet the façade of "business-as-usual" that evolved was, to my mind, damningly responsible for the death of an additional four hundred people: by that incredible margin were the lifeboats short their capacity.

In the light of this appalling discrepancy, one questions the advisability of reassurance in the face of common emergency. We have its modern equivalent in the frozen smiles that airline stewardesses display in moments of turbulence and the taped music played prior to takeoff and, curiously enough, *after* landing. I was on the *Franconia* on one of her last crossings

The *Titanic* in dry dock. The central propeller, of four blades, is turbine driven but each of the triple-bladed outboard screws is shafted to a conventional reciprocating engine. The Belfast workers posing stolidly below had no way of knowing that the same perspective would appear only weeks later, silhouetted against the sky in mid-Atlantic. (*Prints and Photographs Division, Library of Congress*)

and awoke early one morning to find several inches of sea water on my cabin floor. The most comforting antidote to this irrefutable evidence of calamity was the calm announcement shortly thereafter that tea was being served in the lounge. (Later reports that the damage was caused by a random wave and that the ship was in no danger were almost anticlimactic.) We expect Britons to keep a stiff upper lip; imperturbability is a cherished component of the national character.

Yet on the *Titanic,* this stoic determination to carry on as usual had a distressing side effect: it stifled any sense of urgency. When the infernal racket from the steampipes ceased, strains of music drifted up from the lounge. McElroy, the Chief Purser, had mustered the ship's orchestra, which continued to play until the *Titanic* went down. The contradiction in mood on two adjacent decks, coaxing reluctant passengers into lifeboats on one while lulling those on the other with genteel ragtime, was characteristically dichotomous. The desperate nature of the situation was purposely blurred and an aura of surrealistic calm prevailed. Jessop, the stewardess, summed it up cogently: "No one took the seriousness of anything."

Things might have been different had a public-address system been developed and available to the *Titanic.* I have always found lifeboat drill in midocean to be persistently theatrical, despite its familiarity. There is something uncompromisingly authentic about standing on a packed promenade deck, passengers and crew alike bulky in life jackets, the ship silent as all customary activity ceases. From out of this stillness, the captain's voice, even over a loudspeaker, carries with it a very real sense of authority. It was this ultimate reassurance that the *Titanic*'s passengers were denied. An appeal from Smith, or any one of his officers, delivered directly to all those on board might admittedly have unnerved some but would certainly have filled the lifeboats to capacity.

As it was, information filtered down through echelons of command with varying degrees of urgency and accuracy. Stewards who knocked discreetly at cabin doors, advising their charges to don warm clothing and life jackets, did not share the ruthless dispatch of officers on the boat deck sweating from their exertions despite the subfreezing temperature. There was a broad range of credibility. Ismay, party to the horrifying truth, interfered hysterically with the lowering of the boats and was ordered away by a junior officer. Although the rebuke was justified, would that some of the chairman's anxiety had permeated the ranks of subordinate employees.

Below decks, along the ordered spaciousness of the first-class passages, the ludicrous fiction was fabricated that the *Titanic* would somehow proceed to Halifax even though all her passengers would take to the boats.

Edith Russell gave her trunk keys to Wareham, her steward, asking that he check them through to New York from the alternate port. He replied, with uncommon candor, "You go back to your cabin and kiss those trunks good-by. I've got five little ones in Southampton and I'm awfully worried." He did save her toy musical pig, a treasured possession from Paris that played the *Maxixe* when the tail was wound. Incidentally, it saved her life: a fellow passenger threw it into the lifeboat, the only way that its owner could be persuaded to follow suit.

One can hardly blame the women who, urged into lifeboats, saw little reason to comply. It was more than a natural disinclination to leave their husbands. All the preconceived elements of disaster-at-sea were missing: there was almost no wind, the night sky was brilliant with stars down to the horizon, and not far off twinkled the lights of another ship. There was, admittedly, a five-degree list to starboard, but then the *Titanic* had listed slightly to port for most of the crossing. Far better, the women reasoned, to trust in the warmth and security of this great ship than drift about on a cold ocean. Persuasive arguments of all kind were used, including the incredible lie that they would reembark for breakfast the following morning. Those scenes of panic that did ultimately occur on the boat deck involved mostly third-class passengers and stokers, whose common experience was having come from below and seen, firsthand, compartments flooded with sea water. They were quite ready to fill the lifeboats that their complacent shipmates of the first and second class were reluctant to enter.

As the lounge emptied out, as more and more passengers were cajoled onto the upper deck, the orchestra followed suit; wearing life jackets now, Wallace Hartley's bandsmen sawed away. One passenger recalled later that the music itself was not particularly comforting. Left unsaid, I suggest, was that the music, if not comforting, perpetuated a numbing charade of normality.

This anesthetic effect was jolted at quarter to one when a distress rocket streaked up from the bridge, the first overt gesture of despair. Captain Smith was determined to arouse some response from the neighboring ship. The controversy as to her identity and position began that night and continues to the present. Although subsequent findings at both American and British inquiries indicate that she was the Leyland liner *Californian,* Frederick Fleet saw nothing from the crow's-nest except the iceberg. However, at least sixteen survivors did see the mysterious lights; Fourth Officer Joseph Boxhall testified that it was definitely a steamer. Quartermaster Rowe estimates the vessel was no more than four miles away. Captain Stanley Lord, the *Californian*'s master, admitted his ship was nearby but insisted until his death fifty years later that he was not within reach of the *Titanic*. His watch officer saw and reported rockets but, tragically, no attempt was made to investigate.

Jessop was assigned to lifeboat number 16. She had brought no coat from Southampton and came up from her cabin with a Company eiderdown wrapped about her shoulders over her lifebelt. She remembers coming across Captain Smith, Andrews, the doctor and the chief steward standing in the ship's square, the C-deck foyer. Seeing that quartet in that particular place was doubly ironic: like entrances on transatlantic ships to this day, it is pandemonium on sailing day and merely a passageway once land is cleared. Now these four busy men, seldom seen together except on brisk inspection tours, were standing casually in this usually deserted space, as though passing the time of day.

As Jessop came up the staircase, her way was blocked by two pantry boys, impudent cutups she knew from the *Olympic,* struggling up with a Gladstone bag full of money from the purser's office. It was heavy going and in trying to lift the open bag over the doorsill, one of them dropped his end and golden sovereigns rolled about the deck. The two were down on their knees, giggling and joking, not "taking the seriousness of anything," as were the passengers around them, none of whom bothered to retrieve the riches rolling about their feet. A flock of bellboys, dismissed from their duties, skylarked about, smoking and chattering with unaccustomed egalitarian ease; although in their early teens and absurdly young, by today's standards, to be earning a living, they were not permitted to enter the lifeboats. All of them were lost.

The business of launching a lifeboat over the side of a liner is not simple. Well-trained crews, operating in broad daylight while tied up to a pier, have troubles with even an empty boat. The Welin davits, of a recently improved type, newly installed on the *Olympic* class of ships, were unfamiliar to many of the crew operating them. The ropes were new and balky and the winches situated against the deckhouses were not used, either because of the crowded condition of the decks or the shortage of electricity. So the job was done by hand and almost all accounts of that perilous trip down to the water detail an ordeal of jerking and tipping as first one end, then the other was let down too fast. Shouted instructions from boats to officers forty feet above seemed often to aggravate the situation. The list created a different set of problems for each side of the ship. Passengers boarding lifeboats from the starboard promenade deck had to negotiate a gulf between deck and suspended boat, sometimes bridged by a folded deck chair; those on the high port side agonized as protruding strakes bumped over scores of rivet heads during passage down the sloping side.

Just before Jessop's boat started down, an officer found a baby abandoned near the davits. He handed it across to Jessop and she wrapped it in her eiderdown, holding it through the long night that followed. Once on the water, there seemed duplicated in every boat the nerve-racking business of seating the drainage plugs in the bottom; passengers and crew alike groped about in the bilges, feeling icy water flood in as they searched desperately for its point of entry. There was difficulty, too, in shucking the falls once the water was reached. No one could find the pin that released them. One boat, caught in this dilemma, was washed aft by a stream of water pouring from the ship's condenser exhaust. It lay like this, imprisoned against the ship's side, while its terrified occupants watched the neighboring lifeboat descend above it. Fortunately, a stoker with a knife severed the ropes in the nick of time, allowing the boat to float free.

So one by one, some full but others less than half so, the white lifeboats creaked down the sides of the *Titanic* to drift about on the calm water. They remained clustered about the ship as though deriving some comfort from the presence of that enormous hull ablaze with light. Through the crisp air came the thump of the band, the squealing of the blocks, the hoarse exchange of orders on the boat deck. It was a sight granted to few transatlantic passengers—their own ship in midocean. Despite the jarring novelty of this vantage point, the *Titanic* looked almost normal. Almost but not quite: every five minutes another rocket soared up from the bridge to explode with a *flash-crack* above. More alarming still was the ominously growing disparity between water line and the rows of lighted portholes.

Far below, Chief Engineer Joseph Bell ordered all superfluous electrical supply curtailed. Steam pressure, down alarmingly since the *Titanic* stopped, was further reduced as furnaces threatened by rising water in boiler room number 4 had their fires drawn. On the main feeder switchboard, ammeter needles flickered to zero as electricians ruthlessly shut down a host of suddenly redundant services: refrigerating engines, electric baths, radiant fires, kitchen machinery. Even the circulating fans were cut off and the boiler rooms were stifling, steam from the wetted grates adding to the discomfort.

Ironically, the five furnaces in boiler room number 1, farthest aft, were cold, having been put out days before; the Southampton coal strike had prohibited use of all the boilers, just as it had on the *Olympic*'s maiden voyage a year previous. In the remaining operating boiler rooms, numbers 2 and 3, desperate men toiled on sloping tank tops, keeping the fires stoked. Over the clatter of the pumps, they could hear the forward bulkhead groaning, racked by the weight of sea water it resisted. The solitary, inspired work of those brave men, not one of whom escaped, kept the lights burning to the very end.

All over the ship, for those hundreds who remained on board, the most fortunate must have been those who could lose their emotions in a job of work. On the after end of the boat deck, Andrews and the chief deck steward moved about, unlashing deck chairs from the night storage ranks and throwing them over the side. Passengers who had no duties grasped pathetically at shreds of life to fill those awful waiting minutes before the final plunge. Having seen their families safely into lifeboats, one group of friends retired to the tranquility of the empty smoking room. Others drifted into the gymnasium, where McCawley, the gym instructor, immaculate in jersey and white flannels, held open house. A few joined ship's officers on the deckhouse aft of the bridge, trying to manhandle the last two lifeboats to the ship's side. (These were the famous Englehardt collapsibles, with wooden bilges and folding canvas sides: two of them had already gone down the forward davits.) A crowd of immigrants gathered about a priest in the second-class lounge, praying. It was all understated, grim and tight-lipped, unbearable final moments made unreal by those gallant bandsmen who played on until the deck canted up to such an angle that they lost their footing.

Somewhere below, a bulkhead gave, the bow lurched down and a wave raced along the sloping deck, driving those in the open even further aft. Some, embracing the inevitable, stepped off bravely into the water that by then was slopping over the edge of the bridge. With a final reddish flare, the lights went out.

The surrounding lifeboats, fearful of being pulled down when she went, moved away. Jack Thayer, still in the water, thought he saw the ship breaking up. In point of fact, she didn't, although a sketch he later concocted with the enthusiastic assistance of a *Carpathia* passenger gave wide credence to the notion. What he did see was the collapse of the number 1 funnel. As the *Titanic* nosed down, the massive weight of the stern leaving the water opened an expansion joint aft of the bridge, parting several guy wires. Unsupported, the funnel toppled over with a shower of sparks and soot, providently washing clear one of the collapsibles.

There was an epic jumble of crashes as cargo, machinery, fittings, boilers, furniture—anything wrenched loose by that violent upheaval—thundered down into the bows. Then, astonishingly, the *Titanic*'s stern rose straight up—looking like the Flatiron Building in New York City, Edith Russell remembers—her counter, rudder and propellers thrust up to the sky. The internal avalanche continued until slowly, majestically, deliberately, the glistening hull plunged out of sight.

The dreaded suction proved a myth. One crewman, a baker, rode down to the water as the ship sank, clutching the poop railing, and didn't even get his head wet. Another man, treading water under the stern and momentarily hypnotized by the sight of three monstrous propellers overhead, remained undisturbed on the surface right next to the stern as it disappeared under water. Yet some of those in command of the boats played on the ignorance of their passengers, and continued to pull away, not only from the *Titanic* but hundreds of her people screaming for help in the icy waters.

Mindful that a son or husband might be among those haunting voices, some women entreated the rowers to return; others, terrified of swamping, joined their efforts to those of the crew. This appalling failure to render assistance is understandable among those boats fully loaded—there was little enough room as it was, let alone space to row properly. But a boat that carried only twelve people, over half of them seamen, had no earthly reason for refusing. One sailor forestalled the request by striking up a verse of the hymn "Pull for the Shore, Boys!", ostensibly to assist the rowers but in reality to drown out the cries. In Edith Russell's boat, the women were urged to cheer ". . . 'because they've all been saved! What you hear now is a hallelujah from the ship!' And we poor fools cheered. . . ." she recounts. It is doubtful whether any of their singing or cheering outlasted the dreadful chorus from the darkness that continued, in pitiful diminuendo, for nearly an hour.

One lifeboat did finally go back. In among the flotsam that came gouting up from the wreck long after she sank were hundreds of bodies, sustained on the surface by lifebelts that were useless against the twenty-eight-degree chill of the water. Of the four they rescued, one was clinging to a piece of ice and another had lashed himself to the top of a sideboard.

The traditional catchall word that lumps crew and passengers together is "souls." The term has gone out of fashion these days and "souls" never travel in airplanes, trains and buses. But in 1912, it was a standard maritime collective that appeared on manifests at either end of the crossing or in the event of a disaster. For those seven hundred souls who passed the remainder of the night in open boats, it was not the great leveler that it picturesquely implies. Hardly had the lifeboats touched the water than rankling animosimosities broke out, mainly between women and crew, in many cases packed in more democratically than either would have wished. Women in several boats complained bitterly about the men smoking. One grabbed a bottle of whiskey from a stoker and threw it triumphantly over the side; that it might have restored some circulation to his limbs seems not to have discouraged her. Many criticized the seamanship of those handling the oars.

I think the woman who later expanded on this, comparing the crew's fumbling incompetence with the bravery of the men who remained on board, articulated a point of view common to those newly made widows: although most of the men in the lifeboats were there under orders, their mere presence, in preference to an absent husband, was a source of bitter resentment. It was a sentiment that would be shared later by observers on both shores. In defense of the crew, they were just as vulnerable to the shock of the night's events as the passengers who expected them to be supermen. They were not supermen—they were ill-trained, confused, frightened and cold. The boats were poorly equipped and in some cases, oars were still lashed together with the builder's heavy twine.

One of the more outrageous games we have sometimes played on long crossings is to make a list of the talky, irritating or hysterical shipmates we should hate to find in our lifeboats. Fortunately, we have never had to put these fantasies to the test, but the *Titanic*'s people did. The resulting blend of bravery, resignation and recrimination seems fairly predictable. What those wretchedly cold survivors couldn't know for several days was that twice their number had perished.

Of all the ships that heard the *Titanic*'s distress call, first on the scene was the Cunarder *Carpathia*. She had raced fifty-eight miles through the night, her engines pounding out an incredible seventeen knots, threading at high speed through the ice in the predawn darkness. Her arrival, firing rockets as she came, her portholes ablaze with light, was a glorious antidote to the terrors of the previous night.

She hove to within sight of the boats, maneuvering gently to provide a lee shelter for each as it struggled alongside. During the slow process of embarking the survivors, the sun came up, tinging the white ice and lifeboats alike an orange-pink. The breeze freshened, ending the provident calm that had sustained all night. Most of the *Carpathia*'s passengers lined the rails, watching the survivors climb stiffly up the sides. Women had slings placed under their arms and children were taken up in ash bags and mail sacks on the after crane. There was almost complete silence as they stumbled onto the deck, were wrapped in blankets and led below. When her arms could relax their frozen embrace, Jessop's baby was taken back by its mother.

During the days that followed, the woman made no attempt to communicate with, let alone thank, the stewardess who had saved her child's life.

All on board the rescue ship did their best to comfort the new arrivals. Public rooms were turned into dormitories, women made clothing from steamer rugs and ship's blankets, toilet articles were distributed. At Captain Arthur Rostron's suggestion, a minister conducted a memorial service in the lounge as the *Carpathia* steamed about in a vain search for further survivors; his words were lost in outbursts of grief as thawing limbs and sensitivities took in the events of the last tragic hours. So began a sorrowful passage back to New York; Rostron chose to return there rather than closer Halifax or Boston for fear of additional ice. The ship's orchestra played nothing for two days and broke their self-imposed silence only with hymns on the third.

On the eastbound *Olympic,* which had been too far away to help, the same hushed atmosphere prevailed. The ship's concert was canceled, the orchestra played no more and crew members who had friends or relatives on the sister ship moved through their duties overcome with grief. The *Olympic*'s radio picked up the *Carpathia*'s weaker signals and relayed them on to New York so that there was a close rapport with the disaster and the names of those who survived it. Indeed, all ships equipped with radios picked up the news. On some of them, it was first kept secret, then imparted in confidence to the men. Theodore Dreiser, crossing home on a German liner, was one of a group of men called outside the smoking room and whispered the awful news. Within hours, it was all over the ship.

During that four-day trip to New York, the *Carpathia*'s radio, manned by two exhausted operators, poured out streams of personal messages as survivors among the passengers cabled their next-of-kin. Incomprehensibly, the same privilege was withheld from the crew, and two wives in Southampton died, quite literally, from suspense. The list of names that reached the White Star Line's office at 9 Bowling Green was read aloud by the chief clerk as he stood on top of the booking office counter. Outside, traffic had been diverted because of anxious crowds. One of the first to hear news of his father was young Ismay, who was working in the New York office at the time.

But there were still no details, nothing reliable that newspaper editors could inject into the inventive stuff that filled their front pages. On Thursday evening, when the *Carpathia* arrived at Quarantine, a flotilla of chartered tugs, crammed with newspapermen, surrounded the ship, following her as she steamed upriver. Reporters bawled through the rain: "Throw over a note in a bottle!" and "Jump overboard—we'll pick you up." One reporter

R.M.S. *Titanic* at Southampton the day before she sailed. The white-banded funnels immediately to the left belong to the liner *New York*, pulled from her moorings by the *Titanic*'s wash the following day. (*National Maritime Museum, Greenwich*)

Below, anxious New Yorkers outside the offices of the *New York American* at William and Frankfort Streets. The *Carpathia* has passed on news of survivors via the *Olympic*'s radio. (*Brown Brothers*)

managed to get on board the *Carpathia* but was summoned to the bridge by Rostron and put on his honor to disturb no one. A boatload from the *Herald* missed the rendezvous at Quarantine altogether and returned to her pier full of queasy and disgruntled newsmen. They had to join the dense crowds, numbering in the tens of thousands, that lined Manhattan's western shore from the Battery to 14th Street; never before had so many watched a ship come in. Flashes from photographers' flares lit up the scene like lightning as the *Titanic*'s boats were lowered and towed away. At nine-thirty, the Cunarder tied up. As the first survivors came down the gangplank, they were greeted by C. W. Thomas, the assistant New York manager, weeping openly. At the end of the pier, a human chain of police and company personnel held back the crowds. Those who had passes to meet a relative went to the appropriate overhead customs letters; in many cases, the costumes of those off the ship were so bizarre that recognition was difficult.

Ismay was no sooner ashore than he found himself a particularly vulnerable target for those in search of a scapegoat. When a brand-new liner sinks and most of the passengers drown, who better to crucify than the Managing Director of the company that ran her? Any male survivor on board the *Carpathia* had, in effect, to justify his existence and it became apparent that Ismay had less reason than many. The surreptitious nature of his departure from the *Titanic* was added to gossip on the *Carpathia,* particularly among those bunked together in the lounge who wondered bitterly why Ismay rated a cabin to himself. His intercepted message to New York headquarters, signed "Yamsi," ordering the *Cedric* held to take him and the crew back to England, seemed confirmation that this arrogant man was trying to run away. Typical of the vilification that followed was this final stanza of "Master and Man," a poem that appeared in the Chicago *Record-Herald,* written by a young reporter named Ben Hecht:

> To hold your place in the ghastly face
> Of death on the sea of night
> Is a seaman's job, but to flee with the mob
> Is an owner's noble right.

One cartoonist, amending the name to J. *Brute* Ismay, pictured him as a rapacious ogre who, having urged the *Titanic* along her suicidal course, fled from the sinking vessel hidden among the women.

In point of fact, although tempting to label him simply a coward, it is probable that Ismay was not totally responsible for his actions. His behavior, from the moment that he first knew the ship was doomed, was erratic enough to be classified today as an acute stress reaction with periodic psychotic episodes. I have already noted his hysterical interference with lowering the boats. In his own lifeboat, when Quartermaster George Rowe, nominally in command, asked what he should do, Ismay blurted out: "You do what you like! You're in charge!" and then lapsed into silence, neither speaking nor moving for the remainder of the night. When the *Titanic* went down, Rowe and his mates touchingly doffed their caps; Ismay didn't even turn around. Contrary to his own testimony, he never laid a hand to the oars. Once on board the *Carpathia,* he raced down to the dining room, demanding that he be fed instantly, and tipped the astonished steward who served him two dollars. It was then that he retired to the surgeon's cabin, from which he did not emerge until the ship reached New York.

This wide variation in mood, total withdrawal punctuated by irrational outbursts, indicates that the White Star Chairman was emotionally overwhelmed by the disaster, to the point where he did not function as his normal self. In any event, it was his particular embarrassment to have survived a catastrophe that engulfed so many of his fellow passengers. What is the answer to the question asked by a White Star counsel at the British Inquiry: "Was it the duty of Mr. Ismay to have remained, though by doing so no other life could have been saved?" His only crime, in reality, was that he was alive.

Whereas Ismay's behavior was frequently criticized, Captain Smith's was not. He went down with the ship, a traditionally heroic end. He was last seen in the water, leaving a collapsible that could have saved his life, swimming back toward the *Titanic*. A Royal Navy colleague, speaking at the dedication of his memorial, confided that his last command was "Be British." Passengers who saw him that night spoke admiringly of his concern and distress.

Smith is customarily pictured as a flunky of the line, forced to drive his vessel recklessly in an attempt to establish a record. This is arrant nonsense. The *Titanic* couldn't have approached the *Mauretania*'s speed even with all of her boilers fired. In any case, to assume that Smith would endanger the ship on Ismay's behalf is absurd. He was a sailor of vast experience, about to retire, with no reason to risk his command at the whim of an owner. In his defense, fellow captains later admitted that keeping speed up in the vicinity of ice was a common practice, given the same conditions of visibility; rigid adherence to mail schedules meant that Captain Smith and his contemporaries habitually violated the rules of good seamanship. Unfortunately, the odds caught up with him and the fact that he chose to die with his ship in no way mitigates the enormity of his guilt. Only the *Titanic*'s captain can assume full responsibility for the ruinous speed at which the ship plowed through that calm April night.

Meanwhile, to the north, the White Star Line chartered two cable ships to proceed with the business of locating and identifying the bodies. Two days after the sinking, the first of these, the *MacKay Bennett,* sailed from Halifax with Canon Hind of All Saints Cathedral and an embalmer; stacked in the cable well was a supply of coffins and large quantities of ice. As they approached the area of the sinking, they encountered fog and some ice. The sea temperature dropped from fifty-seven to thirty-two degrees. It was on the twenty-first of April that they came upon the first of the bodies and wreckage, in company with two giant icebergs. One of the cable engineers, Frederick Hamilton, kept a diary of the voyage and it is worth quoting here:

> April 21st: The ocean is strewn with woodwork, chairs and bodies, and there are several growlers about, all more or less dangerous, as they are often hidden in the swell. The cutter lowered, and work commenced and kept up all day, picking up bodies. Hauling the soaked remains in saturated clothing over the side of the cutter is no light task. Fifty-one we have taken on board to-day, two children, three women, and forty-six men, and still the sea seems strewn.

Unidentified bodies were buried at sea:

> 8 P.M. The tolling of the bell summoned all hands to the forecastle where thirty bodies are to be committed to the deep, each carefully weighted and carefully sewed up in canvas. It is a weird scene, this gathering. The crescent moon is shedding a faint light on us, as the ship lays wallowing in the great rollers. The funeral service is conducted by the Reverend Canon Hind, for nearly an hour the words "For as much as it hath pleased . . . we therefore commit his body to the deep" are repeated and at each interval comes, splash! as the weighted body plunges into the sea, there to sink to a depth of about two miles. Splash, splash, splash.
>
> April 22d: . . . All around is splintered woodwork, cabin fittings, mahogany fronts of drawers, carvings, all wrenched away from their fastenings, deck chairs, and then more bodies. Some of these are fifteen miles distant from those picked up yesterday. 8 P.M. Another burial service.
>
> April 24th: Still dense fog prevailing, rendering further operations with the boats almost impossible. . . . Noon. Another burial service held and seventy-seven bodies follow the others. The hoarse tone of the steam whistle reverberating through the mist, the dripping rigging, and the ghostly sea, the heaps of dead, and the hard weather-beaten faces

of the crew, whose harsh voices join in the hymn tunefully rendered by Canon Hind, all combine to make a strange task stranger. Cold, wet, miserable and comfortless, all hands balance themselves against the heavy rolling of the ship as she lurches to the Atlantic swell, and even the most hardened must reflect on the hopes and fears, the dismay and despair, of those whose nearest and dearest, support and pride, have been wrenched from them by this tragedy.

In all, more than three hundred bodies were recovered, among them that of Wallace Hartley, the bandleader, his music case still strapped to his side. Colonel John Jacob Astor's body was badly crushed and heavily ingrained with soot, indicating that he was doubtless killed when the *Titanic*'s funnel collapsed. At the end of the month, the ship returned to Halifax. The port was in deep mourning, church bells tolling and all flags at half-mast. The dead were transferred on carts to a makeshift morgue in a curling rink. Hamilton closes his entry with the reflection that earlier that year, when their ship had rescued six men from a foundered schooner, they had tied up unnoticed; now, "with not one life to show," thousands waited on shore.

In mid-May, a full month after the sinking, two hundred miles from the *Titanic*'s last position, the *Oceanic* came across collapsible "A." There were three bodies in it, a passenger from Chicago and two crew members, left there by Officer Lowe when the surviving occupants had been transfered to boat 14. The canvas sides of the boat had never been raised and there was a foot of water in the bottom. Yet this sluggish condition of the boat had miraculously preserved, as though just arranged, neat little piles of jewelry, hairpins and combs left along the thwarts by the women. A crew of volunteers rowed over from the ship and prepared the bodies for burial. Passengers on the *Oceanic* watched the scene in grisly fascination. The luncheon bugle was ignored until the last canvas-wrapped bundle was slipped over the side.

A series of sensible transatlantic reforms went into effect almost immediately. Passengers sailing on the *Adriatic* demanded and received assurance that they would follow a more southerly route. In point of fact, summer tracks for all vessels were shifted sixty miles further south, where they remain to this day. Moreover, masters were advised that the practice of "cutting the corner" was to cease immediately; this tempting detour was habitually used to make up lost time. There was a dockside showdown in Southampton when stokers on the *Olympic* quite simply refused to work until more lifeboats were provided. At the end of the year, their ship was taken out of service and returned to Harland & Wolff. Hordes of workers toiled for six months, nearly gutting the hull. When they had finished, wa-

Wishful thinking from the *Graphic*, April 27, 1912.
(*Radio Times Hulton Picture Library*)

tertight bulkheads extended up to the promenade deck and the double bottom turned the corner of the bilge. Her return to sea was heralded by company flyers that read in part: "In her will be embodied everything that human foresight has devised for the safety of passengers and crew."

The same drastic hull revisions were incorporated into hull number 433, which lay on the ways next to the fitting out basin. This was the third of the *Olympic* class ships. There is an apocryphal story that she was originally to have been christened *Gigantic* but that company officials opted for the less pretentious *Britannic* after the *Titanic* sank. Her profile was radically altered by enormous gantry davits, the largest ever constructed on any ship. Central stacks of lifeboats, three high, could be lowered over either side of the vessel. The davits' height gave them additional horizontal clearance over the side of the hull so that even a substantial list would not hamper launching operations.

In Germany, the *Imperator* and *Vaterland* were festooned with red lifeboats and a powerful searchlight was mounted under the crow's-nest to pinpoint any icebergs in the ship's path. Although the British Merchant Shipping Advisory Committee rejected the use of searchlights, it was not lost on the astute Germans that it *looked* safe; there is no record that they were ever used to spot icebergs.

Marconi, haunted by the *Californian*'s ignorant proximity, worked for a dozen years to perfect an automatic radio alarm that would ring when triggered by a series of four dashes. But by that time, radio operators worked in relay aboard ship and there was always someone monitoring a set. Sir Hiram Maxim announced that he was building a device that would broadcast signals and detect their reflection from anything in the path of a vessel. It was a crude and evidently unsuccessful attempt at a kind of acoustical radar; nothing more was ever heard of it.

One British naval architect proposed installation of a detachable poop deck on all transatlantic liners that would remain on the surface as a floating haven should the hull sink beneath it. A Frenchman came up with a scheme to span the Atlantic with a chain of illuminated buoys, connected by insulated cable; ships in trouble could tie up and telephone to either shore for assistance. Although neither of these latter proposals ever came close to fruition, it is symptomatic of public concern at the time that they were taken seriously.

Throughout the world, the disaster touched a responsive chord in all who heard of it. Plaques, plinths and memorials sprouted on both sides of the Atlantic: to the musicians in Boston's Symphony Hall, to the engineers in a Southampton park, to Captain Smith himself outside Lichfield. Thirty thousand heard five brass bands play at Wallace Hartley's funeral in a Lancashire mill town. Every fifteenth of April, a wreath is placed at 41 degrees 46 minutes North and 50 degrees 14 minutes West, the position where the *Titanic* lies. It is dropped from either a ship or plane of the International Ice Patrol, which was formed immediately following the sinking and is now operated exclusively by the United States Coast Guard.

Almost everyone, it seems, was moved to write verses about the *Titanic* and enough doggerel was produced to fill several anthologies. One irreverent ballad passed into popular musical literature and was soon sung quite openly to a rollicking chorus:

> It was sad, it was sad
> It was sad when the great ship went down.
> Husbands and wives
> Little children lost their lives
> It was sad when the great ship went down.

But for sailors, the impact of the *Titanic*'s loss never assumed the proportions of a joke. Bertram Hayes, a White Star Commodore who wrote his memoirs in 1925, makes no mention of the ship anywhere in the book.

Astonishingly enough, there were those in the shipping establishment who comforted themselves with the thought that, although lamentable, the disaster really resulted from a freakish accident to a unique class of ship. Two years later, the *Empress of Ireland,* proceeding cautiously down the fog-shrouded St. Lawrence, was rammed by a collier and went to the bottom within twenty minutes. Even though in sight of land, a thousand lives were lost. The tragedy never assumed mythic proportions and few people today are familiar with it. Perhaps it occurred too close to a war, when wholesale slaughter became commonplace. But in our own time, the loss of the *Andrea Doria,* equipped with sophisticated equipment undreamed of in 1912, points up exactly the same lesson: disaster at sea is never predictable and seldom consistent. The only sound provision against it is adherence to impeccable seamanship.

One approaches the job of researching the *Titanic* disaster determined to resist the mystique that surrounds it. Up to the moment of collision at eleven-forty on the evening of April 14, 1912, one can detail the train of events with detached clarity. But the human drama that ensues, juxtaposed against the tragic inevitability to which we are privy, is so compelling that objectivity is blurred. The *Titanic* just missed avoiding the iceberg and the nightmare that followed seems made up of a series of near misses, any one of which, slightly varied, might have averted the ghastly finale.

We must seize the trident.
      —KAISER WILHELM II

4.
The Kaiser's Fleet

One of the most enthusiastic visitors to Britain's Naval Review of 1889 was the new German Emperor, Wilhelm II. As grandson of Queen Victoria, his welcome in England was particularly cordial. What impressed him at Spithead more than the dreadnoughts was the glistening new liner *Teutonic*. He was intrigued with the size, power and luxury of the British ship and determined, shortly after his return by battleship to Kiel, that Germany too should have a share of the profit and, more important, the prestige of the North Atlantic. Thus was implemented the same kind of grandiose national decision to which President Kennedy committed the United States in connection with landing on the moon. If Wilhelm's vision was not necessarily warlike, it was ambitious and practical. Nor was it lost on the admirals who surrounded him that battleships were not enough. Merchant ships were inextricably involved in the superiority of Britain's seapower.

So a strong government-supported building program was initiated with electrifying success. Eight years later, only four months after *Turbinia*'s performance at Spithead, the *Kaiser Wilhelm der Grosse,* a lean four-stacker of fourteen thousand tons, took the Blue Riband. She was a ship of Bremen's North German Lloyd, only rival to the great German company the Hamburg-Amerika Line (or HAPAG, to use an early and convenient acronym far easier to master than *Hamburg-Amerikanische Packetfahrt Actien-Gesellschaft*). HAPAG's *Deutschland* recaptured the speed prize three years later but in 1903 lost it back to their Bremen rivals, whose *Kaiser Wilhelm II* boasted the largest reciprocating steam engines ever built to that time.

How or when the Blue Riband changed hands during this decade is less important than that it was a uniquely German contest, a friendly battle within the Hanseatic family; Britain was, temporarily, out of the running. It was this humiliation, together with the specter of Morgan's Atlantic combine, that ensured the British government subsidy to Cunard, already discussed in another chapter.

Fortunately for the Kaiser's mercantile pretensions, guiding the Hamburg-Amerika Line was a genius named Albert Ballin. He had joined the company in 1886 as head of the Passenger Department; soon afterwards, he was elected to the Board of Directors and, by the turn of the century, had risen to leadership. Ballin was indefatigable, an extraordinary man whose almost total preoccupation with the Company was reflected in its excellence. He spoke fluent English and was in constant touch with his colleagues across the Channel, where he kept a relentless eye on the competition. His infrequent trips to New York were seldom relaxing, for he spent the entire crossing filling notebooks with suggestions for improvements.

He traveled in a state suite, unless it was booked by a paying customer, and was hardly awake the first day out before recording that the bathroom towels were too small. Why did there have to be so many notices strewn about? He scribbled a recommendation that they be included in the passenger list or framed attractively. Then down to breakfast and more notes: the toast would be better served in a warm napkin, the butter dishes were inadequate. The eleven-o'clock bouillon on deck was good but needed an improved cup to prevent it from slopping. Some Westphalian ham sandwich should accompany it. Back in the cabin, the desk drawer lock was defective and the furniture could be rearranged thus to provide more room for all those trunks the Americans carry.

En route to dinner, in a boiled shirt but still writing, the tag end of a dirty sheet showing under a linen cupboard door rated as explosive an entry as the inadequacies of the Moselle that the sommelier would produce in the dining room. Then a quiet game of bridge in the smoking room was disrupted twice: the backs of the cards should bear the HAPAG crest and the steward's jackets should be modeled after those on the White Star ships. And then to bed, recording a final complaint that the pillows should be bigger and softer, before closing the notebook for the day. By the time the ship had returned to Hamburg, the notes, amplified by a secretary into memoranda marked *"Obligatorische,"* were delivered to chief steward, chef and shore-based commissariat with fearful dispatch. Ballin's all-seeing eye, though infuriating to subordinates, was nevertheless responsible for the superb standards of comfort and service on the HAPAG ships.

On one of his visits to London, Ballin came across the work of two men who were cutting a wide swath in European hotel circles: César Ritz and Charles Mewès. The first is well known and his name has passed into the language, synonymous with opulent grandeur. The other deserves to be remembered, particularly in this book, because he was largely responsible for the interior design of nearly all the giant liners that still plied the Atlantic into the thirties; but for the Kaiser's petulance, he might have done them all. It is not an exaggeration to say that he founded a whole new school, if there is such a thing, of seagoing architecture that lasted long after his death.

The Paris Ritz was opened in 1898, situated within the stunning façade that surrounds the Place Vendôme, surely one of the handsomest squares in the world. It was the first of a glittering chain of Ritz Hotels that would stretch across Europe to America. Mewès really invented the modern hotel and today, seven decades after it was built, it still bears his impeccable stamp. The sweep of staircase rising effortlessly from the lobby and the inviting coolness of the garden contribute to a remarkable sense of quiet and serenity.

The collaboration between hotelier Ritz and his architect was extremely close. Mewès was the kind of artist who pursued the execution of his vision down to the last doorknob. He supervised the finish of the paneling, selected the fabrics for the walls and curtains, even for the silk of the lampshades, and did his best to discourage contemporary enthusiasm for antimacassars. This tireless supervision of every last detail resulted in a whole that was nowhere less than perfect. On the floors above, double-hung windows insulated the rooms from the noise and dust of the streets, and, for the first time, there was a bathroom connected with each one. And what bathrooms they

Charles Mewès as sketched by his
British partner, Arthur Davis.
(*Courtesy of Georgette Mewès*)

were: grand, almost vaulted chambers, with gigantic tubs and enough marble for a piazza.

But despite the grandeur, nothing offended. The scale was human, manageable and regal. By adhering, with refreshing purity, to the best of Louis XVI, Mewès avoided the pretentious vulgarities of *deuxième empire* eclecticism. And if he attempted to recapture a world of muted good taste and spatial elegance that no longer existed, at least it was a welcome change from the epic monumentalism that stifled much of French nineteenth-century architecture. Finally, Mewès' choice of style was doubly fortunate in that it imparted a sense of refinement to those newly rich from across the Atlantic, who have always found the Ritz irresistible, as though some of the *noblesse* they crave might rub off.

Within two years of their Paris venture, Ritz and Mewès repeated their success in London, where the Carlton Hotel's interior had been rebuilt to their specifications. Ballin, his ear to the ground for anything new and fashionable, was one of the first to dine in the splendor of the Ritz-Carlton Grill. He was on his way back from Belfast, where Harland & Wolff were building him a new ship. It can only be supposed that his notebook was on the table before the soup was cleared. Why not a restaurant high up in the ship, with lots of windows, done in this handsome French style . . . ? If the king of German shipping was unable to define precisely the ambience he sought, at least he would go directly to the men who could create it for him. He was then pleased to discover that Mewès had designed the townhouse of the Warburgs, old friends in Hamburg.

As a result, Mewès was asked to take on the interiors for the new liner, to be called the *Amerika*. She would be large, the largest in the world, and like the White Star ships which served for so many years as models for German inspiration, sumptuous. (Speed was out; HAPAG's one experiment with a fast ship had been a disaster. The *Deutschland* had broken the record but the cost, in terms of fuel and vibration, had been so catastrophic that Ballin and his co-directors were quite happy to leave that kind of thing to their Bremen competitors.)

In search of exactly the right touch of topical chic for the *Amerika*, Ballin engaged a man whose work ashore was the height of fashion. His decision to assign the planning of a vessel's interior to one qualified architect was significant. The contemporary alternative was a selection of stifling revivals. Ships' interiors were customarily a pastiche of period rooms: Tudor, Jacobean, Olde Englishe, Italian Renaissance; almost any style that took the shipping executive's (or his wife's) fancy was slavishly copied down to the last detail. Even innovative ships like the *Mauretania* and *Olympic* were prey to this museum mentality and it was on the *Amerika* in 1903 that an architect, for the first time, was given the opportunity to achieve some kind of total design harmony, implementing a scheme of uniform decoration in all the public rooms throughout the ship.

Mewès had engaged Arthur Davis as partner for his London work, a young protégé who had earlier been apprenticed to him in Paris. It was a practical move, since Mewès spoke no English. That most of the firm's prestige came from the older man is suggested by the fact that Mewès had another partner for his German work; although born in Strasbourg, he spoke no German either. Yet whether the work was from the office of Mewès & Davis in London or Mewès & Bischoff in Cologne, there should be no confusion that the guiding hand in both cases was undoubtedly the Frenchman's. The first bombshell he dropped into the offices of Harland & Wolff was that the uptake casings on the *Amerika* should adhere to the sides of the hull, leaving him exclusive use of a spatial preserve in the center. The Belfast builders rejected the scheme out of hand as impractical, and it must have given Mewès intense satisfaction to have used it so successfully several years later on the *Vaterland*.

Although not particularly rakish looking, the *Amerika* enjoyed the distinction of being the most fashionable ship on the Atlantic until the advent of the *Lusitania*. She is remembered less for Mewès' interiors than for the restaurant that was the brainchild of his German employer. Ballin sensed unerringly that the traveling public was ready for an à la carte restaurant, separate from the ship's dining room, that would feed passengers at all hours for an additional charge. His instincts were right. The evolution of transatlantic dining saloons had been slow. Although more pretentiously decorated, they were scarcely an improvement over the "hearse with windows" that had so offended Dickens on the *Britannia*.

In October of 1904, William Harris, on behalf of the Carlton's Board of Directors, announced that the Hamburg-Amerika Line had asked them to operate the restaurant on board the *Amerika*. Shortly thereafter, a team from the London establishment journeyed to Dover and boarded the *Deutschland* for a voyage to New York. They were greeted by von Holtzendorf, the Company's director of catering, and spent their time for the next two weeks snooping about the ship, interviewing the New York purveyors and listening unobtrusively to their fellow passengers on the subject of food. After their return to London and a series of top-level meetings, the decision was taken to separate the proposed restaurant from the main kitchen entirely; provisioning, preparation, and service would be under the exclusive supervision of a Ritz-Carlton staff.

Here again, Ballin stole a march on his competitors with the provision of a service unobtainable on any but a HAPAG ship. Rival companies had regularized competition among themselves to the extent of standardizing fares; anything else was fair game. They were not victims of the ludicrous condition of uniformity self-imposed by today's airlines: flying the same planes over the same routes for the same price, competition in any real sense is reduced to skirmishes over the contents of a sandwich or the length of stewardess' hemlines.

Moreover, Ballin was not content to sell his inspiration short. The whole idea was conceived and carried through in a characteristically first-class style. The staff of captains and waiters were to be trained by Ritz himself and Escoffier would handle matters beyond the green baize door. The most luxurious thing about the room itself was that passengers could dine at twenty-five separate tables. There were large windows on three sides. Stanchions disguised as serving islands indicate that Mewès had learned by then to live with the realities of naval architecture. Ormolu sconces and individual table lamps shed a warm glow on the cream-and-gold walls and mahogany woodwork. Underfoot was a dark blue carpet. The china and linen carried the Carlton crest. The only item not made especially was the silver; it had come from the *Hamburg,* on which Kaiser Wilhelm had once made a cruise, so that brochures could hint grandly that the Kaiser's silver service was used in the restaurant. It was the only demeaning aspect of an otherwise superb presentation. Nagel, maître d'hôtel of the Carlton Grill, was persuaded to officiate for the first year, and his only instruction was that meals ordered thousands of miles at sea were to be indistinguishable from those served in the London grill. It was a commission that he and his successor never violated and, given the difficulties of victualing in 1905, it was an astonishing record.

Passengers on the maiden voyage of the *Amerika* seemed to have two major diversions; the first was the elevator, the operator of which was so proud that he tallied the exact number of round trips made: one thousand eight hundred and twenty-five. The other was the restaurant, which did such a land-office business that Ballin's first note of the voyage was to double the size of its kitchen. Passengers who chose to eat exclusively in the restaurant were permitted to deduct twenty-five dollars from their first-class fare. There was some question as to whether it was possible to eat exclusively in the restaurant for that price; one enterprising passenger who tried was rather peckish by the time he reached New York.

Nevertheless, the most expensive meal of the crossing, the Captain's Dinner, seems good value for eighteenpence, even pre-1914 pence: Caviar,

Soup, Fish, Lamb Cutlets, Roast Pigeon, Salad, Ice and Petit Fours. In addition, for this penultimate meal of the crossing, there were table favors of little notebooks with silver pencils. The "Ice" was, appropriately, *Glace Amerika,* evidently one of those gastronomic fireworks so dear to Edwardian palates: the lights were dimmed and from the kitchen came squads of waiters bearing overhead a sizzling combination of fire and ice. A breathless reporter for *Leslie's Weekly* who was present spoke also of "grotesquely costumed attendants," but it is more likely that, in the hysteria of the moment, she mistook the scarlet-coated Tzigane band who bowed and scraped among the diners without ceasing. In any event, the dinner climaxed a triumphant voyage and the Hamburg-Amerika Line was delighted with the sobriquet "Floating St. Regis" that the *New York Herald* offered the next day.

It is probable that the *Amerika*'s Ritz-Carlton restaurant was, pound for pound, the finest of the lot—finest in that it was the first and benefited from all the care and attention lavished on the first-born. It was a time, also, when the care and preparation of food both ashore and afloat was a loving art. The restaurant chef on a steamer had the advantage over his land-based colleague of being able to select the finest food of four countries, at which he called weekly. At Dover there was fish, including the famous sole, and the best lamb in the world. Across the Channel, dairy products, poultry and fruit came on board at Cherbourg. In New York he took on beef and oysters, the latter fresh up from Baltimore the night before. All these provisions came on board by hand. Eggs were immediately coated in butter and turned daily. Peaches were bedded down in straw nests, to be removed from the cold storage room a precise two hours before serving. On the after deck was a greenhouse where, behind the flowers that passengers could buy in mid-ocean, there were flats of mushrooms, strawberries and lettuce for use in the restaurant. It is doubtful that cuisine anywhere on the Atlantic attained such heights as it did on those German ships around the turn of the century. Chief stewards nowadays shop internationally for reasons of economy, but before 1914 the criterion was excellence.

Excellent, too, was the lounge aft of the restaurant, which Mewès had executed in the style of Robert Adam. Again, characteristically, he drew from the purity of style found in the eighteenth century. There was also a subtle appeal to the tastes of those English and Americans who would travel on the German ship. So impressed was Ernest Cunard that he sensibly inquired if Mewès might be interested in taking on the prestigious commission of the *Lusitania* and *Mauretania*. Ballin quite naturally demurred, pointing out that Mewès was under contract to the Hamburg-Amerika Line and could not possibly work for a competitor.

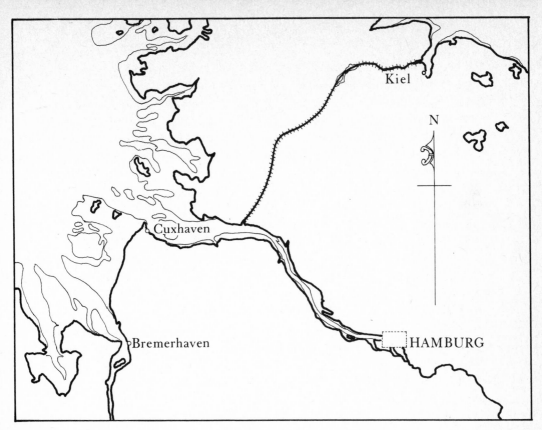

Kiel

N

Cuxhaven

Bremerhaven

HAMBURG

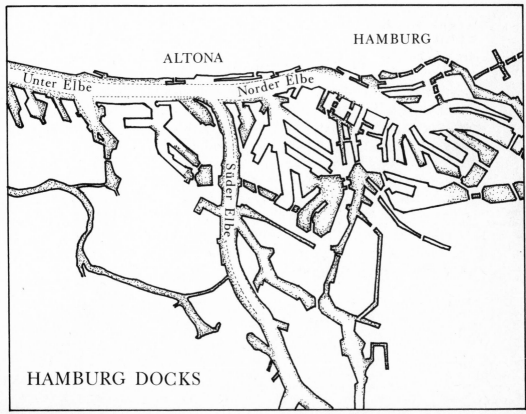

HAMBURG

ALTONA

Unter Elbe

Norder Elbe

Süder Elbe

HAMBURG DOCKS

So Mewès stayed on and designed the interiors for a series of vessels, moving from strength to strength. On his next ship, the *Kaiserin Auguste Victoria,* he created a charming ladies' cabin or saloon, a delightful confection of treillage. This imaginative use of a new material on board ship became an abused standard on many to follow; endless winter gardens, verandas and café terraces, for the most part inferior adaptations of Mewès' original perfection.

Although he became the HAPAG's resident architect, he was by no means exclusively concerned with liners. The following year, he completed the Ritz Hotel in London. It is today, unfortunately, shabbier than its Paris counterpart; but if its original luster has dimmed, the masterly proportioned central hall and dining room more than justify the sensation they created in 1906. Lunch at the Ritz, by one of the great windows overlooking Green Park, is as pleasing to the eye as to the palate. In fact, the restrained elegance of Mewès design has survived more perfectly than the cuisine. After the Ritz, two more ships for Ballin, the *Cleveland* and the *Cincinnati,* then a series of country and town houses in England, climaxed by a monumental addition to Pall Mall, the Royal Automobile Club.

This imposing edifice is significant in foreshadowing the scale of the last three ships of his career, and was built at a time when there seemed no limit to the funds put at his disposal. If in creating a gentlemen's club he tended to stray back toward an epic style which he had hitherto avoided, at least we can admire the taste that still contained it. He employed the same treatment as with the London Ritz but double the size: the elliptical oval just inside the entrance was fifty feet high and rose through two stories. Not only there, but in all parts of the incredible structure, everything is in the grand manner. In the basement, there is a swimming bath which could only be described as, and was, Pompeian. Those first delighted members who reveled among its mosaic columns would never have dreamed that a duplicate of their splendid pool would shortly appear on an ocean liner.

For by this time, Ballin had irrevocably committed the Hamburg-Amerika Line to the reality that his two British rivals had long since faced, the three-ship service. He had little trouble enlisting the Kaiser's support for such an ambitious scheme. Plans to award the contract to Harland & Wolff were canceled when a new government mail contract stipulated that the ships be constructed in German yards. That they were, built and launched with clockwork regularity, one a year for three years, is a tribute to the vigor and technical diligence of those Hamburg shipwrights. It must be remembered that it was as natural then for Germany to buy ships in England as it is for most of the world to shop for airplanes in the United States today. For an infant industry to embark on such a colossal program, let alone carry it off, was an extraordinary feat.

The first of the HAPAG's new class was laid down at Vulkan Werke in June 1910. There were benefits to be derived from starting third after their two British competitors. The ship's design and specifications could incorporate all the lessons learned from the front runners. From Cunard's *Lusitania* and *Mauretania* came the system of quadruple screws driven by steam turbine; from White Star, details of the *Olympic*'s extravagant interiors and, just in time, the hideous lesson of the *Titanic*. There was, too, the incontestable advantage of assigning a length that would establish a world's record. It was a source of great pride that the new liner's length of over nine hundred feet would exceed the *Olympic*'s by a comfortable margin.

The practice of selecting names for the Hamburg-Amerika ships was an informal business and bore no relation to the rigid system employed by either Cunard or White Star. It seems to have been a matter of choice made arbitrarily by whatever was tactful near launch time. A good case in point was the abuse, perhaps symbolic, of the name *Europa,* which although finally used in 1929 was initially scheduled for 1906. Ballin had intended it for the *Amerika*'s sister ship, thus establishing a symbolic continental identity for the two vessels. But at the last moment, in deference to the Empress who christened her, the name was changed to *Kaiserin Auguste Victoria*. The name was thus available and planned for the first of the three superliners. But HAPAG's Board of Directors chose the name *Imperator* as a flattering gesture to Kaiser Wilhelm, who not only exhibited a proprietary interest in the ship but decided that he would launch it himself. So the second ship was to become *Europa*. But the intrusion of a national crisis in 1913 made it expedient to have Prince Rupert of Bavaria christen her *Vaterland* instead. Incidentally, it is interesting that two of the three German ships were christened by men, assuming a role almost universally accorded to women.

The ship was ready for launching by the spring of 1912 and on the twenty-third of May the Kaiser arrived by train to perform the ceremony. It was fortunate that he was not subject to attacks of vertigo or he would never have made it to the top of the launching platform. It was an incredible structure, built to get within striking distance of the *Imperator*'s massive stem. Twenty feet above the ground, a covered pavilion was superseded by yet another, in the form of a gazebo perched on the roof and connected by a separate staircase. There were elaborate bleachers arranged on either side and the entire yard, together with the ship's prow, was garlanded in looped evergreens.

The Kaiser, dressed as an admiral, strode solemnly around the hull at the head of an extensive inspecting party. Then, with much clatter of sabers and heel-clicking, he ascended to the first level and shook hands with a score of silk-hatted functionaries. Then another thirty steps up to his private platform on which he and Ballin stood, probably rather out of breath.

It was at this moment that the first of two *faux pas* occurred. A piece of planking, improperly secured to the forepeak, fell to the ground under the bow. It passed within feet of the Emperor and there was an instant when it seemed to horrified officials that he had been struck. But he had leaped back in time under the roof of his aerie and moments later resumed the ceremony. It was all hideously embarrassing. The trigger was pulled and a bottle of wine, nationality unknown, swung on the end of a metal arm and caught the stem on cue as it started down the ways.

There was a second rhubarb as the *Imperator* thundered bravely into the water. She had been launched carrying both anchors and, to help arrest her, the port one was let go. Literally "let go," for the inboard end of the cable was unattached and roared out of the hawsepipe, depositing the anchor and several fathoms of brand-new anchor chain into the mud of Hamburg harbor. Despite this failure, the hull came to a stop with three hundred feet to spare between the rudderless stern and Kaiser Wilhelm Quay on the opposite shore.

Only a month had passed since the *Titanic* disaster and fitting out was delayed by the addition of an inner skin, extending well above the water line in the forward compartments. To check the soundness of the work, the methodical Germans hoisted on board a fire engine from the Hamburg Fire Department, the largest pumper in Europe. The five-foot space between the plates on each side was filled with water from the pier-side mains and pronounced tight.

This optional refinement on the part of her builders was almost more easily solved than the problem of lifeboats. There were new safety regulations in effect, including a sensible proviso guaranteeing "lifeboats for all." "All," in this case, involved a staggering number of souls. The *Imperator*'s passenger-crew complement worked out as follows:

First class:	700
Second class:	600
Third class:	940
Fourth class:	1750
Crew:	1100
TOTAL:	5100

Above, the *Imperator* ready for launching in May of 1912. Workmen complete the Kaiser's special cupola at lower left. Assembled in silk hats and spiked helmets, the *Honoratioren* gaze raptly as Kaiser Wilhelm II launches his favorite ship, left. (*Kurt Innecken Collection*)

Decked out like a Christmas wreath, the *Imperator* thunders into Hamburg Harbor. Moments later, the port anchor was gone. (*Kurt Innecken Collection*)

By crowding, an additional four hundred could be accommodated. Somehow, room had to be found for no less than eighty-three lifeboats, over four times the number carried on the *Titanic*. If all of them were stacked on the boat deck, the stability of the ship would be threatened. The ultimate solution was to place half of them in bays carved out of the after shelter deck.

Below decks, there were new water-tube boilers and an ingenious device to discourage rolling. It was the invention of a Dr. Frahm of Hamburg, and Frahm's antirolling tanks became standard equipment on many ships to follow. The system incorporated half-filled water tanks on either side of the hull, connected by a pumping system. In theory, flow between the tanks could be so directed as to counteract the attitude of the hull. Yet the problem of anticipating roll was more difficult than originally suspected; early versions of Frahm's invention couldn't keep up with the sea and corrective reaction lagged hopelessly behind the roll. But the shortcomings of the *Imperator*'s stability were yet to be revealed and as she lay alongside her fitting-out berth, the ship that grew was, both inside and out, an impressive sight.

Mewès, now at the summit of his career (and unfortunately near the end of his life), was charged with the interior design of all three HAPAG giants. Davis, meanwhile, was awarded a contract to design the *Aquitania,* building on the Clyde. This division of labor resulted from an extraordinary compromise hammered out by Cunard and the Hamburg-Amerika Line: Mewès would work in Germany and Davis in England, but neither partner could disclose details of his work to the other.

It was a ludicrous arrangement and one that was doubtless circumvented. Although the *Aquitania*'s public rooms had an English flavor, certain aspects of the work, particularly the dining room, bore Mewès' unmistakable stamp. However, close collaboration between the two for over a decade, together with the compatibility of taste that originally brought them together, meant that by 1912 their work was perhaps interchangeable. Certainly Davis must be credited with the *Aquitania*'s Carolean smoking room, an adaptation from a room in Greenwich Hospital, as well as the Palladian lounge; they are both as faultless as anything that has ever appeared on the Atlantic.

Mewès was presented with the most taxing commission of the five he had already fulfilled for Ballin. On the *Imperator* class, he dealt with dimensions essentially the same as those of the Royal Automobile Club, surpassing anything ever seen on board ship. The Germans were determined to surpass the *Olympic* in every particular. This pretentious ambition pervaded the *Imperator*'s entire design philosophy. It is to Mewès' eternal credit that, in his climactic work, he avoided the temptations to which a man of less disciplined tastes might have succumbed.

Once again, he chose as style the best aspects of eighteenth-century France, a choice that seemed to sit well, surprisingly enough, not only with the Company but the Kaiser as well. Mewès' relationship with the Emperor was cordial on the subject of ships. But on political matters, there were predictable differences. At the launch of the *Vaterland,* Wilhelm asked the architect if he would undertake to enlarge a portion of Strasbourg's principal boulevard; Mewès, an Alsatian, replied coldly that Napoleon had always found it adequate.

The key to the two mammoth interior spaces on the *Imperator* class lies in the number of funnels: with only three, there was correspondingly more uninterrupted space between them. On the second and third ships, this largesse was further increased by division of the boiler uptakes, so that Mewès could finally design a suite of public rooms along a central axis, as he had hoped to do years before on the *Amerika.* Both the *Vaterland* and the *Bismarck* share with the later *Normandie* the distinction of being the largest ships ever to have adopted this design feature. Yet if the central funnel casings on the *Imperator* hampered Mewès planning in any way, it was not apparent in the two splendid rooms that took shape on her promenade deck.

Grouped below number 2 funnel were the inevitable staircase, elevators and hall. Forward of this was a lounge, a hundred feet long and narrower than the hull only by the width of promenade deck on either side. It was a room that could absorb, quite comfortably, all seven hundred passengers traveling first class. The Germans called it the social hall and, despite a vaguely institutional ring, that is exactly what was intended. It was indeed a very social place—to gather, to talk, to have tea, to play cards or to dance. Comfortable chairs grouped about low tables in an amorphous mass were the very antithesis of the *Olympic*'s formal arrangement.

This total reversal of White Star's treatment is interesting and, I think, revealing: on the German ships, Mewès' design ensures that husbands and wives join each other in a room not only large enough to accommodate them but of a character that encourages participation. The ceiling was hung from a series of girdered trusses overhead which effectively obliterated the forward end of the boat deck but freed the lounge beneath from any pillars, columns, alcoves or corners. The monstrous skylight, as opposed to the central dome on British ships, was not much smaller than the ceiling, with the result that it embraced the entire space beneath it, encompassing all

Near the end of her fitting out,
the new HAPAG flagship is
towed to dry dock. (*National
Archives and Compagnie
Générale Transatlantique*)

corners of the room into one. It was thus subtly but firmly designed for the pursuit of a common purpose. One must not assume that either Mewès or his employers neglected those who wished for seclusion; there were traditional havens of privacy and separation of the sexes on the same deck. But the creation of this central meeting room, both handsome and useful, was a noteworthy development.

An Englishman who later described the *Imperator*'s lounge as a place of "Teutonic gloomy majesty" was more prejudiced than knowledgeable. "Majesty" there was, but a room of that scale needed it; it was never overpowering. I also find it difficult to be gloomy in a room with a thirty-foot ceiling, and anything less "Teutonic" than the restrained elegance of the ill-fated Louis would be hard to imagine. One shudders to think of the pedantries of Potsdam rococo that might have appeared in the Frenchman's absence. Similarly, one might also carp that the room seems crowded with furniture. Yet it has been my experience that people placed close together tend to enjoy themselves more than those spread out esthetically over a wide expanse. Perhaps it explains, somehow, the gaiety of tourist as opposed to the occasional stuffiness of first class today. It was a lesson learned by designers of the *Queen Mary*'s lounge and so disastrously ignored by their successors responsible for the equivalent space on the *Queen Elizabeth 2*.

On the other side of the entrance hall, there was a room of equal dimension that seemed at first glance to be a baroque theater. There was a gold-and-white auditorium, filled with chairs, bisected by a broad aisle which led, up a short flight of steps, to the stage. Within the proscenium, framed by massive columns and a wrought-iron railing, was a lavish set, all mahogany and gilt. To the left was space for a string orchestra. This was the treatment that Mewès had chosen to combine winter garden and restaurant; if I have stressed, quite literally, the theatricality of his solution, it is for a very sound reason.

The Ritz-Carlton restaurant, the permanent production that was to play on that stage, was larger than any of its predecessors. Yet its greater size and pretension were effectively balanced by a trick of illusion. There were, center stage, beneath an imposing rotunda, some set pieces of restaurant scenery: some tables, a basket of flowers, a buffet, a glass screen. But the majority of tables were concealed, hidden in the wings. Although giving the appearance of an open space, the restaurant had all the privacy lacking in the social hall. Research conducted long after the *Imperator* was scrapped confirms that restaurant patrons crave a paradoxical combination of isolation and community. The total seclusion of a private dining room (excepting, of course, those discreet rooms that provide for the satisfaction of other appetites simultaneously) is evidently less desirable than the proximity of others. Whether one respects this conclusion or not, it is evident that Mewès instinctively anticipated it. Diners en route to the restaurant ascended the staircase, performing the ritual of the grand entrance, and were then accommodated in the seclusion of its recesses, rather as though on a screened balcony, removed from yet in touch with their fellow passengers below.

And those who watched comfortably from among the palms and hydrangeas of the lower room were not in any sense mere spectators. They were participants as well, just as occupants of sidewalk cafés are interchangeable with passers-by on a Parisian boulevard. Indeed, the reference is appropriate, for Mewès' design of the winter garden and the delightful restaurant that adjoined it gratified a sense of impromptu. Life on board any well-run ship is and should be improvisational. There is ample time to greet friends, join a group, put off lunch; in short, to ignore the clock. (There are those who are no sooner on board than they set about creating a substitute set of obligations indistinguishable from those they suffer ashore. Personally, I make as few plans as possible and don't understand those who flock like lemmings to tournaments, competitions and lessons, effectively destroying one of the most priceless blessings a crossing can offer.)

There were also within easy reach a smoking room, ladies' salon, writing room, gymnasium and, strangely enough, a grill room. This latter was situated at the end of B-deck and could only be achieved by traversing the promenade deck crossover. It was the only aberration in an otherwise sensible deck plan and proved a superfluous facility that didn't last very long, for various reasons, nor was it repeated on either succeeding ship. In point of fact, its interior, together with that of the smoking room, betray by their anonymous banality that Mewès was not involved in their design. The only other facility to rival the magnificence on B-deck was the aforementioned Pompeian pool. Mewès had prevailed upon the Vulkan Werke to leave him adequate height so that, although smaller than the London original, the pool's proportions were just as striking. There was at one end a double staircase giving access to a balcony running the length of the room, creating a spectators' gallery above and a series of changing rooms below. The swimming pools on all three of those HAPAG ships were breathtaking, conceived and executed on a scale that has never been equaled.

That the dining room was an almost total disappointment is not really surprising. Mewès had given his all on the promenade deck and the decorative leftovers served up for the regular diners were essentially tasteless. It was a pattern that emerged on all the great ships. The restaurants were

Copied from his Royal Automobile Club original in London, Mewès' stunning "Pompeian Bath" on board the *Imperator*. (*Avery Library*)

enormously popular and to passengers who had already paid their fare, the additional expense was negligible. So steamship companies, always ready to capitalize on success, quite naturally increased not only the capacity but the prestige of their restaurants. The self-contained little room that Ballin had introduced on the *Amerika* a decade earlier had blossomed into an extravaganza that dominated the center of the vessel.

It was a preoccupation that was unfortunately accompanied by a perceptible deterioration of catering standards previously established for all. Inevitably, there was a division of both resources and priorities with the promotion of a kind of super-first-class alternative. By the end of the twenties, when the new thousand-footers were on the drawing boards, the whole question of restaurant policy was redefined. It is interesting that the grill rooms on both the *Normandie* and the *Queen Mary* were located on the after end of the top deck, where they had, admittedly, a magnificent view aft over the stern. But they were also tucked out of sight, so to speak, removed from the center of things, and were presumably less of an irritant to passengers who resented any double standard within the first class. What began as a convenience ended as a club. It is revealing that the finest cuisine available on the Atlantic today is served in the dining rooms of the *France*, a ship that has no restaurant whatsoever.

Shortly before the *Imperator* was to depart for trials, an enormous crate from Berlin arrived at her fitting-out pier. Perched inside it was a monstrous gilt bronze eagle, the work of Professor Bruno Kruse. The pugnacious creature, wings outstretched, gripped in its talons a globe, over which was draped a banner bearing the HAPAG motto: *Mein Feld ist die Welt*. With great care, it was hoisted up and bolted in place on the prow, from which vantage point it scowled down the river Elbe. It was, if not quite the last, certainly the most preposterous figurehead to appear on the Atlantic, tacked onto a hull whose architect had quite obviously made no esthetic provision to include it. It was, in addition, a dangerous obstacle to visibility, both for a docking pilot and forward lookout. Press releases hinted that its hollow interior incorporated space for a seaman to peer through a plate-glass panel in the creature's breast. This was as untrue as the companion tale that the bird's weight forward was essential to counterbalance the opulence aft.

The simple truth was that the *Imperator*'s eagle was nothing more than a means of lengthening the ship. The Germans were desperate to retain statistical superiority and, having outclassed the *Olympic*'s tonnage, length and width, they were determined not to be eclipsed by the *Aquitania*. In point of fact, the *Imperator*'s hull would have been slightly longer than the

A decorative ruse to add overall length to the
Imperator: Professor Kruse's improbable eagle
adorns her prow. Note the comparative height
of the man perched on the anchor, lower left.
(*National Archives*)

new Cunarder's without the lamentable addition of the eagle. Perhaps the precious extra ten feet that it afforded were held in reserve for the *Britannic*. As it was, the record for length was taken bloodlessly the following year by German competitors from across the harbor, Blohm & Voss. Both the *Vaterland* and the *Bismarck* were larger, made so by the arbitrary introduction of two extra frames into the hulls during construction. It is ironic that both experienced serious hull fractures in later years, which were the result, I am quite sure, of this idiotic one-upmanship.

In May of 1913, the proud new *Imperator* started down the Elbe. Within hours, she was aground; nothing approaching her thirty-foot draft had ever negotiated that tortuous sixty-mile channel before. Additional tugs were sent down river from Hamburg and she was freed without damage on the next tide. The following day, she dropped her pilot at Cuxhaven and sailed into the North Sea.

It was only then that a condition hinted at earlier manifested itself with uncompromising reality. The *Imperator* was top-heavy or, in the delicate prose of naval architects, deficient in initial stability. To the crew, she was a tender ship, "tender" in the sense that she heeled alarmingly at the slightest provocation; worse, she "hung on the roll" or seemed reluctant to return to the vertical. However, there was nothing that could be done about it at short notice. Only a laborious rework of her tophamper could correct it and there wasn't time. Literally and figuratively, there was too much riding on the *Imperator,* and she was handed over to the company as was.

Unhappily, there was worse to come: a workman, having filled his lighter from a storeroom tin of benzene, tried it out and started a flash fire. Although the fire was confined to one compartment, five crewmen were burned to death. Company officials had to postpone the maiden voyage while the damage was put right, releasing a bogus report that blamed a combination of bad weather and inadequate docking facilities at Cuxhaven for the delay. Uppermost in their minds was fear that the fire, together with the grounding in the Elbe, recalled the incidents that had marred her launch. Ever since the *Titanic,* the public was very sensitive to what they considered bad omens in connection with vast new liners, and it is not to be wondered at that the Hamburg-Amerika Line were anxious about the *Imperator's* image.

But they needn't have worried; the first voyage to America was an unqualified success. Although her regular English port would be Plymouth, she first touched Great Britain at Southampton and was accorded the full pomp of a civic welcome. Following a call at Cherbourg, she started across the Atlantic with thirty-one hundred passengers, a record for a maiden voyage but nowhere near her capacity. In command was Commodore Hans Ruser, who had under him a staff of four additional "captains"; this was a clever piece of subliminal promotion, the implication being that such a huge ship needed a radically new command structure. In mid-Atlantic, Ballin remembered to send a congratulatory cable to Berlin, marking the occasion of Kaiser Wilhelm's twenty-fifth year on the throne.

The *Imperator* arrived off Hoboken on the eighteenth of June, just as the *Amerika* was pulling away from the pier that had been specially enlarged to take the new liner. As the two ships passed, each had its bands on deck, serenading the other's passengers with "America" and "Die Wacht am Rhein." It was a brave sight, the Hudson sparkling in the sun of a summer's morning, tugs fussing and hooting about the new ship and music floating clearly over the water to watchers on either shore. There was a particularly festive air, for the *Imperator* was, apart from the *France,* the first great new ship to arrive in New York since the *Titanic*'s aborted maiden voyage the year previous. Passengers who came ashore announced that they were highly pleased with the crossing and with their magnificent accommodations. Not a word was said about the new ship's stability.

But during the summer that followed, passengers less hesitant to disrupt the euphoria of a maiden voyage became more articulate. The *Imperator* listed to port, she listed to starboard, she listed with even a moderate breeze on her vast flank. Coming into New York with her bunkers depleted and immigrants crowding the port rail for a glimpse of the Statue of Liberty, she listed worst of all. Even Frahm's celebrated tanks were useless, since they were designed to prevent rather than correct rolling. There are very few photographs of the ship that don't show her tipped to one side or the other. Publicity pictures of the pool, taken in port, show a water line that doesn't match the row of horizontal tiling. The Sandy Hook pilots said that she never came in on an even keel, and rechristened her the "Limperator." Despite this adverse publicity, she proved not only popular but enormously profitable: passengers of all classes booked on her in record numbers. Ballin amended her sailing schedule in July to give the Emperor and his family an exclusive overnight excursion into the North Sea.

On her fourth voyage to New York, she carried over five thousand passengers, more people than had ever crossed in one vessel before. Pier officials, overwhelmed by sheer weight of numbers, requested that the eighteen hundred in steerage remain on board for an additional night.

At four the following morning, an indicator on the *Imperator*'s bridge alerted the officer of the watch to the presence of smoke in the dry-stores room forward on the starboard side near the water line. He immediately

Painting the *Imperator*'s rudder and underwater hull. Like the *Mauretania,* she had quadruple screws driven by turbines. (*Frank Braynard Collection*)

HAPAG's new flagship, the *Imperator,* sails past the Battery on the second leg of her maiden voyage. Apart from the problem of vertical stability, it had all been a great success. (*Prints and Photographs Division, Library of Congress*)

The *Imperator*'s narrowly-averted disaster at Hoboken. A stubborn fire has been drowned by tons of water and the ship recovers her vertical stability. In a brave show of business-as-usual for Manhattan-bound commuters, paint crews touch up the tops of all three funnels. (*Frank Braynard Collection*)

The *Imperator*'s lowered profile seen at Cuxhaven. The funnel tops are gone but the eagle remains. (*Frank Braynard Collection*)

closed off the compartment and ordered steam piped into it from the boiler room; he also set off the pier alarm. Below, fire parties raced to the forward end of the ship and off-duty stewards were instructed to rouse the immigrants and get them ashore. It is doubtful whether many of them needed waking, for the ship was being bunkered through the night and the roar of coal rattling down the chutes was enough to wake the dead. There were inevitable scenes of panic as steerage passengers were herded ashore, pouring down gangplanks up which firemen from Hoboken were trying to drag hoses. The blaze, though still contained, was a stubborn one, filling the forward passageways with clouds of choking black smoke. One officer, who had recently fought a blaze on the *Fürst Bismarck,* died in the burning compartment, overcome by smoke.

News of his death concluded a familiar argument up on the bridge. A ship tied up to a pier with a fire on board is often in more danger from shore-based firemen than flames. It is their quite natural inclination to put out the fire at any cost, to drown it, if necessary. It was this very course of action, which sailors are reluctant to follow, that was put into effect on the *Imperator.* More than a score of hoses, threaded into the ship's starboard pier side, filled the compartment to a depth of thirty feet, aided by a pair of enthusiastic fireboats that jostled the coal barges still moored to port. Tender ship that she was, the *Imperator* leaned ominously toward the pier, assuming a near-critical list before the blaze was extinguished shortly after nine. Remarkably enough, she was delayed in sailing only two additional days. Ship's personnel, their summer whites smudged from the smoke, worked round the clock to complete the turnaround and clean up the mess. Immigration officials managed to round up all the steerage passengers, including two who were unearthed in an Elizabeth, New Jersey, boardinghouse miles from the pier.

If those who fought the *Imperator* fire can be censured for overreaction, it is probable that still fresh in the minds of most of them, firemen and sailors alike, was the tragic Hoboken fire of 1900. On a hot Saturday afternoon in June, several ships were loading at the North German Lloyd piers. Bales of cotton, waiting to be loaded on Pier 3, somehow ignited, and within minutes the entire complex was ablaze. The *Kaiser Wilhelm der Grosse,* with crew on board and steam up, managed to back into the Hudson and extinguish the flames which had leaped, with frightening rapidity, from pier to ship.

Three other vessels were not so lucky: their hawsers burned through, the *Saale, Bremen* and *Main* drifted out with the tide. The latter two went aground at Weehawken while the *Saale,* blazing fiercely, her red-hot bow steaming at the water line, drifted further down and caught on the mud flats north of Ellis Island. From a passing ferry, horrified commuters saw, through the smoke, a line of white faces at the portholes. Yet the tugs and fireboats that quickly surrounded her were powerless to assist: each imploring face, only inches away, was framed in a brass port less than a foot in diameter. Escape was impossible. There was no way to break through the shell plating and access from above was out of the question. Two men with fire axes who managed to get on board the blazing liner were unable to pierce the steel deck plates that lay directly under the teak planking. Crews on the tugs, reduced to tears of helpless rage, could do no more than try and comfort the German crewmen trapped in the burning hulk. Those who were not burned to death mercifully drowned as the flooding tide crept up the sides of the grounded vessel and lapped into the portholes.

The only survivors from any of the three ships were fifteen coal passers found in the *Main*'s bunkers, cut free from the beached ship twelve hours afterwards. The death toll topped two hundred and the North German Lloyd's Ocean Terminal was incinerated down to the low-water marks on the piles. Following the holocaust, officials at all passenger piers in New York were extremely sensitive about fire, and shortly thereafter portholes on all new liners were made significantly larger.

The *Imperator* finished her inaugural season two voyages later and spent the winter back in the Vulkan Werke yard, undergoing some radical surgery to lower the center of gravity. Nine feet were taken off the top of each funnel, cutting them down to the height of the steampipes. Easily the most dispensable of her upper-deck facilities was the grill room on the after end of the promenade deck; it was removed and the space turned into a veranda café, open to the weather and filled with cane furniture. More wicker was also introduced into the large public rooms, a design indignity that Mewès must have found as irritating as the replacement of some of the Ritz-Carlton's paneling with lightweight fireproof sheeting. The social hall, happily, retained its original appearance intact. As a final clincher, two thousand tons of cement were added as permanent ballast.

When she went back to sea the following spring, the *Imperator* had lost her thoroughbred look with the tops of her stacks. As she had originally appeared, that enormous bulk was offset by proportions that worked, eagle and all, to make her unconventional, perhaps, but distinctive and proud. Like the prototype of any new class, she was experimental, a hybrid whose builders had attempted to combine huge capacity and unparalleled luxury with a quite remarkable speed; despite her massive appearance, the *Imperator* could average nearly twenty-four knots. But all this had been achieved at the expense of stability, which was only partially remedied by the winter's refitting. The problem remained to plague her for the rest of her long career.

The *Imperator*'s first crossing with her new silhouette was in the early spring of 1914. One day out of Cherbourg, she ran into a gale with winds up to ninety miles an hour, a classic Atlantic storm. Her captain wisely headed her into the wind and rode out the worst of it for six hours. All he could see from the bridge was a fog of spindrift. Passengers who were well enough to eat in the Ritz-Carlton could not speak over the shrieking of the gale. When dawn broke next morning, four lifeboats had been washed away and the famous eagle, which had survived the remodeling back in Hamburg, had been shorn of both wings by a monstrous wave; one had disappeared and the other was wedged under the starboard anchor cable on the forepeak. What remained of the proud figurehead was later taken off at Cuxhaven and never replaced.

The *Vaterland* joined her in service later that spring, completing the westbound leg of her maiden voyage on May 22. Her designers had profited from the *Imperator*'s shortcomings and the new ship was far more stable. However, both her arrival and departure were complete with opera buffa overtones. She came up from Quarantine escorted by no fewer than twenty-five tugs, a flotilla that HAPAG's marine superintendent had deemed sufficient. But he underestimated the combined effect a strong north wind and falling tide would have on the new arrival's record displacement. The pace up to Hoboken was appallingly slow and the ship's band, stationed on deck to play her into the berth, had run through several refrains of "The Star-Spangled Banner" before they downed instruments and waited for a signal from the bridge.

Just as the ship was abreast of the pier, a string of Lehigh Valley barges cut blithely across her bows. The *Vaterland* gave an agonized bellow and backed water; one of the tugs only just escaped being drawn under her counter as she slid back downstream, threatening yet another rail barge astern. The agonizing approach was repeated and the ship docked five hours late. Among her first-class passengers was a group including Nelson Aldrich and Joseph Ochs who, in a roseate glow following the ship's concert two nights earlier, had cabled Ballin:

THE MOST SANGUINE EXPECTATIONS OF THE PASSENGERS HAVE BEEN FULLY REALIZED. THE VATERLAND IS A VERITABLE PALACE AFLOAT AND ITS COLOSSAL PROPORTIONS, AMPLE ACCOMMODATIONS AND SUPERB COMFORTS ARE ONLY SURPASSED BY THE SENSE OF SAFETY AND SECURITY THAT IN EVERY DIRECTION IMPRESS THE INTELLIGENT OBSERVER.

As these same men paced the promenade deck impatiently, it must have occurred to them that docking their "veritable palace afloat" under adverse weather conditions had its disadvantages.

The same frustrations no doubt prompted the *Vaterland*'s master to depart New York with a redeeming flourish. At twelve noon sharp, against the advice of his docking pilot, Commodore Ruser pulled smartly away from the Hoboken terminal with a burst of full astern power. The ship hurtled across the Hudson and, despite a series of desperate commands from the bridge, seemed loath to abandon her rearward surge. It was established later by a white-faced chief engineer that the valve stems on the after turbines had somehow failed; at any rate, to crowds gathered on shore to watch her departure, it seemed that the *Vaterland* was determined to take revenge on the small craft that had so interfered with her arrival four days earlier. Her stern was actually between two Manhattan piers before steam was admitted into the high-pressure turbines and the quadruple screws thundered ahead. The turbulence in the slip swamped a coal barge and damaged two others. Only by a few feet was the German vessel saved from a collision that could have seriously damaged her rudder.

When the *Aquitania* came into service, Cunard was the first to have a three-ship service in operation. Their new ship, together with the two HAPAG liners, were the most popular ships on the Atlantic during that brief summer season of 1914. Their interiors were quite incredible and the unanimous reaction of their overwhelmed passengers was that they were still on shore. This was precisely the effect that steamship companies were anxious to achieve. Arthur Davis, addressing his colleagues at the Royal Institute of British Architects in 1922, summed up the companies' case as follows:

> When I was first engaged, some fifteen years ago, to start this work . . . I said to the directors of the company that employed me: "Why don't you make a ship look like a ship?" . . . But the answer I was given was that the people who use these ships are not pirates, they do not dance hornpipes; they are mostly seasick American ladies, and the one thing they want to forget when they are on the vessel is that they are on a ship at all. Most of them have got to travel and they object to it very much. In order to impress that point upon me, the Company sent me across the Atlantic. The first day out I enjoyed the beautiful sea, but when we got well on to the Atlantic, there was one thing I craved for as never before, and that was a warm fire and a pink shade. The people who travel on these large ships are the people who live in hotels; they are not ships for sailors or yachtsmen or people who enjoy the

The *Vaterland,* second of Ballin's super trio, was
launched on schedule in 1913. The following
year, the *Bismarck* joined her two sisters—a
remarkable *tour de force* for German shipwrights. (*Frank Braynard Collection*)

Left, Mewès' splendid social hall on the *Vaterland*, seen at teatime and after dinner in midocean. It is doubtful that this handsome room has ever been surpassed on any other North Atlantic liner.

Before adjourning to the smoking room, male passengers on the *Vaterland* take their ease in the winter garden, above. Up the short staircase is the entrance to the Ritz-Carlton Restaurant. (*Frank Braynard Collection*)

Two remarkable B-decks: far right, the *Imperator* and right, the *Vaterland*. It is interesting to compare options afforded by the second ship's divided uptakes. From the stage of the social hall aft to the back wall of the Ritz-Carlton Restaurant, Mewès could plan around a magnificent central axis. Also on the *Imperator* plan, note the splendid treatment he has been able to use for the grand staircase. (*The Mariners Museum, Newport News, Virginia*)

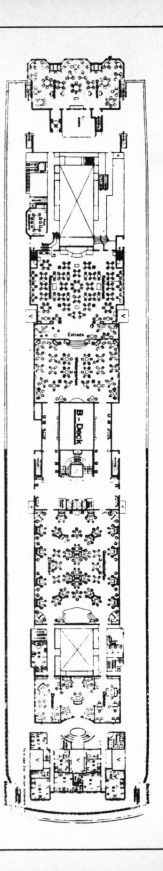

sea. They are inhabited by all sorts of people, some of whom are very delicate and stay in their cabin during the whole voyage; others, less delicate, stay in the smoking room all through the voyage. . . . I suggest to you that the transatlantic liner is not merely a ship, she is a floating town with 3,000 passengers of all kinds, with all sorts of tastes, and those who enjoy being there are distinctly in the minority. If we could get ships to look inside like ships, and get people to enjoy the sea, it would be a very good thing; but all we can do, as things are, is to give them gigantic floating hotels.

It was clear that when passage of the Atlantic between Europe and America could only be made by ship, fear of and discomfort from that most dangerous ocean were still potent forces. So it was company policy to lull passengers into the comforting fiction that they were nowhere near the ocean that lay, in point of fact, just beyond the columned, curtained, tapestried interior that housed them. Acknowledgment of its existence was first to appear on another line, notably in the P & O liner *Orion* of 1935; Brian O'Rorke, an Australian architect whose lack of previous ship experience was considered among his better qualifications, designed a ship's interior that was, for the first time, in communication with the elements that surrounded it.

But she was a ship designed for a different kind of service, traveling through sunnier and calmer waters for six weeks at a time. The last eastbound crossing I made was on the *Queen Elizabeth 2,* an anomaly whose service requirements dictated a scheme of design half Atlantic and half Caribbean. We traveled in a bank of fog for the entire five days and the white blanket that remained outside those large dining-room windows designed for the tropics became increasingly oppressive.

Number three in the German series, the *Bismarck,* was launched that same spring of 1914, christened inadvertently by the Emperor. Hannah von Bismarck, naming the ship in honor of her grandfather, swung too late and missed. The Kaiser, snatching the bottle from her hand, managed to hit the target before it got out of reach. The giant vessel was still fitting out at Hamburg when Blohm & Voss, like all the shipyards of Europe, turned their attention to more pressing matters. Charles Mewès died that year too, having completed drawings for the *Bismarck.* Had he lived, he might have found time in the twenties to sail on one of the ships whose rooms he designed; most of the traveling elite did. As it was, he never once crossed to America. His output was so enormous that I suspect he never had time. The *Aquitania,* the last of his ships, was in service until 1950, a victim of superannuation rather than outmoded taste. The characteristic purity of Mewès' style survived well past the orgy of Art Deco that succeeded it.

Of course, he was fortunate enough to have lived and worked in a momentous shipbuilding era, the golden age of transatlantic competition. Those impressive ships were conceived, laid down and launched with an optimism and vigor that the postwar world would never recapture. Never again would one company build three passenger vessels of over fifty thousand tons. Ships in the future might be bigger and faster, but there would never be as many. For another battle was to rage over the Atlantic and the shores of Europe that it washed. There would be changes in the ships, in the ways that they were built and in the people who would sail on them.

5.
War

Hostilities began in the summer of 1914. Two years earlier, a German Navy Act had proposed that all German merchant vessels should carry guns below decks, thereby simplifying the process of mobilization once war was declared. There is no evidence to suggest that this recommendation was put into effect, but dockyard workers at Southampton reported that the *Kaiser Wilhelm II*, in for emergency repairs following a Channel collision, had gun mountings installed on her decks. Later that same year, an observant British visitor to Kiel saw a row of doors set in the wall of a dockyard warehouse. Above each, the name of a different German liner was lettered neatly. If the ordnance was not actually on board, it was at least stored and allotted against the day of need.

In Great Britain, the Admiralty too was strongly in favor of reviving the ancient tradition of the merchant navy as a fighting auxiliary. The faster vessels in service would be equipped with enough guns, armor plate and naval personnel to qualify them as armed merchant cruisers, flying the White Ensign, among them the *Mauretania, Olympic* and *Carmania*. It was planned, however, to fit the remainder with a pair of 4.7 guns mounted on the after end. Although reducing their striking power to a sting in the tail, it was quite in line with Their Lordships' stated policy that armed merchantmen should fire only while retreating as hastily as possible, thus incidentally presenting as small a target as possible. There was the additional necessity of presenting a low warlike profile while in neutral ports.

From the day war was declared, Liverpool was the scene of dozens of forty-eight-hour conversions as ship after ship was provided with armaments and sent down to Portsmouth for ammunition. The *Laconia* loaded seventy-five tons of cordite on board, which the Navy insisted should be kept in the cold-storage rooms among the beef and cabbages. They also insisted that the *Oceanic*'s carpenter be equipped with a sword, a solemn precaution that rocked the fo'c's'le for weeks.

Those ships not in British home waters received on their wireless a message advising them to abandon regular tracks, reduce the brilliancy of their lights and complete the voyage without bunkering. It is incredible that there were no collisions anywhere during those first hectic days of August while ships scuttled for cover. As declarations of war crackled between European chancelleries, traffic on the North Atlantic was thrown into the kind of confusion that would only be repeated a quarter of a century later on the eve of another world war. The *Mauretania,* westbound, cut off all communication and raced through the fog to Halifax; an extra watch of stokers was put on and the ship attained a dazzling twenty-eight knots. Limping along after her came the *Cedric*. The *Olympic* stayed on course for New York, steaming at top speed to avoid reported German warships. There were more than thirty German ships caught in American ports, including the brand-new *Vaterland,* held at Hoboken in the midst of her fourth voyage. The *Imperator* was in Hamburg.

Several of the Germans tried to make a run for it but turned back. Both the *Grosse Kurfürst* and *President Grant* came back to New York, followed shortly thereafter by the *Friedrich der Grosse* which had sailed from Baltimore two days earlier and narrowly avoided a British cruiser. The only ship that successfully departed the neutral sanctity of United States territorial waters was the *Kronprinz Wilhelm*. She sailed on the third of August, carrying two thousand tons more coal than she would ever need to reach Europe. In addition, besides hundreds of pounds of seastores, there was lashed to her forward railings a suspicious wooden crate, twenty-five feet long and in the shape of a Maltese cross. Ship's officers said that it was a spare crankshaft stowed temporarily on deck, but to observers on the Hoboken piers, it looked more like a gun. She slipped out of harbor that night, showing only her running lights. The pilot who left her at the end of Ambrose Channel noted that she steamed south rather than east.

Midnight sailings were suddenly furtive rather than festive. The *Lusitania* left her New York pier at one o'clock the following morning, the same day that England declared war. She carried only three hundred passengers and those cabins that were occupied had their portholes covered by Company blankets. In the passageways, the electric lights were disconnected and replaced with oil lamps. With no ceremony and few awake to see her, the black Cunarder crept down to the Narrows and shortly thereafter made contact with the cruiser *Essex,* which had just escorted the *Olympic* in. On the same morning that the *Olympic* tied up at the Chelsea piers in New York, astonished residents of Bar Harbor, Maine, reported that she was anchored out in Frenchman's Bay.

But the long black liner that lay peacefully outside their yacht anchorage was actually the *Kronprinzessin Cecilie.* She had sailed for Hamburg in late July, carrying twelve hundred passengers and, locked in her specie room, twelve million dollars in bullion. Four days out of New York, Captain Charles Polack heard by wireless that war was imminent; he was also advised that two French cruisers were steaming to intercept him. Without a moment's hesitation or advice to his passengers, he turned the ship about. Couples who found the dance floor harder to negotiate due to the unfamiliar motion of a quartering sea were stopped in mid-turkey trot by a chord from the orchestra; the men were asked to assemble in the smoking room.

There, they were informed by the master that the ship was headed back to America. As he spoke, the stewards were extinguishing all lights on the ship. Some groped their way below to spread the news to their families while others stayed in the blacked-out smoking room for the night. Presumably the bar stewards were kept busy, for the next morning, a delegation of Americans, whose outrage matched their bank accounts, offered to buy the ship outright from Polack so that she could legitimately fly Old Glory. The Captain refused and ordered paint crews aloft to add a black band to the tops of the yellow funnels, thus masquerading as the *Olympic.* When the *Kronprinzessin Cecilie* ran into fog (the same fog that the *Mauretania* had encountered), he sounded his foghorn and reduced speed only when presented with a written request to do so by his terrified passengers. By the

Photographed together by chance
for a Cherbourg post card in 1911,
the *Kronprinzessin Cecilie* (right)
and the *Olympic*. The German
vessel masqueraded briefly as the
larger British ship in the first days
of the war. Although Bar Harbor
residents were momentarily taken
in, the disparity in size and profile
would scarcely have deceived the
Royal Navy. (*Compagnie Générale
Transatlantique*)

526. - Les Transatlantiques " Olympic " de la White Star Line et " Kronprinzessin-Cecilie "
de la Norddeutscher Lloyd en rade de Cherbourg

night of August 3, having successfully avoided the Canadian mainland, Polack knew he could never reach New York with his remaining fuel. So, with an American yachtsman next to him on the bridge, he put into the Maine resort unannounced, in the pitch dark. The next morning the elusive "Treasure Ship," as the press had dubbed her, was found after a week of wild speculation.

The inevitable disruption of sailing schedules stranded thousands of Americans in Europe. In the manner of their countrymen summering abroad, they had calculated their expenses to a nicety so that even a day's delay in boarding a ship was ruinous. (Stewards on the North Atlantic have always disliked westbound crossings near Labor Day because tips are so low.) The *Imperator*'s cancellation alone sent hundreds of suddenly impoverished Americans to camp, quite literally in some cases, on the doorsteps of the Paris and London embassies. Ambassador Herrick in Paris was so completely drained of cash that he was unable to pay off embassy servants called to the colors. President Wilson ultimately had to send a battleship, the *Tennessee,* with a shipment of gold to provide emergency funds. Even getting from Paris to Le Havre by train was an obstacle. *The New York Times* reported that "millionaires rode in cattlecars"; actually, they were neither millionaires nor cattlecars but first-class passengers crowded thankfully into fourth-class French rolling stock, complete with *poilus* perched on each roof. No luggage was allowed beyond what could be carried by hand.

Every available berth was taken on all the ships that came into New York during the following weeks. There was silk among the steerage, as the saying goes, and quite often the reverse: a young Armour of the Chicago meat-packing family gave up his deluxe suite on the *Laconia* to thirteen women and slept in the ship's hospital. Contrasted with this was the *Olympic*'s departure on the eighth of August with no passengers whatsoever. For the second time in two years, she carried coal in her public rooms. Her promenade deck windows were painted brown and as she left her pier, crews were tackling the white superstructure with what White Star officials fondly termed "invisible gray." As she turned her vast bulk in midstream, her crew waved derisively at their opposite numbers lining the stern of the *Vaterland* on the Jersey side of the Hudson. Unspoken among those wistful German seamen was the wish that they too were heading back to their home port and families.

In Halifax, the Naval Depot had finished arming the *Mauretania* before the last of her disgruntled passengers had departed, protesting, by train to New York. At the same time, hundreds of miles to the south, the *Kron-*

prinz Wilhelm's crew sweated in the tropical heat of the West Indies, transferring coal and stores to the cruiser *Karlsruhe*. The naval vessel in turn carried guns that were hoisted up and mounted onto the liner's decks. It was apparent that this rendezvous was part of a methodical German scheme of emergency conversion, effected on the high seas and explaining the significance of the row of marked doors in the Kiel dockyards. Off Buenos Aires, the *Cap Trafalgar* effected the same liaison with the *Eber*. It is more than probable that other German warships patrolling the western reaches of the Atlantic immediately following the outbreak of hostilities carried ordnance for those German liners interned in New York.

The *Kaiser Wilhelm II,* fresh out of Hamburg the day after war was declared, was carrying weapons mounted precisely where sharp-eyed Southampton dock workers had predicted she would. Within four days, she closed with her first adversary of the war, a small British trawler weighing all of two hundred twenty-seven tons. The British vessel, called the *Tubal Cain,* was stopped off the coast of Iceland and boarded by a German crew, who confiscated her papers and instruments and returned with her crew to their own ship. Safely back on board, the German gunners zeroed in with their new weapons and, after expending no less than forty-five rounds, managed to sink their diminutive, unarmed and derelict opponent. Their next victim, the five-thousand-tonner *Galician,* might have made an easier target. But she carried women and children on board and was spared. In those early, almost courteous days of the war, certain standards of conduct obtained that would be neglected only a few months later. The German steamer's second kill, a New Zealand ship called the *Kaipara,* proved as difficult to sink as the first. Even with the addition of guncotton charges placed next to open condenser doors, the stubborn little vessel remained on the surface for most of the fifty-three rounds sent in her direction.

The sad truth emerged that ships designed as fast passenger liners, carrying armaments operated by unskilled gun crews, were ineffectual and amateur warships. The naval staffs of both belligerents also discovered an elemental fact that any steamship company's cost accountant could have clarified with ease: the amount and cost of the coal necessary to keep these ships operational was quite prohibitive. Docked at Chatham in the Thames estuary to take on ammunition, the *Aquitania*'s furnaces consumed every lump of coal in the depot's reserve bunkers. The *Mauretania,* which arrived back in Liverpool bearing proudly the prefix "H.M.S.," worked out at Admiralty charter rates costing over thirteen hundred pounds a day. The bumptious First Lord, Winston Churchill, was heard questioning the wisdom of his predecessors in urging government support for the Cunard sisterships.

The upshot was that the *Mauretania* spent the first years of the war tied up at her pier, a slightly embarrassing white elephant.

There was only one textbook confrontation between armed merchantmen during the entire war. In early September, the *Carmania,* one of Cunard's "Pretty Sisters," engaged in action the *Cap Trafalgar* of the Hamburg South America Line, recently armed at sea. The battle was fought off the island of Trinidad and was marked by a furious exchange of gunfire. Captain Noel Grant, R.N., in command of the Cunarder, kept his vessel just outside the range of the German heavy machine-guns but was less successful in evading their heavier ordnance. The *Cap Trafalgar*'s gun crews were more accomplished than their colleagues on the *Kaiser Wilhelm II* but made the mistake of concentrating their fire on the upper works. The scraps of armor plating, bags of coal and woven rope splinter shields that were supposed to protect the *Carmania*'s superstructure were woefully inadequate and a high percentage of her gun crews were wounded. Despite a high casualty rate, they directed their fire against the enemy's water line and the German ship began to capsize. By the time the *Cap Trafalgar* lay on her side, Grant had transferred his command to the after docking bridge, and the *Carmania*'s upper decks were a shambles. Fire control parties worked under hopeless conditions in that German fire had ruptured the water mains. It was a close thing and pointed up the appalling vulnerability of hulls and superstructure not specifically designed for war; a hit almost anywhere at or above the water line could create havoc.

There were other frustrations for German Imperial Navy strategists besides the failure of their armed merchantmen. To precipitate a grand naval battle, a set piece confrontation on the order of Trafalgar, was clearly inadvisable until the High Seas Fleet could be brought up to a strength rivaling that of their opponents across the North Sea. During this process, they were locked in port and the Royal Navy remained firmly in control of all the seas surrounding Europe. The only effective weapon with which Germany could subvert this blockade was the submarine. At the start of the war, Germany had only two dozen short-range U-boats and part of the building program initiated to strengthen surface units at Kiel was the construction of a new class of long-range submarine, vessels that could remain on station for weeks at a time. It was a lesson the Germans learned in the First World War that was equally appropriate for the Second.

The *Lusitania,* spared the ignominy of a lay-up, was retained on the North Atlantic run, making one voyage a month between Liverpool and New York. Although there was no profit in it for Cunard, at least they broke even on the service by making economies in fuel consumption. The *Lusi-*

tania ran on only three quarters of her boiler capacity. It was a piece of complacency that seemed incongruous with other precautions that the Company took. The ship carried no national or even house flags, and her name and port of registry were painted out. All watertight doors were in a closed position for the entire crossing. Near the Irish Sea, lifeboats were swung outboard between the davits, and lookouts were doubled.

Yet even by May 8, 1915, there was no naval escort to meet her nor did her master, Captain William Turner, take any recommended evasive action. (He admitted at a later inquiry that he misinterpreted standing Admiralty orders on this subject to mean zigzag only *after* a submarine had been sighted.) From the time the *Lusitania* cleared the Narrows, there was only the one customary lifeboat drill, poorly and casually attended. Company officials, as well as passengers, were not put off by a small, black-framed notice that appeared in the New York papers the morning of her departure. It had been inserted by the German Embassy in Washington, a warning to Americans traveling on British vessels that they were liable to attack. In some editions, it appeared adjacent to Cunard's own announcement of the *Lusitania*'s sailing, a chilling coincidence in the light of subsequent events. But it was no indication that the Cunarder was to be ambushed. The sea off Ireland's south coast was the scene of intense submarine activity as it was a natural turning point for vessels heading east or west. It is scarcely to be wondered that U-boats would collect there, and the skipper who sighted the *Lusitania* that Saturday morning had no idea of her importance.

It was just after lunch, the same lunch that crews of three motor torpedo boats were enjoying ashore in Queenstown. The crossing was nearly over, and Captain Turner, within sight of land, was more concerned with adjusting speed to make Liverpool on the right tide than with two Admiralty submarine warnings received earlier. The weather was clear and warm, and stewards had opened portholes in the dining rooms. At ten minutes past two, with no warning other than a white track racing under the sea to starboard, the *Lusitania* was torpedoed. Kapitanleutnant Walther Schwieger fired only one torpedo. (It is probable that those on board who later disagreed with him were misled by secondary explosions from the boilers.) The enormous damage caused by a direct hit amidships had a devastating effect. He saw at once that what he had first thought to be a steamer towing another was one ship, swarming with people and mortally wounded. There was no need for a second torpedo.

The ship sank within twenty minutes. During that time, she continued to make way but effective control was lost. Communications with the engine room were out and when it became apparent to Turner that he could not

THE ONLY WAY TO CROSS

A sinisterly prophetic photograph
taken in 1911. R.M.S. *Lusitania*
steams past the Old Head of Kinsale
off the Irish coast. Four years later,
she sank in the same waters, victim
of a German torpedo. (*The Peabody Museum of Salem*)

beach her in the shallows, he had no means of stopping her. Somehow, from the appalling wreckage of her boiler rooms, there was steam enough remaining to drive the ship until the last. The wide sweep of her wake was littered with debris. A severe list to starboard rendered the port-side boats useless. On the low side, there was the familiar agony of panicky crewmen, tangled falls and overhead, the monstrous funnels bearing down. What additional time might have been afforded by the extensive watertight subdivision was nullified by the large number of open ports on D-deck and below. When she did go, her propellers above water and her bow already on the bottom of the sea, the last vicious swipe of her radio antenna nearly killed several passengers struggling in the water.

Even with the relative warmth of the water, hundreds drowned in the wait for rescue. Others without lifebelts clung to chicken coops and deck chairs, and a British officer and his mother sat on top of the grand piano from the main lounge. A small armada of tugs and fishing boats put out from shore. The first load of survivors to enter Queenstown had to contend with the obtuseness of a harbor official who, his superior having gone out for tea, would not let anyone ashore. Had he known how many small craft were inbound through the May dusk, carrying both living and dead from the sunken ship, he would probably have relaxed his official posture. Other locals seemed not at all surprised by the sinking, confessing that they had seen submarines for some days waiting off the coast.

News of the loss reached New York first via the *Vaterland*'s powerful radios which, although prohibited from transmitting, were allowed to receive and picked up triumphant German bulletins. One of her German crew relayed the news to a newspaper reporter in a Hoboken bar who in turn alerted Charles Sumner, Cunard's New York manager. The loss of nearly twelve hundred lives aroused public indignation throughout the world and is popularly credited with bringing America into the war. If this is perhaps an oversimplification, it would not be inaccurate to say that the incident led to a rude awakening on both sides of the Atlantic. In America, the European War, as it was called at that time, took on ominous significance.

With the realism forced on us by two World Wars, it seems the height of naïveté for the British to have presumed that one of their fastest ships could steam with impunity on an announced schedule through hostile waters. To generations who have seen saturation bombing of civilian targets, the contemporary disclaimer that the ship was not involved in hostilities borders on the ludicrous. For, even though the Germans had laid Belgium to waste, even though civilian casualties were already a reality, there was a cherished delusion that war, however frightful, could be confined to confrontations between armies and fleets. Its extension to include noncombatants was incomprehensible in the spring of 1915. The *Lusitania*'s destruction marked a loss of innocence nurtured by too many years of peace. Especially galling was the celebration that Schwieger's kill triggered in Germany. The Kaiser declared a national holiday and crowds thronged the streets of Berlin. In Munich, a commemorative medal was struck, one side showing passengers lined up at a guichet under the legend "Business As Usual" and on the reverse, a representation of the sinking liner loaded with armaments.

In London and other port cities, furious mobs sacked and burned German shops. Still kept in Cunard's vaults to this day is a collection of reports forwarded on by the Royal Irish Constabulary in an attempt to identify some of the *Lusitania*'s dead. One photograph shows a seven-year-old boy washed up on an Irish beach. An accompanying text describes "number four," as he was called, as wearing a blue Lord Fauntleroy suit, with black stockings, one of which was held up by a piece of string instead of a garter; in his lapel was a *Lusitania* souvenir pin. It is difficult to believe that the catastrophe responsible for his death was the occasion for his German contemporaries to be given a holiday.

But the British eventually learned their lesson. It is revealing to contrast the scenes of confusion and panic on the *Lusitania* with precautions taken on board a smaller Cunarder, the *Laconia,* in February of 1917. Passing through the same waters off Fastnet, all passengers and off-duty crew were assembled in life jackets on the saloon deck as a matter of routine. The ship was torpedoed and made water fast.

It is admittedly easier to evacuate a small ship but there were the added complications of darkness, colder water and rough seas. Passengers climbing into boats heard the roar of steam from ruptured lines and the ventilators, whose lower casings were open to the sea, puffed and spouted like blowholes. Despite the shortage of time, every passenger was put in the proper boat with the correct complement of crew. The purser was able to collect the papers and valuables from his safe and bring them with him through the lounge. The ship was in total darkness by this time and he dodged, by the light of a lucky match, the piano which sailed over the edge of the music gallery above his head. The ship went down in less than twenty minutes and only twelve lives were lost.

Following their initial inactivity the larger Atlantic vessels were finally employed, regardless of cost, at the time of the abortive Dardanelles invasion in mid-1915. The campaign was a failure, reminiscent of Britain's Crimean endeavor years earlier. Yet the role played by those great ships

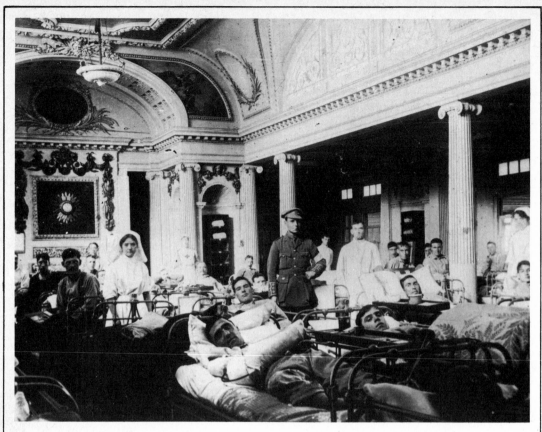

The *Aquitania* turned into a hospital ship. Survivors from the Dardanelles' debacle sail for Southampton in the unlikely elegance of Mewès & Davis' Palladian lounge. (*Cunard*)

Mudros Harbor in wartime. At right is the *Olympic*, newly arrived with reinforcements. In the distance, the white-painted *Aquitania* takes on patients from a smaller hospital ship for passage back to Southampton. (*Imperial War Museum, London*)

was both crucial and, for the first time in the war, practical. The island of Lemnos, chosen as combined headquarters, had an excellent harbor that could accommodate the naval forces assembled in support of the regiments ashore as well as the deep-draft ships of the Western Ocean that had carried them out from England. The flow of traffic in and out of Mudros Harbor was enormous and included the troop carriers *Aquitania, Olympic, Mauretania* and, from Le Havre, the *France*. Rather than masquerading as impractical warships, they were employed in the service for which they had been designed, the transport of large numbers of passengers at high speed.

Local evacuation of the wounded from Gallipoli was initially carried out by the *Franconia*. She sailed from Mudros to Alexandria with five thousand wounded packed into her staterooms. There were only three doctors on board who operated nonstop in one of the deluxe suites. But as the toll ashore mounted, Alexandria and Malta hospitals were soon filled to overflowing. So there was put into practice the system of the "black carriers." These were merchantmen chartered to bring troops from Britain and take the wounded back. For convenience, unwounded armed services personnel were sometimes included on the homebound manifest, direct violation of their noncombatant status. Several of them were sunk and, to put an end to the unfortunate abuse, the big liners were converted to hospital ships, carrying back to England the broken men they had originally brought out as troops.

Joined into this service was the *Britannic,* third of the *Olympic* class, completed too late for peacetime mail service on the Atlantic. She was taken over by the government immediately after trials and repainted white with a five-foot green band around the hull, interspersed with enormous red crosses. For identification after dark, she had an additional illuminated red cross suspended between the first two funnels and a circuit of green bulbs carried in the rigging and around the promenade deck. Then she sailed, under heavy escort, from Belfast to Liverpool for the remainder of her conversion.

It was the custom to carry the wounded as high up in the ship as possible so that they would be near the boats in the event of an emergency. Furniture from the lounge and smoking room was stored ashore and replaced with hundreds of cots. All A-deck public rooms were converted into wards as well as the children's playroom, gymnasium and restaurant. Upper-deck capacity was further augmented by slinging hammocks for the walking wounded along the enclosed portion of each promenade deck. From B-deck down, cabins were left in their original condition, providing luxurious accommodations for the medical and nursing staffs.

By November of 1916, the *Britannic* had completed five voyages to the Mediterranean and back. Outward bound on her sixth, she coaled as usual at Naples and put back to sea in the midst of a violent storm. Two days later, at eight A.M., four miles west of Port St. Nikolaos in the Aegean, she struck a mine. By great good luck, there were no wounded on board; if there had been, the loss of life might have been catastrophic. She sank in an hour, going down, as one of her people said to me, "like a lady." That person was, remarkably enough, Violet Jessop, the same stewardess who had survived the *Titanic*.

When the explosion came, she was in the pantry, aft of the main dining room, making up a tray for one of the nursing sisters who lay sick below. It was different from the *Titanic,* she remembers, in that there was absolutely no hesitation; the dining room emptied out immediately. The mine had exploded at a point in the hull directly under the main staircase and medical personnel climbing its mahogany length to the boat deck could smell smoke drifting up the stairwell.

Mrs. Jessop, remarkably calm, finished her tray and went down to the cabin where the terrified nurse still lay. The stewardess helped her eat, dressed her and escorted her up to the lifeboat on one of the last trips made by the elevators, manned by the *Britannic*'s contingent of seascouts. Then Jessop ran to her own cabin through passageways that were already sloping. Besides her rosary and clock, she collected a toothbrush, the one thing she had craved and been unable to procure on the *Carpathia;* she was determined not be sunk without one again. With these items safely in her pockets and her apron turned up to keep them there, she left her cabin for the last time.

By the time she reached the deck, there were only two boats left, aft on the port side. She got into the last one and, as it touched the water, all but the stewardess jumped suddenly over the side. Jessop, glancing to her left, saw that the *Britannic,* still under way, was drawing the lifeboat under her enormous counter into the screws. So she followed her shipmates into the water and seemed to sink down forever. (She was wearing her coat under her life jacket, an offense for which she used to scold her passengers during drills.)

She came back up and struck her head on the bottom of the lifeboat. She was quite resigned to going back down for good when she felt and clutched at a man's hand which, she could tell, was alive. By holding on, Jessop eventually surfaced, having swallowed large amounts of salt water, oil and granulated cork. She was, miraculously, away from the ship, floating

At a Southampton photographer's studio, Violet Jessop poses proudly in her nurse's uniform. She had survived the *Titanic* disaster in 1912 and was about to join His Majesty's Hospital Ship *Britannic*. (*Author's collection*)

Below, the *Britannic* in wartime service. Only five of the eight enormous davits are installed as she sails from Southampton for the first of six voyages to Mudros. (*National Maritime Museum, Greenwich*)

among wounded and dying men from two lifeboats that had been splintered by the port propeller.

Shortly thereafter, she was picked up by other boats and watched the brand-new *Britannic,* in service for less than a year, sink into the calm, sparkling sea. As she listed over to starboard, the last engineers walked along the fourth dummy stack and jumped into the water. Her master, Captain Bartlett, was the last off. Just before he stepped from the bridge into the Aegean, he signaled the final call to abandon ship, one long despairing blast on the ship's whistle. Then the *Britannic* rolled over on her beam ends. The smoking funnels collapsed, the sea poured into the casings and blew up her boilers. Just like the *Titanic,* her stern rose straight into the air at the last and then slid quickly out of sight.

She was gone, one of the world's largest, third of the *Olympic*-class ships so promisingly planned only seven years previous. Her end was kinder than her sister's: only twenty-eight were killed and over eleven hundred saved. Some of her crew later insisted that they had been torpedoed but no U-boat commander ever claimed credit for the kill. However, a submarine had just the day previous left a string of mines in the Zea Channel where she sank, and another hospital ship, the *Braemar Castle,* struck one two days later.

The United States' entry into the war in April of 1917 precipitated, in effect, the Jutland of the German merchant marine. The ships interned in American ports, now legitimate prizes of war, were seized by executive order within hours of the declaration of hostilities. The crews were removed to Ellis Island pending formal internment and their ships overhauled for conversion to troopships. It was obvious employment for what Navy Secretary Josephus Daniels called "the Fleet the Kaiser built for us." Even the great British ships, laid up again since the conclusion of their work in the Mediterranean, were recalled into Atlantic service. For the last eighteen months of the war, the Atlantic liners were back on their original routes, ferrying two million American soldiers to Europe.

The best prize of all, of course, was the giant *Vaterland,* now the largest and one of the fastest vessels in the world. When American engineers boarded her, they expected to find considerable damage inflicted by her crew. Oddly enough, there was none. The only cases of malicious damage were several instances of water pipes having been cut, usually behind paneling. The cut ends had been squeezed together, creating slow leaks that didn't show up at once.

One astern turbine was totally inoperative, its blading sheared off and the casing smashed. After careful examination, engineers concluded that it had fractured while turning over at high speed. It was not sabotage. Perhaps the Germans felt the ship was inoperable without full astern power and refrained from inflicting any further damage on the machinery. Yet it left a mystery which has never been solved: if it was not sabotage, when had it happened? During the near-catastrophic departure from Hoboken in the midst of her maiden voyage? But if that were the case, is it likely that the HAPAG would have kept the *Vaterland* in service for three additional voyages with half astern power? It is possible but unlikely. Her subsequent American captain once crossed westbound in this condition in the twenties but only as a last expedient; that low-pressure turbine seems to have remained a source of constant trouble. But as for the damage found in 1917, no answer was ever forthcoming. If the Germans knew, they weren't telling. Even more disastrous than the damaged blading was the absence of a complete set of plans. A partial set found ashore in the Company offices was of no use and obtaining a replacement set from Blohm & Voss was quite clearly impossible during wartime.

By November, seven months to the day after she had been seized and the last German ship to be converted, the U.S.S. *Vaterland* was ready for trials. (The Navy had taken over conversion of the vessel from the Shipping Board.) Even then, there were problems. Off Guantanamo, more piping gave way and over a foot of water flooded the officers' quarters on the starboard side. The valve stems on both port and starboard steering engines broke while the ship wallowed helplessly. It explained the discovery of a roomful of replacement stems found in the bowels of the ship, each one of which broke as quickly as its predecessors. Finally, Lieutenant Woodward, the engineering officer in charge, machined a new prototype which lasted for a hundred thousand miles.

The public rooms, although retaining their handsome paneling, were otherwise unrecognizable. The winter garden was fitted out with steel tables as an officers' mess while the dining room was stripped of all tables and chairs to provide standing accommodation for relays of over eight thousand enlisted men. The famous Roman bath, long since drained by the Germans, was filled with deal shelving to hold officers' baggage. Troops traveling on British ships were berthed in hammocks but Yankee ingenuity had produced an improvement called the standee bunk, a series of hinged beds on two upright stanchions. By this means, a triple-decker bunk could be and was installed in almost any free corner of the vessel.

Strangely enough, there seems to have been absolutely no thought for her future or postwar career. There were no company officials to oversee storage of the furniture, carpeting and hangings that were put ashore. Bits

Internment and seizure. The *Vaterland* lay at her Hoboken pier, a prisoner in New York for three years. (*Frank Braynard Collection*)

By November of 1917, she had been taken over by the United States. Although painted out, the elaborate scrollwork remains, complete with German shields. (*Hoboken Public Library*)

and pieces of the *Vaterland* have turned up for years all over the East Coast: the extravagant bust of Kaiser Wilhelm from the social hall has a place of honor in an Italian restaurant in central Connecticut. Just prior to her first crossing, the ship was renamed *Leviathan,* at the suggestion of President and Mrs. Wilson, a name that was promptly amended to "Levi Nathan" by the first doughboys to swarm aboard.

She sailed in December of 1917 from the same Hoboken berth: Pier Number 4, each side of which had been dredged in 1912 to a depth of forty feet to take the two new ships. She could carry ten thousand soldiers at a time, who boarded on four double-decked gangplanks in under two hours. On the pier, Red Cross volunteers handed each man a postcard, which he addressed to a next-of-kin with a noncommittal message announcing a safe arrival "over there." They were left in large mail sacks on each deck and collected just before sailing. Only upon wireless notification that the ship had arrived safely in France were they mailed from the Hoboken Post Office. On her first crossing, the cable to the steam whistle contracted from the cold and the huge siren bellowed in the middle of the night, sending the fear of God throughout the ship. It is an extraordinary fact that in both world wars, no troopship of comparable size was sunk. Although festooned with doughnut-shaped life rafts, there is no doubt that a well-placed torpedo on a ship carrying over ten thousand passengers would have created a hideous record that would make the *Titanic*'s death toll seem insignificant.

After disembarking her first load of troops in Liverpool, the *Leviathan* was taken into the Gladstone dry dock, an operation that required considerable boldness. In the absence of a proper docking plan, recreating the precise arrangement of blocks on which she was built, dockyard officials risked serious damage to the hull; but their estimates were successful and over three years' accumulated growth was removed from her bottom.

She was also dazzle-painted, a system of ship camouflage adopted by the Admiralty during the last year of the war. Warships up to that time were gray, ever since an observer at the Kiel Naval Review of 1895 had remarked that the British dreadnoughts, with their smart black hulls and cream upper works, were considerably more conspicuous than their French and German counterparts. So battleship gray was adopted until October of 1917, when Norman Wilkinson, a marine artist, headed a dazzle scheme, housed, appropriately, in rooms formerly used by art students at Burlington House. The principle involved eradication of vertical and horizontal lines by application of black, white, blue and gray paints, supposedly making it impossible for enemy commanders to guess the course of the vessel. Although its effectiveness was queried by skippers of British submarines who shadowed the dazzle painted *Aquitania* on an exercise, it was nevertheless a protective device of modest cost which was subsequently adopted by all big troopships including the *Leviathan*. The effect on any U-boat captains that saw her is unknown; however, her return to New York with what looked like an enormous set of grinning teeth on either side of her bow occasioned considerable surprise.

In May of 1918, the *Olympic* was involved in the second major collision of her career. Loaded with American soldiers, she was proceeding up the Channel under escort when a submarine was spotted inside the destroyer screen. The *Olympic* turned sharply and rammed her, one of her propeller blades slicing through the U-boat's pressure hull and forcing it to surface. It is the only recorded case of one of the giant liners sinking an enemy vessel. The German commander later said that, in attempting to run too close a parallel course to the *Olympic,* he had been drawn, like the cruiser *Hawke,* into her side. It was a moment of great drama for the troops on board, and the 59th Regiment later presented the ship with a commemorative plaque that hung in the grand staircase for years. The *Olympic* had another close call when she was actually struck by a torpedo which turned out, mercifully, to be a dud.

The most horrifying passage of the war was the *Leviathan*'s eastbound crossing of September 29, 1918. Shortly after the ship left New York, loaded with nine thousand officers and men, an epidemic of flu broke out. Seven hundred men were stricken by midnight and the next morning, one man was dead and the chief Army surgeon was taken ill. Each succeeding day, there were fewer men to take care of the sick, and the death rate mounted alarmingly. Entire sections of the vast ship were declared hospitals. In all there were ninety-one dead, some of them wearing blank dog tags and impossible to identify. A hospital ship met the *Leviathan* at Brest and took off hundreds of the sick.

The day before the Armistice, the *Mauretania,* under Captain Rostron of *Carpathia* fame, sailed from New York with thousands of green American troops. The soldiers reached Liverpool as scheduled, went ashore for two days and then reembarked on the same ship for westbound passage back to the States. They were the first men to arrive back in New York and, in the emotion of the moment, the peculiar limitation of their overseas service was overlooked and they marched, sheepishly, up 5th Avenue. The war was over.

Eleven million tons of shipping had been sunk by the Germans who, in turn, no longer had a merchant marine. The Hamburg-Amerika Line

The *Olympic*, dazzle-painted and packed with troops, is restored to service in the North Atlantic. She has a pair of five-inch guns on the poop and carries extra boats; those in davits are swung out as a precaution. (*Imperial War Museum, London*)

The first American detachments to come home crowd the dazzle-painted *Mauretania*'s side as she pulls into her Hoboken pier. (*Frank Braynard Collection*)

and North German Lloyd fleets were either at the bottom of the sea or, worse, flying allied flags. By the terms of the Armistice, the victorious powers took over intact all ships remaining afloat, including Ballin's giant trio, two of which had dominated the Atlantic during the last irretrievable summer of peace. Normal schedules were not resumed for a year as trooping continued in reverse. Americans sailed back from the trenches to a United States that would never, like the rest of the world, be quite the same.

The maritime irony of the Allied victory was that Ballin's ships survived, the only giant trio to do so. The German merchant fleet sustained no loss the equivalent of the *Lusitania* or *Britannic*. The *Imperator* passed through the war without incident, literally under wraps. The entire ship and neighboring pier were draped in a patchwork of tarpaulins to disguise them from the air. She entered service as the U.S.S. *Imperator*.

Predictably, with such a rich haul, there was considerable disagreement between Great Britain and the United States as to how the "ex-Germans," as they were called, would be parceled up. For some time, the most heated arguments raged around the *Imperator* which Britain, in all fairness, claimed as just reparation for her greater losses in a longer war. The British also pointed out that America had retained most of the German vessels seized in her ports when she entered the war. By January of 1920, the issue was finally resolved in Britain's favor: the United States would retain the *Leviathan* while Cunard and the White Star Line would jointly take over the *Imperator* and the still unfinished *Bismarck*. Although never specifically stated, the two lines were in effect given a replacement for the big ship each had lost.

It was with some satisfaction that Cunard's Company Dinner of 1920 was held in the dining room of the *Imperator,* tied up in Liverpool. She was put into service shortly thereafter and it was apparent that if her house flag had changed, her stability problems had not. When the Americans had carried troops on her, included in the crew were half a dozen cooperative German engineers whom Cunard had sent back to Cuxhaven; they probably wished them back on board during a gale two days out of Cherbourg near the end of her second voyage. Seawater poured into the ash ejectors and backed up in a gray slurry that quite effectively clogged the pumps. Several coaling ports leaked also and water rose in the bilges, increasing the customary list. Unable to dispose of the ashes, engineers let several fires go out.

Alarmed passengers, who were initially told nothing, knew only that the ship was listing critically and that speed had been reduced; as if in final confirmation that disaster was imminent, there was a plague of rats all over the ship, displaced by floods from their lairs below. Access to the bilges was finally achieved by breaking through the tank tops and pumping out from above. The *Imperator* reached Southampton, out of danger but listing heavily, and found herself at the center of a land-based storm as passengers articulated their concern to the press. Questions were asked in the House of Commons and Cunard announced in April that the vessel's after funnel would be removed as part of a drastic scheme to increase stability. Fortunately for the ship's appearance, this threat was never carried out, but ultimately several other changes were effected. The restaurant was turned into a ballroom, all marble bathtubs in the first-class suites were replaced with galvanized iron and an additional thousand tons of pig iron were added as permanent ballast. The ship was also given a new name, *Berengaria*. It was the first time that the Company, although retaining the identifying -*ia* suffix, had used a person's name, in point of fact a queen's name, for one of their ships. Poor Queen Berengaria, wife of Richard the Lion-hearted, saw very little of her husband and nothing of the land over which she reigned.

In March of 1922, Blohm & Voss were ready to hand over the *Bismarck*. Completion of her fitting out had been delayed by conversion of her furnaces to oil burners and because most of her brass and copper fittings had been stripped during the war for scrap. News of the ship's impending departure stirred resentment and rumors circulated in Hamburg that she would never leave Germany. But her passage down the Elbe passed without serious incident. Crowds that gathered along the shore were silent; many of them wept as two boatloads of young men, sailing along in the *Bismarck*'s wake, sang laments. Ballin had died in 1918 and was spared the heartbreak of losing his last great ship.

After successful completion of her trials with Hans Ruser in command, the vessel was officially handed over. In a simple ceremony on the bridge, she changed owners, nationality and name. Germans clambered over the *Bismarck*'s port railing into a waiting ferry as a White Star crew simultaneously embarked over the *Majestic*'s starboard side under Bertram Hayes. The British immediately painted the ship's new name on her stern. The next day she arrived in Southampton, a bloodless prize of war.

As if to confirm British pride in her acquisition, the *Majestic* was honored in August of that summer by a visit from King George and Queen Mary. After discharging passengers and mails at Southampton, ship's crew worked through the night sprucing up first and second class. The following morning, she was anchored in Cowes Roadstead and a yeoman of signals bearing the royal standard came over from the royal yacht. It was broken out from the *Majestic*'s masthead the moment Their Majesties stepped on board.

Abandoned at her fitting-out pier, the *Bismarck,*
above left, Ballin's third great ship, as she
appeared after the Armistice. (*Frank Braynard
Collection*)

Below, left, as the *Majestic,* the White Star
Line's new flagship, she enters Southampton for
the first time in the spring of 1922. (*Echo
Commercial Photo*)

A quartet of ex-Germans lies rusting in the
Chesapeake in the late twenties (left to right):
the *Monticello* (*Kaiser Wilhelm II*), *Mount
Vernon* (*Kronprinzessin-Cecilie*), *America*
(*Amerika*) and *George Washington* (her name
remained the same). (*The Mariners Museum,
Newport News, Virginia*)

Their tour of the ship was far more exhaustive than White Star's chairman, Harold A. Sanderson, had anticipated. On the bridge, the Queen was unimpressed with the revolving screen windows, remarking to the King "Why, they're no better than the squeegees on our car." But Her Majesty in turn dawdled during the inspection of the kitchens, fascinated in particular by a new type of can opener. At the conclusion of Miss Winnie Elliot's swimming demonstration in the *Majestic*'s Roman Bath, lunch was hopelessly behind schedule. Compounding the delay, Queen Mary moved firmly toward the third class, an unscheduled decision that created havoc behind the scenes. But fortunately, those cabins into which Her Majesty peered were quite presentable and the remainder of the visit passed happily.

As the Sovereign was about to leave the ship, the *Mauretania* appeared inbound from New York and dipped her ensign in salute. It was fitting that she should be there for she was the only other merchant vessel ever visited by royalty. Her crew was drawn up on deck and the ship's bugler sounded "Attention" and then the "General Salute" as the Cunarder steamed slowly past her White Star rival. The two brave ships, one brand new, the other a prewar favorite, offered ample indication that the war was finished. The twenties had begun, an indomitably British decade on the Atlantic. Business would pick up again and the sweetness of peace seemed assured.

*It cannot be urged too strongly that it is a
gross breach of the etiquette of the sea
life, and a shocking exhibition of bad
manners and low inquisitiveness, for
passengers to visit unasked the quarters
of an inferior class.*
  —R. A. FLETCHER, TRAVELLING PALACES

6.
Stokers & Steerage

The *Majestic*'s adaptation to oil burners was common to all the great
Atlantic ships of the twenties. There were many reasons for this change,
among them the labor unrest that made bunkering liners at Southampton a
perpetual headache for marine superintendents. Cunard once sent the *Berengaria* to Brest for fueling, a detour that, combined with the inferior quality
of French coal, added four expensive days to the crossing. So in the year
following the war, companies in competition on the Atlantic withdrew their
ships one at a time for conversion to oil.

Bunker C oil, the stuff used to drive ships, is a treacly black goo, the
residue remaining after a variety of profitable components has already been
removed from the original crude oil. Use of the new fuel meant additional

plumbing as well as radical reconstruction of storage space. All bunker rivets had to be punched out and countersunk to make them oiltight. A system of wash bulkheads was installed to restrict sloshing and heaters incorporated into the tanks to increase fluidity.

It took eight months to convert a large ship. Yet the resulting economies in manpower, speed of bunkering and maintenance more than offset the temporary loss of revenue. Two hundred men could be eliminated from the engineering department, men who had formerly performed the back-breaking task of keeping up steam. Firemen on oil-burning ships would acquire a white-overalled respectability that their blackened predecessors had never attained.

Stokers were without question the toughest men on the ship. The rigors of their brutal employment ensured that. Their very presence on board was a strange anachronism of the express liner: despite the glittering interiors and sophisticated propulsion systems, no attempt had ever been made to automate the stokehold's incredible labor. In point of fact, there was no room between transverse rows of boilers for the stoking machinery used on shore so the work had always been done by men with shovels. It was a soul-destroying occupation that began to be phased out in the early twenties.

Gone would be the distinctive, sulphurous reek of coal smoke, part of steam's image for a hundred years. The changeover precipitated a crisis in Britain's strife-torn collieries and New York, where oil was cheaper, became the major fueling center for Atlantic liners. Among the first to profit were the ships' surgeons, whose main occupation heretofore had been the removal of cinders from patients' eyes.

Although passengers were always encouraged to tour the ships that carried them across the Atlantic, boiler rooms were seldom included on the itinerary. It was not because of the heat and noise, but rather that stoke-holds were the crucibles of company ambition, where nothing that might distract from the deadly serious work should intrude. No matter what schedules might be selected in company board rooms, no matter what speed requests might be rung down from the spotless bridge, both owner and master relied completely on the endurance, brawn and skill of those awesome men who kept up the steam.

At the bottom of the engineering hierarchy was the trimmer who worked inside the bunker, shifting piles of coal so that a ready supply could spill, on demand, down the chute into a coal-passer's barrow. Not very demanding work with full bunkers, but near the end of a crossing there was a laborious amount of shoveling. The coal-passer delivered a load to each boiler, upending his barrow next to the fireman. Under each boiler were

In the U.S.S. *Leviathan*'s stokehold, the
Navy stoker seems about to coal the
center of three furnaces under one enormous boiler. However, his costume as well
as the unnatural cleanliness of hands and
face indicate that he is posing rather than
working. The firehose at left is for wetting
down hot clinkers. (*Frank Braynard
Collection*)

three or four furnaces, each with a separate door, sometimes one at each end. To conserve heat in these double-ended boilers, stoking was arranged so that their doors were never opened at the same time.

The routine of tending was exacting and had to be done in a specific order, at great speed and with considerable skill. First, a slice bar, in reality a ten-foot skewer, was thrust home four times, once along each track of the grate, showering ashes down into the pit and raising clinkers or fused lumps of impurities to the top of the coals. The next operation involved raking these out, white hot, onto the steel tank tops and spreading the fire evenly. Finally, each furnace was stoked with usually no more than four shovelfuls of coal. A skillful fireman could spread a new black carpet uniformly over the entire glowing bed, so that the total height nowhere exceeded four inches. Similarly the water-tenders, who governed the amount of water in each boiler, never let the water rise to more than two inches in the glass gauge. Maintenance of these two levels, rigidly enforced by the leading fireman, made for optimum steam production but required constant attention.

Near the end of their watch, the fireman and coal-passer would rake out the ashes, hose down the clinkers and dispatch both over the side. This was done by a mechanical hoist in canvas bags, the same bags that carried the *Titanic*'s children up the sides of the *Carpathia*. On grander ships, there was a floor-level hopper, into which ashes were shoveled, mixed with sea water and pumped up inclined pipes to ejectors above the water line.

To systematize the men's work, a device was patented in England which became standard equipment in all boiler rooms: Kilroy's Stoking Indicator. It was, in fact, a remorseless metronome, which could be set for any rate of firing from three to twelve minutes. Normal cruising speed on the *Aquitania,* for instance, necessitated a setting of seven. A gong would echo through the stokeholds every seven minutes, indicating seven minutes for slicing, seven minutes for raking out and seven minutes for stoking. The next shrill of the gong signaled repetition of the entire cycle. The lower the number selected by the duty engineer on the engine-room starting platform, the more relentless the pace, since the same series of operations had to be completed in a shorter time span.

In rough weather, firemen learned to stoke as the bow plunged down, slamming the door shut as the ship rose again, to avoid a shower of red-hot coals on their feet. In a particularly bad gale, trimmers carried the coal in baskets rather than wheelbarrows and were usually able to keep pace with the reduced demand for steam. But slow speed carried with it a guarantee of harder work when calm seas returned, to make up for lost time. Even at the best of times, stokers worked under appalling conditions: stripped to the waist, coal dust and ashes adhering to the sweat of their bodies, their feet shod in clogs as protection against the red-hot debris underfoot. By the end of their four-hour watches, bodies were dehydrated, faces and chests seared by radiation from open furnaces and hands inflamed from the heat of the slice bar that penetrated insistently through the double layer of canvas used as a mitt. The assault on their senses included a constant raucous cacophony of shovels ringing and crunching on steel, the roar of the drafts, the interminable banging of furnace doors and over all, the relentless peal of the indicator gong.

It is not surprising that these hideous conditions nurtured a breed of ruthless men. On British ships, they were invariably Liverpool Irish and on others, the brutal dregs of half a dozen nationalities; whatever the blend, violence seemed preordained, often lethal. Drunken stokers, sometimes wheeled in barrows back on board ship, used to embark upon fearful battles, going after each other with slice bars, tongs, shovels, anything that came to hand. Mates had a standing order when the black gang fought: close the hatches and stay clear. Charles Lightoller, one of the surviving officers from the *Titanic*, tells of a hard-driving engineering officer who intervened in one of these rows and was never seen again; rumor had it that he was brained with a shovel and his corpse incinerated in a furnace.

Legend or no, deaths were not uncommon. Another Atlantic horror story took place on the Cunarder *Ultonia*, carrying immigrants between Fiume and New York. One day out from her destination, the men of the stokehold went on a rampage, broke into the wine stores and seemed about to take over the ship. Order was ultimately restored and the men confined to their quarters. Although this removed the threat of mutiny, it also crippled the ship and replacement stokers were recruited from the deck department. Their best efforts reduced maximum speed to two knots. When the *Ultonia* reached New York, the entire black gang jumped ship.

However, most disturbances were confined to port; the routine at sea devoured too much energy. The men took pride in their work and there was often keen competition between rival watches. On smaller ships, gamblers among the passengers used to promote such contests, despite stringent company regulations to the contrary, by lowering notes down the boiler-room ventilators on the ends of weighted strings. The winning watch would receive their prizes the same way, usually a small amount of money or occasionally a bottle of whiskey. In the early nineteen hundreds, there was a rich American whose return home was delayed by a strike in Liverpool. He let it be known in the boiler room that he would stand drinks all round if they reached New York according to schedule. The ship not only made it

A rare photograph taken on the *Mauretania* in 1908. The stokers' band is celebrating capture of the Blue Ribband from the *Lusitania*. Most of the Black Gang was notoriously camera-shy. (*Brown Brothers*)

Coaling the *Mauretania* at her 14th Street Pier. Before the perfection of automated coaling barges, each quarter-ton load was hauled and dumped by hand into the ship's bunkers. (*Brown Brothers*)

but the man's reputation as a stoker's friend spread to other lines and company records were broken whenever he took passage.

Despite the gallons of water they consumed, the black gang were a thirsty lot and a traditional penalty for rare visitors to the stokehold was to be "chalked," to have their boots encircled with a chalk ring that meant forfeiture of drink money. Another stokehold perquisite of long standing was the black pan. This was the name given to the best leavings from the first-class dinner, particularly plentiful after a spell of rough weather. Stokers off the four-to-eight P.M. watch devoured these choice left-overs in return for keeping the galley fires supplied with coal. Stokers on the *Mauretania* when she took the Blue Ribband celebrated noisily on the fantail in New York Harbor, complete with a small but vociferous band. But in general, scenes of benevolent horseplay among the black gang were the exception and they were usually a bitter, truculent lot.

The agonies inflicted by coal were not confined to the boiler rooms. Getting it on board the vessel at either end of the run was a messy and time-consuming business, particularly in New York. Soft, bituminous American coal had a high dust content. After the last passengers and their luggage had departed, the ship was boomed twenty feet out from the pier so that coal barges could tie up along either side. They had come up from Perth Amboy on the flood tide, each carrying about a thousand tons that sold, in 1914, for $3.25 a ton. Before any was put on board, every ventilator cowl was covered with canvas, air-vent louvers were closed, and all interior spaces sealed off.

Then carpenters went over the sides and removed the eight bolts that held each coaling port closed. These were openings in the shell plating, ten feet above the water line, with bottom-hinged flaps that took a temporary sheet-iron scoop. In addition, a row of simple derricks was rigged above, their heels secured in concave indentations in the hull, together with precarious two-man platforms adjacent to each coal chute. Winched up from the lighter, quarter-ton buckets of coal were tipped into the chute, two of which fed each bunker. It took twenty-four hours to coal one of the larger ships, after which carpenters sealed up the ports with a buckram gasket soaked in red lead. Following that, every railing, deck, staircase and passageway had to be cleaned thoroughly, to remove the fine coating of black dust that seeped everywhere. Near the end of the coal-fired era, there were some improvements made by mechanizing coal barges. They were equipped with a tall tower amidships which contained an endless motorized chain of scoops. This reduced coaling time by ten hours but made just as much mess on board.

Coal for steamers was always sold by the bargeload and it was not uncommon for the fuel to be shored up underneath with a mule carcass or two. Mediterranean coal merchants were the most unscrupulous and often constructed elaborate wire cages that gave the illusion of a full load. Another deception popular in that part of the world was to provide full barges but to drop a large proportion of the stuff overboard during bunkering, to be retrieved by divers following the ship's departure and sold again.

One fortunately isolated hazard resulting from coaling endangered the *Mauretania* during a westbound crossing early in World War I. Having coaled in the Sloyne during a bad blow, the ship sailed with two of her coaling ports improperly secured. In midocean, an astonished trimmer reported sea water seeping into the bilges from a midships bunker on the port side. By the following morning, continued heavy seas had increased the flooding so that the ship had a noticeable list to port. The pumps, continually clogged with coal dust and debris, could not keep up with the inflow and several furnaces were put out before the leak was located and made sound.

The expense of converting their ships to oil was only one of the financial hardships faced by steamship companies following the war. In 1921, Congress acted to cut off the flow of immigrants to the United States, depriving the companies of one third of their total revenue. During the peak years prior to World War I, more than a million immigrants a year had arrived from Europe, part of an epic westward migration unparalleled in the history of mankind. The packed steerage deck of liners coming into New York Harbor was to vanish with the same finality as the coal smoke that poured from their funnels. It was an ancient traffic, older than steam, and one that had purged itself of its worst abuses by the time it was ended.

Charles Dickens traveled back to England by sail in 1842 and like many another first-class passenger, compelled either by curiosity or a social conscience, he sometimes left the saloon to see the wretched squalor of the decks below. He was obviously moved by what he saw, and the waggish reportage of the *Britannia* passenger is replaced by the zeal of a pamphleteer.

The holds of the vessel were crowded with the pathetic eastbound backwash of immigrants, including some who had arrived only weeks before on the same vessel. One man dressed in rags had sold his clothes for the price of his ticket and another, who had no money to buy food, subsisted on scraps for the entire crossing. Living conditions were hideously inadequate, the inevitable result of indifference displayed by the captain and crew of the vessel. The 'tween-deck spaces on ships at that time were leased out wholesale to groups of traders, whose agents were paid so much per immigrant delivered to the pier. As a result, the holds were overcrowded, a condition that was only slightly remedied by the appalling numbers, including children, who died before the ship reached Liverpool.

Fifty years later, companies had realized that provision of even the most primitive conveniences for their poorest passengers was good business that could turn a profit. Although immigrants still brought their own bedding and eating utensils, there was a marked improvement in services. The sexes were segregated, unless married, and there were stewards, although no stewardesses. It was common, therefore, for some married couples to separate for the voyage, the wife traveling in the second cabin, or intermediate, as it was called, while her husband traveled in the men's steerage dormitory.

These latter compartments were little more than hold space, filled with sixteen bunk units. The bunks, or rather shelves, were about six by three feet, four to a tier separated by an eight-inch board, and served not only as bed but bureau and closet as well. In the center of the compartment was a table, on which three meals were served daily, including one which duplicated the fare given to the second cabin. Despite this vast improvement over the communal potato pot of the *Britannia,* it was still customary for passengers to bring supplementary rations of their own or to tip stewards in return for delicacies from the saloon galley. In rough weather, with the ship tossing about and spray drumming on the shell plating that formed the walls of the compartment, shrieks of terror combined with the moans of the seasick to create an atmosphere of hideous suffering. However, the ship's captain inspected their quarters daily and there was a doctor on board in whose care the company also placed them.

In the late 1880s, Robert Louis Stevenson, traveling on an unnamed ship from Glasgow to New York, recorded his impressions under the title *The Amateur Emigrant;* he was "amateur" in the sense that he booked second cabin, masquerading as a steerage passenger during the day but retreating to the relative comfort of his own class by night. For a ticket that cost him eight guineas, two more than he would have paid in steerage, Stevenson had the privacy of a cabin. He chose to sleep on its floor rather than its bunk in order to capitalize on the draft that came in under the door. His latent tubercular condition would explain his reluctance to berth permanently in the fetid holds. All of his free time was spent, by choice, with his friends in the steerage. When the weather was calm, his description of the endless songs, dancing and storytelling sounds almost festive, comparable to the idle moments of passengers who traveled above and with whom he was united only once, on the occasion of divine services on Sunday.

Despite his concern for their life on board ship, Stevenson appears to

Brought on lighters from Immigrant Village, third-class passengers board the *Imperator* en route to New York. (*National Archives*)

Below, living and eating accommodations for steerage passengers on *La Provence,* circa 1906. Eating utensils were provided by the company, a fairly recent innovation. Straw from the palliasses on each platform was thrown overboard the last morning of each crossing. (*Compagnie Générale Transatlantique*)

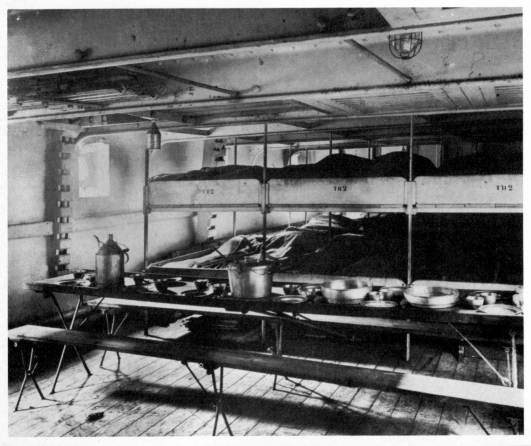

have had little admiration for the emigrants. They were, he wrote, "a company of the rejected; the drunken, the incompetent, the weak, the prodigal, all who had been unable to prevail against circumstances in the one land were now fleeing pitifully to another; and though one or two might succeed, all had already failed. We were a shipful of failures, the broken men of England."

This was an attitude he shared, unfortunately, with many of his contemporaries, but one I find harsh and unjustified. Emigrants to the New World displayed a remarkable courage and resourcefulness which cannot be equated with cowardice. Even in flight from persecution, injustice or quite simply starvation, surely theirs was not the easy way out. The decision to uproot their lives, the sacrifices to raise the price of passage, the perseverance to obtain passports and often bribe officials to validate them, and the struggle overland to a port were steps not easily taken. They were the most vulnerable of travelers; most had never left their villages before, let alone the region. Traveling by train was a terrifying novelty to most of them, a journey that would carry them within hours to a country where they understood neither language, customs nor currency. Yet they set out bravely, carrying their most precious possessions, lured by the promise of a land and a way of life so remote that it staggered the imagination.

In the last decade before the First World War, emigration involved a huge volume of business for the steamship companies. It is no accident that the peak year of all time, 1907, when one million two hundred thousand were admitted to the United States, also saw the maiden voyage of the *Lusitania* and *Mauretania*. Other superliners that followed on their heels were designed with this huge demand in mind, and the economic foundation that made such fleets of enormous vessels feasible was the seemingly endless flow of humble passengers. Half of the *Imperator*'s thirty-five hundred passengers were immigrants. Companies might publicize the splendor of their swimming pools and restaurants, but their most profitable clients never used them. Even the eastbound traffic was substantial, for the westward flow was sensitive to American economic conditions and a recession could momentarily reverse it. The practice of sending cattle back to Europe in empty immigrant holds was suspended and ships like the *Olympic* even offered cabins.

Like all gigantic human enterprises, the emigrant boom was not merely subject to natural fluctuations. There was also judicious manipulation on the part of the companies who, having ordered the ships, now promoted a hard-sell campaign to keep them filled. The offices of steamship agents hundreds of miles from the sea were decorated with posters representing, in easily comprehended graphics, the fabulous rewards of the land that lay a transatlantic passage away. Cunard paid Austria-Hungary a stipend on condition that the government deliver annually to continental ports twenty thousand emigrants. (It was this particular kind of scheme that backfired and ultimately brought an end to mass immigration. Government agents, beating the provincial bushes to furnish the year's quotas, rooted out thousands of undesirables that they were only too happy to be rid of who washed up, hopelessly inadequate, on America's doorstep.)

German ships carried the bulk of those prewar immigrants for their ports were ideally situated for central and eastern Europeans. Companies that had neglected their steerage passengers for years now went to inordinate trouble to sustain them from the moment they arrived at the port. Ballin, typically, was one of the first to realize that each immigrant who reached the United States as a contented HAPAG passenger would be more likely to recommend the same carrier to relatives anxious to join him. One of the most frequent abuses, common to all ports of Europe, were bogus company officials who would steer emigrants to shoddy boardinghouses, charging them an exorbitant daily rate against the day their ship sailed.

Ballin ended this victimization by construction of a picturesque Emigrant Village on fifteen pleasant acres next to the Elbe. Completed in 1906, it was divided into two sections by a rigidly observed line of demarcation: the Unclean side, inland, and the Clean side, which faced the water. Passengers arriving by cart from the Hamburg Station (railway tickets courtesy of the company), were given a shower and a physical examination; their luggage was fumigated separately. Upon completion of the process, they crossed to the Clean side where they could obtain inexpensive food and lodgings. There was also a church, a well-run infirmary and a canteen. The night before embarkation on lighters that would take them downriver to the ships, outgoing visitors to Emigrant Village were entertained at a dance.

If it was all vaguely prisonlike, it was at least clean, honest and reasonably priced. Furthermore, Ballin's preoccupation with the health of his passengers was sound business. Immigrants who failed the Public Health examination at Quarantine were returned by law at company expense to the port of embarkation. Thousands who occupied the slums of European ports were these pitiful rejects who, brought back to their port of origin, had no money to take them home again.

It has often been suggested that emigrants were content with conditions in steerage because their previous experience had been restricted to even meaner quarters. My own suspicion is that, having finally boarded the

On the bigger ships, steerage was called third class.
Ballin's sensible preoccupation with the lot of his most
profitable passengers paid off. On the *Vaterland,* they
had their own kitchen, dining room and stewards.
(*Frank Braynard Collection*)

ship that was to transport them to America, these grateful people would have settled for anything. Among the most delighted to embark were women in the last stages of pregnancy. By the early twentieth century, the medical care available on the bigger vessels was of such good quality that it was common practice for emigrants to arrange, when possible, to have their children born while crossing. Third-class passenger Joseph Imperator Schnapp, born in midocean on the ship that inspired his middle name in March of 1914, was one of hundreds of babies delivered in the steerage hospitals of that period. His parents were the recipients of a generous collection raised among the cabin passengers.

An invaluable commentary on contemporary attitudes toward the steerage is a book called *Travelling Palaces,* written by an Englishman called R. A. Fletcher in 1913. It is a source of both information and advice, covering a variety of subjects: hints for correct decorum in the dining and smoking rooms, what to take and when to wear it. Then suddenly, we are in third class, or rather near it, for the author reveals instantly his heritage and particular sensibilities:

> Most British liners will not carry emigrants from Central Europe because of their dirty habits. This may seem unkind but if you were to see the disgusting condition of some of the men and women who come from that part of the continent, you would not wonder at the restrictions but would be surprised that they were allowed to enter a railway train—even a fourth class continental—for a seaport or were allowed to embark.

But emigrant passengers have their uses. Fletcher continues on the subject of laundry, suggesting that a woman traveling first class can:

> . . . arrange through the intermediary of a stewardess for a female third class passenger to receive a few more articles when she was cleaning her own in the wash-house provided for third class passengers.

Savor the delicacy of Fletcher's discretion, that the contact can be best effected by a third party to avoid the danger of contamination. His reference to the wash house is interesting, presumably the only facility in transatlantic history that was denied the first class yet common in the third.

Pompous though he may have been, Fletcher spoke out strongly against a common violation of taste—cabin passengers who went slumming. His verdict is contained in the quote at the head of this chapter. It was a popular diversion for first-class passengers, resplendent in evening dress, to explore the third, a habit which companies did not condone but often found hard to prevent. Anything more patronizing than a party of arrogant youngsters thrusting themselves into these simple quarters is hard to imagine. Stevenson had written feelingly about it during his passage as quasi-immigrant:

> Picking their way with little gracious titters of indulgence and a lady-bountiful air about nothing which galled me to the quick. . . . They seemed to throw their clothes in our faces. Their eyes searched us all over for tatters and incongruities, a laugh was ready at their lips; but they were too well-mannered to indulge it in our hearing. Wait a bit, till they were back in the saloon, then hear how wittily they would depict the manners of the steerage.

The third-class promenade, so-called, was in either of the two well decks. There were no deck chairs or games for it was a dreary expanse of space given over to cargo-handling in port. Once a day, all the emigrants were sent there while their quarters were cleaned. If it was cold, they brought with them the gray company blankets that were, by the turn of the century, included in the price of their fare. They perched on winches or in the lee of the hatches, the old people huddled about the steampipes. Sometimes there were impromptu concerts or dances on the hatch covers that would attract a gallery of spectators from the second cabin. Slumming from above, they would lean over their promenade deck railing and throw candy and pennies down to the steerage children.

But celebrations of this kind were comparatively rare; what distinguished the mood of third from either of the two superior classes was a lack of frivolity. Beneath the boredom, the mindless singing and dancing, was anticipatory dread as the ship drew closer to New York. For the cabin passengers, landfall meant a return to the familiar, for the crew, the halfway mark of a routine voyage; but among the emigrants-turned-immigrants on the lower decks, New York and its officials were the last hurdle before entry into the United States. Ahead lay not only the promised land but a brush with an alien, incomprehensible bureaucracy, the ordeal of Ellis Island.

Just inside the Narrows, on the Staten Island side, inbound ships would anchor at Quarantine off the Public Health Station at Clifton, flying a yellow flag, the letter "Q" in international code. The system of quarantine originated in fourteenth-century Venice in an effort to control bubonic plague, and the name has its roots in the Italian *quaranta* or forty-day detention period. For most of the ships coming into New York, it was a matter of an hour or more unless they had to wait their turn behind other vessels. A team of inspectors would come on board, pass through the first and second class at a brisk pace and settle down in third for examination of the immigrants. Each one in turn passed before the inspectors under a bright light.

Although the inspectors could and did find anything from typhus to leprosy, their task was made easier by the compulsory examination conducted by the companies themselves at the time of embarkation. One of the main concerns was the detection of trachoma, a disease of the eye that betrays its presence by a reddening around the pupils. Incurable in adults, it had been carried to Europe by Napoleon's soldiers returning from the Egyptian campaigns and the Public Health Service was determined to resist its spread to America by immigrants. After 1904, those found infected with trachoma were expelled from the United States.

In 1892, there was a cholera scare in the harbor and the *Normannia,* a HAPAG ship, stayed anchored at Quarantine for days on end, even though she had no cases on board. Prevented from landing her passengers in New York, authorities finally disembarked them on a bleak stretch of Fire Island, where they finished out their "forty" and were ultimately returned to the city under protection of the Army.

Following pratique, or clearance, the yellow flag came down, New York reporters were allowed to board and the ship proceeded up the harbor. En route to the piers was Bartholdi's famous statue of Liberty Lighting the World, a harbor landmark since 1886. The sight of it had enormous emotional impact on the immigrants. They fought for a place at the rail, fell to their knees or wept tears of joy. When the ship tied up at the pier, all the cabin passengers were ashore before the immigrants were allowed to disembark, only to board lighters for the trip to Ellis Island. Prior to 1892, they would have gone to Castle Garden on the Battery, but operations had moved that year to the fort off the Jersey shore. The land fill that had been added to the island's original three acres was composed largely of ballast from inbound sailing ships; Ellis Island was itself as cosmopolitan as the clients it served.

The new arrivals were lined up in serpentine rows, corralled by railings in the reception hall. There was another cursory medical examination and those whose illness might have escaped previous scrutiny had their lapels chalked in different colors, coded to indicate the suspected disease. These unfortunates, together with those whose papers were incorrectly validated or who lacked the required twenty-five dollars in cash, were herded into the detention room, tagged "Public Charge." This was a dreaded dead end where the incompetent, the epileptic and the insane might languish for weeks on end. Conditions were inferior to the meanest third-class accommodation, the diet often a hideous monotony of prunes and rye bread. In most cases, the only release from detention was passage back to the European port of embarkation. So confinement in the stateless limbo of

The first of two transatlantic inspections for trachoma. Doctors at Le Havre examine immigrants for the dreaded eye disease. U.S. Public Health doctors repeated the examination at Quarantine. (*Compagnie Générale Transatlantique*)

Below, the *France* (left) and *Mauretania* awaiting clearance by health officials at Quarantine off Staten Island. This photograph was taken in August of 1913 by Alice Austen, pioneering woman photographer, whose front lawn is in the foreground. (*The Staten Island Historical Society*)

Representatives from each of three divergent classes line the forward decks of the *Imperator* as she approaches her Hoboken dock. Third-class deck space, expendable as usual, has been appropriated by a mountain of cabin trunks. (*Frank Braynard Collection*)

Ellis Island was, curiously enough, preferable to that ultimate rejection as unfit for admission.

But for those who passed muster, departure from the island lay through one of three halls. To the left and right, under signs marked simply WEST and NEW ENGLAND respectively, were rooms to purchase rail tickets and American currency. These moneychangers used to keep a supply of polished pennies on hand which they could pass off to the gullible as gold pieces. Between the two railway halls were stairs that led directly down to the ferry terminal. At the bottom, immigrants bound for Manhattan would link up in hysterical reunion with friends and relatives who waited at the kissing post where millions were welcomed to the New World by relieved New Yorkers. A new life was just a ferry ride away and many of those who stepped ashore at the Battery would never leave Manhattan.

Having been drawn into a European war, the United States tried to turn her back on the world in the years succeeding it. Postwar unrest produced an ugly new mood, a species of national paranoia to which twentieth-century America seems peculiarly vulnerable. Wholesale victims of this hysteria were the immigrants, among whom might be reds, anarchists or, indeed, any bent on subversion. Congress passed the Dillingham Immigration Restriction Act in May 1921 and the vast influx was over. Within five years, Ellis Island was deporting more than it admitted. The ships that had brought the new Americans had to find new sources of revenue and an irrevocable reversal of Atlantic traffic was to follow.

Cunard's share of the spoils. After using her as a trooper, the United States Navy handed the U.S.S. *Imperator* over to the British company. As the *Berengaria*, she continued as flagship of the Cunard postwar fleet, if not the fastest, certainly the most prestigious ship of the twenties. (*Hapag-Lloyd, formerly Hamburg-Amerika Line*) (*Cunard*)

. . . went to Europe each year as good
New Yorkers do.
—ALICE B. TOKLAS, WHAT IS REMEMBERED

7.
Eastbound:
the Twenties

Peacetime service resumed in the twenties was essentially unchanged, apart from a welcome absence of coaldust. British transformation of their ex-Germans was largely cosmetic: a new flag at the masthead, a new name across the stern, new funnel colors and a new berth on the Hudson's eastern shore. In the *Berengaria*'s working spaces, her German origins had disappeared; plates identifying switches and valves had been reversed and inscribed in English. But in the cabins, the bathtub drains were still marked AUF and ZU and ashtrays bore the legend ZIGARREN. The playroom's little rocking boat was still there but with a new name painted on the side.

The Ritz-Carlton restaurant was no longer. Cunard used the space for a ballroom instead. The winter garden became the palm court, "skillfully schemed," suggested a contemporary brochure, "to give the *Berengaria* passenger the illusion of being in a patio at Monte Carlo." By accident, the British copywriter made at least oblique reference to the national spirit that gave the public rooms their character, something that the original owners had failed to acknowledge. The swimming pool remained unchanged but for the addition of a diving board and some trapeze rings overhead. As a sop to Anglo-American superstition, all cabins which the Germans marked "13" were renumbered.

Of the largest ex-Germans, it was ironically the least successful which received the most lavish attention. Charged with the reconversion of the *Leviathan* was William Francis Gibbs, America's leading naval architect and a man of uncompromising diligence. He sailed to Europe and called on Blohm & Voss. The German builders, smarting at the prospect of losing their brand-new *Bismarck,* were less than cooperative. They demanded the prohibitive price of a million dollars for a set of the *Vaterland*'s original plans. Gibbs' reply was probably unprintable and he returned to New York determined to make his own. He organized a task force of a hundred naval draftsmen who swarmed all over the ship, down each staircase, passage and ladder, measuring every square foot of her. Since there was no dry dock in New York capable of taking the *Leviathan* at the time, the measurements included her exterior dimensions as well, calculated from inside the hull. It was a formidable, heroic and unique task.

After twelve months of incredible labor, a complete set of drawings was presented to the United States Shipping Board and the *Leviathan* was taken down to Newport News for a vast job of refitting. Eight million dollars and another year later, she emerged with red, white and blue funnels, rewired, strengthened, converted to oil and a thoroughly Americanized vessel. Captain Herbert Hartley sailed her from Virginia to Boston's Navy dockyard where a tug captain was heard to remark exasperatedly: "Where do you tie a line to this goddamned hotel?" On shore, fifty thousand Bostonians jostled each other in such an unruly manner that a battalion of Marines was called out. Many of the crowd had missed seeing the *Majestic* the previous year, and ships that size seldom appeared in Boston harbor.

She sailed east on her second maiden voyage in July of 1923. Poor, proud *Leviathan*—she was hopelessly betrayed by circumstances: she had no running mates her size and, worse, could offer her passengers nothing more bracing than sarsaparilla. As a result, she lost money consistently and spent as much time laid up as in service. Near the end of her career, one of her owners cracked: "The *Aquitania* is the most popular ship in the world and it cost us nine million dollars to find it out."

One reason the *Imperator* was top-heavy: A first-class bathroom with lavish marble paneling and a steel tub. Evidently there had been blithe unconcern among the Vulkan Werke sanitary engineers for economy in weight. (*Hapag-Lloyd, formerly Hamburg-Amerika Line*)

A single faucet, rivets, pipes and precious little
privacy characterized the spartan confines of
Tourist Third Cabin on the S.S. *Ballin* in 1924.
The almost total absence of frivolity, save for
a single potted plant, in no way discouraged
Americans willing to forego luxury in return for
economy. (*National Archives*)

Her entry in service in the early twenties precipitated a series of ridiculous squabbles between companies for title of the world's largest ship. The White Star Line, whose *Majestic* was in fact the longest, went so far as to call her the fastest as well. This brought demands of instant retraction from Cunard, whose *Mauretania* still held the Blue Ribband. The United States Lines claimed the title of largest for the *Leviathan* based on gross tonnage figures arbitrarily boosted by enclosing a weather deck. A Cunard steward, conducting a party of Southampton trippers through the *Berengaria,* had perhaps the last and most ludicrous word in this battle of superlatives. "The lounge," he announced proudly, "is the largest public room in any ship afloat—and you will notice that the roof is entirely supported by no pillars!"

If most ships remained essentially unchanged, their human cargoes had not. For the first time, the majority of steamship clients were American; in fact, eighty percent of them, not only rich Americans of prewar vintage but an entirely new breed of mass passenger. Their presence in such vast numbers on board the Atlantic ships was, curiously enough, the result of American legislation. Although Congressional restriction of immigration reflected a strong isolationist sentiment in postwar America, one of its effects was to make Europe available to large numbers of their grass-roots constituents.

Faced with large expanses of inferior berthing space, the companies had done some nimble footwork. Those suddenly redundant quarters were upgraded to accommodate teachers, students and tourists, Americans anxious to travel abroad in high season but unable to pay any but the minimum fare. "Steerage" was banished from the copywriter's lexicon and in its place was created tourist third cabin, quite clearly something for everyone. The clever new title implied, generically, respectability ("tourist"), frugality ("third") and privacy ("cabin"). The White Star Line put it this way: "If, however, you are contemplating passage in Second Class, Tourist Third Cabin or Third Class, you will find in these classes respectively the same careful thought for your comfort. The fittings, of course, will be somewhat less luxurious, but no less pleasing." It was not uncommon to share a cabin with strangers and the food, according to one passenger, was "plain, substantial, utterly uninteresting but eatable." Neither of these shortcomings discouraged applicants. The delighted companies discovered that with a little fresh paint, improved service and a monogrammed company bedspread, space that had seemed suitable only for minimal subsistence was quite acceptable to the new white-collar steerage.

Bunking in with strangers was only part of it; the refurbished decks were also shared with remnants of the true third class. Listed in company projections as the "old home traffic," these were immigrants whose success in the New World enabled them to visit their birthplaces in the Old. This they did, more discriminating and independent travelers than on the occasion of their original westbound crossing. They absorbed in their midst these new, educated travelers with bemused indifference. Conversely, devotees of tourist third cabin welcomed the continuity with the past that their multilingual shipmates provided. For the real secret of tourist third cabin's appeal was not only its economy but its flavor. It was christened the Left Bank class. Making their first crossing, passengers who booked in it were having an adventure, a brief experimental descent into the lower depths that would have been impossible in the bourgeois familiarity of second class. The scheme was enormously successful, and even though the *Berengaria*'s capacity was reduced from forty-one hundred to twenty-seven hundred seventy, the new third class was a godsend in those postwar years.

As the travel impetus changed direction, so did companies assiduously work the other side of the street. New York offices were enlarged and, with the same zeal that had enticed the persecuted from Europe's ghettos, steamship publicists unleashed a more sophisticated campaign to sell "Abroad" throughout the American hinterland. European travel was marketed with a variety of subtle appeals: culture, luxury, snobbism and, predominately, thirst. America had been in the grip of Prohibition since 1919 and the public was quick to realize that the Atlantic Ocean was wet in more ways than one. If the Volstead Act did nothing else, it led to the creation of a new transatlantic stereotype, the drunk American. Noisy, argumentative but generous, they transformed smoking into drinking rooms. Pantry stewards kept later hours and the largest among them doubled as bouncers. In the early twenties, before Americans learned to live with their bootleggers, the eastbound crossing proved too much for some. The *Aquitania*'s surgeon grew familiar with delirium tremens and often put passengers onto the boat train in stretchers.

Consider the inducement of a French Line brochure:

> As you sail away, far beyond the range of amendments and thou-shalt-nots, those dear little iced things begin to appear, sparkling aloft on their slender crystal stems. . . . Utterly French, utterly harmless— and oh so gurglingly good!

The French in particular made their ships a haven for suppressed drinkers. *Mousses,* their boys in buttons, were taught more than to remove their caps when addressed. Following daily calisthenics on the sun deck, there were

compulsory English classes, complete with blackboard and pointer. The heaviest word drill centered about "dry martini" and "manhattan" and sample vignettes were rehearsed literally as follows:

Mousse: Good morning, sir (madam)!
Passenger: Where is the bar?
Mousse (bowing): This way, sir (madam)!

The *Leviathan*'s smoking room became a mockery, although drinking continued elsewhere. In any passageway after the dressing gong had been sounded could be heard a sustained rattling and clicking. It was nothing more than the surreptitious song of the shaker.

New York, greatest and gaudiest of the Atlantic ports, was the undeniable focal point, not only for Americans who made it their place of departure but also for the foreign-flag companies that sought their patronage. No matter what subsidiary traffic might sail to Canada or Boston, the westbound tracks of the greatest ships converged at Ambrose Light. The forests of bowsprits that overhung South Street in the eighteenth and nineteenth centuries was symbolic of New York's involvement with its port, an involvement that continued into the twentieth century as well.

This very oneness with the sea was something that Europeans never fully expected. Manhattan stood with its feet wet, a cluster of futuristic spires rising improbably from the waters of the harbor. It was a geographical characteristic shared to some extent by Venice and Copenhagen but on a much vaster scale. Passengers on the decks of incoming vessels were suddenly involved with an astonishing metropolis whose pulse they could hear across the water. No city-port in the world so dominated the ships that entered it, a gigantic backdrop against which superstructures that towered over European quays were forced into humbler perspective. It was a sight that never failed to impress. Though environmentalists tell us our air is poisoned, there are mornings even now when the clean-washed sparkle of New York seems close to the vision seen by Rupert Brooke when he arrived in 1913:

But there was beauty in the view that morning, also, half an hour before sunrise. New York, always the cleanest and least smoky of cities, lay asleep in a queer, pearly, hourless light. A thin mist softened the further outlines. The water was opalescent under a silver sky, cool and dim, very slightly ruffled by the sweet wind that followed us in from the sea. A few streamers of smoke flew above the city, oblique and parallel, pennants of our civilization. The space of water is great, and

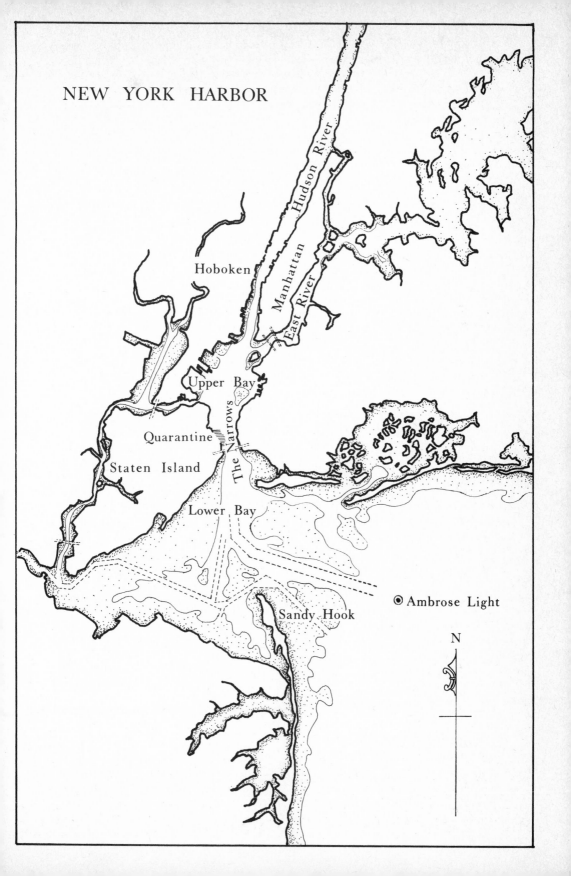

NEW YORK HARBOR

Hoboken

Hudson River

Manhattan

East River

Upper Bay

The Narrows

Quarantine

Staten Island

Lower Bay

Sandy Hook

⊙ Ambrose Light

N

Taken in the early fifties, this aerial view
of Pier 90 indicates Manhattan's extreme
accessibility from New York harbor.
From left to right: the *Britannic, Queen
Mary* and second *Mauretania.* (*Cunard*)

so the vast buildings do not tower above one as they do from the street. Scale is lost, and they might be any size. The impression is, rather, of long, low buildings stretching down to the water's edge on every side, and innumerable low black wharves and jetties and piers. And at one point, the lower end of the island on which the city proper stands, rose that higher clump of the great buildings, the Singer, the Woolworth, and the rest. Their strength, almost severity, of line and the lightness of their color gave a kind of classical feeling, classical, and yet not of Europe. . . . Our boat moved up the harbor and along the Hudson River with a superb and courtly stateliness. Round her snorted and scuttled and puffed the multitudinous strange denizens of the harbor. Tugs, steamers, queer-shaped ferry-boats, long rafts carrying great lines of trucks from railway to railway, dredges, motorboats, even a sailing-boat or two; for the day's work was beginning. Among them, with that majesty that only a liner entering a harbor has, she went, progressed, had her moving—English contains no word for such a motion—*incessu patuit dea*. A goddess entering fairyland, I thought; for the huddled beauty of the buildings and the still, silver expanse of the water seemed unreal. Then I looked down at the water immediately beneath me and knew that New York was a real city. All kinds of refuse went floating by: bits of wood, straw from barges, bottles, boxes, paper, occasionally a dead cat or dog, hideously bladder-like, its four paws stiff and indignant toward heaven.

Perhaps the poet's most significant observation was New York's particular dualism, a persistent aspect of this alluring and repellent city. As a converted and consequently manic New Yorker, I have to agree with him. I live in the intellectual, artistic and financial center of the United States, a city that lacks only the seat of government to legitimize its obvious role of capital. In its own ruthless way, New York City has attracted many of the bright, tastemaking people of the world, the investors to underwrite their creations and the adventurous consumers to try them. It also happens to be noisy, dirty, expensive, dangerous, frantic, corrupt, cynical and noxious. But overall, there is vitality, sprung from the rich diversity of the port's human traffic, no less from the anonymous immigrant who landed and stayed than the statesman embarking for Europe.

The end result is this irresistible, impossible city where everything in America happens first. New York's pace has always awed the European, enervated the Midwesterner and exhilarated the native, spoiling him for permanent residence in any of the imitation New Yorks scattered across the continent. "A nice place to visit but . . ." is the traveler's inevitable verdict. This is fortunate, for New York is almost impossible *not* to visit if you would travel eastward. This is less true today, but it was practically inescapable in the twenties.

Despite a look of impregnability, New York was astonishingly accessible from the harbor. One was hardly through the agony of the piers before being engulfed in it. The ship's passenger was in a hotel or office almost more quickly than he embarked on a boat train in Southampton or Cherbourg. Sailing from New York was characterized by the same ease of departure. In the late forties, there was a silly snob joke to the effect that one went to the West Side only on the way to Europe; this is not just a joke but an incredible convenience. All other Atlantic ports are subsidiary cities, milestones in the progress from ship to capital. New York is uniquely a terminus and center combined. The same skyscrapers that provide such a handsome setting for inbound vessels effectively hide them from the land. Approaching the piers, one turned a corner and there, gloriously bright, was that white superstructure towering inviolate over Manhattan's shoreside clutter. I know of no more exhilarating sight, nothing that raises the spirits more than that sudden dramatic revelation. The now-derelict piers that line lower Manhattan's western shore were all operational in the early twenties. In fact, the whole Hudson was operational; there were neither bridges nor tunnels to New Jersey and ferries carried all traffic from shore to shore. At its mouth, the Hudson is still called the North River, an ancient name used in the early days of American exploration to distinguish New York's waters from the Delaware and Chesapeake inlets to the south.

The baggage had gone ahead, mountains of it. Trunks were indispensable then, great leather and brass creations that still appear on New York sidewalks, consigned to the Department of Sanitation. In those days, they were picked up by one of several companies exclusively concerned with the movement of luggage. This efficient shuttle of transfer men and trucks streamed back and forth between hotels, apartments, stations and piers. It was a time when trunks dispatched from anywhere in the country would reach the docks on time, when railways still had expresses and Railway Express was not a joke.

Americans have always excelled in the amount of luggage they carry and it is no accident that the wardrobe trunk was an American invention. But it was more than a matter of trunks—it was the conglomerate that astounds in retrospect. A cousin of mine still uses a sturdy relic of that era, a leather suitcase that belonged to his grandmother. She was a woman who traveled with a vast assortment of luggage. The particular suitcase that my cousin cherishes has the number 47 painted neatly on one end and it was by no means the last of the collection. Equally astonishing, despite the maid who accompanied her everywhere, she packed them all herself.

No matter how much luggage was sent ahead, there was always more with the passengers. On arrival at the pier, it was seized by the longshoremen. These affable pirates, standing with palms extended under large company signs renouncing any charge for their service, always made a killing on sailing day. They were particularly intimidating to the new tourists of the twenties. If there was anything the neophyte passenger dreaded, it was the embarrassment of not knowing the form, of doing the wrong thing. As the hapless tourist scrambled from a taxi, wallet in hand, it was a simple matter for the longshoremen to press their case. It was the first and not the last unnecessary gratuity with which those green travelers would part during the following weeks. (Longshoremen were one of two parasitical groups that used to prey on steamship clients; the others were dishonest taxi drivers who worked the piers on arrival days and have since transferred their attentions to the airports. Both were figurative descendants of the rogues who waited at the Battery for inbound immigrants and it seems quite probable that their consummate villainy will be part of New York's passenger image indefinitely.)

In its cavernous upper level, the pier had an honest, practical ugliness about it. For those outbound, there was little reason to linger there. The ship's hull, seen through the raised sides of the shed, seemed to go on forever. This close-up of black, rivet-studded plating, streaked with salt and rust, was not as pretty as the glistening upperworks seen from afar, but infinitely reassuring. Someone once wrote that a ship is the largest thing that moves. It seemed extraordinary that such a jettylike wall was actually afloat and would be at sea in a matter of hours. Novices arrived early during boarding time and stood in a line at the ticket barrier opposite their gangplank. Old hands knew to cut their arrival time as fine as possible and go almost directly on board.

Passage from shore to ship was brief but symbolic. In those days, the way lay across a broad plank equipped with handrails, rather than through a steel and canvas tunnel. During daylight, there was a flash of sunlight between the two worlds, dizzy suspension over pilings, flotsam and discharging condensors, before entering the beguiling warmth of electric light, panelling and concern that was a ship's interior. Waiting on their home ground just inside the shell plating were the master-at-arms and a brass-buttoned, starched detachment of stewards and bellboys. Underfoot, there was an enormous bristly doormat, part of a ship's never-ending battle against the dirt of a port.

On larger vessels, there might have been as many as five thousand visitors on sailing day, particularly in early summer. It was not unusual for visitors to outnumber passengers. Despite the appalling confusion they helped create in the passageways, their presence on board was encouraged. Companies reasoned quite rightly that this year's visitor might be next year's passenger. So they were welcomed at a subsidiary gangplank further aft, their ticket of admission a donation to charity. The ship's lobby or embarkation hall, severely congested this day and empty for the following six, was a maelstrom of porters, passengers, stewards, visitors, shore staff, golfclubs, handcarts, flowers, trays and telegrams. There was no greater test of a chief purser's skill than sailing day. From his office, located at the storm center, he supervised assistants, dispensed advice, greeted familiar passengers and coped with the company officials who invariably chose this crucial hour to pay their respects. Small wonder that the opening pages of Cunard's Routine Book for pursers were concerned with the minutiae of this assault on their sanity.

I have often seen friends off on ships and have as many times regretted doing so. Worse than the midday champagne hangover was a keen sense of deprivation that I was not sailing myself. Then again, for someone who had never sailed, the ship was not at her best. Tied to a pier, the cant of the decks was wrong. There was no engine tremor, and the light through the porthole had none of the brilliance it would later have at sea. The cabin seemed crowded, unbearably hot in summer, with not enough places to sit; the noise from a party next door was overwhelming and even the ministrations of the steward curiously remote.

If companies profited from visitors, stewards did not. They had just completed a laborious turnaround and were as anxious as their passengers to get to sea. In the meantime, they struggled through choked passages, fetching ice and vases, giving directions and reassuring distraught passengers about suitcases. In particularly busy seasons—westbound from Southampton in late August, for instance—it was not unusual for spaces to be double-booked through an agent's error ashore. Stewards would summon an assistant purser to make peace between two families, one ensconced in a suite and another camped furiously on suitcases in the passage. On occasions of this kind, possession was not nine tenths and the earlier dated ticket won out. It was not uncommon for the displaced passengers, allotted whatever space could be found, to have their fares refunded.

It was and still is a tradition for visitors to ignore the first as well as the subsequent half-dozen calls ashore. On the old Cunarders, a boy in buttons paraded up and down the corridors thumping on a Chinese gong and intoning the time-honored "All ashore that's going ashore!" White Star ships used a bugle and the French a discreet little set of chimes. More recently, the ship's loudspeaker system has been substituted. But the only infallible signal was the ship's whistle, a ludicrously inadequate name for that shattering, majestic blast that rattled the cabin. Tugs whistled but liners bellowed, on a device with no appropriate name that could be heard for miles.

The *Leviathan* had three of them, one on each funnel, while her British sisters were content with two. The *Ile de France* had a trio of steam sirens with ascending scales. But the Germans outdid everyone on the *Bremen* with five. One of them was a new device called a Nautophone which was really a loudspeaker that whistled, an early model of the directional signals that ships have today. When she steamed out of Bremerhaven, she used to blow a triple blast on all five simultaneously, a jolt for those not expecting it. Steam whistles became obligatory on all Atlantic vessels after the fogbound collision of the *Arctic* in 1854; astonishingly enough, they were rare before then. On New Year's and Armistice Day, British ships tied up in port used to serenade the town for minutes on end, until the chief engineer turned off the steam. E. B. White once said: "I heard the *Queen Mary* blow one midnight and the sound carried with it the whole history of departure, longing and loss." From the shore, the poignancy was very real but for passengers thus summoned to sea, it was a thrilling, definitive cadence that sent visitors hastily seeking the way out.

Only after they had gone did the cabin make sense. It was a small, admirably planned space that, despite its low ceiling, seemed to grow as each day passed. Companies went to great care and expense to make them attractive. Visitors took lasting impressions away with them, and in the event of rough weather they might become sickrooms occupied for a large portion of the crossing. There was, in fact, a kind of cabin mystique that made it far more personal than temporary quarters of any other variety. Siegfried Sassoon once wrote on the *Berengaria:*

> I like it—this creaking, heaving, vibrating, white, polished box. . . . Mischa Elman's cabin was quite close to mine and I often heard him playing. . . . The memory of those evening hours has a strange serenity; the drone and thud of the turbines, the pad and patter of feet on the deck above, the smell of new paint, the lapping of waves on the side of the ship, the sunset seen through my porthole, and Elman practicing Bach's *Chaconne.*

Even without the splendid coincidence of a neighboring virtuoso, Sassoon's

New York reporters and camera-men board the *Olympic* at Quarantine. On this occasion, in 1921, they will interview Madame Curie, just arrived in New York to accept an ounce of radium from America's school children. The famed French scientist seems at ease under the scrutiny of five newsreel cameras. (*Edwin Levick Collection, The Mariners Museum, Newport News, Virginia*)

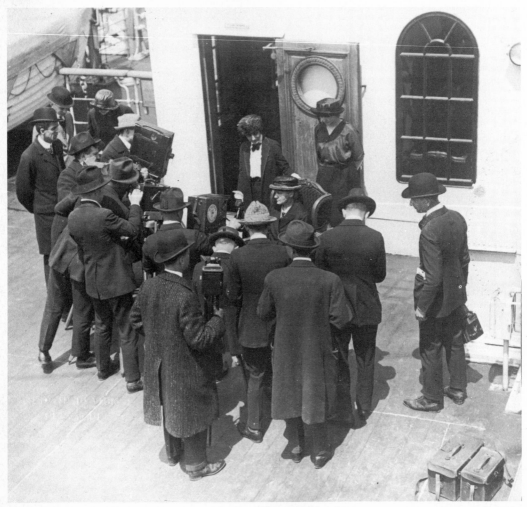

image is evocative and strangely peaceful, infinitely superior to the negative charm of most hotel rooms.

Predictably, the most lavish suites made the least successful cabins because their designers had successfully insulated them from the ocean. Bunks were replaced by brass beds, and portholes, those perfect windows unique to a ship, were concealed behind conventional land-based casements. This determination to disguise honest nautical features has always seemed to me a grave error in judgment. Occupants of less pretentious accommodations, with steel ceilings, exposed pipes, proper bunks and portholes, were reminded that they were indeed on board a ship.

Portholes could be opened in those days, adding the unmistakable aroma of the sea that is sadly lacking on today's air-conditioned ships. This was best done by a steward with a port key, thus avoiding an agonizing contusion known as porthole thumb, a crunch of brass against knuckle that ship's surgeons learned to expect the first day out. Despite this occupational hazard, outside cabins were desirable, not only to passengers who craved light and air but to companies which could, in good conscience, charge more for their occupancy. The Bibby cabin, so called after the line that first implemented their design, was converted from inside to outside by addition of a narrow passage to the ship's side terminating in a single porthole. These doglegs served to reduce the dimension of legitimate outside cabins they displaced, but proved enormously popular and profitable; the *Olympic* had many of them.

On the *Aquitania,* light was admitted to a double rank of inside cabins by the ingenious provision of a platform on the inboard side of the promenade deck. It not only raised occupants of deck chairs conveniently high enough to see over the rail but also left space, within the riser, for a six-inch clerestory window into the cabin directly below. A similar window in the wall immediately behind the chair provided light for a cabin even further inside. It was a clever inspiration, unique, as far as I know, to the *Aquitania.*

Bunks began to disappear around the turn of the century, victims of the pretension of increased tonnage. One of HAPAG's boasts about their *Imperator* was that there were none in first class. They had been a necessity on small, hard-riding ships like the *Kaiser Wilhelm II,* for instance; she was christened "Rolling Billy" by those who sailed on her. During severe storms, when sleeping passengers might be flung to the floor, they served as an admirable restraint. There was also the old steward's trick of stuffing a folded blanket under the edge of the mattress away from the wall, effectively cradling the occupant. But there was a strong prejudice against bunks, particularly the upper ones which children used to fight for.

There were other design aspects common to all cabins, regardless of class or ship, that exist to the present. Bureau tops and shelves had protective rims to keep things from sliding off. Beds and bunks never ran athwartship but fore and aft. Cabin and closet doors could be secured in an open position. A thermos and accompanying glass rested in wall-hung brackets. Bathroom doors had a two-inch sill to prevent slopped-over water from reaching the carpet.

If there was a trunk in the cabin rather than the hold, it was invariably a steamer trunk, so called for the simple reason that it held clothes to be worn exclusively on board. Companies used to store these trunks in European ports free of charge against the passenger's return. This tradition remained long after the original need for special clothing had passed. Salt damp air required an especially serviceable brand of outerwear, and on earlier ships there was in addition a distinctive and presumably unwelcome smell compounded of engines, salt, tar and bilges. A North German Lloyd brochure for 1908 advised passengers to include sachets among their clothes to keep it out. By the twenties, however, passengers on board large Atlantic liners were unaware of any smell at all, or at least any that could be termed objectionable. A frequent passenger on the *Aquitania* said that the ship smelled only of flowers, soap and the sea.

Almost everyone who might remember nothing else about a crossing retains an uncanny sense-memory about the way something smelled or sounded. A middle-aged man of my acquaintance still finds that a freshly cut orange takes him back instantly to a cabin he had occupied as a boy on the *Majestic*. (My suspicion is that he had broken into one of those preposterous fruit baskets that were popular *bon voyage* gifts. Why people insisted on sending each other mountains of citrus, I have never discovered; I can only assume that there were those who still associated ocean crossings with scurvy.) Teak decks wet with salt spray gave off a distinctive aroma. A woman who crossed only once in her life remembered the smell of fresh paint, another the particular lavender salts used by the bath steward in second class, yet another the unique pungency of a tub full of hot salt water. I remember sailing on the *Queen Mary* on my honeymoon, the first British ship I had been on since the *Georgic* seventeen years earlier; a familiar smell came flooding back, an evocative blend of tea, flowers, floor wax and whatever stern British antiseptic had survived the war intact.

Sounds were just as familiar. Inextricably associated with those summer crossings from New York was the endless susuration of electric fans behind their marcelled wire guards, hundreds of them swinging back and forth all over the ship. There was also, often unwelcome but like no other sound, the early morning noises of an overhead deck: the scrape of holystones, the wash of the hose and the thunder of the early walkers. Or again, the *slap-slap* that grew and faded as a child in sneakers raced past the cabin along rubber-tiled passageways. Finally, there was the chorus of chattering and creaking as the vessel moved through even a moderate sea; but that was a sea sound, heard only after the harbor had been cleared.

Perhaps the best time to board was for a sailing at midnight. These were quite common in New York between the wars and had been for some time. This most romantic of departure hours was prompted by nothing more exotic than the reluctance of the French to put sleeping cars on the train between Cherbourg and Paris. To ensure that the journey would be taken in daylight, companies using the port scheduled midnight sailings from New York. The Germans had initiated the practice in 1904 for the very same reason; the crossing was thus timed to conclude off Cuxhaven at dawn. Midnight sailings from New York were features of a three-and-four-ship service, a practice with which the two *Queens* could dispense following World War II.

Yet whatever the practicalities involved, night departures achieved a mystical chic that had nothing at all to do with Cherbourg. Part of the ritual was a farewell dinner ashore, at a friend's apartment or a speakeasy, followed by a race through deserted streets to the Chelsea piers. The ship seemed incredibly romantic, floodlit and overrun with people in evening dress. Private gatherings were augmented by dancing in the lounge. This was an effort to focus the noise away from cabins where children, protesting through yawns, had been sent instantly to bed. However, the gaiety was contagious and every child was probably glued to a porthole, determined to remain awake until the moment of departure. To them, it was of no consequence that the ship's log did not acknowledge the start of a crossing until after the pilot had been dropped; their crossing began the moment the view through the porthole moved. There were some children who filled the tub and, risking a wet pillow, thrust their heads under water the better to hear the engines throbbing below.

To their parents on the boat deck above, the lights of New York glittered beyond the bow, somehow already part of another world. There was an extraordinary detached quality about being on board ship even an hour after boarding; perhaps it had to do with the height above land, exaggerated by the darkness. At any rate, it was the hardest time to tear visitors away. The almost hypnotic appeal of sailing at night proved irresistible to many.

On more than one occasion, the pilot boat brought in through the dawn chill dinner-jacketed bons voyageurs. If not out-and-out stowaways, they were certainly susceptible celebrants unabashed by lack of a ticket.

Not all departures from New York were accomplished in good weather. I know of no more penetrating winds than blow up the North River in January and there were many midnights when standing on an upper deck was a test of endurance. Manhattan's famous lights could be obscured in gray murk or there might be three inches of slush underfoot. Similarly, conditic `ed as we are now to summer sailings, all teeth and Instamatics, it is as well to remember that many passengers who boarded then did not do so in a state of high anticipation. As Arthur Davis pointed out, some quite simply loathed the sea and everything on it. A few sailed for desperate reasons, absconding, eloping or running away from something. There were those who remained on deck long after a face at the end of the pier had dwindled to nothing, and those who retired to their cabins for six days. They blended in with those on business, those on vacation and those with nothing else to do. Behind the neat columns of alphabetized names on any ship's passenger list lay a wealth of compelling drama. Some of it would be exchanged, relished and forgotten before the crossing was over. Somerset Maugham remarked once that he derived inspiration for some of his best work from observations made on countless sea voyages.

The business of selecting which ship to take was a different matter for each kind of traveler. The professionals, buyers or salesmen who had to be in London or Paris on a certain morning chose the fastest ship that sailed east as close to their deadline as possible. Although companies welcomed their patronage, they realized that convenience rather than loyalty to any particular line was involved. At the other end of the spectrum were the newcomers, on vacation and sailing for the first time. If the companies knew what dictated their often laborious choice, they did not divulge it. Recommendations from friends, the nationality of the ship, the image of glamor— there were countless reasons.

It was obvious that the large, fast ships were popular with these novices, not only because of their speed but also their prestige. Just as tourists in New York want to see only Broadway's newest and most unattainable hit, so then did passengers want a crack ship's name plastered on their suitcases when they went home. Unfortunately, this particular cachet was denied them since baggage labels never carried the ship's name in print, only the line's. But there were always postcards of the ship, dozens of them bearing an appropriate "X," to be stuffed in the library mailbox before the ship cleared the Narrows. Later, of course, there would be time for a snapshot,

Bon Voyage on board the *Mauretania*. Although the ship is still at her pier and the bar is closed, the dance floor is packed. How many were passengers and how many visitors would not be revealed until the vessel sailed at midnight. (*Cunard*)

The *Majestic* sails from the White Star piers in the waning light of a bitter January afternoon. The Atlantic ferry was a year-round operation with little relation to leisure or vacation for most of the winter. (*Frank Braynard Collection*)

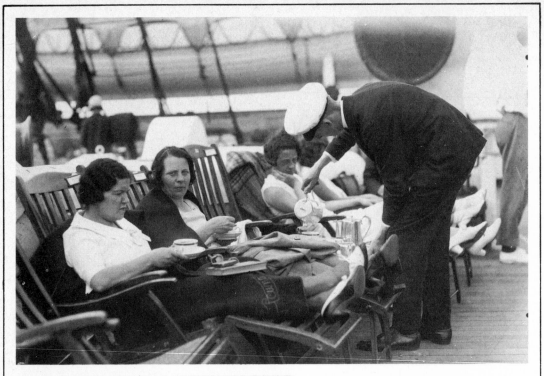

Mid-Atlantic summer, 1924. Tea on deck with a steamer rug over the shoulders. Left, forty years later on the *Queen Elizabeth*. Neither chair nor rug has changed, but there is a welcome postwar refinement in the shape of a mattress. The quality of midocean wind and sun is curiously invigorating and exhausting at the same time. (*Cunard*)

taken at the rail by an obliging steward. Included in the photograph was a lifebuoy, irrefutably stenciled with the ship's name.

In between these two extremes of professional and novice were the regulars who sailed annually, always on one ship or on ships of the same line. Families used to book the same cabins and stewards year after year. There was a hard core of passengers who disliked big ships, confessing intense uneasiness on such vast and impersonal vessels. They always sailed on small ones and found the slower pace and traditional appointments more to their liking than the excesses, in decor, tonnage and shipmates, of the flagships. These intermediary vessels were delightfully conventional and as late as 1925, still carried signs advising passengers that the smoking room was reserved for gentlemen. Christopher Morley was a confirmed small-ship addict but acknowledged some boredom at the length of the slower crossing:

> The Channel is opening her arms to us, the queer uneasiness returns, a whole continent of irregular verbs is waiting. And this morning, when I went on deck, I distinctly smelled England. For seven days we had the universe to ourselves but even God, I think, was restless on the eighth.

Immediately after boarding, already fitted out in plus fours and caps, knowledgeable passengers would hunt out the deck steward to reserve a deck chair. This was an errand of some urgency, for the best locations were limited. Companies used to reserve a choice half dozen for last-minute decisions by steady clients, rather the way theatrical producers retain house seats for every performance. Eastbound, the starboard side was booked first, sheltered as it was from cold northern winds and sunny for most of the day. For Americans, it was the reverse of the old Mediterranean bromide POSH— Port Out, Starboard Home—that used to prevail for Englishmen sailing to India.

To many, the matter of sun was of less importance than the attraction of one's neighbor. For ambitious mothers, a first-class ticket was a strategic weapon. It was not uncommon for women with daughters of a marriageable age to choose their ship on the basis of its passenger list. Having pored over the gossip columns for weeks in advance, these determined creatures booked only when convinced that a rich bachelor, preferably titled, would also be on board. After embarking, their first move was to bribe the chief deck steward, heavily and quite shamelessly, to obtain not only the chair location of their quarry but the privilege of engaging the one adjoining it. There was no more ideal opportunity for initiating a friendship. It is curious that people insistent elsewhere on the privacy of spatial insulation submitted quite cheerfully on deck to an intimacy reminiscent of Coney Island. With scarcely an inch separating one from a supine neighbor and bundled in rugs, two adjacent deck chairs in blustery mid-Atlantic had much of the coziness usually associated with a double bed. The impulse to reply to comments on the weather, a book or the ship in general was almost irresistible. Professional gamblers had known and used the trick for years.

Another ritual observed as the ship cleared New York was reserving a seat in the dining room. There were some passengers who, incredibly enough, intimated to the chief steward that they would consider dining with the captain. Such gaucherie betrayed their ignorance of the tradition that a seat at the head table might be refused but never requested. The captain's table companions were selected only after exhaustive conference, sometimes necessitating careful research by company officials and other pursers of the line. Many among the famous had crossed swords ashore and to revive a feud on board was considered unfortunate. There was a dreadful flap on the *Majestic* once when a distinguished politician found himself seated at the captain's table with his ex-wife's co-respondent. Henri Villar, a fixture on French ships between the wars and dean of Atlantic pursers, was astute at avoiding precisely this kind of gaffe. He was blessed with an encyclopedic memory for names and scandals, and his diplomacy was unmatched.

Failing meals with the captain, parvenus insisted on a table nearby, again unaware that the best ones were elsewhere. Chief stewards usually assigned their new men to the middle of the room where they could be kept under observation; older and more experienced stewards were given tables to either side. The most exclusive tables apart from the captain's were those situated on the balcony (a piece of inside chic obviously restricted to those ships whose dining rooms boasted more than one floor). On the *Olympic* there was only one level, but on the *Berengaria, France, Paris* and *Mauretania,* the smart set invariably booked upstairs in advance. To do so meant that entrances and departures could be made unobtrusively, and since the upper level was smaller, greater privacy was assured.

It is indicative that the famous were willing to have their soup a trifle colder in return for protection from unwanted attention. A first-class ticket was, in effect, an invitation to a house party for a week and for arrivistes, basking in the reflected glow of celebrity was heady stuff. On larger ships, the passenger list always had its quota of important names. Short of remaining in their cabins, there was little their owners could do to maintain their privacy. Pursers were sensitive to any persecution of their eminent clients, and whenever possible discouraged the more insistent boors who could make a crossing unbearable.

Passage down New York Harbor was nearly always auspicious. Astern, the city receded, its glitter cloaked in haze. Attendant gulls breasted the cutting edge of an ocean breeze that came over the bows. The ship passed between Brooklyn and Staten Island through an opening that could only have been called the Narrows. Then a sharp turn to port, into a channel newly dredged at the turn of the century to replace the serpentine curves of the Gedney Channel farther south at Sandy Hook.

This latter had been a natural channel into New York that became increasingly difficult for large steel hulls to negotiate. So a new East Channel was dug, straight to the sea, ultimately named after John Wolf Ambrose. This was particularly appropriate for an immigrant whose success as a contractor in Brooklyn was coupled with a vital concern for New York's waterfront. Ambrose was a rare, avant-garde ecologist who devoted considerable energy to discouraging the practice of harbor dumping. At the end of the channel lay a red lightship with his name lettered on both sides.

Down the ladder went the pilot, clutching the last of the mail under his arm as he stepped onto the bobbing tender. Engine revolutions, reduced for his transfer, were stepped slowly up to cruising speed, a process that would take several hours. Cargo booms were secured, hatches sealed and sea routine begun. For the crew, this meant that double watches, mandatory while in pilotage waters, could stand down. For eastbound passengers in the twenties, sea routine meant the opening of the bar and the start of the crossing.

*Say, when you go to Europe, be sure not
to miss the boat trip!*

                —ED WYNN

8.
On Board

If the time elapsed between this and the previous chapter were a theatrical intermission, the program would carry a notation to the effect that the action was continuous. Yet a subtle change came over the vessel and its passengers: both were in their native element. It was at this point, following departure of the pilot, that bows began their regular lift and fall. I know of no better moment to discuss the only bane of transatlantic travel, seasickness. Charles Dickens spoke for legions of his fellow sufferers when, faint with nausea on the *Britannia,* he penned the definitive symptom: "Not ill but going to be."

Until the early 1940s, when the Royal Canadian Navy pioneered a series of exhaustive tests, no one had done much to investigate the problems of motion sickness scientifically. Steamship companies, acutely sensitive to negative publicity, tended to play down the entire subject. Although they were prepared to install bilge keels, antiroll tanks and stabilizers, very little of their concern was bruited about among the passengers.

Instead, they condoned an attitude of jocular insensitivity to which all but those afflicted cheerfully subscribed. Seasickness was popularly dismissed as a momentary disposition, restricted to small vessels of other lines, that would disappear when passengers "found their sea legs." For those slow to achieve this promised state of grace, there was bemused tolerance bordering on outright ridicule. But then, seasick passengers have traditionally been figures of maritime fun, the butt of endless jokes and a rich source of amusement. One of the most popular comic postcards, sent by the thousand to and from the North River piers, depicted a row of bilious passengers lining the side of a pitching vessel, captioned: "Some of our shipmates made the crossing by rail."

Speaking from a position of painful authority, I am able to state that those cursed with this odious affliction find it less than hilarious. That it produces no permanent disability in no way diminishes its very real discomfort. Contrary to popular supposition, crew members were sometimes seasick too and those originally prone remained so for life. There were varying degrees of susceptibility, ranging from a morning's vertigo to those who began trembling within sight of the pier. When it was the only way to cross, prospective passengers who knew of their shortcomings as sailors used to book only in early summer, while chronic sufferers literally never went abroad. Those whose business made year-round Atlantic crossings a necessity suffered the tortures of the damned.

When that diabolical combination of pitch and roll set some demon to work in the inner ear, when potted palms swayed and trembled, when luncheon ordered moments before seemed a threat, when a hasty ascent from the dining room was hampered by stairs that refused to function properly, then those unfortunate souls sought oblivion in their cabins, immune to all but a heartfelt longing for shore. For my part, I have never seen seamen stringing ropes across open halls, never had the tablecloth dampened to keep the plates in place and never, God forbid, completed a meal from a table with fiddles or edges raised. Long before any of those hideous eventualities, I have retired from the scene, dosed heavily with dimenhydrinate, without which I would no more sail than without my passport.

In the twenties, there was something called Mothersills Seasick Remedy that many swore by. But there were also unpatented remedies to be had for the asking all over the ship, usually offered by those never in need of them. In the smoking room, heavy favorites included a glass of brandy every two hours, champagne, rum straight up or mixed with grapefruit juice, even humble lemonade. From the dining room came prescriptions of grapes, chicken, oysters, raw celery or baked potatoes or, curiously, the total avoidance of jam. But treatments were not restricted to ingestions. There were behavioral cures for every taste: lying down, standing up, staying below, fresh air, earplugs, nose plugs, walking, running, exercising, resting, sleeping, reading, not reading, drawn curtains, sunshine. Some recommended inhaling as the ship rose and exhaling as she fell. One hoary antidote was a bandage about the abdomen to keep the viscera in place, and Dickens' whist-playing doctor prescribed that Victorian cure-all, the mustard plaster. Perhaps the only sound advice came from a wag who recommended eating nothing that you couldn't lift.

Sustained heavy seas raised havoc with catering schedules. Sauces and desserts returned to the kitchen untouched and there was a run on cold meats and boiled vegetables. One chief steward sympathized with but refused a woman who, felled for the duration of a stormy February crossing, requested her unordered allotment of caviar delivered to her cabin the morning of debarkation. Deck stewards counted these days among their most trying, ministering to rank after rank of sudden invalids, their pale faces shrouded in steamer rugs, bouillon congealing untouched beside chicken sandwiches with one tentative semicircle removed. They were the highest tipped servants on the ship, and in rough weather they earned every penny they made.

Seasick passengers were least inclined to find sympathy on German ships. In 1909, HAPAG surgeons announced that sick call was dramatically reduced on board vessels equipped with elaborate athletic facilities. Seasickness became synonymous with malingering, best thwarted by a regime of violent physical activity. From this unshakable conviction emerged a mania for sea sports which spread like the plague to lines of other nationalities. For the British to embrace the idea was understandable—severe exercise was a notorious Anglo-Saxon predilection. But it was extraordinary for the French, traditionally antisport, to subscribe to the same ludicrous hypothesis. The same cumbersome German devices installed in the *Olympic*'s gymnasium had their counterparts on the *France*. So it was that a symptom of Teutonic callousness passed into the realm of Atlantic convention. Even in 1929, when a Dr. Dammert patented an elixir of oxygen and atropine to combat *Seekrankheit,* it was dispensed on the *Bremen* exclusively by deck stewards. In other words, passengers could obtain their two-mark whiffs only if they made it on deck; slugabeds could languish untended below.

The first to pursue the matter of deck games seriously had been the passengers on the *Great Eastern*'s maiden voyage. Prior to that time, diversions to combat ennui were confined by cramped decks to the mental gymnastics of the saloon: spelling bees, quizzes and whist parties predominated. But Brunel's vast ship changed all that. Passengers weary of climbing out on the sponsons to gawk at the paddlewheels set about utilizing seven hundred feet of deck space. History's first midocean marathon was run. One man had brought along a set of ninepins as a joke, little guessing the profusion of deck sports that would follow in their wake. The provision of games on board ship became a universal company fetish that, by the 1920s, had become a deck steward's nightmare.

Requiring more stamina than talent was walking. Five times around most promenade decks was a mile, and this impressive statistic was as indispensable a part of steamship publicity as representations of locomotives driving through funnels. It encouraged passengers who never gave the matter a second thought ashore to become ardent hikers afloat. Year-round, redoubtable enthusiasts would tramp out their rounds, on the boat deck in fair weather and promenade in foul. Purists kept coins in a right-hand pocket, one of which was transferred to the left to mark completion of a circuit.

There was a state of constant war between the walkers, usually vigorous early risers, and the occupants of deck chairs in their path, who had probably been driven from their bunks by the racket overhead. Sax Rohmer, creator of Fu Manchu, used to reel off ten miles daily on the *Aquitania* whenever he crossed. An extraordinary walker was Dr. John Finley of the *New York Times*, who achieved a hundred miles on one crossing. He had struck, at his own expense, a platinum medal in celebration of the event and offered it to a more ambitious successor; but his record was never equaled. The *Queen Mary* carried on her promenade deck a plaque commemorating the occasion when Lord Burghley, the Olympic runner, completed a quarter-mile circuit in under sixty seconds while in evening dress.

Shuffleboard was the granddaddy of all deck sports. The game was derived from the "shoveboard" of Shakespeare's time, played with coins or disks that were "shoved" along a "board" in an attempt to cover numbers at the opposite end. When the game was transferred from land to sea by White Star passengers in the eighties, the etymology was not surprisingly distorted to *shovelboard,* since the maritime version involved the use of shovel-like sticks with which to propel the oversize disks along the deck.

Although quite obviously passengers rather than models, occupants of the *Vaterland*'s gymnasium seem a self-conscious lot as they experiment with the motorized devices at their disposal. (*Frank Braynard Collection*)

The quieter side of German deck sports. First-class children on board the *Imperator* in the midst of a game. At left is a corner of the sand box. (*Steamship Historical Society of America*)

Midocean boat deck, photographed in the summer of 1912 and unchanged to this day. The weather is fine and the *Lusitania* rolls easily. A pair of walkers have just marched through a shuffleboard game. Passengers at left exchange the latest ship's gossip while crewmen in boat number 10 sustain an endless program of maintenance. (*Radio Times Hulton Picture Library*)

A staged bout on the *Berengaria,* supervised by Mason, the gym instructor, in sweater at left. On a later crossing, he served as sparring partner for the Prince of Wales. (*Radio Times Hulton Picture Library*)

Below, one of the *Majestic*'s officers takes on a woman passenger at deck tennis. (*Library of Congress*)

Inevitably, "shovel" became "shuffle" and the game a permanent Atlantic fixture.

For years, the numbers were chalked on deck daily by the crew; it seems not to have occurred to anyone to have them painted there permanently until after the First World War, although chalking them meant that the game could be moved about to accommodate other activities. The length of the court was a matter of contention among the various lines. Those on the *Ile de France* in 1927 were the longest, necessitating a forty-foot shot for gentlemen. Ladies were traditionally permitted to use their own foul line closer to the target. Gridded numbers at either end were laid out so that in any direction, including diagonally, they added up to a total of fifteen. This arbitrary arrangement was all the more surprising in that it had no effect on the scoring itself.

The other great ocean game was deck tennis, played without rackets or balls but with quoits flung back and forth over a badminton-height net. (Beanbags were sometimes used but this was a Pacific innovation that didn't prevail on the Atlantic.) Aficionados of the game, sometimes called tenikoit, became adept at the macaroni shot, in which body English was imparted to the ring as it left the hand so that it wobbled unpredictably and was harder to catch. Blinko, a popular White Star refinement, was played with an opaque net extending down to the deck; opponents could not anticipate the origin of the returned shot. Quoits were also thrown into a bucket, lobbed over spikes on an inclined board and occasionally thrown over the side either in error or fury.

Whatever the deck game, and there were dozens, balls were only used if tethered or confined. Giant Holo, for instance, a brainless struggle to coax a ball through a tunnel with a stick, was restricted by a boxed-in court. The same applied to a German variation called the Mousetrap Game, together with the *France*'s open-air bowling alley and deck billiards on the *Bremen*. A rare exception was an experimental croquet court extending over the *Paris*' sun deck.

There were three varieties of golf. A device with a ball on the end of a cord was provided at which addicts en route to St. Andrew's could swing and swear to their heart's content. There were also driving ranges, complete with canvas walls and fairway bull's-eyes. Universally popular was miniature golf. It appeared on board the big ships prior to World War I, predating the fad ashore by a decade. The impression of size conveyed by a ship that could advertise a golf course on its upper decks made installation mandatory for all ships from the *Olympic* on. It was played with shuffleboard equipment over a tortuous course. Real obstructions such as scuppers, stanchions and people in deck chairs alternated with chalked-in hazards. Until the advent of the *Empress of Britain,* tennis players had to content themselves with Bubble-Puppy or Spiro-Ball, a kind of tennis solitaire played with a regulation racket and a tethered ball.

One afternoon of each summer crossing there was a series of competitive games on deck. These midocean gymkhana inevitably attracted more spectators than entrants, but there always seemed to be enough passengers willing to make spectacles of themselves. On German ships, running races were extended to other decks by installation of canvas chutes strung between companion railings, so that entire circuits of the ship could be made at high speed. Descent of these chutes involved a sitting or kneeling posture that discouraged female entrants. But ladies were invited to join other races— egg and spoon, potato sack, threading a needle and, a curious fixture, the cigarette race. A group of men, each carrying an unlit cigarette, would race from a starting position to female partners who had to light the cigarette with a match, using neither a matchbox, a shoe sole nor any part of the ship. Presumably the only alternatives were the thumbnail, the teeth or the seat of a muslin skirt. It was an inveterate crowd-pleaser, although a writer for *The New York Times* found it "not the least exciting or amusing."

On British ships, there was the biscuit-and-whistle race, in which the winner was the first to whistle a popular air through a mouthful of dry soda crackers. British pursers also offered a piece of dormitory nonsense called "Are You There, Mike?" a battle between a pair of blindfolded opponents who squirmed about on their bellies swatting at each other with furled-up newspapers. Contestants on the *Olympic* tried to dislodge their fellow passengers from the after cargo booms with feather pillows. Like all participant spectacles, these seem nonsensical viewed from afar, but their durable appeal lasts to this day. Deck games that are just as asinine, if slightly more risqué, draw enormous shipboard crowds on Caribbean cruises. During the winter months, there were two great indoor substitutes: ping-pong and, on ships with adequate pools, water polo. This latter was a great German favorite, and national teams competed furiously on the *Imperator*'s maiden voyage.

It was an era, shortly to end, when nearly all shipboard entertainment was passenger originated. There were no social directors and, by mutual consent between members of the Atlantic Conference, no professional cabaret. Radio was in its infancy, talkies a decade away and television a laboratory experiment. As a consequence, games abounded on board, serious ones in the smoking room and endless rounds of charades, treasure hunts, amateur theatricals and competitions elsewhere. Improvisation of

Third-class passengers on the *Homeric* engage in a tug-of-war, the inevitable finale to deck sports. (*National Archives*)

this kind was a tradition on steamships, and made crossings a paradise for children old enough to enjoy it.

On the *France* today there is an adolescent hangout called the *Salle des Jeunes,* a soda fountain complete with jukebox, pinball and shooting galleries. Undeniably popular as it is, there were none of these electronic assists on board ships of the twenties, but in their place, a kind of innocent fun that seems to have largely disappeared. Admiral Lord Charles Beresford, for instance, used to assemble the ship's children in the *Saxonia*'s dining room and tell them stories every afternoon. Lord Beaverbrook's "Rich Uncle" to Princess Zenia's "Fairy Godmother" were not unusual aspects of impromptu theatricals in the *Aquitania*'s playroom. Walter Lord remembers the thrill of finding a treasure hunt clue that had eluded his elders, taped to the bottom of a piece of silver in the *Olympic*'s dining saloon.

On English ships in particular, there was a passion for masquerade competitions that consumed hours of intense preparation. A young officer named Bisset, who rose later to command both *Queens,* wrote an excellent little book called *Ship Ahoy* in 1924 which sold briskly on board many transatlantic vessels. It was full of advice for travelers as well as assorted nautical trivia. Subjects covered included everything from Propellers to Ice Patrol to Fancy Dress. The seriousness with which this latter was pursued can best be gauged by the following quotation regarding sources for costume material on board:

FROM THE OFFICERS: Flags; strips of red, white, blue and yellow bunting; coloured thread and needles for sewing same; oilskin coats; sou'westers; seaboots; white duck suits; brass buttons; uniform caps; telescopes; whistles; revolvers.

FROM THE PURSER: Coloured inks; cardboard; twine; printed notices; paste; glue; paper fasteners; crayons; baggage labels.

FROM THE DOCTOR: Cotton wool; adhesive tape; Red Cross badge; nurse's cap.

FROM THE CHIEF STEWARD: Linen; towels; curtains; table covers; trays; empty bottles; bottle straws; brushes; ship's biscuits; goblets; curtain rings.

FROM THE BOATSWAIN: Rope yarns (for combing into wigs, beards, etc.); lanterns; canvas; broom handles; lifebuoys; burlap; jerseys; knives; sailor's caps; thin wire for stiffening; silver and other paints.

FROM THE BARBER: Fancy coloured papers; hair ornaments; jewelery; slippers; hats; walking sticks; bathing costumes; pipes.

NOTE: A lady's black silk stocking pulled on the head and twisted

Fancy dress competition on the *Mauretania*. The ice-cream wagon is a deck steward's tea-trolley and at least three of the apparent females are male. (*Cunard*)

STOP ME AND BUY ONE

A children's Christmas party in the
Berengaria's dining room. The
young jockey, whose mount is composed of both parents, is about to
win first prize. (*Cunard*)

makes a good Chinese pigtail. Burnt cork is a good method of blacking one's face and is easily washed off. A round tray covered with a flag makes an excellent shield. Curtain rings make splendid Oriental earrings. Wonders can be worked out of cardboard and paper fasteners.

Cunard passengers in need of costume suggestions were advised to dress up as mannequins, witches, brides or Elizabeth Arden. A consistent winner was something called "Spring," a modest but startling assemblage of green chiffon and flowers. In that naïve, pre-Freudian age, gentlemen who won first prize invariably impersonated women, usually French maids or hula dancers.

By the mid fifties, fancy dress was retained on the *Queens* for children only and a Funny Hat Contest was the sole vestige of prewar adult competition. I met an Englishwoman once on the *Queen Elizabeth* who told me that she never traveled without a trunkful of splendid professional costumes for her children. She confessed that when she was a child, her parents had never been prepared for the fancy dress competitions and she was not about to make the same mistake with her own family. Sadly for her, the tradition of improvisation still won out. The winner on that crossing was a magnificent St. George, brandishing a flag-covered tray and a broom-handled spear, his tabard a company bedspread, an inverted saucepan on his head; he slew, many times, a dragon which was in reality his sister, swathed in green crepe paper. But the poor Englishwoman's children didn't even get honorable mention.

Each day promptly at noon, the ship's whistle sounded a long blast. For certain passengers, it served less as a time signal than a summons. From all over the vessel, plum-colored from the Turkish bath, roused from the torpor of a deck chair or a sound sleep in their bunks, these anxious ladies and gentlemen converged on the smoking room. Simultaneously, a messenger arrived from the bridge, with a slip of paper signed by the officer of the watch. Written on it was the ship's noon position and, most vital to the assembled passengers, the number of miles traveled during the preceding twenty-four hours. This number determined the winner of the ship's pools, of which there were always several in each smoking room as well as in the crew's quarters. In all but the first class, they were hat pools, in which players drew or chose a number that could win by matching the final digit of the day's mileage. These simple decimal pools, together with the "anchor pool" or time of arrival at Ambrose Light, are the only surviving ones on the Atlantic today. But the spirit has gone out of the game and bar stewards on the *QE2* are hard pressed to fill a roster of ten among a thousand passengers. It is a sad comedown from the old days when the auction pool, a financial extravaganza restricted to first class, was a daily ritual.

Wagering heavily on the day's mileage grew historically out of the larger gamble that characterized Atlantic competition. It was only natural that a company's intense concern for the performance of a new ship should be shared by the clients she served, all of them anxious to cross as expeditiously as possible. This preoccupation with the speed of passage between continents was such that mileage pools on all steamer routes in the world derived from the Atlantic original. They were an institution on board ship until the airplane made surface speed records academic.

In an auction pool, a field of twenty consecutive numbers was selected, grouped about the ship's mean daily run for that period of the year. The span of numbers varied, of course, from vessel to vessel, but on the larger ones it was in the vicinity of six hundred miles. A score of passengers would each contribute anywhere from five to twenty-five dollars to join the pool and were assigned, by lot, one of the numbers. They could dispose of their number by submitting it for auction; one half of the proceeds realized from this sale swelled the pool and the other half went into the owner's pocket. If his number was near the center and consequently popular, he could quit then, already ahead. But more often than not, depending on the persuasiveness of the auctioneer, he might reenter the pool, bidding on another number that for some intuitive reason took his fancy. Then again, he might bid instead for the high or low field in the hope that the actual figure might lie outside the predicted span.

Of the three passenger chairmen selected by fiat on every crossing, chairman of the auction pool was the one that offered the most challenge. The head of the Sports Committee needed only unflagging devotion to the business of arranging tournaments, while the concert chairman usually had such a glittering reputation that his greatest contribution was often his presence. But the man selected to run the auction pool needed a variety of skills. His talent lay less in chairing than auctioneering. In addition to the respect of his fellow punters, he needed a rapid line of patter, overwhelming charm and a set of leather lungs. William A. Brady was commonly acknowledged as one of the best.

In point of fact, the midday announcement of the winning number lacked the drama of the auction that took place the previous evening. It was a noisy performance that preempted all other activities for a raucous hour or more after dinner. The chairman would thunder for order in a room that had surrendered its dignity for the boisterous exuberance of a commodities exchange. The *Mauretania*'s smoking-room table, supported by an octet of mahogany griffins, had its top damascened by the gavels of three decades of auction pools. Smoking-room stewards took ten percent of the winnings. It was thus in their interest to keep glasses and the atmosphere charged so that auction prices would soar. The pace of the bidding was furious, complicated by the formation of syndicates whose members were out to "corner the center." Pools totaling hundreds and sometimes thousands of dollars were routine and although the stewards justified their cut by holding the stakes, they held them in name only and ended the evening by depositing stacks of bills in the purser's safe.

Participants used to badger the ship's officers about the weather that lay ahead. For heavy investors, it was a quite natural preoccupation. Even a small patch of mist could seriously upset predictions and many a favorite number was rendered worthless when its owner was awakened by the drone of the foghorn. What price then a piece of the low field! Eastbound, if the wind was right, the Gulf Stream often boosted mileage over the estimate.

It was not unusual for bad losers to claim that the pools were rigged, although details of this incredible fix were never forthcoming. As a matter of fact, I would have thought it quite impossible. The number that came down from the bridge was the result of calculations made independently by several ship's officers. Furthermore, its function as vital company statistic, affecting schedules and fuel consumption reports, precluded any thoughts of tampering with it.

Although the auction pool was preponderantly a masculine ritual, the greatest winner of all time was an American woman who won for five consecutive nights of an eastbound crossing on the *Aquitania* in 1923. Her feat generated such publicity that on her return passage, all the ship's gamblers tried wherever possible to duplicate her choice of numbers. Predictably, she never won again. As it was, seamen's charities were a thousand pounds richer as a result of her good fortune.

The New York Times reported recently that cardsharps are working the upstairs lounges of planes carrying the big spenders out to Nevada. It is somehow appropriate that swindling passengers should continue as a tradition of the jet age. The wheel has come full circle and the vehicle that displaced both the train and steamer is evidently subject to the same abuses. But gamblers who made a living on ocean liners, known as boatmen by their land-based colleagues, would probably have been at a loss aloft. Essential to the success of their technique was ample time; they were, in truth, craftsmen of a more leisurely and gracious era.

Shipboard work had a variety of built-in advantages. A cardinal rule among confidence men or tricksters of any kind was never to keep a game going too long in one place. The length of a crossing was ideal—six days that were long enough to find and fleece a sucker and short enough to allay suspicion. There were plenty of rich men on any vessel and casual meetings were, after all, a shipboard tradition. One boatman recalled that the choicest mark was a millionaire from Oshkosh, traveling alone. Passengers on their own keenly appreciated making friends and a lonely, flush "egg" just asking to be "hatched" made an ideal victim.

Conversely, those who fell afoul of these crooks were invariably deceived by a superb performance. Gamblers on the liners were the most sophisticated con artists in the business, with an abundance of ready charm and a style far removed from the riverboat stereotype. The successful ones were cultivated, polished ladies and gentlemen who blended smoothly into the first class. The gambler who, when unmasked by the *Campania*'s purser, grappled with his accuser on the smoking-room floor was rejected by the fraternity as a vulgar amateur.

If they were unrecognized by their fellow passengers, their faces and sometimes their names were often familiar to the staff. Some of them switched identities since a name involved in a previous scandal might tip off booking agents; they kept blacklists of gamblers to whom the company refused service. However, false names involved false passports and, since this was one of the few ways they were vulnerable to prosecution, it was a device used sparingly. Curiously enough, their choice of alias was revealingly naïve, indicating a predilection for "society monickers" that never deceived pursers but made ideal sucker bait for susceptible Midwesterners. One boatman was greatly embarrassed, as intended, when he sat down to breakfast the first morning out. His steward enquired in a loud voice "What name *this* time, sir?"

This was one of the two dining-room breakfasts at which gamblers appeared; the first and the last. In between, they were inveterate night people who slept until early afternoon and seldom left the smoking room before three in the morning. Their first day was spent in pursuit of a mark and they invariably found one by evening. Gamblers always booked deck chairs, tipping heavily for a good one but abandoning it the moment contact had been made.

There was a variety of ingenious ploys for effecting introductions. One man posed as a cleric, ingratiating himself with selected children and fleecing their parents before disembarking in France. (Ostensibly en route to missionary work east of Suez, the bogus parson had never been east of Cherbourg, in which port he remained only long enough to catch the first westbound vessel.) Another traveled with a large silver cup, inscribed with a list of prominent names including his own. It had supposedly been presented to him years before by grateful passengers on the *Cedric,* although the incident that had prompted the award varied on each crossing. This impressive trophy made an irresistible conversation piece and somehow bespoke impeccable references.

Others worked with confederates both male and female. An old gentleman whose hands had long since lost their cunning passed on his skills to a daughter who accompanied him everywhere; the pair of them used to clear thousands. Another Raffles-like character worked with a retinue of flappers who worked a formidable series of confidence tricks, not all of them related to cards. Then again, there was a quartet of sharps whose companion was the notorious Girl with the Waxen Arm, a beauty complete with withered limb who steered a succession of gullible unfortunates to ruin.

All ships had a company rule forbidding gambling. It was universally ignored. The rule remained on the books, in fact, only to protect the company from subsequent action by passengers who seemed determined to play for high stakes with imperfect strangers. Doing so violated one of the most cherished Atlantic caveats. The following rather elaborate flight of fancy is reprinted in its entirety from the *Hamburg-American Gazette* of February 1907:

HIS LIMIT

"Have you ever been made a fool of by a woman?"
"Yes, I'm afraid I'm guilty."
"Have you ever lost money on a horse race?"
"Yes, I'm ashamed to say that I have."
"Have you ever rocked a boat?"
"If I must confess the whole truth, I cannot deny that I once did rock a boat, and while I am at it, let me confess all my shame. I once had a fight over a professional baseball game; this scar over my left eye shows where I was kicked by a mule whose heels I attempted to tickle. There is on a certain hillside a gravestone where lies a boy at whom I pointed a gun which I didn't know was loaded. I have written letters with the request that they should be burned after their recipient had read them, but I positively decline to admit that I ever played poker with a stranger on an ocean liner."

Prominently displayed in all Atlantic smoking rooms were large signs warning against the activities of professional gamblers. On White Star ships there were two, one a general cautionary notice frequently supplanted by another specifically acknowledging their presence on board. When movies were shown in the lounge, the slide flashed on the screen between reels carried the same message. Smoking-room stewards on the *Leviathan* additionally displayed a rule sheet advising passengers never to play poker with strangers, to play bridge for no more than a cent a point and on no account to invite newly made friends to drinks in their cabin. This last was particularly apropos. Contrary to popular myth, the big action never took place in the smoking room. It was merely the scene of endless setting-up games. Gamblers who booked on at the last minute, often in pursuit of a dilatory spendthrift, habitually approached pursers in search of larger quarters. Ideally, they wanted a suite with its own drawing room in which they could play privately.

A classic shipboard setup, necessitating a team of three confederates, began the moment the vessel left the pier. A well-heeled gentleman would lose his wallet, which turned up at the purser's office a few hours later, its contents intact. It had been found on deck, the relieved passenger was informed, by a Mr. So-and-so. The grateful passenger would repair straight to his benefactor's cabin, to find it a large comfortable one with a game of three-handed cutthroat bridge in progress. His host, dismissing his thanks, would urge him to join as a fourth. It was the first of a series of convivial games throughout the crossing, at which the newcomer invariably won considerable sums of money, usually a couple of thousand dollars. Remarkably enough, it never occurred to him that he was being allowed to win, any more than he suspected his partner across the table of lifting his wallet in the crush at the rail on sailing day.

After the ship had docked, the four friends shared a compartment on the boat train for a final game. The rubber ended just as the train was pulling into the outskirts of London, and one of the three original players would propose a quick game of red dog. The mark, his pockets stuffed with winnings, could hardly refuse. In five minutes, it was all over. Dealing from a stacked deck, the team took over twenty thousand dollars from their victim, their two thousand in seed money plus a draft written on a London bank for the balance. This was cashed within minutes of their arrival at Waterloo, before the bewildered sucker had time to think things over. The denouement might take place in a cabin, train or hotel but never in a vessel's public room. Gamblers preferred to administer the *coup de grâce* away from a concerned ship's staff. One man was driven from Cherbourg in his friends' car, which "broke down" conveniently outside Bayeux. During an overnight stay at a hotel, the inevitable final game was played.

This was the pattern of most Atlantic gambling conspiracies. If it seems transparent in the telling, it is only because I have neglected to embroider it with convincing detail. But imagine the hours of jovial play, interspersed with good whiskey and conversation. The careful façade of good will, companionship and flattery, set against the civilized pace of shipboard life, made the whole proposition seem quite legitimate. The skill of the gambler lay more in this critical establishment of mood than in the manipulation of cards. My conviction is that these patient swindlers earned every penny they made. The hypothetical trio whose activities I have detailed above had to deduct their round-trip fares, including an expensive suite, before splitting the take three ways. For a week's intensive work, this was not exorbitant.

Most of the victims kept quiet and absorbed both the financial and emotional loss. Some did not, particularly in the common instance of having lost thousands of their company's money. If they were still at sea, they would appeal to the captain. When Rostron was in command of the *Mauretania,* he grew so familiar with one forced bridge hand that he took the trouble to memorize it. A victim would appear and launch into a painfully familiar tale, at which point Rostron would interrupt and ask if the fatal hand had included the ace, king, queen, jack, nine and one other of hearts. Incredulous, the man would nod. Rostron, with nothing more than bluff on his side, used to confront the cheats and threaten them with arrest when the ship docked. Often, he made them settle for considerably less than the original sum. During his command of both the *Mauretania* and *Berengaria,* Rostron reckoned he had reduced crooked gamblers' claims by over fifty thousand dollars. Another Cunard master used the same technique with even greater success by leaving a large revolver on his desk during the interview, untouched but menacing.

Gamblers had further refinements that were quite common. Having pocketed the bank draft, a boatman would seem to relent, suggesting to the mark that, in the light of friendship, he would settle for whatever cash he might have with him. As soon as the money was paid over (usually the amount the gambler had "lost"), the check would be produced, torn into pieces and thrown over the side. But the little pieces of paper that fluttered convincingly down to the water were quite blank. The original nestled safely in one of four waistcoat pockets, each of which contained a blank check in one of the popular colors. Vastly relieved, the sucker seldom stopped payment on a check he had seen destroyed with his own eyes.

Another gambler used to pull the cash-for-check routine as the ship was being berthed in New York. He would pocket the money and go below to get the check. His victim, as instructed, would wait in the embarkation hall. About half an hour would pass before he realized that his friend was already ashore via the second-class gangplank, through Customs and en route to the bank by taxi. Boatmen traveled light for this very reason, never carrying more than a few essentials in one small suitcase. Stewards could always spot gamblers because they occupied such splendid suites with so few possessions.

There was an Englishman who worked a clever switch on the gamblers. He assumed the role of prize sucker, a foppish baronet on his first voyage desperate to make friends. His performance was impeccable throughout, including a convincing loss on the boat train. But he paid off the cheats with a rubber check and made a handsome profit on the seed money which he had deposited in the purser's safe that morning.

The heyday of the ocean gambler was prior to the First World War when, according to one of their numbers, travelers were less sophisticated. There is a dearth of statistics to refute this, since neither party to a crooked gambling incident ever talked much about it: perpetrators had no wish to publicize their methods and victims were understandably reluctant to elaborate on their dupability. But I am quite sure that every great ship had its gamblers right up to the mid fifties. There was one named Yates who went down on the *Titanic,* after sending a farewell note to his sister in Ohio via a departing lifeboat. There were also some experts who played honestly and made a perfectly legitimate living in Atlantic smoking rooms. On one occasion, a passenger who happened to have won handsomely at bridge overheard on the Cherbourg tender a child's voice piping: "There's the man who took all of Daddy's money!" Perhaps the most outrageous story, which I don't believe for a moment but which bears telling for its extravagance, concerns a bridge game on the *Queen Elizabeth.* A player was dealt an astonishing heart hand, perfect but for a queen of clubs. The smoking-room steward swears that before laying down the hand triumphantly on the table, the player secreted the offending card into a caviar sandwich and devoured it. Evidently no one noticed that he had only twelve cards, nor did the player holding the thirteenth heart intervene; perhaps it was his partner.

Swindlers of all kinds preferred flagships. They felt secure in the anonymity of a large passenger list and there was always a richer clientele. (Everything on the larger ships cost more, even the tips.) Then again, fast ships making more crossings per annum meant a better income, for crooks usually devoted their attention to only one sucker a crossing.

However, philanderers were targets of a seduction-extortion parlay that had the advantage of being repeatable on the same trip. Businessmen traveling without their wives were common enough in those days. Such a man, in the mood for a midocean affair, might find himself paying court to the dazzlingly beautiful and accommodating wife of a fellow passenger. She was alone, she pouted prettily, because her husband was always drunk and never gave her a good time. The flirtation crystallized deliciously into an evening rendezvous at her cabin, the sucker encouraged by assurances that her carousing mate never retired before dawn. But within moments, the gentleman in question flung open the "locked" door, chillingly sober and brandishing a revolver. The passenger, *in flagrante delicto,* was easily persuaded to make out a check in settlement of the affair which had turned hideously, from one of the heart to one of honor. If he balked, it was pointed out that his wife would be apprised of the incident.

It was comparatively easy for a team operating judiciously to duplicate this scheme more than once on a crossing, and very few of these blackmailers were ever caught. One who was had a resourceful "wife" who continued alone during her partner's incarceration. Her solo effort similarly involved the near seduction of an attentive male, dispensing with the role of the outraged husband. Incorporated into the plot instead were notes, a plethora of billets that arrived by steward at the victim's cabin, requesting meetings, solace or advice, in all cases begging the favor of an instant reply. The ardent gentleman unwittingly penned as many light-hearted responses on the reverse side. The final message from the woman was more businesslike, in effect a ransom note demanding payment for the safe return of those that had preceded it. Again, the threat to deliver them to a wife was usually effective.

Curiously enough, ships were remarkably free from crime, considering the thousands of people who traveled on them. Crooked gambling and blackmail apart, the only universal aberration was smuggling, endemic among passengers and crew near the end of any crossing. But this was an offense against authority rather than each other. Crew members were honest for the very simple reason that they had no way of concealing the results of any dishonesty. They all lived within a short radius of the company's home port and any increase in a standard of living, even an extravagant purchase, would not pass unnoticed. Thefts on board were restricted almost exclusively to sailing day when the ship was overrun with visitors whose credentials were impossible to check. Personally, I have never locked my cabin door at sea nor had anything taken from it. Furthermore, I never left anything in the cabin on debarking; stewards were fined a day's pay for any article left behind and as a result their care was always meticulous.

In a caustic little volume he wrote in 1924, *Ship-Bored,* Julian Street advised his readers: "If you ever decide to end it all, there is one humane suggestion I would make. End it all before the ship's concert." It was ironic that the concert, having evolved from a desire to combat boredom, became a means of dispensing it. Self-inflicted shipboard entertainment originated when passengers sought distraction from the tedium of a long crossing. It remained a fixture long after the need had passed. One obvious reason for its continuance was the handsome collection made on behalf of seamen's charities. These amateur variety shows survived into the late thirties, although under increasing criticism from younger passengers. One might almost say that ship's concerts were victims of a generation gap. I purposely use a cliché of our own time to describe a phenomenon that had its equivalent in the period immediately following the First World War. It was a time of defiant experimentation when "flaming youth" were similarly suspicious of anyone over thirty. The obligatory ship's concert of their parents' generation seemed an appropriate target for their scorn. In a larger sense, they were quite right. It was a tattered remnant of a cherished Victorian tradition, parlor histrionics, when an evening's entertainment centered about home-brewed innocence.

Consider the program of an actual second-class concert chaired by a Reverend Roberts on the *Aquitania* in the fall of 1921. Among the offerings was a Song by Mrs. Corndoefer, Comic Patter from Mr. Whalen entitled *Mrs. Whalen's Boy Mike,* a Dance by Miss Celeste Rush, a Pianoforte Solo by Miss May Vrabeck, another Song, "The Trumpeter" offered by Mr. J. D. Coutts, *Some Dry Scoth,* arch Highland buffoonery from Mr. Marks and, as finale, Miss Isabel Brown's celebrated *Whistling Solo.* Bracketed with a Gilbert and Sullivan overture and a brace of national anthems, the evening had everything but an intermission; in its stead were some ponderous remarks from the chairman preliminary to soliciting contributions. This was an archetypal ship's concert. To a generation of moderns obsessed with motor cars, gin and free love, it was tame stuff that seemed a relic of the Dark Ages.

Somehow, it had all worked prior to World War I. In those days, crew members often took part; one of the *Saxonia*'s inevitable star turns was a flute solo from her purser, Jimmy McCubbins. On one occasion, a Boston matron consented to act as his accompanist. McCubbins leaned over the keyboard and asked discreetly for a G. The imposing lady obliged and was instantly enveloped in a white cloud. Someone, he never found out who, had floured the purser's flute, and it wasn't played in public again.

From passengers and crew alike, there were magicians, impressionists, monologuists, instrumentalists and a veritable chorus of sopranos and baritones, all of whom clamored for the privilege of entertaining their fellow passengers. Each turn was introduced by the chairman. This was almost exclusively a man's privilege, although the position was once assumed by Lady Astor. As in the auction pool, the take depended on the chairman's persuasiveness, and one of the best was Charles Schwab, the steel magnate. He crossed frequently on the *Mauretania* and had the knack of documenting, with great humor and accuracy, the personal worth of many of his audience. After analyzing a victim's assets, he would send one of the young lady ushers over to him, suggesting in a stage whisper that she ask a preposterously large contribution; to the accompaniment of roars of laughter, she usually got it. Professionals traveling as passengers were asked to and did entertain. Those whose talents were not suited to the lounge submitted items for auction. Helen Wills' autographed racket went once for two hundred pounds and Chief Black Horse, journeying east with a party of Sioux Indians, put up a spare tomahawk.

In the Depression, impulsive public extravagance of this kind went out of fashion. The talkies had also arrived and, together with bingo and horse racing, supplanted the concert in first class. Racing wooden horses about an oval track to the roll of dice had long been an afternoon diversion on the promenade deck. Now the canvas track was remade in felt and moved indoors as after-dinner entertainment, the bettors black-tied rather than plus-foured. The task of moving the horses on British vessels was always assigned to a blue-jacketed seaman, almost the only time that honest apparel ever appeared in the lounge. Pursers in uniform called the numbers too, a practice that was discontinued on the *Queens* towards the end of their careers. By then, Cunard had put the business of passenger entertainment into the hands of social directors, or at least specialist pursers in mufti. I have always preferred to see the crew involved, to have the ritual of evening recreation somehow fittingly related to the sea. Happily, the tradition continues on the *France* where pursers, resplendent in mess kit and faultlessly quadrilingual, run all the games, and *mousses,* the red-liveried boys in buttons, scurry about moving the horses. Fulfilling at least a portion of the concert's function, a cut of the tote or bingo pool always goes to charity.

For those who missed the concert's aura of nostalgia, the Captain's Dinner was revived or, as the French Line would have it, the Captain's Gala. A painless substitute for amateur vaudeville, it had its roots in the testimonial dinners given by grateful passengers on early steamers once they had reached port. In the twenties, it was never celebrated on the last night as the Germans had done prewar, but one night previous. (First and last nights on the Atlantic were universally colorless, as though spirits were lowest near either shore.)

Passengers on White Star vessels were summoned to meals by music; for dinner, a rendition of *The Roast Beef of Old England*. Here, the *Megantic*'s bugler poses on a wintry boat deck tied up in New York. (*Edwin Levick Collection, The Mariners Museum, Newport News, Virginia*)

Cunard White Star R.M.S. Ascania

Captain C. G. Illingworth, R.D., R.N.R.

⚜

Programme of Concert

(In aid of Seamen's Charities)

IN THE

CABIN WINTER GARDEN

ON

SATURDAY, APRIL 17, 1937 at 9.00 p.m.

⚜

Chairman : Mr. J. H. Cooling

Overture ... "Cavalcade"			*Noel Coward*
ASCANIA ORCHESTRA			
Song ... Selected		...	...
Mr. C. J. PYE			
Piano Selections ...	...	...	...
Mr. A. STORER			
In a Tearing Episode ...	...	...	...
Mr. L. DIX			
Violin Solo ... "Hejre Kati"		...	*Hubay*
Mr. B. MUSKETT			
Legerdemain ...	...	...	...
Mr. J. WHITTLE			
Alleged Comedian ...	...	...	...
Mr. H. GRISDALE			

Chairman's Remarks   Collection

Star Spangled Banner   God Save The King

Although larger and more sophisticated ships dispensed with them, the ship's concert survived on smaller vessels well into the thirties. (*The Peabody Museum of Salem*)

The night of the Captain's Dinner was the occasion for which women hoarded their most elaborate dresses and gentlemen their giddiest behavior. As with all celebrations embellished with paper hats and false noses, photographs seem to immortalize only moments of pointless insanity. In the words of the comedian's depreciatory disclaimer following failure of a joke, "you had to be there." One of the most extraordinary pictures I have of my grandparents, pillars of the Perthshire gentry, shows them sitting solemnly at their table on the *Berengaria* wearing crepe-paper jockey caps and brandishing noisemakers. On French ships, there was the *bataille des cotillons* that started during dinner and raged back and forth between tables throughout the evening. Grinning stewards supplied quantities of featherweight cotton balls, symbols of Gallic abandonment whose accuracy was improved by immersion in champagne.

Later, there were the most incredible ballroom games: improbable dance marathons involving one lady, one gentleman and a turnip; relay races with oranges (no hands allowed); hysterical attempts to burst balloons by sitting hard on a partner's lap. These exercises in total lunacy were dredged up from a purser's bag of tricks on that evening only and perspiring winners were applauded wildly for "being such good sports." It was the same madness that inspired early German deck games, brought indoors and of obvious appeal to older and supposedly wiser contestants. In the microcosm of the crossing's season, it was the *Faschingsnacht* or Midsummer Eve, a time of abandoned revelry. Once on the *Berengaria,* there was a Brigade of Guards captain who, disguised in tails and false moustache, hawked seedy neckties in the Palm Court; two days later, this same man changed the boat train name boards at Cherbourg, discommoding hundreds of his fellow passengers and failing to amuse. But on the night of the Captain's Dinner, even the ship's bore was tolerated and all was idiotic fun, labored in the telling but hilarious at the time.

By the following morning, late-night cleaners had removed the last streamer from the chandeliers and put aside a rich haul of discarded noisemakers for favorite nephews. Passengers regained their dignity and the lounge was restored to brochure perfection. It was the last full day at sea. Although the first glimpse of Bishop Rock was hours away, land was somehow imminent. On deck, the air smelled differently, the water had a strange color and there were gulls overhead. The ship's square came to life again, an inevitable barometer of proximity to port. Pursers retired into black and gold, no longer *compères* but sober guardians of schedules and lists. The baggage master, ignored for the crossing, assumed new importance and as-

HAPPY ON THE *OLYMPIC*

Douglas Fairbanks
april 19/1924
Mary Pickford

Typical of steamer publicity in the twenties. Famous passengers oblige for the company photographer. (*The Mariners Museum, Newport News, Virginia*)

Garbed for disembarkation,
homecoming Americans while away
the time on the *Aquitania*'s promenade deck. (*Radio Times Hulton
Picture Library*)

sured querulous passengers, some for the tenth time, that their hold luggage would join them on the pier.

The longest line snaked back from the teller's window at the bank which became an Atlantic fixture shortly after the war. Its establishment put an end to the purser's perquisite of ship's money changer, a lucrative sideline that was the only legal way these hardworking company servants could supplement their salaries on board. The line moved slowly, for it was here that novices had first contact with a currency other than their own. Dollars were transformed into bewildering handfuls of francs and British coinage pulled at the pockets with an unfamiliar weight. Habitual passengers avoided the crush; they carried letters of credit to European banking houses, together with neat bundles of foreign notes, "porter money," made up for them at their American banks.

In the ship's library, there was a final run on stamps and postcards. In those days, companies stocked first-class writing desks with notepaper engraved "On board R.M.S. *Olympic*," or whatever the ship's name might be. Somehow, a letter headed thus carried enormous prestige and was a far more persuasive cachet than the four-color ship's profiles that followed. Reams of the stuff disappeared, some of it to reappear in the mailbox; the balance went unused into suitcases, to serve until something more elegant could be found in a hotel. Wireless traffic, already burdened with coded victualling requests to company headquarters, grew heavier as passengers dispatched last-minute changes of plan to either shore.

Basil Woon, a contemporary observer of the Atlantic scene, wrote: "I have never begun a voyage yet that I didn't swear to myself that I would do two things: I would rest, and I would work. I have never done either." His experience is not unique. Part of this book was written at sea, and completion of those passages required the most rigorous application. There seems ample time free from intrusion on board ship, but midocean insouciance more often than not destroys disciplines carefully nurtured ashore. This is a traditional malaise and even the most trifling task seems insuperable. On eastbound crossings, ship's clocks are advanced one hour nightly. At least the adjustment is painless, unlike the shock to one's metabolic clock experienced after passage by air. Whether it is this series of abbreviated days or the seductive distractions of shipboard life, I am not sure. But time passes with insidious rapidity and nagging obligations are and always have been cheerfully neglected. In addition to the sachets packed in among steamer clothes was indolence, an incurable virus that retains its potency to this day.

These very clothes were packed away that last day. The length of the ship's alleyways, which when empty revealed the graceful curve of the hull, was obstructed with strapped and labeled trunks. Hard-pressed stewards loaded them onto handcarts and worried them forward to the well deck, ready for transfer to the tender the next morning. This was their hardest day. In between assaults on the luggage, there were chores for the purser: collecting customs declarations and distributing landing cards. Then again, passengers recuperating from the Captain's Dinner seldom got to the dining room before ten the following morning, so that pantry annunciator systems buzzed and flashed with nagging regularity most of the day. It was a morning when whichever button was pressed, red or green, a stewardess most often responded. Spared the gargantuan struggle with trunks, stewardesses did their best to lighten the undiminished housekeeping load for their male colleagues. Cabins inclined to chaos that day, unmade bunks awash in a sea of tissue paper, the very floor an obstacle course of devoured breakfasts, half-opened drawers and gaping suitcases.

Stewards assumed the harried look that was *de rigueur* near port. If they seemed unduly pressed, then so were their clients. There were forms to complete, tips to arrange, letters to write, bills to settle, bags to close. Bon voyage books, which Brentano's used to deliver to the ship in bundles of assorted price, were donated to the ship's library. This tradition doubtless arose because recipients had no room to carry them ashore. Flower arrangements nursed across the ocean went out, their vases stored against the next sailing day. (There were never enough receptacles for flowers and this perennial shortage prompted certain passengers to travel with their own. Lady Elsie Mendl was one of these, but then she carried her own linen and little oddments of furniture as well.)

It was one of the ironies of intense Anglo-French competition of the period that passengers on French ships reached London earlier than their opposite number traveling Cunard or White Star. Conversely, British ships could deliver their people to Paris well in advance of the Compagnie Générale Transatlantique. This apparent lapse in diligence arose from the practice of touching base on the opposite side of the Channel before proceeding to home port. British vessels en route to Southampton stopped at Cherbourg, while French ships bound for Le Havre called first at Plymouth; the Germans stopped at both before proceeding on to Bremerhaven.

That each company chose the westernmost port available to them was no accident. By so doing, they could take advantage of the railway's ability to complete the crossing at a vastly accelerated speed. The ploy had its origins in Cunard's experiment, while still based at Liverpool, of having the *Lusitania* and *Mauretania* call in at Fishguard. This was a relatively minor port on Wales' Pembroke coast. Yet from its terminus, crack trains could

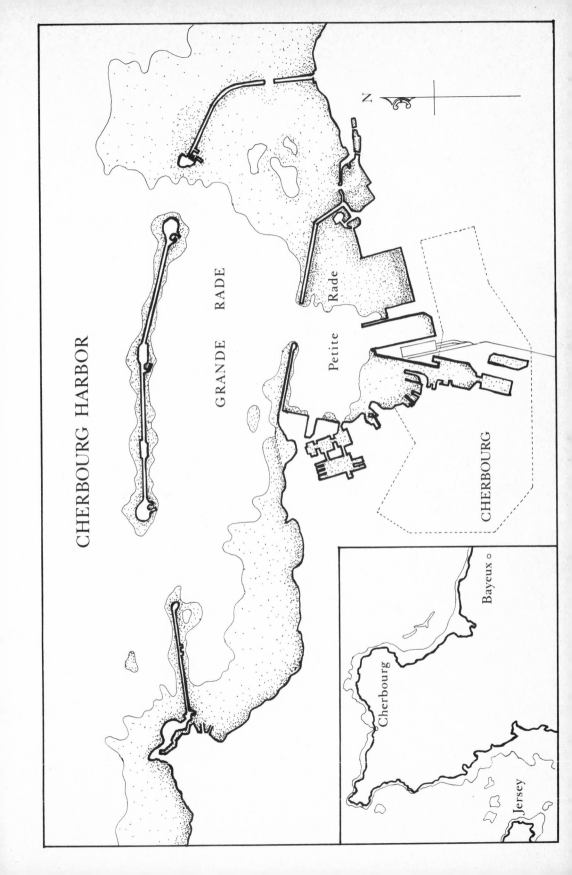

CHERBOURG HARBOR

GRANDE RADE

Petite Rade

CHERBOURG

Cherbourg

Bayeux ○

Jersey

N

have passengers and mails in London long before the ship had docked at Liverpool.

The Hamburg-Amerika Line had been the first to institute a Cherbourg call in 1869. There was no deep-water quay, only a protective breakwater. French Line publicists made much of this inconvenience, pointing out in all their American copy that landfall at Le Havre involved no hazardous transfer to a tender. But despite this disadvantage, use of the port grew and became routine for all British and German vessels. In those balmy days when the balance of payments was not their concern, Cunard was delighted to have as many Paris-bound Americans debark there as possible. "By this route," ran the boldface text in Company brochures, "passengers avoid the much-dreaded Channel passage, disliked even by hardy travelers and good sailors." Cherbourg's real advantage to British companies lay in its superb location. Southampton was due north, only seventy-seven sea miles away. Cunard's only experiment with a double call at a British port came in the twenties, when for a while, the *Mauretania* stopped at Plymouth, Cherbourg and Southampton, all in one day. By the mid thirties, the Cherbourgeois built an enormous iron Gothic terminal which was inaugurated by the *Bremen*. Completion of this elegant facility put the port on an equal footing with their rivals up the coast, *Messieurs les Havrais.*

But in the twenties, before all this grandeur, Cherbourg from the sea seemed little more than a fishing village. It was a splendid first sight of Europe. In terms of strictest accuracy, first contact was near midnight with the sweep of light from Bishop Rock, western outpost of the British Isles and finish line for eastbound attempts on the Blue Ribband. All that final night, in fact, England's south coast glimmered to port. Not till the dawn was there a closeup of the continent. To those making their first crossing, it was a travel poster come to life, totally removed from the concrete metropolis from which they'd sailed. There was the bright green of the Norman countryside, the white and gray houses clustered below the Fort du Roule and, indubitably French, the tuglike craft that came out to meet the ship with the word "PILOTE" lettered on its side.

Once inside the massive breakwater, two tenders (or *tendres,* as Harold Nicolson once punned) came alongside, one for passengers and the other for mail and baggage. Almost half the passengers left the ship. A fragile sense of community was gone; the crossing was over for those remaining on board as well. Stacked with their luggage in the alleyways were giant bundles of dirty linen. Everything on the ship was closed or locked up. Luncheon was taken in the subdued atmosphere of a half-filled dining room. Second- and third-class passengers appeared afterwards, having been given the run of the deserted public rooms. The promenade decks were crowded and, if the weather was good, the upper rails were lined as well. Shuffle-board addicts sometimes finished up a tournament begun two thousand miles back, hatted and suited for shore and looking ludicrously out of place.

If he hadn't already boarded at Cherbourg, the English pilot came on board just inside the Nab Tower. This was the terminal channel marker, Southampton's Ambrose, a Royal Navy relic from the First World War sunk as a substitute lightship; it was originally to have been the first of a series of submarine listening posts extending across the Channel. Trinity House Pilots of the Isle of Wight District could, if companies selected them, serve as pilots of choice. This meant that one man habitually brought specific ships in and out, unlike the New York Harbor pilots who are assigned vessels on a strict rotational basis. The pilot was expected to know the London train timetable by heart, as well as the location of Southampton's best restaurants. If he boarded by tender, he carried with him a set of the day's newspapers and was met by a junior officer who escorted him at high speed to the bridge. It was quite common for the pilot, usually an older man, to fall far behind his brisk guide, still winded from having climbed forty feet of Jacob's ladder up the ship's side. Once on the bridge, his greeting to the master was always: "Are you well, sir? Is there any sickness on board?"

Southampton's excellent harbor, double tide and all, was marred by an enormous shoal called, appropriately, the Brambles. Its position of maximum inconvenience could be duplicated on land by placing an ornamental fountain in the center of the intersection of Broadway and 42nd Street. It complicated the business of getting up to the docks to such an extent that foreign vessels stopped at the Motherbank Anchorage off the Isle of Wight. Even the prestigious *Normandie,* having departed the splendor of the Gare Maritime at Le Havre, used to take on her Southampton passengers by tender rather than waste time docking. British ships bound up Southampton Water followed the Channel's reverse S-turn about the western end of the Brambles, the second half of which was enormously exacting. In daylight at least, pilots had a trick of negotiating the turn when their bearing was such that a visual sighting directly down Cowes' main street indicated the moment to swing the ship about. Once past Calshot Castle, the route lay clear up to Netley and the tugs. There the outward pilot took over, so called because he not only berthed the vessel but ultimately took it to sea again.

Docking a ship in those days was a noisy affair. The pilot had to signal the bow tugs with a police whistle and the after tugs on the ship's whistle. This primitive control system was extremely cumbersome. It was complicated by the fact that the tugs were still coal burning and had to keep a

Left, Southampton in the 1920s. The photograph was taken from the *Leviathan*'s boat deck. Directly ahead of the American ship lies the *Olympic* while across the slip, the *Berengaria* is about to sail. On the extreme left, Cunard's *Aquitania* rests in dry dock. (*National Maritime Museum, Greenwich*)

Below, British Railway Poster of the thirties. (*Museum of British Transport*)

Below left, customs clearance at Southampton Docks, 1937. Passengers, porters, inspectors, constables, Cook's men, representatives from the Savoy and Claridges and inexplicably, a film crew. (*Museum of British Transport*)

SOUTHAMPTON DOCKS
THE GATEWAY TO THE WORLD
OWNED AND MANAGED BY THE SOUTHERN RAILWAY OF ENGLAND

full head of steam up during the entire operation. If the routine of berthing was such that a tug stood by for even a few minutes, the safety valve would blow and steam would roar furiously from the three-inch brass pipe on the stack. Hearing a whistle signal through this appalling racket was impossible and tug skippers had to watch for puffs of steam from the ship's whistle or, if they were working the bow, take a visual cue from a neighboring tug whose skipper could hear.

It was a delicate job at best, fraught with risk that rain and fog often compounded. On rare occasions, there were young passengers with toy whistles who stood under the bridge making their own random signals, blowing conflicting and apparently insane orders to the tugs below. This happened in New York, too, on no less an occasion than the maiden arrival of the *Normandie*. More recently, radio communication and diesel tugs have made the whole matter quieter as well as cheaper. Fewer tugs under tighter individual control now do the job far more efficiently.

There was a final shift in shipboard tempo even before the first lines went ashore. Leave was imminent for many of the ship's people and passengers found only distracted haste in place of the previous week's care. Those members of the crew who remained on board would have no passengers underfoot but might suffer during the day other, more urgent visitors. Time in home port was invaluable. If the scheduling of the New York turnaround seemed pressured, that in Southampton was infinitely worse. There were only a limited number of working hours when maintenance between voyages could be effected within reach of Southampton's technical facilities. Almost the instant the gangplank was down, breasting the tide of shorebound passengers came a swarm of determined men in bowler hats, raincoat pockets bulging with grimy requisition orders. Before the last passengers were gone, cables lay across the carpets, sections of paneling were removed and harsh conferences about drains echoed up and down the passageways. Cleaners, upholsterers, polishers, plumbers, joiners, a veritable army of housekeeping experts that sustained those spotless interiors, scoured the vessel. Any one of a thousand shipboard fixtures—from boilers to music stands to frayed telephone cords—came under their relentless scrutiny. In the lounge, a tuner struggled over the roar of giant vacuum cleaners to put the piano to rights.

Ninety-nine percent of those millions who sailed in and out of Southampton saw at close hand nothing more of the city than the strip of pier between gangplank and railway. During that brief transfer, there were hints of port noises: the hoot of harbor craft, the racket of the cranes and gulls crying overhead. But perhaps most compelling was the particular metallic rhapsody unique to British rolling stock. For Americans whose destination lay to the northeast, Southampton was as much a terminal for trains as ships. In those days, it was a fundamental Company principle that the crossing was complete only after reaching London. Until that moment came, passengers continued under the Company's care, an obligation admirably discharged by provision of a splendid boat train. Before boarding it, there was time for a last glimpse of the ship's profile, at once familiar and remote, which reared over the docks. The ocean passage was over, its only physical legacies a tighter waistband, a passenger list with a few scribbled addresses and a curious sensation that the cement underfoot was afloat.

From the platform, diminutive British trains had a toylike appearance. But the comforts inside were remarkable. Carriages were clean, well lit and charming, the best the Company had, faultlessly maintained. Even to passengers spoiled on board ship, the service on those trains was impressive. They seemed havens of plush cushions, framed sepia views of Bognor Regis, polished windows that could be opened with a broad strap and the best tea and cherry cake in the world. A cavernous fauteuil in one of those cream-painted compartments was ideal in any season. In summer, the vision of lush green country was a perpetual delight, and what better retreat from winter's gloom than the silk-shaded electric warmth of that two-hour race to London?

It was a comforting fact of life that the firm that owned most of Southampton's docks was, in fact, the Southern Railway. Thus there was very real concern for the conditions of trains carrying passengers to and from London. There was even an occasional excursion of a maritime nature arranged by the Company: London trippers who wished to gape at "The World's Largest Ship in the World's Largest Dock" could make a day trip from London to Southampton, seven shillings and sixpence return, to see the *Majestic* in dry dock.

Debarking under Waterloo's grimy vaults was made simpler in that cars could wait right next to platform number eleven. In the cheerful pandemonium of whistles and slamming doors, nimble passengers dashed through pungent coal smoke to collapse in the boxy, leather-lined seclusion of those London cabs. The crossing was done, completed in a series of splendid vehicles that diminished in size but not in character: express liner, boat train and taxi. There were several hours of daylight left, dinner was at hand and all of London's civilized delights lay ahead.

On the *Berengaria*'s passenger list one summer in the mid twenties was a certain Lord Renfrew, in reality His Royal Highness, the Prince of Wales. He was starting what was described officially as an unofficial tour to North

America. Only on the occasion of a White House dinner with President Coolidge would the Prince abandon his incognito. His itinerary included a stay in Long Island's Syosset for polo, a visit to his Canadian ranch and assorted good works. He had come to the United States once before as a naval officer on board a British warship in 1919. On this occasion, he was to travel "anonymously" as a first-class passenger. He was uncontestably the single most famous passenger of the twenties, a distinction he would regain in the forties and fifties.

From the moment that the Palace confirmed the date of his sailing, the *Berengaria* was booked solidly by Americans who sacrificed a few weeks of European vacation for the privilege of crossing with royalty. (When he returned on the *Olympic* in October, the ship was only half full.) Company directors issued a memorandum to the effect that uniforms for officers would include sword and frock coat, finery that had lain undisturbed in Liverpool attics since 1914. Shortly thereafter, the suggestion was withdrawn; one can only assume that Palace spokesmen informed Cunard that the Prince was determined to have no special treatment.

Suiting action to the word, plans for an honor guard and band from Portsmouth were canceled, together with an arrangement whereby the Prince was to have traveled to Southampton by royal train in company with Their Majesties. Instead, he boarded surreptitiously via launch from the Isle of Wight at four A.M., circumventing a hundred reporters and photographers who assembled on the dock later that morning. From on board, His Royal Highness issued a statement apologizing for lack of a conventional embarkation due to fatigue. This disarmingly simple start set the tone for the subsequent crossing.

The last royal occupant of the Imperial Suite in which he slept had been Kaiser Wilhelm II on the occasion of his overnight cruise a dozen years earlier. It was refurbished in the Prince's honor. In addition, the ballroom had been feverishly repainted two days earlier and masses of flowers brought on board to displace the smell of fresh paint. Ship's personnel who might come in contact with the royal party were issued new, albeit regulation, uniforms. Traveling with His Royal Highness were the Mountbattens and a retinue of aides and secretaries.

The following morning, Sunday, the Prince was up early and completed no less than fifteen grueling circuits of the boat deck. Having exhausted a succession of walking companions, he then went to church. Services on the *Berengaria* were held in the lounge, conducted by Captain Irvine who took the opportunity of wearing his frock coat. Those from second and third class, who traditionally worshipped in first on Sunday mornings, were unable to find chairs. The place was packed and the assistant purser who directed the choir reported that in his experience, divine services had never been as popular.

Sunday luncheon was the first meal the heir to the throne took in public. A special alcove had been arranged in the relative seclusion of the balcony but, characteristically, the Prince decided he preferred a neighboring table. It was just as convenient but less pretentious. A mortified chief steward saw his masterpiece transferred in hasty armloads from one table to another. Yet the only concern to which he later admitted was distress at the royal appetite: after all that exercise, the Prince ate nothing more sustaining than some lobster and a grouse wing. The remainder of the day passed quietly, like any Sunday at sea. His Royal Highness appeared neither at tea nor in the ballroom after dinner. Tables full of devastated partners waited in vain, evidently unaware that members of the royal family rigidly observed the Sabbath.

But on Monday, as though in compensation, the Prince embarked on a regime of furious activity. It seemed as though there were two or three royal facsimiles darting about the vessel. Wherever he was attended, he had already departed. He took breakfast in his suite, disappointing dozens of unaccustomed early risers who dawdled over coffee in the dining room. Even before they relinquished their vigil, the Prince had turned up in the gymnasium, throwing himself at every device in sight, pedaling, punching and rowing at a whirlwind rate. He also went three battering rounds with Mason, the instructor, initiating a morning ritual that prompted the royal gloves to be hung on the gymnasium walls for the remainder of the ship's career. Then down by elevator to the Pompeian pool and a brisk swim before miraculously reappearing on deck for bouillon and a further series of breakneck laps that could only be described as a tour de force. His otherwise constant companion Trotter, a gallant old general with one arm, was winded after three turns and was seconded by younger members of the Prince's suite.

That afternoon, a group of Harvard and Yale undergraduates issued a challenge to the royal party, suggesting a tug of war, best two out of three, to climax the next day's deck sports. Lord Louis immediately took up the gauntlet and fielded a team that included himself in the number 1 position, the Prince at number 7 and the portly Counsellor to the British Embassy as eighth-numbered anchorman. Training included workouts with a scratch team mustered from the ship's crew, and it is not surprising that these wise sailors pulled with less than their accustomed vigor. One of these early-morning sessions was monitored by an unnamed American spy. He elaborated to his countrymen on the incredible strength of the Prince's team and the Americans consequently enlisted the heaviest brutes they could find. That afternoon, it was all over in two violent tugs: the British went down to cheerful defeat twice in quick succession.

In spite of his strenuous pace, the Prince did not distinguish himself in competition on board. He was unceremoniously swatted off a pole by an opponent with a pillow and disqualified from another classic race for mislaying his potato. That evening, he won booby prize in the Fancy Dress Competition. Though his disguise as a Parisian apache was successful, other, more dazzling entrants surpassed it. The Prince's talent lay rather in his indefatigableness on the ballroom floor. Whether by accident or design, there was present on board an additional orchestra returning to America which was summoned to play whenever the distinguished passenger appeared dressed for dancing. There was scarcely an evening when the palm court was not heavily patronized by hordes of anxious ladies. The Prince disappointed them, dancing with Lady Louis Mountbatten and the actress wife of Duff Cooper, en route to a part on Broadway. Occasionally, however, an American girl was approached by a discreet aide and subsequently two-stepped blissfully off her feet by the Prince under Mewès' handsome rotunda. It was not uncommon for His Royal Highness to wilt two collars of an evening.

His wardrobe was unusually restrained and disappointed correspondents cabled their editors that he wore nothing more astonishing than a dinner jacket and gray lounge suits. The only item that excited universal comment was a pair of suede shoes. The Prince of Wales was the contemporary arbiter of what is called today "men's fashions," although he was restricted to a limited range of apparel. What pass now for sport clothes were unknown then, at least for men, and it was customary for a game of deck tennis to be played in nothing more appropriate than flannels and rolled-up shirt-sleeves. For a gentleman to appear in something pastel or striped was unheard-of.

Spared the ordeal of U.S. Customs inspection on the pier, the Prince disembarked at Quarantine following a news conference. He transferred to the steam yacht *Black Watch,* thoughtfully lent by Robert Graves. Every passenger crowded the starboard rail and the proud old *Berengaria* listed as if in salute to the departing heir. His crossing had been a marked success and happily free from embarrassment. The Prince's wish to travel without fuss was genuinely respected, affording a rare opportunity to escape the protocol that usually surrounded him. Britain's royal family was far less accessible then than now; for as popular a figure to find even a semblance of anonymity in semipublic was quite remarkable. It speaks well for the re-

His Royal Highness effects a painless debarkation in New York harbor. The Prince can be seen left of center on board the *Black Watch* talking with an officer. His fellow passengers on the *Berengaria* line the rails. (*The Mariners Museum, Newport News, Virginia*)

straint of his fellow passengers and the particular *délicatesse* of shipboard life in the mid twenties. No one misbehaved except for one crestfallen American, who was seen to focus his Kodak during the deck sports and asked instantly to desist by a ship's officer. If any photographs were taken, not one of them was ever published. There were no requests for autographs or any unpleasant manifestations of group adulation.

That westbound passage of the *Berengaria* in August of 1924, so symbolically an epic of the twenties, was both memorable and ordinary. It was typical that the Prince's first contact with America was made on a British ship and that he found a measure of carefree contentment while there. The Atlantic decade following the war was quintessentially British and his debonair good looks and easy gaiety were popular symbols of that age.

One can conclude a look at that era no more fittingly than on the *Berengaria*'s promenade deck nearly half a century ago. It was after midnight the last night out. The public rooms were empty and the orchestra had long since put away their instruments. In the soft light that spilled from the palm court, the Prince and a group of friends sprawled in deck chairs. Conversation was sporadic and from a portable phonograph at their feet came strains of "Dardanella." In the shadows a steward lurked, immobile, caught in a moment's nostalgic peace. Outside, there was an August mist, hinting at a humid New York the following morning. Impervious to regret, the great black *Berengaria* drove through the oily swell, a girdle of foam hissing along her flanks.

Here's to Villar, the France's great purser!
But oh, how much more than a purser you were, sir!
—RING LARDNER

9.
France and
the New Generation

Despite the vast eastbound flow of tourists, no radically new ships appeared on the Atlantic for nearly ten years following the First World War. Those built in the early twenties were small and economical, reflecting a conservative if regretful conviction that the days of the monstrous leviathans had passed. In 1927, however, a new ship flying the tricolor sailed west. She was the famous *Ile de France*.

From afar, she seemed a typical St. Nazaire hull, larger although hardly different from the two ships she joined in service. Before discussing the significance of her interiors, however, it is worth a moment's diversion to examine her immediate antecedents as well as the company that built and operated her. Atlantic steamers have an evolution all their own and discussion of an isolated vessel is misleading. The *Ile de France* belongs in a very particular context, that of the Transat or Compagnie Générale Transatlantique.

Heading the company when it was reorganized in 1861 under its present name were two energetic brothers, Emile and Isaac Pereire. Like the rest of the world, they went shopping for their initial vessels across the Channel, and settled finally on the firm of John Scott. It was no accident that the Greenock yard had also built Cunard's original quartet. The two brothers envisioned a very similar service. They placed contracts for three ships, planning to order others in their own country. But the stiff price per hull demanded by the Forges et Chantiers de la Méditerranée prompted the Pereires to build their own. They found a piece of riverbank near the mouth of the Loire and invited their Scottish builder to supply advice, equipment and cadres of Clydesiders to activate the new yard. Scott accepted and one can only surmise that his contract with the Frenchmen must have been extremely favorable for the company. He was, in effect, providing them with enough expertise to dispense with his services. With only occasional economic lapses, the Société Anonyme des Chantiers et Ateliers de St. Nazaire, Penhoët has flourished ever since.

From this bold opener, the French Line established a tradition of building their own vessels. I would suggest that this arrangement, unique among Atlantic companies, has contributed much to the success of the Transat over the years. Although denied the economies of competitive bidding, they were afforded a unity of design and execution. The relationship of shipowner to shipbuilder is a delicate one at best. In Britain, the special understanding that existed between the White Star and Harland & Wolff was exceptional for its durability and cordiality. Elsewhere, harsher terms sometimes prevailed. It was a fixed policy of North German Lloyd, for instance, to delay final acceptance of a liner until after the maiden voyage. This meant that a vessel's performance had to be consistent throughout an ocean voyage under service conditions rather than two days of trials. In 1897, the *Kaiser Friedrich* became one of these rare but embarrassing refusals, "declined with thanks" and returned to her builders as too slow. She languished for fifteen years at a Hamburg pier before a French company picked her up for a song and put her in trade to South America.

The French Line's home port is Le Havre, originally a fishing village at the mouth of the Seine. Work on its harbor began under Francis I and has not stopped since. Unlike its cross-Channel rival, there is no protective Isle of Wight and no monstrous shoal. Nothing impedes the swift entrance and departure of ships. Today, it is the proud boast of the Port Autonome that they can handle any ship, any day, at any time. But in the early twentieth

THE ONLY WAY TO CROSS

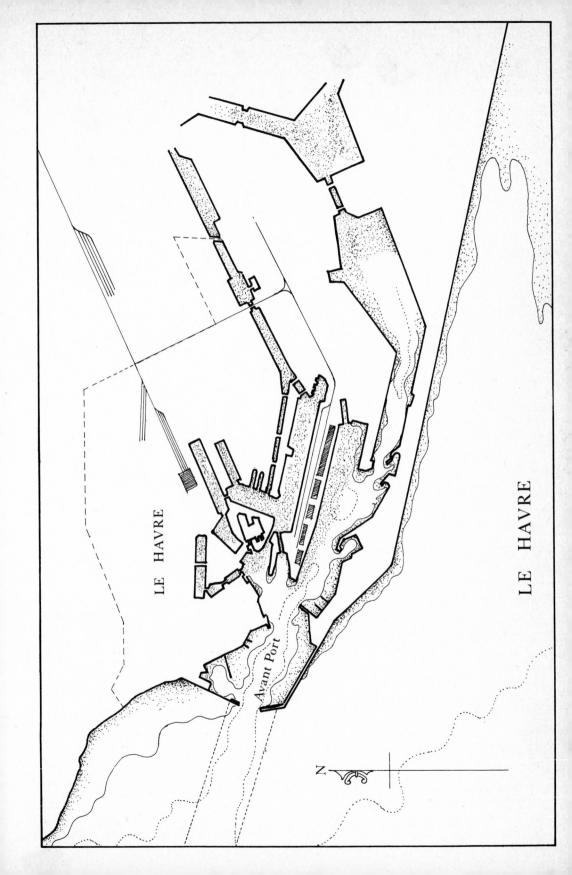

LE HAVRE

LE HAVRE

Avant Port

The sea wall at Le Havre. The French liner *La Provence* sails through a Channel storm into its home port. (*Compagnie Générale Transatlantique*)

century, there were restrictions on the size of vessel Le Havre could accommodate. In the tonnage race that followed the debut of the *Lusitania* and *Mauretania,* the French Line had to limit the displacement of their entry.

She was laid down at Penhoët in April of 1909 as *La Picardie,* in line with a Transat policy prevalent at the time of naming vessels after provinces. Sometime before her launch exactly seventeen months later, the name became *France.* This was a thoroughly appropriate change. The new ship had not only twice the tonnage of any French vessel previously constructed; she was also their first (and only) four-stacker, their first turbine ship and the first to be equipped with quadruple screws. By coincidence, the original *France* was due for demolition that same year. She in turn had been the first paddle-wheeler that Scott and his Greenock shipwrights had launched into the Loire, with forty-five years of service to her credit.

The new *France* was to be engined by her builders under Parsons' license. Experiments on smaller vessels led French engineers to add their own refinements and they constructed the first triple-expansion marine turbine. Her stern frames were cast in Budapest when British foundries quoted an exorbitant figure. How those vast steel castings reached the Loire confounds the imagination. Yet the hull was completed on time. It is interesting to compare French building techniques with the enormously more sophisticated facilities of the northern British yards. There were no overhead structures, few cranes and certainly no elevators for workers to reach the upper decks. Penhoët-built ships to this day seem to rise miraculously from the very mud of the riverbank.

A year and a half after her launch, the brand-new vessel was pulled gingerly through the narrow passage leading from the Bassin de Penhoët to the sea. There was none of the *Mauretania*'s dashing rake about her. The *France*'s four funnels, identical in size to those carried by her smaller predecessors, seemed lost on the greater length of her hull. They were crowded forward in a way that gave the ship a slightly unbalanced look. Aft of number 4 was an expanse of featureless superstructure that continued almost to the counter, as though the after hull had been stretched. Between bow and bridge, her upper strakes were painted with an abnormally wide white band, a feature that served to identify her from miles away. Inadvertently, it achieved a *trompe l'oeil* by apparently lessening the height of black hull below and creating the illusion of a lowered freeboard. All British four-stackers conveyed an impression of overpowering verticality whereas the *France* was emphatically horizontal, diminishing the towering effect of her funnels to produce a long, low look that was quite singular. Embodied in the ship's appearance was a subdued yet powerful dignity.

If her exterior profile was subdued, her interior spaces knew no such modesty. She was to be called the Château of the Atlantic; "Palais" might have been more appropriate. In executing the public rooms of her HAPAG rivals, Mewès adhered to the relative tranquility of Louis XVI. Designers of the *France*'s interiors embraced without hesitation the lavish opulence of Louis XIV. Into her seven hundred feet of hull were packed more gilded paneling and ormolu encrustations than had ever floated before. The expense was astronomical. It was commonly acknowledged by all who saw her that, pound for pound, the richness of her appointments exceeded those of the previous year's *Olympic* by a good margin.

I doubt that any craft since Cleopatra's fabled barge knew such visual extravagance. In the *salon de conversation,* Rigaud's portrait of the Sun King, faultlessly duplicated from a Louvre original, gazed the length of the room at another likeness detailing his return from the hunt. To keep him company in that ornate chamber were portraits of Madame de Maintenon, the Princesse de la Tour and other court favorites stunningly reconvened in this maritime Versailles. Each fauteuil, although faithfully reproduced from those he favored, carried unfortunate antimacassars that he would not have.

A correspondent from the *Marine Review* tried in vain to put it all in perspective: "the main impression aimed at will be one of simplicity, but of calculated intent." "Simplicity" seems a massive understatement for that orgy of Louis XIV, and the "calculated intent" was surely to stun impressionable Americans with an overkill of grandeur. All was curves and flourishes, including an oval embarkation hall and sweeping staircases modeled on the grand entrance to the Bibliothèque Nationale. Aft of the *Salon Mixte* was the celebrated *Salon Mauresque*. Moorish corners, a pervasive North African rage, were immensely popular in France at that time. From a white marble fountain trickled a stream of perpetual ice water in subtle response to an epic American demand. Each evening, balloon-trousered stewards dispensed Turkish coffee.

The smoking room was, curiously, as disappointing as those on the splendid Hamburg-Amerika liners. One critic has described them all as representative of the Alpine Hotel Lobby School of Architecture, redolent of Tyrolean *kitsch*. Oddly enough, smoking rooms on British ships were, by comparison, quite imaginative. This was in contradiction to the supposed predilection of Anglo-Saxon males for somber leathers and woods, enlivened by occasional glints of brass. However, this clubland stereotype obtained on neither the *Olympic* nor *Mauretania,* although an attempt at it was a consistent aberration on continental vessels.

The *France*'s magnificent dining room extended upward through three

decks. ("Low ceilings don't aid the appetite" admonished Company literature; this piece of gratuitous nonsense was nothing but a dig at the *Olympic*'s
single-story saloon.) The lower end of the main staircase debouched triumphantly into the room, a finale for what French naval architects call *la
grande descente*. This seemed appropriate in view of the expectations with
which passengers on vessels of the Compagnie Générale Transatlantique
approach the dining table. One could hardly sweep down the sinuous curves
of that glorious double staircase without the sensation of entering a temple.

Dining on French vessels ever since has entailed this ritual descent
within the *salle à manger*. Some dismiss it as a fashion show, an outlet for
passenger vanity. I think it is all part of an attitude toward food. Concern
for the preparation of a meal is a national fetish monopolized by the French
and Chinese; to find that there is an equal preoccupation with its consumption is hardly surprising. The French excell at presentation, and I think
that there is a strong connection between the presentation of a superb meal
and the presentation of those who are about to eat it. Passengers on the
QE2, for instance, enter the dining room practically on one level, slipping
inconspicuously into their seats at a table devoid of inspiration. Even their
most timid contemporaries on the *France* were obliged to effect a ceremonial entrance, center stage, down to a meal acknowledged as one of the
world's finest.

The *France* sailed on her maiden voyage in April of 1912, arriving in a
New York still stunned by the loss of the *Titanic*. She was a fast ship, second only to the two Cunard record-breakers. Despite the French sailor's
maxim *"Bon rouleur, bon marcheur,"* her stability left something to be desired. Following that inaugural season, her bilge keels were lengthened. At
the same time, two new propellers were installed on the inboard shafts and
vibration was also reduced. Following these improvements, I would hazard
that the *France* came closer to that elusive Atlantic combination, a fast and
luxurious ship, than any of her prestigious rivals. With her low profile and
solid construction, she handled well and her comfort was legendary. Of
course, she had no pool or squash court, none of the White Star extravagances soon to be duplicated by her German competitors. But then, the
France was far smaller than any ship we have discussed thus far, with a
gross tonnage of only twenty-four thousand tons. Despite these limitations,
she was immensely popular and the Company laid down a companion ship,
the *Paris,* two years later.

I have avoided calling the *Paris* a sister ship for the very simple reason
that she was not. The Compagnie Générale Transatlantique exhibited a firm
distaste for identical vessels. During that hectic period before the First

World War, when British and German companies scrambled to build trios of identical liners, the French desisted. When the *Paris* went into service in 1921, she was a different ship altogether from her predecessor. I can only assume that this curious reluctance to duplicate was tied somehow to the limitations of Le Havre, that the French were hesitant to commit to a series of identical ships at one time when, by waiting, improvements in harbor facilities would permit something more ambitious.

In support of this hypothesis, the tonnage of succeeding flagships progressed regularly, seemingly geared to no other factor than the growth of the port. The *Paris* grossed ten thousand tons more than the *France,* an edge that she lost by the same margin to the *Ile* six years later. This unique building philosophy cut both ways. A traditional three-ship service wasn't achieved until the late twenties, and then only by accident. The service maintained up to then by the *France, Paris* and *De Grasse* was not without its disadvantages. The British-built *De Grasse* was, in reality, an intermediate ship whose maximum of seventeen knots was only two thirds the service speed of her two larger partners. In any event, the French were not preoccupied with classes; they never built groups of sister ships and had none of the German or British fixation about balanced trios. Between the wars, a large ship sailed every Wednesday, and in high season a smaller one departed also on Saturdays.

There was one enormous advantage to the system. Passengers were prone to "try" a new ship, an affectation on which the Compagnie Générale Transatlantique was in a unique position to capitalize. The new voyagers of the twenties had been denied the thrill of crossing on a brand-new liner. Cunard's big three, the *Mauretania, Aquitania,* and *Berengaria,* were handsome and compatible running mates but by 1927 were beginning to show their age. They were all prewar ships, decorated to the tastes of an era that grew increasingly remote. So, too, White Star's tonnage was, if eminently serviceable, very much last year's model. It was into this vacuum of topicality that the Transat committed their glistening *Ile de France,* their Now ship of the twenties.

As she was due to leave St. Nazaire for dry-docking at Brest, there was a near disaster. Something went hideously wrong with the turbine controls just as the *Ile* cast off from her berth. Despite frantic signals from the bridge, forty-three thousand tons of liner drove steadily towards a closed drawbridge. Mercifully, it opened in the nick of time, thanks to the quick-wittedness of the port lieutenant. Captain Blancart guided his runaway vessel between the stone quays, only eight feet wider apart than the hull. Halfway through, the engineers finally got astern power and the ship was

The *France*'s first appearance in New York. The *Titanic* had sunk a month earlier, as the profusion of life rafts would indicate. (*Compagnie Générale Transatlantique*)

Proud and aristocratic, the Transat's *Paris* was the French postwar flagship until the advent of the *Ile de France* in 1927. (*Collection Michel Eloy*)

The main lounge and dining room of the *Ile de France:* choices made in a concerted effort to begin anew. Despite the excesses, the ship set decorative precedents that last to this day. (*Compagnie Générale Transatlantique*)

stopped. It was chillingly similar to the *Vaterland*'s control failure when she left New York in mid-maiden voyage.

There were some who felt that the French had overdone things. Words like "hectic" and "gaudy" leapt to mind. Her original interiors do not appeal to me, but then much of the twenties doesn't either. Although the source of an apparently inexhaustible supply of nostalgia for many, I have always thought of those years as essentially a reckless, vulgar decade on both sides of the Atlantic, ending with a frightful hangover.

But the *Ile de France* appealed to those whose business lay on the opposite side of the ocean. She was an instant success, neither the fastest nor largest but certainly the smartest. Eclecticism was dead; there was almost no panel, fabric, railing or motif identifiable with an earlier age. John Dal Piaz, Transat head at the time, had laid the ground rules: *"Vivre ce n'est pas copier, c'est créer."* Guided by this bold credo, his design staff set to work. What emerged was a riot of Establishment Modern, an extension of the International Paris Exposition of 1925, packaged in a conventional hull and delivered to New York.

In the lounge were two score columns, classicism's last gasp. But they were devoid of traditional capitals, lacquered blood red and clustered about the walls in groups as if recoiling in alarm from a blatant geometric carpet. From this monstrous Aubusson sprouted chunky club chairs upholstered in vibrant chintz. It seemed less a *salon* than a hothouse, an impression reinforced by the coffered vaults above. Lighting on the *Ile* was nothing if not indirect and from this ghost of a skylight came a pitiless tropical glare. Less frantic, but monumental, was the entrance foyer. Four decks high, one ponderous arch after another, it was strongly reminiscent of the lower level of New York's Grand Central Station.

This penchant for the colossal was manifested most painfully in the *salle à manger*. Although the largest afloat, it was a hollow triumph; sheer cubic capacity, a novelty twenty years earlier, had no real validity any longer. There was no balcony and all seven hundred in the first class were summoned to one enormous sitting. In place of conventional grandeur, they dined as though on the bottom of an empty municipal swimming pool. Rather than minimize the dimensions, every effort had been made to glorify them. No detail relieved the acres of marble sheathing, not even the rectangular lights that marched overhead as if in step with the rigid formation of tables below. All that broke the rectiserial monotony was an oval Arcadian landscape, hideously overscale, that hung menacingly over the captain's table. In the center of the room was an imitation fountain, its "waters" immobile chromium tubes lit from below. This introduced a favorite shipboard confection of the thirties; there was one in the *Bremen*'s ball-room two years later. The total effect was uncomfortable and overpowering, a preview of the architectural brutality that Europeans of a subsequent decade would call Mussolini Modern.

Illumination elsewhere became an elaborate game: where to hide a light. Tulip or urn, oversized receptacles abounded, each concealing a flood-light directed overhead. In the lounge, it was an apparent conceit that sources of light should remain anonymous; there wasn't a bracket or lamp-shade anywhere in sight. Would that the statuary had been as invisible: The French had always had a weakness for shipboard sculpture. Mirror pediments on *La Lorraine* were supported by a pair of massive caryatides, and on the *France* Nelson's *La Belle France,* modestly draped, occupied a niche on the staircase. But on the new ship, blatant nude groups dominated the public rooms. In the *salon de thé,* a group of three—male, female and stag—even had a sofa incorporated into the plinth that supported it.

Besides a profusion of molded glass and lacquer, there was new application of a traditional material. Wood was everywhere, not the meticulous carving of the *Mauretania* but sheets of veneer that creaked and drummed in midocean. This was such a chronic failing on the *Ile* that most of it was reinsulated during the following winter. In the cabins, brass beds were a thing of the past. The partial bunk was back, sheathed in exotic marquetry. Other woods were tortured, steamed and varnished into blunt-cornered tables topped by frameless oval mirrors.

I don't wish to convey the impression that such interiors were necessarily in advance of tastes on either shore. It was only remarkable to find them established wholesale on board ship. The *Ile de France* was the great divide from which point on decorators reached forward rather than back. No matter what my reaction to those garish rooms, I am forced to acknowledge that they served as models for generations of succeeding vessels. It was the end of period revival.

The new hectic gaiety had no more nautical validity than a Tudor dining saloon but it served as just as unremitting a floating cliché. Gone were plaster ceilings, iron railings and stained glass; gone too, the richness of the *Berengaria*'s paneling, the cool elegance of the *Leviathan*'s winter garden, the cozy teatime fire under the *Aquitania*'s Adam mantel; gone forever the bobbles, tassels and fringes that danced and trembled to the faint music of the turbines. The potted palm was displaced by frozen glass cascades, the string orchestra by muted cornets and the peace of the smoking room by installation of a gigantic bar.

The *Ile de France* had, in fact, twenty-seven feet of bar, an Atlantic record indicative of French solicitude for their parched American clients. In terms of decor, the smoking room was the least frenetic of the promenade-deck public rooms, and its size was inadequate for its popularity. It occupied two levels, and the balcony extending up to the boat deck was open to the stern. When the ship was redecorated in 1932, yet another floor was incorporated across the after end of the sun deck, according the *Ile* the dubious distinction of having the first and only triple-decker smoking room on the Atlantic.

Following this thirties renovation, the space was no longer called a *fumoir* but, more pretentiously, the *Grand Café,* with its topmost level christened the *Café Terrasse.* Due to its exposed position, there was no attempt to make it open to the weather. It was a most delightful little aerie, only twenty feet deep but spanning the full width of the ship.

If the view over the stern was incomparable, it didn't help the ship's profile at all. In fact, the *Ile de France*'s superstructure island had an odd reversible look, as though the *Café Terrasse* were somehow a smaller bridge facing aft. Yet one point must not be lost to the social historian. Smoking-room business in the twenties was so brisk that such an enlargement was essential, even at the expense of valuable space on the sun deck. No matter how the Company might hint at the elegance of their new addition, its raison d'être was quite simply the phenomenal American thirst. One brochure rhapsodized that the little room was "athrob with international repartee." I suspect it was athrob with nothing more than potential cardiacs; bar stewards on the ship must have had incredible stamina to keep pace with a party of serious topers on that third story.

Among the dozens of liners that have sailed the Atlantic within living memory, only three have achieved a kind of maritime canonization: the *Mauretania, Ile de France* and *Queen Mary*. These ships were naturals from the moment they entered service. In common they had a curious blend of prestige, glamor and ambience that created strong passenger affection. Loyalty of this kind cannot be generated artificially. Passengers are easily persuaded to book on a new vessel, but converting that initial novelty into a sustaining preference was a function of the ship rather than promotional diligence. Of course, traditional appeals were always highly marketable: both the *Mauretania* and *Queen Mary* were record-breaking ships and, at the time of their maiden voyages, among the largest in the world.

How then to account for the durable attraction of the *Ile de France?* Though her radical interiors were certainly memorable, that kind of sensational chic is usually short-lived. Besides, the impact of her decoration is seen best in historical perspective, and the *Ile* was popular from the start.

Incredibly enough, no champagne was broken across the bow of the *Ile* when she was launched in March of 1926. Such an omission seems singularly inappropriate for the vessel that proved so popular to thirsty Americans. Below, fifteen months later, she sails for Le Havre and New York. (*Frank Braynard Collection*)

The Department of Police and Sanitation's band crowds into the cutter *Macom*'s bow to serenade the newly arrived *Ile de France* at Quarantine. (*Frank Braynard Collection*)

The French Line never built sister ships. Although the *Paris* and *Ile de France,* below, may seem similar at first glance, the differences in tonnage, speed and, most significant, interiors were considerable. (*Compagnie Générale Transatlantique*)

Excellent food was, of course, a stable attraction. Overeating is the most popular Atlantic sport and clients of the French Line have always abused their digestions to perfection. It is worth repeating here that, apart from the *Normandie,* no liner of the Compagnie Générale Transatlantique has had a supplementary restaurant. Passengers were more than content with standard first-class fare, although it is a happy fact that French chefs seldom produce a "standard" meal.

I think that the *Ile de France* was perhaps the floating incarnation of a consistent American fantasy about France and the French. Just beneath the American consciousness was an unshakable conviction that France, or more particularly Paris, was the sin capital of the world; not biblical sin but momentary and forgiveable deviations from the norm, closely akin to the acceptable indulgencies of a night on the town. This was a perennial Anglo-Saxon myth that outweighed all other considerations for both the American Expeditionary Force of 1917 and the tourists who followed them in the twenties. Paris meant not the Louvre or Versailles but naughtiness, a heady synthesis of champagne, dirty postcards and Mademoiselle from Armentières. Lurking in the background were the ghosts of de Maupassant, Lautrec, Offenbach and whichever impresario invented the indecorous cancan.

In the 1920s, even the mention of "Paris" in middle America elicited a snicker and only "French" was a sufficiently lurid prefix for mass-produced pornography as well as sexual adventurousness. It was no accident that a secret compartment, concealed under the center drawer of a famous American make of trunk and common knowledge to U.S. Customs, was of identical dimension to the slim green volumes of the Olympia Press. Parisians have endured a surfeit of Americans in pursuit of erotica, a condition that explains much of their jaded attitude towards us today.

Oddly enough, the situation is now reversed, and collectors of pornography or aberrant behavior make a far richer haul in New York than in Paris. Yet despite this, the lure of Parisian *ohh-la-la* continues even among the French. Montmartre is as crowded with provincial tourists from Périgord as from Pittsburgh. Americans have consistently misunderstood French society which, as if in compensation for the upheaval of 1789, is suffused with a rigid morality quite as intense as anything in our own Bible Belt.

But to those embarking on their Grand Tour in the late twenties, the *Ile de France*'s mood was both appropriate and irresistible. She was the original whoopee ship, symbolizing an abandonment that was unthinkable in the pompous authenticity of the *France.* The absence of traditional frills and the relentless modernity, coupled with the seductive Parisian dream, guaranteed her success.

She outgrossed all her competitors that inaugural season and remained a consistent moneymaker throughout her life. The timing of her appearance was impeccable. Had she sailed into the Lower Bay after the crash of '29, I doubt that her bizarre showiness would have caught on. But although she was a creation unique to the twenties, her popularity transcended the economic disaster that ended them. She survived the slump of the thirties and a world war and lasted well into the postwar years. Like the *Mauretania* and *Queen Mary,* she was in service for three decades.

The Germans were not far behind. That they were in a position to reenter the Atlantic lists by 1929 says a great deal for their astonishing recuperative powers. They had emerged from the humiliation of defeat with no merchant marine and in the early twenties knew only severe economic distress. Hamburg and Bremen were cities of unemployment, crippling inflation and political unrest. Herbert Hartley, who ultimately commanded the *Leviathan,* arrived in the port in 1919 carrying a cargo of lard. The crossing had been rough and several hogsheads had been fractured. Yet so critical were local food supplies that German stevedores brought crusts of bread to the piers and soaked up the stuff from the bilges.

Yet in the fall of 1926, North German Lloyd placed orders for a pair of express liners that would reestablish a premier German passenger service on the Atlantic. The two ships were to be called the *Bremen* and *Europa.* (Ironically, Ballin's pet name was finally used by his German arch rival.) The former was laid down in the A. G. Weser yard in Bremen, while the latter was awarded to Blohm & Voss of Hamburg. It was 1907 in reverse; an intense German effort to overcome British supremacy since the war, an unspoken but determined effort to win back the Blue Ribband.

This coveted Atlantic award is not something that a new ship just happens to win. As I mentioned in connection with the *Mauretania,* it represents a massive company commitment. If the prize can be taken on the maiden voyage, it is a dream come true. Like the actor and his Oscar, advantages accruing to the recipient are sometimes intangible but historically invaluable. Passengers seldom book on a vessel merely because it crosses in a few hours less time. They book because the ship is famous, and even figuratively flying that glorious blue banner from the main truck makes for fame. Companies never announced they were in quest of it, even though trials indicated that they could have. In point of fact, most were at pains to deny it. Failure to achieve a predicted crossing time, even if only because of poor weather, would be intensely embarrassing as well as damaging to the ship's image. So mid-twenties company ethics dictated an apparent lack of concern for that ancient and much-envied honor, perhaps the most famous award for speed in the world. Architects, engineers and owners might work for it with manic fervor, but this was never a matter of stated policy. But the *Mauretania* had held and improved her record for more than two decades and it was quite apparent to the Atlantic shipping fraternity that the Germans were out for blood.

If there was ever any doubt about it, spectators at Blohm & Voss' launch of the *Europa* were quick to dispel it. Incorporated into the lower forward strakes was an incredible bulge, as if some giant had inflated the steel plating. Even the most unscientific among the onlookers could not fail to be struck by its radical appearance. It was the recent invention of a man called Taylor, an American admiral. Although nothing seems less probable, a bulbous bow lessens the water resistance of a hull. The bow wave thrust up on either side of a conventional cutwater makes for a brave effect but United States Navy tests indicated that the resultant eddies along the ship's flank reduced speed. In simplest terms, the bulbous bow makes a better hole in the water for the hull to slip through. The *Bremen* and *Europa* were the first great merchant vessels to take advantage of this innovation, commonplace today.

More knowledgeable observers who had time to inspect the *Europa*'s hull before the American Ambassador sent it down the ways noted two other experimental features. The butt edges of the overlapped plates faced forward rather than aft, and at the stern hung a streamlined Oertz rudder, aerofoil in section and supposedly better adapted to high-speed maneuvering. The German builders were preoccupied with reducing drag. While Cunard's great breakthrough twenty years earlier had revolved about steam turbines, North German Lloyd was profiting by recent hull refinements.

The *Europa*'s launch was without incident but her fitting out was not. In March of 1929, she was nearly destroyed by fire before she even left her berth in Hamburg. At three o'clock in the morning, the blaze was discovered by a night watchman. Fanned by high winds, it spread rapidly. Shortly thereafter, it was quite apparent that the yard's detachment could not possibly contain the fire and Hamburg's municipal equipment was called in. Within minutes, the same massive pumper used to test the *Imperator*'s inner skin was now engaged in pouring tons of water into the blazing *Europa*. The results were predictably similar to those following the *Imperator*'s fire in New York. However, there was one important distinction. At the time of the Hoboken conflagration, the Kaiser's new merchant flagship was fully manned with a crew that knew the vessel and could operate the extensive fire-fighting equipment embodied in her design. The *Europa,* although

Manhattan piers in the late twenties. From left to right: *Britannic, Olympic, Leviathan, Pennland* and *Paris*. The *Britannic*'s low profile contrasts sharply with the *Olympic*'s towering height from two decades earlier and gave the Germans their inspiration for the *Bremen* and *Europa*. (*Radio Times Hulton Picture Library*)

A year after the *Bremen* had taken the Blue Ribband, the *Europa* makes a belated appearance. Shown here steaming down the Elbe, the North German Lloyd ship had burned and sunk during her fitting out. (*Author's Collection*)

nearly completed, was deserted during the night. There was no one on board except a team of watchmen who, having discovered the blaze, were powerless to combat it. Ships caught in the unmanned limbo of fitting out or conversion are particularly susceptible to fire damage. This same vulnerability accounted for the disastrous plight of the *Normandie* in 1942.

With no captain or crew to discourage them, the Hamburg fire fighters swamped the vessel. At ten the following morning, the starboard list was so acute that the ship was evacuated. By some miracle, she did not capsize; if her funnels, masts and boats had been in place, I think she would have. As it was, the ebbing tide deposited her upright next to the pier. The fire was extinguished later in the day and the proud *Europa* sat in the harbor mud with scarcely three feet of freeboard at the well deck. Her upper works and most of her interiors were ruined and it would take an additional year's work to put her in service. There had been a bitter three-month strike during her construction and although arson was suspected, it was never proved. Thus it was that the *Bremen* assumed the limelight intended for her gutted sister ship. To this day, one speaks of the *Bremen* and *Europa* in that order, whereas it had been North German Lloyd's plan to enter them the other way around. The *Bremen* earned a niche in Atlantic history even though the *Europa* was ultimately faster and lived longer.

Both were long, low racers, reminiscent of their turn-of-the-century forebears. Yet the new bulbous bow made possible a greater beam than would have been proportionally possible on the *Kronprinzessin Cecilie,* for instance. They were comfortable and seaworthy, although low freeboard made the third-class deck space forward inclined to be damp in even a moderate sea.

There was power in the silhouette, but little grace or beauty. The *Bremen* had a squat, almost malevolent look, an appearance compounded by a brace of incredibly short, pear-shaped funnels. Her builders claimed that they had been specifically constructed to minimize wind resistance but I have always suspected that their form was dictated by other considerations. The ships were, of course, driven by conventional turbines. Four years earlier, the Swedish-American Line's *Gripsholm* had crossed the Atlantic, the first diesel-driven liner to do so. She had no boilers and consequently no need for conventional funnels. So by the late twenties, the motor ship's low profile was *de rigeur* and I am quite sure that the Germans seized upon it to give their liners a look of ultimate modernity. Whatever their motives, the choice was disastrous, and even on her trials, the *Bremen*'s after decks were caked with soot. The company tried cutting a vent in the after end of number 2 stack, hoping the slip stream might carry the smoke over the

THE ONLY WAY TO CROSS

stern. On the *Europa,* the shape of the funnels was made elliptical, but the final compromise on both vessels was to double their height.

One of the most distinctive things about the *Bremen*'s funnels was the installation between them of a permanent airplane catapult. Implementing an air link for the last few hundred miles of the crossing enjoyed a brief vogue in the late twenties. The point was to rush selected sacks of mail ashore long before the ship appeared. Unfortunately, the scheme had little more than novelty value and service was limited to only a few vessels. In August of 1927, the first mail plane ever to be launched from a liner flew from the *Leviathan.* The pilot's name was Clarence Chamberlin and the astonishing thing about that pioneering flight was that he literally took off; there was no catapult involved. Carpenters in New York had built a hundred-foot ramp on top of the *Leviathan*'s teak bridge that pointed diagonally over the port bow. Chamberlin's tiny Fokker biplane was poised at its after end. His attempt was made, between rain squalls, eighty miles east of Ambrose. Deck hands had to mop the "field" just before takeoff. By having Commodore Hartley turn the ship to take advantage of the breeze as well as the ship's own speed, Chamberlin was airborne within seventy-five feet. He landed at Teterboro Airport and delivered his precious cargo to the Hasbrouck Heights postmaster.

After this barnstorming experiment, it was the French who inaugurated a regular service the following year. A catapult was erected over the *Ile de France*'s stern, driven by steam from the ship's boilers and capable of launching a six-passenger seaplane. The device was tested successfully in Le Havre and the first operational flight made three hundred miles east of Nantucket near the end of a westbound crossing in August. Passengers crowded the afterdecks for the occasion and with Lieutenant de Vaisseau Demougeot at the controls, the Lioré-Olivier shot into the air. He landed three hours later at Quarantine and an official on the Immigration launch chided the pilot for not having ready a complete list of his crew. (There were two.) Then, with Transat's North American manager as his passenger, he flew the last leg of his flight to the French Line pier at 14th Street. Once there, a precious hour was spent posing for news photographers before the pilot clambered ashore and walked one of the letters to *The New York Times.* The paper was flattered enough to commemorate the event on its editorial page the next day, including the following ominous if not wholly accurate remark:

> . . . It is conceivable that ocean flight between Europe and the United States will be the sequel to a ship-and-plane system of mail delivery,

Dress rehearsal. The *Ile de France*'s mail plane is hoisted onto the launching ramp for a trial take-off at Le Havre. (*Compagnie Générale Transatlantique*)

the distances covered by the plane becoming longer and longer until the steamship can be dispensed with altogether.

North German Lloyd was quite clearly in sympathy with this prediction. Their seaplane boasted not only a swiveling catapult amidships but a baron to fly it. Just forward was the ship's restaurant, the first ever to be located on a top deck. It was superb, in the German tradition, and was even equipped with a tank of live trout, assuring diners fresh fish. The public rooms seemed undistinguished, a pallid imitation of the *Ile de France* yet without their daring.

The maiden voyage in July of 1929 was a press agent's delight. Despite a slow start through the fog-shrouded Channel, speed west of Cherbourg improved dramatically. When the ship swept past Ambrose Light eight hours in advance of the *Mauretania*'s best recorded time, her quintet of whistles and sirens sounded one long victorious blast. A light rain was falling, but nothing could dampen the enthusiasm of passengers who had stayed up all night for that historic moment nor the jubilant welcome she received in the harbor.

The only demeaning aspect of the German's triumph was the location of her terminal pier. She was tied up in Brooklyn at the Army Terminal. Although the largest pier, it was certainly not the most fashionable address in New York Harbor. One of the first to endure that irritating subway ride was MacNeil, Captain of the *Mauretania,* offering his congratulations to Ziegenbein, his opposite number on the *Bremen.* The two men had last exchanged distant greetings off les Casquets, the Cunarder inbound from New York, the German undergoing acceptance trials. It was, if accidental, a significant and symbolic meeting: the old campaigner, still in harness after all those years, signaling bravely through the twilight at the ugly challenger bent on her defeat. In August the *Mauretania* did her best to recapture the record, but although she bettered her own time, she was still over four hours short of the *Bremen*'s. It was less a Company than a crew effort. Cunard authorized the oil expenditure and Chief Engineer Andrew Cockburn and his men coaxed everything they could out of their dependable old engines. But two decades of technology could not be ignored and the gallant old Cunarder permanently relinquished the honor that she had held for an incredible twenty-two years.

It was anticlimactic when the *Europa,* making a stormy maiden crossing the following March, took the record herself by a scant eighteen minutes. The two German ships carried twelve percent of the early thirties passenger traffic and had the unique advantage of being the only big express liners that sailed to Germany. However, this very convenience was self-

Music on board German vessels tended toward marches and male choirs. Band concerts on deck and a steward's chorus as part of an evening gala were staples in the *Bremen*'s repertoire of passenger entertainment. (*The Mariners Museum, Newport News, Virginia*)

defeating. Were it not for the additional distance, North German Lloyd could have inaugurated history's first two-ship weekly service. The *Bremen* and *Europa* crossed from Cherbourg to Ambrose in four and three-quarter days. Given thirty hours for turnaround in New York and a home berth in any Channel port, the pair of them could just have maintained a weekly service. As it was, they were frustrated by geography and the additional seventeen hours consumed from Southampton to Bremerhaven; a third ship was still necessary. They made do with the *Columbus,* launched in 1924. Her reciprocating engines were replaced with turbines and her dignified stacks cut down in imitation of her running mates. But try as she might, the older ship could make no more than twenty-three knots—the entire arrangement was as flawed as a troika with one lame horse.

Within a year of the *Europa*'s debut, the Hamburg-Amerika and North German Lloyd lines were united as the HAPAG-Lloyd. Even amicable Hanseatic competition had no validity in the National Socialist regime then consolidating power under Hitler.

And if German shipping men grumbled about subordinating ancient company identities, their colleagues in Great Britain were faced with the same bleak prospect. There, the move towards merger was urged in Parliament for reasons of economy rather than ideology. The stock market crash of 1929 had triggered a world slump whose impact was felt keenly on the Atlantic. Freight and passenger revenues plummeted in the early thirties and work on Cunard's new giant was temporarily halted on the Clyde. Inevitably, provision of government assistance was predicated on eliminating competition. So, as in Germany, two historical rivals combined into one new company, the Cunard White Star Line. (White Star had been returned to English ownership in 1927.)

The pattern of slump, government intervention and merger was played out in Italy as well, where Mussolini directed that no less than three separate shipping companies amalgamate to form Italia—Societa per Azioni di Navigazione. Embarking on a strong nationalistic program, Il Duce was determined to attract American tourists directly to Italy, diverting to Rome even a small portion of the dollars customarily squandered in northern capitals. Mussolini's timing was perfect. Happily available as flagships of the new company was a pair of gigantic vessels originally laid down as competitors, the *Rex* and *Conte di Savoia.* Their projected speed was such that service to Italian ports could be effected in six and a half rather than ten days.

The *Rex*'s original owners had planned to call their ship after Marconi but the King's presence in Genoa at her launch made *Rex* an appropriate choice. Lloyd Sabaudo, the Trieste builders, then suggested the name *Dux* for their ship. But the Italian dictator demurred and the name *Conte di Savoia* was adopted, in line with a company naming policy. Although Mussolini's uncharacteristic modesty can be applauded, I think he was wrong to discourage the happy euphony of *Rex* and *Dux;* short titles stick in the mind. I have always felt that *Rex* was one of the most successful names ever conferred on a ship, combining majesty, modernity and brevity in one simple three-letter word.

It is a popular misconception that "North Atlantic" refers to that portion of the ocean between New York and northern European ports; in point of fact, it extends to the equator. The New York–Gibraltar run is not only a legitimate North Atlantic route but, surprisingly enough, only slightly longer than the distance to Cherbourg. There the resemblance ceases. I have only once sailed to the Mediterranean and it is astonishing for one brought up to equate a crossing with storm and fog to experience the sunny calm of that southern route. The only similarity to a passage further north was a persistent, irritating breeze. All Atlantic crossings were invariably windy, enriching generations of ship's hairdressers. The vessel's speed alone approached thirty miles an hour. Allied with even a mild headwind, this produced a snappy little tempest that might not ruffle the ocean but made a cap obligatory for both sexes. Following winds reduced the gale but tended to retain a stifling cloud of funnel smoke on deck.

But winds apart, ships destined for the Mediterranean were essentially different from their contemporaries traveling the intemperate lanes to the north. The great Italian deck sport was swimming. The one line that might legitimately have aspired to construct a Pompeian pool below was able instead to install monstrous swimming baths on deck, surrounded by tables, chairs, umbrellas and sometimes sand. (Deck stewards loathed this last refinement almost as much as the children loved it.) The *Conte di Savoia* had a gigantic pool between her two funnels and both she and the *Rex* boasted a series of stepped lido decks aft.

Their hulls were painted black, a color recently eschewed by the company in favor of white. Despite the difficulties of keeping it clean, white gives the ships a distinctive summery look. New York tug crews drape clean canvas over their bows when nudging the *Michelangelo* or *Raffaello* into Pier 86. Italian ships have always been best qualified to double for cruising; the indolent poolside life characteristic of the Caribbean is aimed at in their basic design. It is also a strong and successful aspect of the Company image.

Of the two great Italian vessels of the thirties, the *Rex* was the more

The two Italian entrants of the early thirties. Top, the *Rex* sails from Genoa on one of the most ghastly maiden voyages in Atlantic history. Bottom, the *Conte di Savoia* departs from Trieste for the first time. (*Shipping World and Shipbuilder*)

conventional. She had a traditional overhung counter and her lounge had a familiar look about it. Rich walnut paneling and an endless oriental carpet recalled the conservatism of the *Mauretania*. The more advanced features, both inside and out, emerged from Trieste rather than Genoa.

In October of 1931, the Princess of Piedmont christened the *Conte di Savoia,* sending her down the ways with a giant fasces mounted ominously on the forepeak. On one of the rare occasions when a fire brigade was summoned for a joyous occasion, helmeted firemen hosed down the smoking ways after the hull had passed. (This was one of the hazards associated with increased tonnage: when the *Queen Mary* was launched three years later, her ponderous bulk ignited the ways and they burst into flames.) She had, like the *Bremen,* a new cruiser stern, and below decks, a trio of gyro-stabilizers unique on a passenger liner.

The grand lounge was an explosion of Italian baroque, a floating Villa Borghese. There was marble everywhere, on the walls, columns and under-foot, save for a heraldic carpet. The ceiling was an enormous vault painted with all the verve of the Sistine Chapel. Around the room lay bloated fauteuils covered in zebra stripes and hideously out of period. There was a riot of lush statuary reminiscent of Forest Lawn. Yet this sumptuous interior was unequivocally and gloriously Italian, a colossal brew of stone, gilt and grandeur that was stunning. With the scale was a rich warmth that avoided the sterility of the *Ile de France*'s dining room.

Unique among the Italian fleet, both the *Rex* and *Conte di Savoia* offered accommodations in no less than four classes. In common with all Atlantic vessels, tourist third cabin was discontinued, a casualty of the Depression. Yet in addition to the first, tourist and third that remained, passengers on the two new flagships could travel in a near luxury called special, just below first. The traditional first-class unity of the *ponte dei salone* was destroyed, its forward end given over to tourist and aft the domain of the specials. This profusion of classes had the effect of reducing the number of passengers in each. The main dining room was a modest compartment of identical dimension to the embarkation hall, seating fewer than four hundred. Another impression gained by this intensive subdivision was that the *Rex* seemed smaller than she really was. There was a sensation of small-ship intimacy that did not obtain on the *Majestic,* for instance, only five thousand tons larger.

It was an auspicious day when the nine-hundred-foot *Rex* left Genoa on her maiden voyage to New York. Il Duce himself lunched on board and thousands of ecstatic Genoans saw her off. A pier-side test of the foghorn racketed among the hills surrounding the port. First stop was Villefranche,

El Morocco upholstery meets Villa Bor-
ghese under a vast painted ceiling in the
Conte di Savoia's main lounge. (*Italian
Line*)

three hours along the coast. Anchored in the French port, the dazzling new liner probably never looked more picturesque. Villefranche has always seemed to me the single most perfect anchorage in the world, a deep-water harbor untarnished by industry. Even the naval dockyard seems of a piece with the villas that crowd the hills.

After an hour's stopover, the *Rex* slipped west past Nice and Cannes. In subsequent regular service, her route would lie to the south and Naples. But for this voyage, it lay directly toward the Atlantic. Just as the *Bremen*'s starting post had been Cherbourg's breakwater, so Italian liners running to New York were clocked west from Gibraltar. En route to the Straits, the *Rex* plowed serenely through what her distinguished patron was fond of calling *Mare Nostrum*. Off the Spanish coast, within sight of Malaga, lights all over the ship suddenly flickered and went out. Way was immediately reduced. A failing hinted at during trials returned with nightmare finality: two of the *Rex*'s three turbo-generators ceased to operate. Emergency lighting was restored but ventilation to the engine spaces was severely limited. At three A.M., the ship limped into Gibraltar.

The following morning, passengers anticipating breakfast far out in the Atlantic found they were anchored instead hard by the Rock's overpowering presence. Pinned to the purser's board was a notice that the ship would remain in harbor while certain repairs were made. The scheduled departure was already half a day overdue and it was apparent that the *Rex* was not about to sail anywhere. A pair of tenders had been laid on to ferry people ashore; all afternoon they shuttled back and forth from ship to quay, carrying hundreds who welcomed the excursion as a heaven-sent distraction.

The weather was cool and overcast, discouraging swimming on deck and affording some relief to the engineers laboring in the generator room. Personnel from Gibraltar's Naval Dockyard volunteered their assistance and were ushered immediately below. No public announcement was ever forthcoming as to the exact nature of the damage. During the laborious five-hour passage from Málaga, passengers all over the ship had heard a rhythmic battering, as though something revolving on a shaft was flailing something else that was not. One among a thousand rumors rife in the smoking room was that the generators' violent malfunction had somehow holed the tanks beneath them, tainting the drinking water with salt. If this were the case, the *Rex* had chosen the worst possible port for assistance; Gibraltar's chronic shortage of fresh water was common knowledge. But hard news was at a premium. All anyone really knew was that the ship's capacity to produce service electricity was seriously crippled and the means to repair the damage was not at hand.

Gibraltar was then, as now, a fascinating place, with one understandable limitation: for cruise ships, it was invariably a one-day stop, Trafalgar cemetery, Barbary apes, British raj and all. Two days there were tedious and three too much. It was precisely this realization that began to cloy the next morning. Continuing lack of information as to departure caused increasing and sometimes hysterical irritation. The Italian Line officials were caught in a ghastly dilemma. They could either admit the seriousness of the damage, generating incalculably bad publicity, or they could imply that the *Rex* might sail at any moment. The only safe solution, which they adopted, was to say nothing. The purser's office was shut tight, the master unavailable, and inquisitive passengers who approached the chief engineer were unable to find him either.

A peculiar truth about ocean voyages was brought home to passengers, crew and staff alike. If the "floating hotel" is on schedule, all is well and the range of amenities on board is put to grateful good use. But if she is aground or delayed, nothing will satisfy. Passengers on the *Rex* who clamored the loudest were not necessarily spurred on by pressing engagements in New York. Nor was their frustration appeased by the fact that they were staying at no cost on one of the world's most comfortable ships. Beneath the civilized languor of shipboard life lurks a sense of urgent purpose quite as anxious as the suburban commuter's.

The third morning, the *Vulcania* arrived from Genoa carrying spare generator parts. She also offered alternative passage to those that desired it. Sixty of the *Rex*'s most vociferous clients transferred to the smaller vessel and another fifteen, including Jimmy Walker, stormed ashore. The New York mayor endured a day and a half of arduous continental train travel to reach Cherbourg and the westbound *Europa* in time. That was the unkindest cut of all. Those of the thirteen hundred plus that remained on board the disabled ship settled for a day trip to Seville. More adventurous souls determined on spending a night in Tangiers were discouraged with good reason: early on the morning of October 2, after three days that seemed like weeks to Italian Line officials, the Lloyds surveyor gave his permission for the ship to sail. The abortive maiden voyage was resumed.

Electricity continued in short supply. Elevator service was completely suspended and lighting was only adequate. The engineers could be thankful they were crossing in October rather than in the heat of July. Compounding the discomfort on board was a series of plumbing failures. After a belated but noisy welcome in New York Harbor, the *Rex* was berthed at her pier. The *Weehawken* lay alongside, her direct current a rare source of supply in a city run largely on alternating. During her extended stay in port, work

Passengers on the *Rex*'s monstrous Lido
Deck soak up the advantages of the southern route to Europe. (*Compagnie Générale Transatlantique*)

below decks proceeded at a furious pace. A contingent of shipyard plumbers arrived on the *Conte Grande* and were thrown into the struggle to restore complete service.

One month after the *Rex*'s Gibraltar agony, the *Conte di Savoia* underwent trials in the Adriatic. Her speed was eminently satisfactory; with no drag-inducing bilge keels, she exceeded thirty knots for short distances. Of almost equal interest to yard and company officials was the operation of her stabilizers. They were housed in a forward compartment near the water line, three giant spinning tops each weighing over a hundred tons. They were built by Great Britain's Sperry Company and their novel installation on a passenger liner prompted her owners to advertise a roll-less ship. Severe, uncomfortable rolling results not from one wave but the cumulative effect of several that set up a roll cycle peculiar to each vessel. Gyrostabilizers had the advantage over Frahm's celebrated tanks of a far brisker response. Mounted on top of each large gyroscope was a small pilot gyro which sensed the first infinitesimal aberration and immediately transmitted a corrective maneuver to its larger partner.

However, on both the *Conte di Savoia*'s trials and her subsequent maiden voyage, the sea refused to cooperate. Sperry's engineers must have felt like the harpist who brought his instrument to the party and wasn't asked to perform. Conditions were glasslike and there was no alternative but to rock the ship artificially. Off the Azores, passengers were treated to a display of induced rolling. Two gyrostabilizers were set to swing the vessel through sixteen degrees, at which point the third was employed to restore stable verticality.

It is doubtful whether the *Conte di Savoia*'s gyroscopic devices ever justified their expense. They were temperamental and inefficient. Located directly over the keel, the amount of turning moment they could exert despite their bulk was limited. Stabilizer fins adopted after the Second World War were far more effective. Situated on either side of the hull, their position fifty feet from the center line fulcrum gave them enormous mechanical advantage.

The Italian Line's second maiden voyage of that year produced its own drama. It seemed that the same electrical nemesis hovered over the *Conte di Savoia* as well. In midocean, nine hundred miles from Ambrose, the lights went out at six in the evening and the ship was in darkness for ten minutes. The valve admitting cooling sea water to the turbo-generators had ruptured. Through a hole in the shell plating, a foot-thick jet of the Atlantic poured in.

Acting to save his electrical plant, the *Conte di Savoia*'s master promptly turned her broadside to the wind and had his oil ballast shifted to starboard. The resulting list brought the damaged plate near the surface. A Neapolitan seaman volunteered to go over the side and affix a wooden patch. Four other sailors stayed on rope ladders above him, handing down tools and when possible, maneuvering his life line to keep him from being dashed against the hull. The man's endurance was remarkable. He worked above and below water for two desperate hours, battered constantly against the ship's side despite the care of his shipmates. Passengers packed on the high side of the sloping decks followed the struggle under the glare of emergency floodlights. When the men came up, there was a sustained cheer and the following day eight hundred dollars was subscribed for the plucky seaman.

All ships, particularly when very new or old, are subject to mechanical failure. Owners only pray that the damage can be put right with a minimum of publicity. The inaugural appearance of the *Flandre* in 1952 was perhaps the most humiliating: she was towed ignominiously up from Quarantine by a quartet of tugs, her generators completely disabled. More recently, the birth pangs of the *QE2*'s turbines serve to remind us that no line is immune from the same ghastly misfortune. The *Rex* redeemed her good name the following year by speeding from Gibraltar to New York in four days and slightly less than fourteen hours, taking the record from the *Europa*.

Although they never made money for their owners, the *Rex* and *Conte di Savoia* were handsome, well-designed vessels. Given longer lives, they would more than probably have repaid their initial investment. Together with the *Ile, Bremen* and *Europa,* they dominated the middle years between wars. But already their accomplishments were threatened with eclipse as a most staggering combination of size, power and speed grew on two separate sets of ways in France and England. The last round of prewar Atlantic competition was about to begin.

Va, donc, trouant de feux la nuit éclaboussée,
Bateau-phare, bateau-ruche, bateau musée,
Qui portes l'espérance en tes mats frissonnants,
Et franchis d'un tel vol les immensités bleues
Qu'on verra bien, malgré les milliers de lieues,
Qu'il n'est plus d'Atlantique entre les continents.

FROM *O Normandie!* BY ANDRÉ DUMAS

10.
Ships of State

In 1934, a French marine artist named Albert Sébille was asked by the Compagnie Générale Transatlantique to execute a painting of their new liner. When completed, his canvas was nearly fifteen feet in length. It hangs today in Paris' Musée de la Marine and thousands of reproductions, reduced to convenient size, were used by the line for publicity.

One of them is before me as I write. It shows a starboard view of an enormous steamship, her plating cut away to expose the teeming life inside. Not content with detailing empty interiors, Sébille chose to people his steel beehive with hundreds of tiny figures that give life to the finished work. It is obviously evening in midocean. The *fumoir* and *grand salon* that fill the space between funnels 2 and 3 are nearly empty, only a handful of tailed and lamé Lilliputians dotted about the rooms. A glittering assembly throngs the *salle à manger* directly beneath, while some latecomers drift down the blue carpeted staircase. Forward of the grandest of *grandes descentes,* the chapel is not surprisingly devoid of worshipers, although a party of indefatigable swimmers cavorts in the *piscine* below. Are they dieting or, more likely, are they interlopers from second class using the pool while the first class dines?

Credibility is momentarily reestablished by inspection of the theater on the promenade deck's forward end, a sloping auditorium deserted but for an impresario and his assistants who huddle in the front row while a crinolined diva trills a cappella onstage. Other artists can be seen applying last-minute *maquillage* in the dressing rooms. Overhead, a cinema operator, doubtless jumping his cue, rear-projects an image onto the movie screen. On the sun deck, the playroom skillfully incorporated into the base of number 1 funnel is packed with children engrossed in Guignol.

If one might query the suitability of such late-night diversion for juveniles, a glance at adjacent figures on deck reveals a startling truth: although it is evening below, on deck it is unquestionably midday. Strollers in belted overcoats enjoy the sun, although a distraught nanny grasping a child's hand seems in danger of losing her veiled toque in the wind. There is a game of doubles on the tennis court and further aft, dog lovers exercise their pets.

The bridge is deserted save for a shadowy helmsman, and seated near the windows that give into the winter garden, a solitary correspondent occupies the writing room. Behind immaculate engine spaces below, we can inspect rows of beef carcasses hung in cold storage. Forward on the same deck, a hundred-car garage is comfortably filled with expensive automobiles. Tongue in cheek, Sébille has parked a small monoplane among them.

The vessel whose image bewitched the artist was, of course, the *Normandie.* That her awesome dimensions disrupted his sense of chronological unity is quite understandable. For the *Normandie* and her rival *Queen Mary* were extraordinary creations. Perhaps the most astonishing thing about them is that they were built at all. Conceived in the euphoric optimism of the twenties, both keels were laid in the midst of the thirties Depression.

Neil Potter and Jack Frost, British coauthors of books about the three *Queens,* subtitled their first volume "The Inevitable Ship." In one sense, they were quite right. Thousand-foot monsters racing at thirty knots were inevitable, if only to effect that traditional weekly crossing with an irreducible minimum of two vessels. Yet it is astonishing that such extravagant enterprises should have been countenanced at a time when economic distress was so widespread. White Star's ambitious last gasp before merging with Cunard had been her own thousand-footer, to be driven by diesel engines and called *Oceanic*. She was actually laid down at Harland & Wolff in 1928 but abandoned shortly after the crash; some of her steel went into the smaller *Britannic*.

Work on John Brown's hull number 534, Cunard's great new ship, was suspended for nearly two and a half years. During this untoward hibernation, she had the most exquisite care. Dan Wallace, now Cunard's naval architect, was a yard apprentice in those days, part of a dwindling work force kept on to maintain the unfinished hull. They outdid themselves, painting, scraping and polishing in a desperate effort to justify their continued employment. No scantlings ever received better care. In the Parliamentary debates that raged over government proposals to subsidize completion, one member suggested that the American millionaires for whom the ship was designed no longer existed. In point of fact, many of them did not. Another member whose memory was short argued that an eighty-thousand-ton express liner would have no value in wartime. His remark deserves a booby prize for ignorance of World War I.

What finally passed the measure in Britain was the same jingoistic pride that had effected subsidy to Cunard for the *Lusitania* and *Mauretania*. The spirit of intense nationalism spawned both in Germany and Italy made creation of competing superliners a matter of immense prestige in Britain as well as France. Just as the *Bremen* and *Europa* restored the maritime dignity of a resurgent Germany, just as the *Rex* and *Conte di Savoia* were manifestations of aggressive Italian sovereignty, so the *Queen Mary* and *Normandie* were essentially expressions of national pride. Record-breaking Atlantic vessels were no longer company pawns. Their increased size, speed and sophistication made them prohibitively expensive. They became quite literally ships of state. What but a government-sponsored enterprise could expend the sixty million dollars needed to build a *Normandie?*

The necessity for enlarged facilities arose again, the same expensive ramifications faced by the *Olympic*'s owners two decades earlier but on a grander scale. Construction of the *Normandie*'s berth took longer than the twenty-one months required to erect the hull. Dealing with a launch weight of twenty-eight thousand tons, nothing was left to chance. Penhoët engineers extended the ways three hundred feet under water, insuring the smoothest possible transition from land to sea. Common to all those responsible for the ship's launch was the feeling that more than particular care was necessary. She was not only the largest mass ever moved on dry land; there was considerable resentment about her very existence. Passions were easily

Below, the *Normandie* at St. Nazaire. Notice how the three funnels diminish in height, an artistic subterfuge that aided the impression of speed. (*Compagnie Générale Transatlantique*)

Interiors. The North Atlantic's first theater had everything, it seems, except an orchestra pit. Models fill the pool in an elaborate charade of gaiety. The protected area for children and beginners was quite unique. (*Compagnie Générale Transatlantique*)

aroused among the unemployed in other sectors of the French economy. Many saw the *Normandie* as a symbol of reckless extravagance in times when the vast sums expended on her could have been put to better use. If rumors of sabotage proved groundless, open discussion of a launch catastrophe was common. Betting was three to one against success. I think it is safe to say that construction of a ship had never before aroused such conflicting emotions. The pride of her builders contrasted strangely with the indifference and outright hostility rampant in the French press near the launch date of October 29, 1932.

Among the two hundred thousand assembled to witness the event, none were more concerned than a delegation from the Clyde. There were probably more Scots on the banks of the Loire that day than had been there since the launch of the first *France* in the eighteen-sixties. Had it not been for the Depression, their *Queen Mary* would already have been in service. As it was, the French were the first to conduct the experiment of setting such a gigantic mass in motion.

The wife of President Albert Lebrun had consented to name the vessel, thus assuming the special role of *marraine* (godmother) to the *Normandie*. It was an obligation that she discharged by not only christening her but sailing as guest of honor on her maiden voyage three years later. In company with a priest who blessed both ship and undertaking, Madame Lebrun completed a circuit of the ways through the clangor of workers initiating the launch. Their activity climaxed a fortnight's rigid countdown, threatened two days earlier by high winds which had mercifully dropped that morning. At three in the afternoon, to the strains of "La Marseillaise," Madame Lebrun cut the ribbon, champagne burst against the stem and Penhoët hull number T6BIS took to the Loire. Spectators near shore were nearly swept away by the enormous backwash.

She was to have been called *La Belle France*. But changing the name to *Normandie* did nothing to abate a curious argument that had raged for months. No less an august body than the French Academy felt obliged to offer its verdict on the correct gender of the ship's name. It was their learned opinion that although one might refer to *"le paquebot Normandie,"* *Normandie* by itself should be preceded by the feminine article. The logic of this argument was lost on the Penhoët workers, who adhered to the French convention that ships are always masculine. This is a unique Gallic conviction, in opposition to the British and Germans who subscribe to the opposite theory. There had been an identical debate between Potsdam and Hamburg over Ballin's second great prewar ship. No one ever satisfactorily decided whether neuter *"das Vaterland"* should legitimately change gender to feminine *"die Vaterland"* when applied to a vessel. One of the rare logical advantages of English was that reference to the *Queen Mary* could always be made with the unspoken knowledge that she was indubitably and definitely feminine. As regards the confusion about the French flagship's name, it is interesting to observe that the maritime faction had the last word: Edmond Lanier, current head of the French Line, who began his Transat career on the ship, refers to her in his admirable Company history simply as *Normandie*.

Responsibility for the lines of her hull rested with a Russian named Vladimir Yourkevitch. He had been a designer of battleships for the Imperial Navy until the Revolution terminated his employment. Like so many of his contemporaries, he drifted to Paris. His first job outside of Russia was as a laborer for Renault. By 1928, he was back in naval architecture, this time at St. Nazaire. At the end of his first year, he submitted a series of proposals for an innovative hull design. André Levi, director of the Yard, was sufficiently impressed to order models tested at an experimental tank near Versailles. A backlog of naval orders and a leak curtailed their work there after sixteen months, and Yourkevitch and his staff entrained for Hamburg. There, a twenty-eight-foot paraffin model was subjected to further testing. After countless changes and refinements, German engineers endorsed the ultimate design as *"nicht verbesserungsfähig"*—"unimprovable." Yourkevitch's subsequent report was adopted. Very much as Cunard had risked their all on the *Mauretania*'s turbines, the French Line opted to follow the extraordinary recommendations of a very junior and sometimes incomprehensible colleague.

Out of water, the *Normandie*'s hull was not particularly impressive. In section, her midships frames appeared to sag ponderously like the thighs of a supine fat lady. They were unmistakably and distressingly pear-shaped. Yet this unsightly waist provided a reserve of buoyant displacement that permitted Yourkevitch his astonishingly efficient bow. Afloat, the spread of her bilges concealed, the *Normandie* had a remarkable stance, her forward thrust assured by a beak-headed stem that terminated in a bulbous forefoot after the *Bremen*'s example. An abnormally long and fine entry at the water line, hollowed out under flaring upper strakes, reduced her bow wave to a minimum and served to neutralize flanking turbulence. The paint scheme for her upper hull plating was skillfully conceived to accentuate the dashing prow: the white banding so pronounced on the *France* was sharply tapered on the new ship, transgressing the porthole line and swooping gracefully up to a fine point. On the forward deck, there was a giant white whaleback

A portion of the *Normandie*'s vast sun deck between funnels one and two before the covered bench appeared. It is doubly astonishing when compared with the *Mauretania*'s, right, built thirty years earlier. (*Top: Compagnie Générale Transatlantique, right: Walter Lord*)

which housed beneath it the clutter of winches, chains and capstans *de rigueur* on every other Atlantic liner.

It was this cleanness of line that characterized the ship's appearance. The trio of ovoid funnels, with a ten-degree rake and diminishing in height to the rear, had scarcely a rivet head breaking their smooth proportions. Nothing marred the teak expanse between them. Even the stepped decks aft, beautifully curved and connected by neat companionways, had the cosmetic perfection of a Busby Berkeley set. Only the hybrid stern was a disappointment, a combination of cruiser and counter that housed a massive central anchor bed. Here, as forward, deck machinery was concealed and the clean-swept look continued all the way to the taffrail.

In the *Normandie*'s engine spaces, the link between prime mover and screws was electrical rather than mechanical. Each of the four double-expansion turbines was shafted directly to an alternator that supplied power to a quartet of electric motors. Reducing the turbine's incredible speed to the relatively placid three turns per second required of the propellers was thus accomplished without a complex of massive gears. Similarly, turbine diameters were smaller. The French were very proud of this system, although in point of fact it offered only one operational advantage over geared reduction: full astern power was available if needed. I suspect that the French felt more secure with electrical technology than with their capacity to machine enormous gear components. So the workers of Belfort, miles from the Loire, had a share in the contracts. Most far-flung of the ship's structural elements came from the Skoda Works in Czechoslovakia, where once again, the French had turned to central European foundries for the giant steel castings that made up the stern frames. From Edinburgh came the steering mechanism, including the teak commutator or wheel that sits now in my front hall.

The painter Sébille wrote of the *Normandie* that no ship better combined power and elegance. In his cutaway broadside, one of her splendors was not apparent to the layman. As on the *Vaterland,* boiler uptakes were divided and remained at the sides of the hull. They joined just under the funnels, necessitating a sloping flange around the base to accommodate the juncture of the casings. This remarkable feature allowed a handsome central vista. From a kneeling position center stage in the theater, there was an uninterrupted view terminating in daylight nearly five hundred feet away. One's eye traveled unimpeded through a succession of extraordinary public rooms: up the center aisle, through the grand hall and main gallery, into the *grand salon* and neighboring *fumoir,* up the great staircase, across another hall, and through the café grill's curved glass wall out onto an open promenade.

On C-deck, the same design peculiarity dictated the novel shape of the dining room. Divided uptakes denied lateral access to the hull, but the astonishing length of the room more than compensated for it. Like no other ship's dining room before or since, its three-deck height sustained from side to side, end to end, with no intervening balcony or clerestory. It was a corrected version, so to speak, of the monumental errors incorporated into the same facility on the *Ile de France*. Here, a similarly enormous chamber was a feast for the eye. The scale was colossal, almost Imperial Roman, with columnar twenty-foot lighting fixtures that glowed from the walls, a coffered gilt ceiling overhead and a perspective that receded dramatically into shimmering light a hundred yards away.

French Line publicists were fond of pointing out that the *Normandie*'s dining room was slightly longer than the Hall of Mirrors at Versailles. It was a thoroughly appropriate comparison in more ways than one. Not only was there a built-in implication of grandeur, but reference was made to the same extravagant use of glass. This was not mere decorative pretension; glass is an admirable sheathing material on board ship, noncombustible and maintenance-free. A dozen enormous glass cascades, lit from within, served as further lavish enrichment. The *Normandie*'s dining room was breathtaking, surpassing anything built before or after and fulfilling its function admirably.

It is easy now to talk glibly of theaters on a ship but in 1935, the *Normandie*'s was first. With the advent of talkies, movies had become standard passenger diversions. On older vessels, they were screened in the lounge, the projector grinding noisily away on a card table and late arrivals tripping over wires. Now, on this magnificent ship, there was not only a proper cinema but a stage for legitimate drama as well.

If the *Ile de France* had the first chapel, it was modest in comparison with the *Normandie*'s, which could seat ninety on one level and an additional dozen in a balcony. "Sliding doors," deadpanned *Fortune* magazine, "shut off the altar to make the church safe for Roundhead orisons."

Conveying the effect of the lounge and smoking room is difficult. They were nearly identical in size and adjacent to one another amidships. The French had recognized, long before their British colleagues, that the days of the *fumoir* as a restricted male snuggery were over. The *Normandie*'s smoking room was sensibly designed as an ancillary chamber to the lounge, to which it could be joined by merely pressing a button. An immense fireproof lacquered panel was drawn aside like a curtain to form a cathedral of space for a concert or gala.

Even the use of sculpture, monumental as it had to be, was selective

Dinner in the *Normandie*'s first-class dining room. As in all great French ships, ladies performed a ritual descent. White tie was *de rigueur* for gentlemen. The doors to this room are presently in Our Lady of Lebanon Church in Brooklyn. (*Roger Schall*)

and seemed to fit. A towering matron called Peace loomed over the Captain's table, vaguely reminiscent of the *Ile de France*'s overwhelming soap carvings. But Baudry's over-life-sized *La Normandie,* a sturdy, tunicked peasant girl atop the smoking room staircase, was in perfect scale with her surroundings. It is more than can be said of her today, poor thing, standing desolately in the center of a littered reflecting pool, staring with sightless bronze eyes at the sinuous façade of Miami's Fontainebleau Hotel.

The ship's third sculptural extravaganza was a sea god, poised with curled tail above a sea of dolphins. It appears in lavish renderings as though about to belly-flop onto the after esplanade. I have taken the liberty of using the term "after esplanade" to describe that portion of the promenade deck that formed a delightful terrace beyond the café grill. It was another and most successful attempt at that elusive outdoor Atlantic fixture, the veranda café. Open to the skies, it was sheltered at the front by superstructure and along each side by ranks of high-backed benches arranged in Art-Deco zigzag. These eminently practical devices were not only windbreaks but their reverse sides served as duplicate seating for tourist class as well. The enclosed space was lit at night by gay lamp standards and would have terminated nicely with the seagod as a point of focus. But the colossal statue was never installed, not even for the maiden voyage: its weight proved too much for the deck and it remains to this day on the pier at Le Havre, rearing up from a parking lot. The following year, the handsome space for which it had been commissioned was no more, overbuilt by a new tourist lounge. The handsome teak and mahogany decks were gone forever, the café grill all the poorer without its complimentary exterior vista.

Between the second and third funnels there was a fenced-in tennis court. Just aft of the number 1 funnel was a kind of double-sided, sheltered bench running fore and aft, bisecting that glorious open space. The lesson to be learned from the French experience is that sheltered decks belong aft, tucked in behind the protection of superstructure. Open decks are best left open, not encumbered with ugly little kiosks. Cunard White Star made the same mistake, spanning the first *Queen Elizabeth*'s sports deck with a row of useless little bus stops facing aft. However, the company redeemed itself on the *QE2* with an admirable solution: on the top deck amidships there is a well, open above but glass-walled and almost completely shut off from the wind. This is an area given over to games and deck chairs rather than feeding, but it is clearly the solution to Atlantic out-of-doors. Of course, I suspect that the space is almost untenable in the Caribbean except for the most devout sun worshipers.

Just one deck above the *Normandie*'s café grill, on the after end of the sun deck, were the two *apartements de grand luxe à terrasse* named appropriately Deauville and Trouville. They were the only sleeping accommodations on that entire deck available to passengers. (Engineering officers, traditionally granted as much off-duty light and air as they were denied at their work, occupied a series of cabins grouped just forward beneath the dummy funnel.) Deauville and Trouville each had four bedrooms and its own living room, dining room and serving pantry. In addition, there were two bedrooms obviously designed as accommodations for whatever staff traveled with the caliph occupying the suite. Companies were loath to identify these rooms as such. When not occupied by domestics, these "studios," as they were called, made suitable first-class cabins in a very rarified quarter of the ship. However, passengers might understandably balk at spending heavily for cabins designed for servants. Curiously enough, a special dining room for servants adjacent to the children's playroom was never identified on deck plans that reached the public.

It was not unusual for deluxe suites to be quite splendid. Given certain changes in taste, I doubt that those on the *Normandie* were any more dazzling than their equivalent on the *Imperator*. But they were unquestionably larger. Space on the French ship was as generous a commodity as it had been on the *Olympic*. The *Normandie,* largest of all ships to date, carried fewer than two thousand passengers, an incredibly low density that had never been equaled.

Moreover, the entire vessel was furnished with the same lavish touch that had characterized the interiors of the *France* in 1912. Everything was of the very finest quality and workmanship. It was as though the men responsible for her design had met every obligation and then gone one better. Every first-class bath had fresh water supplied and each adjoining cabin was decorated differently, necessitating over four hundred separate schemes with no repeats. There were even a dozen done entirely in steel and aluminum, experiments in advance of the fireproof perfection of the *United States* twenty years later. The swimming pool was enormous, a hundred-foot-long paradise of blue mosaic and bronze railing, the only one in Atlantic history to incorporate a shelving "beach" for children and cautious swimmers. Dogs on board were housed in an oval kennel room quite as elaborate in its own way as the children's dining room decorated by Jean de Brunhoff with trunk-to-tail chains of Babars. Forward under the bridge was a winter garden, whose elaborate greenery was enriched by exotic birds caged in plate glass and delicate jets of water that plashed in marble basins. The extraordinary dining room was air-conditioned and for the first time, third-class passengers had their own elevator.

The handsome space aft of the Café-Grill, complete with high-backed benches and lamp standards but without the proposed merman. Notice the lavish joinery of the staircase that achieves it. Above it, at right, is Trouville's private terrace. Directly behind the *Normandie* is the *Paris* and behind her, the *Ile de France* in dry dock. (*Compagnie Générale Transatlantique*)

A view of the *Normandie*'s bridge, the quietest place on board. The helmsman stood, traditionally, on an ash grating even though there was little chance of getting his feet wet. (*National Maritime Museum, Greenwich*)

In short, the *Normandie* was unrealistic, impractical, uneconomical and magnificent. The particular standard of shipboard luxe for which the Compagnie Générale Transatlantique strove was unquestionably the most ambitious ever attempted. There were always those who might quarrel with a decorative intent. Some found the ship too imposing. There were, additionally, problems of vibration. But above and beyond these inevitable criticisms, the *Normandie* more than justified her owner's promise. Furthermore, no other Atlantic company has ever provided that same glorious combination of speed and splendor.

Fitting out consumed three rather than two years. Last-minute changes in design, logistical failures, and the reluctance of shipyard workers to hasten completion of such a lucrative contract all contributed to the delay. It was, also, a simply enormous job. During the final year, key officers took up residence at Penhoët to supervise completion of the work. Commandant Pugnet joined Chief Engineer Jean Hazard, who had spent the past three years commuting between Belfort and the Loire. Villar, the obvious choice for post of *commissaire,* occupied the chaotic shell of the purser's office, somehow retaining his customary elegance in a boiler suit and beret.

These were the advance guard of an ultimate crew of thirteen hundred. Competition was keen for a berth on the *Normandie* and the cream of the Transat fleet was selected. One of the first tasks of the catering department was the reception of thousands of bottles of wine, allowed several months in their seagoing *cave* to settle in time for the maiden voyage.

In May, 1935, trials were held at Les Glénans off the Brittany peninsula's south coast. This was the French equivalent of Scotland's Skelmorlie Mile and the new ship outdid herself, averaging over thirty-one knots with ease. Local sardine fishermen, stern critics of not only the *Normandie* but other vessels before her, were awed by the absence of monstrous waves radiating from her wake; they reported that she slid over the water like a gull. They were not the only observers. The Company had invited representatives of the world's press along as part of an elaborate public relations campaign on behalf of the ship. They had only one nervous moment, when Commandant Pugnet executed without warning a crash turn to starboard. The *Normandie* heeled over sharply and righted herself without any delay. Quantities of Transat crockery did not survive the exercise and portions of the dining room were knee-deep in shards. But the reporters were impressed. "The Normandie," wrote A. C. Hardy, "is the most remarkable and luxurious liner of this epoch." This was strong stuff, particularly from an English journalist who might very well have to compromise his exuberance the following year when the *Queen Mary* sailed.

The French ship steamed into Le Havre later that month, already the center of world interest. Vast amounts of work remained to be done: some of the cabins had no beds, the plumbers were woefully behind and the entire ship's exterior had to be repainted for the maiden voyage. Prior to sailing on May 29, three days of unremitting gala had been scheduled, the kind of white-gloved, tricolored pomp without which Gallic officialdom can never commit itself. Magrain, *chef des cuisines,* galvanized his staff of seventy cooks in preparation for an avalanche of visitors. Freight cars were shunted alongside the hull, disgorging tons of produce from the Paris markets. From New York came supplies unobtainable or inferior in Europe: hominy grits, cranberry sauce, dry cereals, buckwheat pancake flour, ketchup, maple syrup and malted milk powder. Cases of these items had sailed eastbound in the dry-stores room of the *Paris.*

On the morning of the twenty-ninth, a special train brought members of the Paris Opera's *corps de ballet,* who went into rehearsal in the *grand salon,* clouding the flawless parquet with resin. They were to perform as part of that evening's spectacle marking the ship's last night in port. The first passengers, permitted to board a day early, were actors scheduled to open the *Normandie*'s theater at sea with the first performance of a new comedy by François de Croisset. On that same morning, Villar discovered to his horror that Trouville, the suite selected by Madame Lebrun, was still a shambles and that basins were being installed in first-class cabins to be occupied that afternoon. Blue-denimed plumbers, incongruous admidst the glitter, bolted porcelain *lavabos* into place, their canvas carryalls agape on fawn-colored carpet. Even late that evening, after the last exhausted *ouvrier* had departed, there was no running water in some parts of first class. Overnight guests were brought ewers of shaving water by a brigade of stewards.

But despite these crises, common to every noble undertaking, nothing could eclipse the luster of that final week. Not only the ship but the splendid new Gare Maritime was unveiled, and the President of France stepped off his train onto a specially carpeted platform under vaulting ferroconcrete. From the roof rose an illuminated tower with giant numerals on three sides, by which pilots and masters alike could take distant readings of tide conditions. The final evening's entertainment was a *succès fou* and President and Madame Lebrun forsook the scheduled delights of Le Havre's principal hotel to pass the night on board instead. A *matelot* from the Navy mounted guard with a pike outside the President's door. In the words of Edmond Lanier, head of the company today: *"Le navire était si beau, le dîner si raffiné, la soirée si élégante que toute cette foule parisienne et critique fit trêve et adopta enfin Normandie."* In addition to Madame Lebrun, the passenger

Above, last days at St. Nazaire. The *Normandie*'s bow viewed at sunset shortly before departure for trials. (*Compagnie Générale Transatlantique*)

Left, the new flagship of the *Compagnie Générale Transatlantique* sails from St. Nazaire for Le Havre. (*Compagnie Générale Transatlantique*) list carried a heady array of names: Pierre Cartier, Colette, Mrs. Morgan Belmont, Mrs. Frank Jay Gould, Madame Jean Lanvin and the Maharajah of Karpurthala, who was booked in Deauville with his own cook.

I have never sailed on a maiden voyage and by now it is extremely doubtful that I ever shall. In point of fact, the ship cannot be at its best. Everything is too new and stewards and pursers are finding their way almost as much as their clients. It takes at least a season for ship and staff to settle down. But if it were possible to be granted the retrospective privilege of sailing on any inaugural crossing, I would choose without hesitation either the *Normandie*'s or, for totally different reasons, the *Queen Elizabeth*'s. The incredible size (nearly 80,000 gross tons), speed and luxury of the French vessel gave the occasion a special panache.

The send-off from Europe and the reception in New York were perhaps no more enthusiastic than for any ship; maiden sailings were rare enough that chroniclers tended to forget the previous one and declared the latest to be just that much more overwhelming. The first American to sight the ship was a surfman at Fire Island's Coast Guard Station. Shortly afterwards, just past eleven on the morning of June 3, 1935, the great black hull swept past Ambrose Lightship. Among the vast quantities of stores brought on board in France had been boxes of medals, inscribed with the ship's name and the date, suspended from a blatant blue ribbon. These incomparable souvenirs were now unearthed from the purser's safe and distributed among jubilant passengers. From the top of the after mast, a giant blue pennant, thirty meters long (a meter for each knot of speed) was unfurled. It had been cut, sewn and grommeted back at Le Havre. There had been little doubt in anyone's mind that the ship would take the honors from the Italians although, traditionally, no public acknowledgment was made of it until that moment.

If the *Normandie* left chaos behind in her home port, the same inevitable disorder awaited her at the New York terminus. She was the first vessel to tie up at one of the three super-piers just completed in the Hudson River at West 50th Street. Harbor engineers had spent years gouging out an additional two hundred feet from Manhattan's West Side, lengthening inland in preference to extending out into the channel. Twelfth Avenue and subsequently the elevated West Side Highway dimpled in at that point.

But though the slips were completed, the interior of Pier 88 was not. Workmen hung bunting over temporary scaffolding still tacky with fresh red paint. On the lower level, two hundred and fifty work-checks were flung indiscriminately among a thousand longshoremen anxious for work and police were called in to quell the resulting fracas. Union electricians on the

THE ONLY WAY TO CROSS

First occupant of the super piers: The
Normandie tied up at Pier 88. In the foreground, 12th Avenue's cobbles are not
yet obscured by the West Side Highway.
(*Compagnie Générale Transatlantique*)

pier chose that moment to take violent exception to newsreel sound men assembled to film the *Normandie*'s arrival. Predictably, a Company representative paid the union an exorbitant ransom to avoid a stand-off.

Passage up from Quarantine was a magnificent sight. Fireboats thrust up plumes of water and ferries filled to capacity veered as close as possible to the armada of small craft that raced along in company with their giant sister. One tug towed a helium-bloated Mickey Mouse and in the sky, dirigibles with loudspeaker systems brayed a nasal welcome to the French. A flight of Army Air Corps planes swooped back and forth in V-formation. Twenty tugs stood by but only a dozen of them were used to turn the ship around the knuckle of the pier. It took an hour to berth the *Normandie,* including one hideous attempt when her gigantic bow, most of its black paint flaked off by the Atlantic, grazed a floating fender and only just missed crushing a man to death. The flaring hull loomed over the pier, sending hundreds of spectators racing panic-stricken inside. On her second try, the bow nearly probed Cunard's unfinished Pier 90 to the north and a warping hawser snapped. Its loose end was retrieved by a bathing-suited longshoreman.

Mayor La Guardia turned on his and New York's charm and gave an official dinner for Madame Lebrun at the Waldorf. She returned the honor on board the *Normandie* the following night, graciously presenting the Mayor with a five-hundred-dollar check "for the poor of New York." Rival companies were less than exuberant in their praise, although Captain Tarabotto signaled from the *Rex:* "Extend sincere good wishes to this great ship for a happy crossing over the ocean of time." From Hamburg's *Boersen Zeitung* came an editorial devoid of praise, hinting that the *Bremen* and *Europa* had purposely been held in check against the possibility of just such a challenge. Sir Percy Bates, Cunard White Star's chairman, admitted in Liverpool that the *Normandie* "seems to have done pretty well"; as for a committal that the *Queen Mary* might recapture the record for Britain, he quite sensibly refused any official speculation. Passengers were delighted with the ship while regretting the brevity of their passage. Vibration was commonly acknowledged as the only distressing failure. Although Madame Lebrun's suite must have felt the worst of it, she wisely refrained from any comment. Cabins located directly over the screws had been evacuated the second night out and their occupants moved elsewhere.

There is an ironic aftermath to the *Normandie*'s vibration that is worth detailing. In November of that year, the ship was withdrawn from service for her first annual lay-up. Dozens of experts offered advice on the subject of vibration and put forth conflicting proposals to remedy it. Strengthening

THE ONLY WAY TO CROSS

members were introduced into various after compartments and the first-class terrace was displaced by a new tourist lounge. This latter addition I suspect, had much to do with an attempt to stiffen the hull.

A Company engineer recommended a new set of propellers with four blades rather than three. They were designed, cast and installed over the winter and tested in the Channel the following spring. At thirty knots, Commandant Thoreux (who had replaced Pugnet) stood on Deauville's private terrace and could not feel the slightest *tremblement*. If this seems inconsequential, it is worth pointing out that water glasses had never been more than half-filled in the café grill, to prevent saturating the tablecloths. Walking back to the bridge, Director-General Henri Cangardel paused and balanced a pencil with its unsharpened end down on a smoking-room table; it remained serenely upright. A triumphant coded message flashed back to Company headquarters and when the *Normandie* appeared in Le Havre two days later, her master was besieged with newsmen requesting confirmation that the problem of vibration had been laid to rest. Thoreux gave it.

The ship was due to sail the following day, inaugurating her second season. Just after the press conference, the chief engineer knocked agitatedly at his captain's door. A diver sent down to make a routine hull inspection reported that all *three* propellers seemed in good shape. On a quadruple-screw vessel, this kind of intelligence induces both mystification and alarm. After some incredulous cross-examination, a Company diver was sent below to refute or confirm the initial report. Half an hour later, he surfaced and told his uneasy listeners that the port central tail shaft was indeed bereft of its new propeller.

It is almost impossible for a screw to be lost in service without at least one engineer having knowledge of it. In this singular case, it is probable that through oversight or mechanical failure, a locking device was improperly secured. The propeller must have dropped off moments after *"Stoppez les machines!"* had rung down from the bridge. The ship was due for departure the following day. She was fully booked and company officials were determined to maintain their schedule. It was decided to use one of the old three-bladed propellers. To do so meant a hazardous nighttime entry into dry dock. It was accomplished without incident and a double shift of workers labored through the night and following morning replacing both inboard propellers. (This was necessary to retain correct synchronization.) With only a few hours delay, passengers embarked that afternoon.

But the reporters who had interviewed Thoreux upon his return from trials had done their work too well; all who came on board could talk of nothing else but the wonderful new propellers and their lack of vibration.

Needless to say, with half of her original set back in use, the vibration was as bad as ever. The *Normandie,* the French Line and the unfortunate Commandant took a frightful verbal drubbing at the hands of the exasperated passengers, who quite naturally felt that they had been victims of a public-relations hoax. Although the weather was good, Thoreux wisely took most of his meals in solitude on the bridge. The incident proved only one thing conclusively: that the *Normandie*'s vibration had resulted from faulty propeller design—all that stiffening and reconstruction of the after end had made precious little difference.

The French ship's entry into service dominated the maritime news of 1935, just as the *Queen Mary*'s did the following year. John Brown's hull number 534 was named after the queen who christened her, the decision kept secret until launch time. There is an apocryphal story still making the rounds that the Company had planned originally to call their ship *Victoria.* Lord Royden, a Company director, was supposed to have been grouse shooting with King George and asked the Sovereign's permission to name the ship after England's greatest queen. His Majesty is quoted as replying that he was delighted with the idea and would ask her the moment he got home.

The story is charming but untrue. Cunard and White Star had chosen *Queen Mary* themselves as a suitably neutral compromise that avoided the *-ia* and *-ic* suffixes cherished by each of them prior to merger. Her Majesty quickly consented but the Board of Trade pointed out that they already had a vessel by that name on their list. This was a small Scottish coastal steamer whose owners were finally convinced that calling her *Queen Mary II* would not confuse potential clients. Cunard White Star profited from their experience. When the *Mauretania* was about to be scrapped shortly thereafter, Cunard passed on the name to a small vessel whose owners agreed to relinquish it when a second *Mauretania* was ready at Birkenhead.

The *Mary*'s launch took place in a cold, driving rain on September 26, 1934. The King and Queen entrained from Balmoral, arriving in the sodden yard at noon. Nestled under the ship's starboard bow was a suite of five specially constructed reception rooms, legged up thirty-five feet above the ground. Although it was accessible by elevator, Their Majesties elected to walk instead up a long sloping ramp, sharing at least a taste of the discomfort experienced by thousands of their subjects huddled under acres of dripping umbrellas. Her Majesty named the ship, cutting with a pair of golden scissors the cord that released a bottle of Australian champagne against the *Mary*'s stem. A world-wide radio audience heard the Queen whisper near an open microphone: "Shall I press the button now?" She did and the gigantic mass of steel, two thousand tons heavier than the *Normandie,* ground triumphantly into the Clyde. Poet Laureate John Masefield dubbed her "a rampart of a ship."

The *Normandie* and *Queen Mary* were the ultimate prewar Atlantic rivals. Together with the *Bremen* and *Europa,* the two vessels dominated the late thirties. Coincidental with their appearance, the slump that had introduced the decade showed signs of ending. Passenger revenues for 1935 actually increased over the year preceding it, reversing a pattern that had endured since the crash.

Why, one might ask, have I dismissed the fabled Cunarder with a brief acknowledgment, following an elaborate panegyric about her competitor across the Channel? It could be argued convincingly that the *Normandie* sailed first and that statistical repetition might pall. The *Queen Mary* was a vessel of equal pretension, of almost identical size and service capability, that proved slightly faster. She took the Blue Riband in August of her first season, if not on her maiden voyage, at least the first ship in history to crack the four-day crossing.

I prefer to justify my predilection for the Penhoët ship by the double rationale that she was the more daring of the two as well as the more unfortunate. The *Normandie*'s career was tragically brief, in service for only four seasons. She scarcely completed seventy voyages before the war ended her career forever. In contrast, the legendary *Queen Mary* went on, like her namesake, to grand old age, accruing an enviable record of dignity and dependability. She crossed more than a thousand times and, with the *Elizabeth,* carried millions of loyal passengers.

There were relatively few who knew the *Normandie.* Her radical hull, her central suites of rooms, her advanced profile, the turbo-electric power plant combined in one astonishing ship to make her unique. Before the war, Yourkevitch hung in his office two framed aerial photographs, one of the *Queen Mary* and the other of his beloved *Normandie,* each cutting through the ocean. He was fond of pointing out to visitors the lack of turbulence around his hull in contrast to the lather of white water surrounding his Scottish-built rival's. Also, he was likely to remind these same visitors that the *Queen Mary* needed her forty thousand additional horsepower to obtain that fraction of a knot faster speed. The British ship's unquestionably sound and seaworthy hull was, apart from its cruiser stern, scarcely novel. In fact, the Cunarder's appearance on the ways suggested nothing more than a longer and bulkier *Aquitania.* With a conventional cutwater, aristocratic entry, well deck and air of four-square solidity, she was reminiscent of any number of Clyde-built hulls. Her sole distinction was size.

September 26, 1934. R.M.S.
Queen Mary, just christened
by Her Majesty, afloat for the
first time on the River Clyde.
(*Cunard*)

THE FORWARD FUNNEL of the "QUEEN MARY" IS 70 FEET IN HEIGHT FROM THE BOAT DECK.
(A FOOT HIGHER THAN THE EGYPTIAN OBELISK IN CENTRAL PARK, NEW YORK CITY)
THE DIAMETER OF EACH FUNNEL IS 30 FEET AND WOULD PERMIT 3 MODERN
LOCOMOTIVES, PLACED ABREAST, TO PASS THROUGH, OR TO ENCLOSE THE
HULL OF THE FIRST CUNARDER, THE "BRITANNIA."

Above, Cunard White Star publicity. Pre-occupation with the number of vehicles that can be squeezed through a new ship's funnels dates back to Swan Hunter's initial experiment with the *Mauretania*. (*The Peabody Museum of Salem*)

The *Queen Mary* at sea. Just under the after mast are the fourteen windows of the veranda grill, the North Atlantic's most famous restaurant. (*Laurence Lowry for Cunard*)

Maiden Voyage. The *Queen Mary* seen
from the deck of a New York tugboat.
Her riveted hull conveys an impression of
enormous strength. (*Edwin Levick Collection, The Mariners Museum, Newport
News, Virginia*)

When completely fitted out, traditional funnels and ventilators gave her a profile hardly different from the ancient ships she was designed to replace. Her interiors were disappointing too. Inside, the *Mary* had the look of a Leicester Square cinema palace, an effect that *Architect and Building News* described as "mild but expensive vulgarity." Veneered in the boiserie of Empire, the ship drummed and chattered with glistening woods. It seemed that every commonwealth and colony had contributed its most exotic trees and somehow the designers had fitted them all in. Paradoxically, near the end of her life, her looks were restored effortlessly to a kind of popularity: a resurrection of thirties tastes made both *Queens* bizarre floating museums in the late sixties, something their original designers could never have envisioned.

But no French forebear prepared one for the *Normandie;* neither the *France, Paris* nor *Ile* conveyed in their appearance any hint of their magnificent successor. She is a stunning departure from anything that has ever sailed the Atlantic. Not since the *Imperator* had such vast interiors been realized as well. Shortly after the fire that destroyed her, Ludwig Bemelmans wrote:

> I have always extended to her more affection than I have to any other ship. I loved her for her gaiety, for her color, for the familiarity with all the world that was in her passenger list. She leaned to excesses in her *décor;* there was something of the fatal woman. She took a *seigneur*'s abusive privilege of frowning on the lesser, fatter, longer, more solid boats. Like all aristocrats, she had abominable moods. I think she was more female than all other ships I have known. I think that's why I loved her so.

When the cabin port-holes are dark and green
Because of the seas outside;
When the ship goes wop (*with a wiggle between*)
And the steward falls into the soup-tureen,
And the trunks begin to slide;
When Nursey lies on the floor in a heap,
And Mummy tells you to let her sleep,
And you aren't waked or washed or dressed,
Why, then you will know (if you haven't guessed)
You're 'Fifty North and Forty West'!
> —RUDYARD KIPLING, JUST-SO STORIES

11.
Westbound:
the Thirties

Most Americans sailed from Europe in late summer, joining with flocks of their fellow countrymen headed for New York and home. Passage west seemed slower, and often was, because of the adverse Gulf Stream. The pace on board was also retarded, the gaiety less spontaneous and the spirit of eastbound adventure totally absent. It was a time of snapshots and souvenirs, a time of reckoning and disillusionment, of tales about victimization and bargains, of fabrications about who had been where and an intense exhaustion that even twenty-five-hour days did not dispel.

There was no carnival air about sailing. Instead of flowers in the cabin there were stacks of parcels, loot, the spoils of the dollar crusaders. Suitcases were familiar now, even despised, erupting with clothes sorely in need

THE ONLY WAY TO CROSS

Platform 11, Waterloo Station, in 1926.
Only Americans ever seemed to miss the
boat train. (*R. C. Riley Collection*)

of attention that they would not get on board. There were no steerage women to wash them, no wash house and, obtusely, no ship's laundry. (Provision of this luxury on board Atlantic vessels is one of the few recent improvements; passengers embarking on cruise-oriented ships today find the laundry that their predecessors in the thirties did not.) Steamer trunks reappeared in staterooms, dusty from storage in the heat of a Le Havre or Southampton warehouse over the summer, their contents as fatigued as their owners. The innocence of June was displaced by the cynicism of September, the promise of dawn in the east by the nostalgia of a westering sun.

Westbound ships called, in reverse order, at Channel ports that had been points of original European contact. Passengers hung over the rail in search of familiar or interesting faces. Friendships ripened fast in the flush of continental summer and new/old friends shrieked back and forth over the roar of the stack that sent acrid fumes into open promenade deck windows.

The succession of outward-bound ports gave latecomers a sporting chance. Taxi drivers used to haunt the Gare St. Lazare in search of Americans who had missed the boat train. Europeans never seemed to miss this crucial departure, only Americans. Drivers knew that no fare would be too excessive for these desperate travelers if they reached Le Havre or Cherbourg in advance of sailing time. Suitcases were strapped to the roof and many a wild ride disrupted the peace of the Norman countryside as Parisian taxis faced their ultimate test.

Those who had urgent reasons to cross on a particular vessel pursued it relentlessly cross-Channel. One determined passenger hired an airplane. Even so, he missed both Southampton and Cherbourg sailings before he finally caught up with his ship at Cobh. He bribed a boatman to row him out and climbed triumphantly on board as the lace sellers and gnarled old men peddling blackthorn canes were being shooed off the promenade decks.

Cobh's most popular souvenirs were those delicious little lobsters, features of the next day's luncheon menu. Mention of lobster brings to mind the *Normandie*'s great lobster glut in early 1938. The occasion was an imminent southern cruise. From mid-Atlantic, purchasing agents in New York were notified by wireless to stock up on American comestibles, among them a quantity of Maine lobsters. In transmission, "dozens" was somehow garbled into "gross" and every fish purveyor in sight was alerted by the French Line commissariat to fill a monumental order. At Pier 88, trucks delivered crustaceans in their thousands, twelve times the number requested and far in excess of the kitchen's live storage tanks. Having scoured the East Coast to find them, suppliers were not about to take them back. Passengers and crew of the *Normandie* bound for Rio spent a week surfeited with an apparently inexhaustible deluge of *homard américain*, broiled, boiled, mayonnaised, stewed, bisqued, thermidored and moussed.

In late summer, the Atlantic tended to be rougher. The promoters of the seven-hundred-foot *Great Eastern* had declared in the 1850's that the ship's length exceeded the longest recorded distance between storm crests. Deceived by this comforting statistic, they took the position that an optimum sized hull had been achieved to defy the ocean's worst. This was a dangerous assumption and one they learned to regret. Following a hurricane off the coast of Ireland which disabled her steering gear, the *Great Eastern* was so battered that luggage was later removed from the hold in scoops.

The builders of the *Queen Mary* exhibited the same curious optimism and neglected to provide handrails along the passageways; in addition, there were no anchoring devices for most of the furniture. An October storm of 1936 made it abundantly clear that even ships of her astronomical size are vulnerable to uncomfortable and terrifying motion. The *Mary* was a tender ship that hung on the roll for an alarming length of time before recovering. In 1958, at the insistence of Cunard's board chairman, two sets of Denny-Brown fin stabilizers were shoehorned into her crowded engine spaces. Critical rolling was eliminated, as was the china replacement bill which, in one prestabilizer season, accounted for twenty-five thousand pieces.

The *Normandie* was not tender. She was instead a snappy roller. Her large metacentric height meant that the speed of return to the vertical was brisk. But avoiding the Scylla of her rival's sogginess, she encountered the Charybdis of a destroyer's resiliency, whipping herself and her passengers back upright with ruthless efficiency. Helen Hayes and Ruth Gordon shared a cabin on the *Normandie*'s first eastbound crossing. While waiting for breakfast to arrive, Miss Hayes was momentarily stunned as a heavy Lalique vase, its base weighted with shot, hurtled off an adjacent bureau and struck her on the head. The resulting downpour of Nyack roses, water and buckshot revived her at once, in time to watch in fascinated horror as the plate-glass top of a circular table, dislodged from its base, spun around the cabin like a giant demented half-dollar. There was a knock at the door. Timing the lethal disc's progress, the two women shouted in unison *"Now!"* to the steward who stood, uncomprehending, with trays outside.

Storm damage on these huge ships was seldom as severe as it had been on earlier vessels. A famous blow of 1912, for instance, reduced much of the *Carmania*'s interior to chaos. The ship went through a series of violent fifty-degree rolls that carried kitchen ranges away and sent them grinding back and forth across the tiles. Deck chairs, in the words of one observer, "floated through the air like pieces of paper." Some cabins were made untenable as beds, only recently introduced as a luxury, battered their way through wooden partitions. Passengers thus dispossessed finally lay flat in the ship's square, clutching the base of the pillars.

On the *Mauretania* one night, the purser's cabin was split open by a wave as a group of passengers were taking their coffee with him. The lights went out and until the sea water drained out the way it had come in, there were a few uncomfortable moments. In 1926, the *Leviathan* encountered a storm with waves a hundred feet high. Captain Hartley navigated from an open bridge wing and ordered all passenger entrances onto the deck locked. One woman, insane with fear, somehow found her way on deck and clambered up a ladder onto the bridge. There she assaulted the master and demanded over the shriek of the gale that he turn back. The poor creature was completely unhinged and it took five men to get her below to the surgeon. Another unfortunate woman literally died on the *Queen Mary* from a combination of exhaustion, seasickness and fright.

There is a device called by American seamen a "dummy," a kind of metal umbrella used as an emergency plug for broken portholes. They were used with good effect on the *Ile de France* one winter's night in the mid thirties when a wave smashed against the side of the ship and burst in no fewer than fifteen dining-room portholes. Luckily, the room was unoccupied, for before the ship could be hove to, water was waist-deep. The same storm broke two windows in an *appartement de luxe* fifty feet above, occupied by Mrs. Frank Jay Gould. Everything she owned was soaked with sea water, but she was able to move immediately across to the companion suite, which was fortunately unbooked. It is typical that her belongings were washed and ironed that night, also that passengers who came down for breakfast at nine the following morning found no evidence of damage other than plugged portholes. It was after storms like this that ship's surgeons were kept busy setting fractured limbs and that ambulances were on call at terminals on either shore.

Once a monsignor, traveling on the French liner *Providence,* was pacing the deck hysterically during a storm. The captain took him down to the fo'c's'le. "Look," he remarked comfortingly, "these are men of the sea, playing cards and swearing. If there were any danger, they would be on their knees praying." The cleric seemed reassured and went back on deck. A little later, the storm grew worse and the master sent one of his subordinates down to the priest. The startled officer was taken by the arm and led

The *Ile de France* plunges
through some dirty weather
on the Western Ocean. (*Compagnie Générale Transatlantique*)

down to the fo'c's'le, where the relieved monsignor turned to him and said "Thank God, they are still swearing."

French sea captains had a way with passengers terrified of rough weather. Commandant Maurras of the *France* used to descend to the smoking room in even moderately heavy seas, clad in oilskins and sou'wester, having been doused by a seaman with a bucket of water. He would stagger into the room, his oilskins dripping puddles of water onto the carpet, demanding of his astonished passengers how they could relax and continue to play cards when such a storm, the likes of which he had not experienced ever before in thirty years at sea, raged unabated outside. Then he would stamp out, leaving a slightly uneasy but reassured assembly behind.

This same captain had another trick. He would invite passengers up to the bridge just before land was sighted and wager that he could guess the exact moment when it would appear. He never lacked for takers and never lost the bet. An accomplice, stationed in the crow's-nest and able to anticipate anything over the horizon by a minute or so, used to transmit the intelligence by removing his cap and scratching his head. Passengers were continually baffled by the captain's skill.

Sea captains have always been a breed unto themselves. One of them said once that they combined "great seamanship, ruthless conservatism, blasphemy and strange inarticulate warmth." Up to the Second World War, all who rose to command the Atlantic mailboats had begun their careers on sailing vessels. Something about that exacting apprenticeship gave them an indestructible fiber. They tended toward doughtiness, their eyes had a clarity and sparkle and their faces a wind-burnished weathering.

Long exposure to the sea and the men who served on it gave their speech a color of its own. Their table conversation in the first-class dining room sometimes strayed beyond the limits of convention. Captain Alec Hambleton of the *Adriatic* had a repertoire of sea stories that he relished on every crossing. My grandmother had heard them all several times and used to kick him under the table whenever she thought he was about to offend feminine sensibilities. One of his stories concerned the day when, as a junior officer, he was charged with getting passengers on board from a tender. The sea was particularly rough and he followed the last one, a plump lady with voluminous skirts, up the ladder. He held onto the ladder with one hand and with the other kept a firm grasp on her skirts to keep them from flying in the wind.

Halfway up the side of the vessel, she looked down, saw that the tender had gone and began to panic. Hambleton relinquished his hold on her skirts in case she should fall. They immediately blew up and over his head, on which the distraught woman sat, refusing to budge. He had only one alternative: he bit her as hard as he could. She flew up the ladder, taking the skin off his nose with her heel as she did. "She hurt me," he used to say, with a twinkle, "but I guarantee she slept face down for a week." Then, if she was there, would come my grandmother's kick. "What are you kicking me for?" he would demand. "It's true, every word of it. I wouldn't tell it if it weren't true." He had another he used to tell about helping deliver twins on board a sailing packet; if it seemed too far-fetched to be true, it was also too bizarre to be a fabrication.

Cunard Captain Arthur Rostron once said that every ship had three sides: port, starboard and social. In company with most of his colleagues, this last was a side he would quite happily have relinquished. It was time-consuming and boring, I suspect, to make the same polite conversation crossing after crossing, answering a succession of predictable inquiries. One master made a collection of queries which included the following perennials: "Does Cunard pay for your uniforms? What time do you get up in the morning? Do you know a reliable tailor in London? Why are the deck lights left burning all day?" To this last, he sometimes replied with a perfectly straight face that it was done in the event they had to pass through any tunnels.

An enormous bearded captain, when confronted by an inquisitive passenger, launched into a prepared recitative:

I have crossed the Atlantic four hundred and twenty-two times this will be my four hundred and twenty-third I have not been shipwrecked or cast away on a desert island or been burnt at sea or marooned or shanghaied or caught by sharks and I don't want to be the ship is doing fifteen knots and could do more if she were going faster you will be able to go ashore as soon as we are alongside the jetty and not before and if you have anything you want to smuggle I don't want to know about it and I don't know the best way to get it ashore without paying duty I hope to retire from the sea some day *Is there anything else you would like to know?*

All this would be delivered at increasing speed and volume so that near the end he was roaring into the unfortunate questioner's ear. Captain John Jamieson of the *Saint Paul* solved the problem of talkative passengers by selecting the best table in the dining room the first day out, seating himself and then ordering the steward in a loud voice to remove the other chairs.

Nowadays, all Atlantic vessels have a staff captain, an alternate master who removes some of the appalling load of social responsibility from his superior's shoulders. On French ships he is the *Commandant Adjoint* and

Archetypal Captain: Arthur Rostron,
who served as master of the *Carpathia,
Mauretania,* and, as Cunard's Commodore, the *Berengaria. (Cunard)*

on Italian the *Comandante in Seconda.* One of the four captains under the *Imperator*'s Commodore, although perfectly qualified to command the vessel, was wisely selected on the basis of his ease with celebrated passengers. Nowadays, there is no captain's table, mainly because there are fewer social lions traveling by sea. On the *France,* there are two Captain's Dinner Parties per crossing when a dozen passengers are invited to dine with the *Commandant* (or his *Adjoint*) at a long head table that remains unused for the rest of the crossing. This is an admirable compromise: it not only dazzles the nucleus of passengers who feel it their due but is a splendid way for the company to reward their *amis de maison.* On the *Raffaello* and *Michelangelo* the captain eats regularly in the dining room, but with only his officers at table.

Captain Jamieson was a short man, as was Hambleton, as well as Smith of the *Titanic.* I suspect there may be some connection between shortness and the kind of competent pugnacity that took men to the maritime top. But regardless of height, all captains were superstitious to a marked degree and possessed of a quick temper; if "temper" is perhaps too harsh a word, it would at least be accurate to say that they suffered fools impatiently. They were, not surprisingly, devout men, despite occasional lapses into picturesque temerity.

On British and American vessels, divine services were regularly conducted by the captain, a role that French and Italian masters had perforce to relinquish to passenger priests. If Protestant captains had one class of passenger they found more troublesome than loquacious females, it was men of the cloth who felt it their prerogative to conduct the Sunday morning service. A Methodist bishop on the *Homeric* once had to be almost physically restrained from confronting the congregation in the lounge. It was ultimately made clear to him that a ship is exclusively the captain's parish.

Fewer marriages were performed by captains than is popularly supposed. The number of giddy couples who requested the service far outnumbered those who actually received it. Captain Herbert Hartley of the *Leviathan* performed only nine marriages during his years on board. The last, between *Mutt-and-Jeff* cartoonist Bud Fisher and the Countess de Beaumont, ended in such a scandalous divorce that the United States Shipping Board discouraged their masters from repeating similar performances. Marriage became, like gin, taboo on American vessels.

Social hazards for Atlantic masters included being mistaken for stewards on their own ships. Captain Irvine, nicknamed " 'Aughty Bill" by his contemporaries, was once summoned by a female passenger as he walked the promenade deck. "Steward," she trilled from her deck chair, "please take this tray away." There are two versions of his reaction: one, that he turned, drew himself up to his full height and roared "And what the deuce do you suppose, ma'am, the Captain looks like?" The other, which I prefer, is that he took the tray obsequiously, stepped back a pace and let it fall to the deck with a glorious clatter. "There, madam," he purred dangerously, "you can see what a very poor steward I am."

A White Star captain, known as "Dismal Jimmy," delighted in the chore of burying the dead. For reasons of his own, perhaps because they were occasions of relative infrequency, he took particular pleasure in delivering those measured cadences while a canvas-draped bundle, one end weighted with iron, was poised on a tabletop over the after railing. Once, just as he was about to begin, the foghorn summoned him to the bridge and he turned matters over to a subordinate. But the patch of fog was a small one and moments later, he raced back down, struggling into his frock coat. He seized the prayer book, barking at the same moment: "Like hell you are, *I* am the resurrection and the life!"

Fog was a dreaded enemy. When the weather closed in, watches for other members of the crew continued as usual but the captain always stayed on the bridge till it cleared. Nowhere did this mean so much loss of sleep as on the North Atlantic. Commodore Bertram Hayes once spent sixty-nine consecutive hours in the wheelhouse of the *Majestic*. Marathons of this kind were not uncommon in the days before radar. On one of the bridge wings was an elevated swivel chair reserved exclusively for the captain; no one else ever sat in the fog chair. Their ears fine-tuned by exhaustion, masters could often hear faint engine noises through fog that none of their supposedly more alert juniors could detect. Mothers of sick children are often blessed with this same acute hearing.

Even more astonishing, masters also *sensed* something out in that clammy whiteness. There is scarcely a captain's memoir that doesn't acknowledge this fortunate phenomenon. Countless ships were saved from collision at the last moment by an intuitive sixth sense, the *Normandie, Mauretania* and *Majestic,* to name but a few. Steaming cautiously through fog, the captain would suddenly order all engines stopped; within moments, a vessel would loom out of the mist, on a direct collision course only narrowly avoided. There were many more close calls on the Western Ocean than passengers ever heard about, near misses that never even went into the log.

Fog has a sinister capacity to distort the nature and direction of sound. Acoustical patterns in the air are upset to such an extent that experienced

S.S. LEVIATHAN - - AT SEA
August 10th, 1923

President Harding
Memorial

ORDER OF SERVICE
Starting 5-45 p.m.

Prayer - - Rev. C. E. Scott

Solo - - Miss Helen Stover
"Lead Kindly Light"

Addresses by James M. Beck,
      Solicitor General, U.S.A.

      Martin B. Madden,
      U.S.A. House of
      Representatives

      Reed Smoot,
      U.S.A. Senator

      James J. Davis,
      Secretary of Labor,
      U.S.A.

Solo - - Miss Helen Stover
"Abide With Me"

Prayer - - Rev. C. E. Scott

*Corresponding to the time the President's
Body is being lowered into the grave, in
token of respect, the Leviathan's engines will
be stopped for five minutes*

Albert D. Lasker - - Presiding

A midocean memorial service.
(*Frank Braynard Collection*)

The *Olympic* in the floating dock at Southampton. Workers are examining her bow plating following collision with the Nantucket Lightship. (*Cunard*)

mariners are perpetually misled by its effect. Relying on the ear alone is as hopeless as relying solely on radar. This particular devilment was at least partially responsible for the *Olympic*'s third and most awful collision one fog-shrouded morning a few hours out of New York in May of 1934. Her foghorn had sounded monotonously all the way from Southampton six days previously, and it is more than likely that her captain, John W. Binks, was red-eyed with exhaustion.

There were only a hundred and fifty-eight passengers on board, one of whom was talking with an off-duty engineer on the boat deck. Through the wall of mist that surrounded them, they could hear the bleat of the Nantucket Lightship. The engineer was literally in the midst of explaining how the sound was actually much farther away than it seemed when the *Olympic*'s steam whistle roared over their heads in desperate emergency. The lightship had appeared directly in their path. It was six hundred yards away, the helmsman later testified. The engines were stopped, rung down from a speed of sixteen knots, but the *Olympic*'s vertical stem moved relentlessly forward and sliced the tiny red vessel in half. (There is a chillingly familiar ring to the incident, the same graceful black hull that cannot effect a crash turn in time to avoid a floating body in its path.) Seven of the lightship's crewmen were killed, the remaining four rescued by the *Olympic*'s boats which had started down her sides moments before the fatal impact.

The tragic collision was significant because a wireless safeguard was also involved. The signal bearing that pulsed from a transmitter on board the Nantucket Lightship could be used by incoming masters in conjunction with others (Pollock Rip, Chatham, Block Island and the Vineyard Sound Lightship) to determine their exact position. Binks, the *Olympic*'s master, suggested at the New York inquiry that the system might have been defective or that the very fog itself had created freak atmospheric conditions affecting reception. Others on the bridge at the time supported him further, testifying that they had heard the lightship's foghorn to starboard and purposely turned a few degrees to port to ensure avoiding it. But Captain Eaton, superintendent of the Lightship Service, claimed that the *Olympic* was a notorious offender, always passing perilously close by the lightship. Actually, it was common navigational practice at the time for all masters to head directly for the lightship, skirting it only at the last moment; the liner *Washington* had accidentally brushed her earlier that year. Like both her sister ships before her, the *Olympic* ran afoul of the odds, suffering awful retribution for a common violation.

The incident was catastrophic for her master. Binks had been close to retirement anyway but the shock and resultant strain finished him. He never commanded a White Star ship again. (Technically speaking, very few of his fellow captains did either: in July of that same year, the two British rivals were officially joined in a merger. The *Aquitania*'s house flag had the White Star hauled up beneath it in midocean.) But he came out of retirement four years later for one last bizarre crossing, in command of the *Leviathan* on her final voyage from Hoboken to the Scottish breakers. The attachment of these men to their ships was extraordinary. Captain Parker of the *Olympic* once remarked in all seriousness: "You only have to will her to do something and she responds."

Retirement from service meant separation from the ships they had served in varying capacities for years. Sir James Charles, Cunard's Commodore prior to Rostron, died in command of the *Aquitania* as he docked her at Southampton for the last time. The emotional stress of the moment was too much. Sir James was remembered as perhaps the most elegant of British captains, a gourmet who insisted on white tie for his table on the *Aquitania* and ran Blancart of the *Ile* a close second as most *soigné* master on the Atlantic. Later on in the thirties, Sir James Netley died in his cabin on the *Aquitania* between Cherbourg and Southampton; again, it was his final voyage and the ship's surgeon attributed his death quite simply to a broken heart. It became customary, following this second incident, for Cunard White Star to withhold the actual date of retirement so that masters due for it never knew which was to be their last crossing. Yet they understood and honored the last wishes of Captain Sorrell in 1958, scattering his ashes from the stern of the *Queen Mary*. Sometimes the position of master combined with host on board one of the new giants proved too great a responsibility. Captain Sir Edgar Britten of the *Queen Mary* collapsed the morning his ship was due to sail for New York. Five hours later, he died in a Southampton nursing home.

Harold Nicolson was one of the passengers who traveled west on the *Normandie* during her first summer of service. Ben, his younger son, was with him but his wife, author Vita Sackville-West, stayed in Kent. Nicolson missed her dreadfully and it was her absence that prompted a long account written during the crossing and posted from New York. The letter constitutes an invaluable commentary on a thirties crossing, penned by an observer as entertaining as astute. The date is July 4, 1935:

> I lolled in my pullman and woke at Southampton docks. Then I embarked on the tendre [*sic*] and sat in a wicker chair reading a detective novel.
>
> It was hours before they got the luggage on board and at last the tendre trembled and began to move. We swung round out into the fair

way and from my chair I observed yachts at anchor sliding past the porthole. Then suddenly the tendre begain to tremble again even more violently. Passengers rushed to the side. There are cries of "We are putting back" "Someone has been forgotten". A grumble of grievance spread through the ship. . . . The tendre churned backwards into the pier and against a sister tendre upon which stood the culprit. He was a young Catholic clergyman, very spotty about the chin, holding a small suit case covered in black American cloth. He faced the five hundred indignant eyes without any of that courage which I believed to be resident in the Order of Jesus. He cast down his eyes at his little black suit case and when the moment came to spring he did so as lightly as he could, making up by his agility for our loss of time. . . . I returned to my chair and my detective story. It was a lovely afternoon. We swung out into the Solent and towards Spithead. Miles away a huge white shape could be discerned and a red funnel. This was the *Normandie.* I returned to my book and in ten minutes I went out again. She was now quite close looking dangerously top heavy. And in a few minutes we stopped dancing up and down and crept motionlessly into the lee of that huge black precipice. I looked up the precipice wondering if I should see a familiar face. But it was like trying to pick out a friend on top of Gibraltar. And eventually, when I crossed the gangway, there was Ben waiting all pleased. We went straight to our cabins. Mine is Martine with satin wood cupboards and every form of gadget conceivable including a telephone. Ben's is prettier but smaller, being light blue shiny stuff with a faint pattern of Chinese effect in gold. . . . It is just like the very best hotel one can conceive. What they have been so clever about is the arrangement on the different levels. That makes the boat look even more enormous than it is. You know how the big rooms on the *Bremen* were all on one floor. Here they are on different floors communicated by vast decorative staircases. This one has a series of vistas seen from above. The decks are also arranged on the same system and there is a really superb deck at the back rising in slight terraces and lit by lampposts like an exhibition. Out of this opens a circular grill room with modern steel chairs and glass all around. Very Le Corbusier. But the rest is Lalique at his most extravagant. It is variegated and amusing but scarcely restful. There is a lovely little catholic chapel with a lit altar and little wooden carvings. The whole ship gives one exactly but *exactly* the impression of an *exposition des arts décoratifs.* Even now we have not explored it thoroughly.

We did not leave until 8.0. Ben and I watched a lovely sunset succeeded by the lights of Bembridge. We waited for the famous vibration but it never came. Even now I can feel no throb even. There is only one part of the deck where I notice it at all.

Nicolson's first impression of the *Normandie* was a good one. Had the ship called at Cobh, it is probable that he would have mailed that first day's portion of his letter and convinced his wife that the mood of the crossing was to have been consistently gay. However, it was not, as we shall see:

Friday, July 5: We had *café complet* in our cabins and divine it was. We then filled out our forms together. Ben decided after some hesitation that he was neither *estropié* or *polygame*. . . . Yesterday was Independence Day and the doorways were draped with huge American flags and French tricolours. Ben and I felt rather out of it. Now that we are in full Atlantic I can see what is meant by the vibration. At the stern where the Le Corbusier circular grill room is, the flowers on the little tables wobble about something dreadful and it would be difficult to read for long. Moreover in the smoking room just behind the panels suddenly start shaking in fury. It must be even worse in the tourist class and I can well imagine that in some cabins it is really intolerable. But where we are one does not notice it in the least and I have never known such luxury as that in which Ben and I live. The food is really delicious and although I am still careful Ben eats a lot. Caviar and *pâté* for dinner yesterday. And underneath it all he faintly disapproves. As he observes the whole place is like a setting for a ballet. Choruses of stewards, sailors, firemen, stewardesses, engineers. There are also some fifty liftiers in bright scarlet who look like the petals of salvias flying about these golden corridors. That is the essential effect—gold, Lalique glass and scarlet. It is very gay but would drive me mad after a week.

Prophetic words! The vibration, the richness of food and decor plus the absence of kindred souls among the other passengers starts to take its toll. The only acquaintance thrust on him proved disastrous:

[July 5th continued] There was a good film and then Ben and I went and bicycled in the gymnasium. After dinner there was an auction pool. I had taken a ticket. When my name was called out there was some turning of heads and a ghastly German woman rose and came towards me. "You are not really Harold Nicolson?" I did the look down my nose face. She is obviously a bore. She implies that T. E. Lawrence had been murdered. Now people who regard Lawrence as a mystery and a romance are obviously bores. . . . So I see this German woman is going to be hell.

Saturday, July 6th: We are now more than half way across. All this speed fuss is rather nonsense. An extra day makes very little difference and going at this pace has very definite disadvantages. In the first place, there is the vibration and in the second place the wind. For

A gala in the *Normandie's* main lounge.
At right is one of the quartet of lighting
columns whose removal proved so disastrous in 1942. (*Compagnie Générale
Transatlantique*)

unless the wind is strong behind one the rush of air on the sun deck is really terrible. It is like being in an aeroplane. One is thus mainly confined to the promenade deck which is enclosed in glass and thus protected and a trifle airless. Then there is the winter garden, where Dorothy Perkins romps in all her splendour and budgerigars hop in vast glass cages from jade green arum lily leaves by Lalique to pink glass hydrangeas by ditto. . . . I managed with great skill to avoid the German woman yesterday. I know not a soul on board and thank God for Ben. . . . I am completely recovered from my tummy upset and can eat anything. I shall go on with this tomorrow, I hate the diary form of letter. I do not know why. But it seems unsuited as a form of composition, to the writing of a letter.

Harold Nicolson may have disliked writing letters like a diary but this *Normandie* letter serves as an invaluable barometer of his mood. One can see between the lines that growing disaffection with extravagance, his petulance with the speed and irritation with decor that had amused only two days earlier. How fragile a thing is passenger enthusiasm and how cloying the riches of steamer life!

[Entry for July 6th]: Ben is well so far but I do think a trifle livery. I gave him a strong dose last night and he is now chirpy again. He bathed in the swimming pool and bicycled a mile and a half. He finds it difficult to work or read serious books. So do I. There is something about a boat which upsets one's brain. . . . His [Ben's] French is really much better than I thought. He orders all his meals and things in French and is perfectly fluent and correct.

Sunday July 7th: We reach New York tomorrow morning. I shall close hoping this finds you in the pink as it leaves me. Poor Benzie is feeling rather livery and bored. He says his mind feels like a lump of dough. He has not felt sea sick for a second but he is obviously a livery person and the sea has hit him hard. [Our fellow passengers] shout and show off the whole time—and try and air their idiotic French in order to be funny. I got caught by my German fan—but escaped. Otherwise we have hardly spoken to a soul. In fact, it is the worst ship-load I have ever struck and I thank God that Ben is with me. . . . The *Berengaria* sails on July 26th and it should be at Southampton August 1st.

Nicolson's disillusionment after a brief four days on board bears out the truth of a wise observation made by my wife: the length of any crossing always seems right; on the final day, one is ready to debark.

Ludwig Bemelmans, a habitual *Normandie* passenger, did not share the Englishman's distaste for his shipmates; he found them entertaining. The American writer sailed east in splendid luxury, awarded the sybaritic delights of Trouville because all the *cabines de luxe* were booked. The first morning, he ventured out of doors:

> I sat the next morning in my *dodine* (rocking chair) rocking on my private terrace and regarding the morning sun and the sea. After five minutes of the most profound rocking and silence, except for the rocking, I thought I would blow up because a man stood on my private terrace looking out to sea.
> I shouted: "Excuse me, have we met?"
> "Oh, I am sorry. I just arrived," said the man.
> "Do you happen to know that this is my private terrace, alors?" I said to him.
> "Oh, I'm so sorry. I'm just admiring the view," he said and left, and I kept on rocking. He walked over to his own private terrace.
> We were introduced later. It was Jules Bache. We are great friends now. I call him Julie.

Bemelmans fell in love with the ship, most particularly the lounge, a "room of silver, gold and glass, large as a theatre, floating through the ever clean, endless ocean just outside the high windows." Two passengers especially intrigued him and his daughter Barbara, the first:

> . . . a dark fortress of a woman . . . an old countess with a face made of Roquefort and eyes like pebbles. . . . She sat wrapped in her sables in the front one of three rows of deck chairs outside the Salon, and on her lap, covered by a small hound's tooth blanket, asthmatic and dribbly, sat a Pekingese with thyroid trouble. Whenever Barbara passed her chair, the old countess lifted her blanket and pushed the dog whose name was Piche, and she said to him—"*Piche, regarde donc la petite fille, qu'elle est mignonne!*"

The other was a devastating widow with long, "glamour-girl" blond hair whose dresses were so astonishingly well fitted that "a doctor could have examined her as she was." She was the sensation of the ship:

> The arms were weighed down with bracelets, all of them genuine, and she had, of course, a silver fox jacket. An ice-box full of orchids helped her bear up throughout the voyage. She was in new flowers at every meal, and she had with her a sad little girl, pale and not allowed to play with other children, who wore a little mink coat—the only junior mink I have ever seen.
> The entrances to dinner, which the young widow managed, re-

minded me of Easter at the Music Hall. She waited until the orchestra played Ravel's *Boléro,* and then she came in, in expensive vapors, heavy-lidded, the play of every limb and muscle bare as on a python. At the first landing of the long stairs, she bent, and everyone held his breath; she succeeded in picking up the train of her dress—a faultless ten inches of ankle and calf came into view—and with industrious little steps, she climbed up the rest of the stairs to the restaurant. There she smeared caviar on pieces of toast and garnished them with the whites of eggs so that they looked like the cards one sends to the bereaved, and she looked out over the ocean and drank champagne. The sad little girl said nothing all day.

The last night on board, the widow fell out of her role. A beautiful, an exquisitely modeled, long, slim, gartered leg came dangling from a high-held knee, out of black satin and lingerie. She danced like Jane Avril and let out a wild cowboy yodel, "Whoopee," and blew kisses to everyone.

There was no more commonplace pastime than passenger watching. The pair that Bemelmans observed, the countess and the widow, seem best to typify the chic, Fellini-esque *haut monde* that tended to travel on the *Normandie* those prewar years. By the end of the crossing, Bemelmans was overwhelmed with attention:

I think the tips on that voyage amounted to more than the whole passage cost. I have never enjoyed such service. The elevator had not only an operator, but a second man, who squeezed himself into the cab and pushed the operator against the wall; he then asked for the destination and handed this information on to the driver. He opened the door, ran ahead to guide us to whatever room we were going. It was altogether too much service.

On his return, the writer was short of cash and tried booking third class on the *Normandie* in Paris. The booking agent would not hear of it. Trouville was free and despite Bemelmans' every objection, he was about to be installed therein again. Finally, the American leveled:

"I would now like to experience," I said, "how a man feels who has no money, or very little, and who has to eat and live in the third class."

(Shades of Robert Louis Stevenson!)

"Ah," he said. "Monsieur Victor Hugo did not become a hunchback in order to write *Notre Dame de Paris,* and if Balzac had lived like Père Goriot—" An icy look stopped him. He folded his arms and waited. When I had said my piece, he pushed the suite over to me and pointed at it with his pencil—"It is all arranged," he said. "You will live in the suite, and every day somebody will take you to the third class, where you can observe life. For your repast, of course, you will come back upstairs. Madame and *bébé* stay upstairs. It will mean a lot of writing and paper work, explanations and confusion, but that is what I am here for."

Bemelmans finally prevailed and traveled back third. He describes his new fellow passengers:

> The glass of *vin ordinaire* is good, and the *cuisine bourgeoise* is fine, the vibration and the pitching are bad, but there was a sharp-faced youngster who, for the first time, had ice-cream and ate himself sick with it. We sat at a table with a man who had dirty finger-nails, and at the next table, there was a missionary who had brought his own savages along in the form of three children, who had to be carried out several times during meals.
>
> There was a man in a sweater and a cap—a German who had left a fortune of several millions behind when he was dragged out of bed in the middle of the night by the Gestapo. He still hid himself behind ventilators, and he crept along the corridors. He was still followed by ghosts. He walked at the side of the corridors, he stood alone on the deck, he seemed to apologize for his presence, and he was afraid that it would all end . . . that from somewhere a hand would reach and push him back into his misery. He slowly healed . . . he was looking up the last day—he smiled.

The unfortunate refugee's smile probably faded near the end of the crossing and he might well have wished back some of his confiscated Reichmarks. Although tipping was less an ordeal in third than in first, Bemelmans' horror at the amounts he felt obliged to lay about him was a consistent passenger sentiment near port. A word, then, about stewards, without whom the most magnificent ships had no life at all.

The personal steward who looked after the captain was called his tiger. The name had originated years earlier when masters of East Indiamen vied with one another for the most elaborately dressed personal servant. Vibrant silk liveries were made to order in Far Eastern ports, creating a brand of maritime major-domo beside whom a palace footman might have paled; tricked out in this brilliant finery, they were christened "tigers." Like their colleagues in all passenger spaces on board the Atlantic liners, they worked long hours for little pay. A month's wages averaged twenty-five dollars and their day began at seven and wasn't over until ten at night. Meals were taken on the run whenever possible.

The steward's great redeeming perquisite was the tips he collected at the conclusion of each crossing. In the twenties, it was not unusual for a good deck steward to make two hundred and fifty dollars a crossing, one third of which he gave, by tradition, to the pantryman. A steward's income usually exceeded his captain's, particularly if he worked a good section of the promenade deck or the smoking room. A new ship's surgeon about to join the *Majestic* was taken for a drink to a favorite merchant marine hangout in Southampton, the bar of the Polygon Hotel. The swells he took for first-class passengers, lining the bar and throwing down double whiskeys, were actually stewards about to report on board. Joseph Blancart, the flamboyant Transat master, could never afford a car during his six years in command of the *Ile,* although many of his stewards could. In the preunion twenties and early thirties, when college boys on summer vacations used to work their passage to Europe, few of them landed jobs as stewards. Most of them ended up instead at the deep sink in the kitchen, ankle-deep in filth from a backed-up garbage chute.

Oscar of the Waldorf once suggested that a good steward's prime asset lay in being a diplomat. Although there were moments during his working day (or night) when diplomacy was doubtless required, I think he needed more a love of hard work. A chief steward on the *Leviathan* kept about him men who were "strong, serious and clever." The best were British, French or German, but never American. Americans have traditionally made poor servants and most American vessels prior to World War II were heavily staffed with Europeans. There are still good stewards on board ships to this day but the number of applicants dwindles almost as fast as the number of positions open to them.

One of the ironies of mid-twentieth-century life is that the role of professional servant has become so unpopular. An expanding pool of unskilled workers rejected from industry by increasingly sophisticated technology shuns the very thought of it. At a time when more people are able to afford servants than ever before, fewer are available. There is a fundamental belief that a service occupation is necessarily undemocratic and demeaning. Whoever discovers a method of attracting people back into service jobs without either offending their dignity or compromising their independence will make a fortune.

Those who formerly thrived on this kind of work now demand and expect an eight-hour day, terminating near sunset, within convenient reach of home. But the popular hours of the office worker are hardly compatible

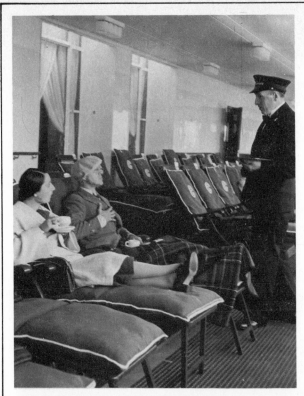

Left, eleven o'clock bouillon on the *Normandie*'s promenade deck. The steward listens patiently and will probably be well tipped. (*Roger Schall*)

Below, crew's lunch in midocean. The carafes of wine, outnumbering the water pitchers, as well as the long loaves indicate that the ship is indubitably French. *Normandie, 1938. (Compagnie Générale Transatlantique)*

with the concept of service to others. Indeed, the reverse is usually true: waiters, chambermaids and cooks cannot expect to keep the same hours as the clients they serve. Stewards and stewardesses on board liners saw their homes and families with the same infrequency as the rest of the crew. Violet Jessop, the *Titanic* stewardess, reminisced about her days "at sea." She was in a sense as much a sailor as the men who stoked the furnaces or hosed down the decks.

Passengers who disliked tipping ship's personnel had a variety of reasons: some found it embarrassing, others weren't sure of the form and many simply disliked parting with money. Although stewards claimed that poor tippers abounded in any season, class or direction, September was consistently their leanest month. The European adventure was over. Money set aside for shipboard expenses had a way of being lavished on last-minute frivolities in Paris shops. Economies in tips were inevitable. New travelers had, by that time, been surfeited with a procession of grasping guides and porters; they looked with a jaundiced and practical eye on the same attentions they had so gratefully rewarded two months previously. One-time crossers were notorious skinflints, for they knew they would never be back.

For the past three years, the Holland-America Line has dispensed with gratuities altogether. A service percentage is added to the price of each accommodation in the manner of European hotels. The scheme is eminently successful. Dutch stewards refuse tips not only in public but in private as well, when there is no superior about to remind them of the company rule. I doubt that the same system would have worked between the wars. Salaries were so low then that supplementing them with tips was the only way stewards could support their families. Company officials knew that passengers were, in effect, meeting a substantial portion of the ship's payroll directly and it was not in their interest to discourage them.

Furthermore, passengers' tips initiated a cash flow throughout the ship. The space where stewards bunked was called the "glory hole" and one of their number took care of it, expecting quite naturally to be tipped himself. He always was, collecting the same shilling or two from each of his clients at the end of every voyage. Dining-room stewards who wanted quick service in the kitchen were sure to pass along a regular gratuity to the countermen. On rare occasions when stewards sat down for a meal, the man who brought their food to them was taken care of as well. There was, then, all over the vessel, a network of small favors or services performed in return for money. Mercenary, perhaps, but like all spontaneous fiscal phenomena, it was effective. To deprive the ship's subeconomy of this basic source of revenue was obviously in nobody's interest.

Fortunately for Atlantic crews, excessive tipping has been a consistent American fetish. For every passenger who found the system offensive, there was another it gratified. The man who showered bills of large denomination about the smoking room or inadvertently pressed a month's wages on a Cherbourg porter was not necessarily as vulgar as his behavior. I suspect that the heavy tipper's weakness is rampant insecurity; he is uncertain of how much is expected and bolsters his ego by creating satellites of obligation about him wherever he goes. For my part, I have mixed emotions. Although the profusion of open palms on debarkation day is depressing, I think the principle of direct reward for excellent performance is sound. A man whose tip is in potential jeopardy works harder than the man who knows it is guaranteed. Service is, and always has been, the name of the game on the Atlantic. Prompt, courteous and efficient service gives shipboard life its particular luster.

In the late thirties, cabin and dining-room stewards were tipped five dollars and a bath steward two. If these sums seem insignificant for a crossing's work, it is worth remembering that dollars were more substantial in those days. Deck stewards made smaller tips but had many more clients. The men in the smoking room made drink tips in addition to their cut from the pools. Good tippers on the *Leviathan* were referred to as "three star," poor ones as *"toqué."* (This is actually a French word that means cracked or daft; the choice of word doubtless grew out of the need for an alien euphemism, incomprehensible even when voiced in an offending passenger's presence.) French stewards had their own word—a stingy client was *"un figaro."* Their British colleagues described the same kind of passenger as a *"walkoff."*

Intelligence about a tipper, good or bad, spread as though by bush telegraph. Once branded by the first to be tipped, the passenger's reputation for extravagance or avarice preceded him from cabin to dining room to deck chair to smoking room and onto the pier. A bad tipper invariably advertised himself the first day out by announcing in a hectoring tone: "You take care of me, steward, and I'll take care of you." Among the worst tippers were film stars, who had a habit of passing out eight-by-ten glossies of themselves eastbound and compounding the insult by autographing them westbound. Some passengers voyaging on the same ship both directions used to tear a bill in two and retain one half until the return passage. A few simply ran out and left nothing. Perhaps the most abused steward of all time was the man on the *Paris* who paid off a bridge debt for one of his passengers, amounting to a thousand francs. The passenger in question, who happened to be a duchess, paid back a third of the sum and then only grudgingly after a series of desperate letters from her benefactor.

If I have dwelt on stewards and their tips, it has not been my intention to characterize them as grasping opportunists whose zeal was governed by passenger exorbitance. They were, in fact, loyal company servants whose cheerful competence was one of the enormous attractions of ocean travel.

It was a boon to steerage passengers when, at the turn of the century, companies saw fit to staff the lower decks with stewardesses. Those neglected passengers had hitherto been denied the sympathies of a responsive company representative and having one finally in their midst made up for any number of shortcomings. On British ships, they were called "Mrs." regardless of their marital status. This was indicative of the high esteem in which they were held. In the hierarchy of the English domestic, it was customary to confer the title only on senior household employees: butlers and housekeepers were referred to as "Mr." and "Mrs." whereas footmen and scullery maids were summoned simply by Christian or surnames. Stewardesses had a knack of comforting children and harried mothers. It is a kind of ministration still available on the *QE2* today although on the *France,* stewardesses have practically disappeared. The few that are retained do little more than zip up dresses and assist with a chignon. They never put a hand to a tray and all the cabin cleaning is done by men.

Stewards on all lines had a keen sense of humor. Commodore Bisset remembers once finding dust on a ledge during inspection of some obscure quarter of the ship. He called it to the attention of the man responsible and surreptitiously left a penny there. The following morning, the ledge was spotless, the penny was gone and two bright ha'pennies lay in its place.

Just as steerage became a dirty word in the twenties, first class was renamed in the thirties. The *Queen Mary* inaugurated the new nomenclature by calling her most prestigious quarters "cabin" rather than "first." The whole name switch was nothing more than a clumsy device to sell more space. I cannot imagine that the same cabin at the same price with a different name would attract more customers. However, the conviction that it did swept the Atlantic fleets and even the *Normandie* became a cabin ship.

Whether first or cabin, however, one universal practice remained unchanged: the determination of the curious or ambitious to vault barriers separating them from choicer quarters amidships. It was a game as old as passenger liners, one that had originally been discouraged by stringing a rope across the deck. In a huge liner, the deterrents had grown into a complex of baffles, one-way doors and grills designed to thwart those in search of upward mobility. On occasion, pursers turned a blind eye to company rules; if there was a shortage of dancing partners for the daughters of families traveling first, eligible young men were discreetly recruited from inferior classes for one evening at a time. Eligibility in this instance included possession of a dinner jacket. Indeed, black tie was the single most effective weapon for one determined to crash the class barriers. With it was achieved an aura of anonymous respectability that even the sharpest-eyed purser hesitated to question.

Individual sorties were not uncommon. One young tourist passenger on the *Leviathan* booked a first-class deck chair the first morning out and ate a series of elegant luncheons from a tray on his lap before he was unmasked near Cherbourg. His acumen contrasted vividly with that of another deck-chair inhabitant on the same crossing, in one of the saddest stories I know. He was rather a shabby man who consistently ate sandwich lunches and suppers on deck, tipping the deck steward a quarter each time from a worn leather purse. On the last day, he confided to the steward that he had enjoyed himself immensely and hoped that the next time he crossed, he would be able to afford to eat in the dining room.

But there were few permanent incursions from below. Most were visits of impulse, made for reasons of curiosity, the same motive that had prompted saloon passengers in their lamentable slumming descents into steerage years earlier. Sometimes it was to see a movie—in the early days, talkies were exclusive attractions of first. Lounge stewards on the *Berengaria* knew that when chairs ran out, a massive infiltration from the lower decks had been effected under cover of darkness. It was on this same ship, incidentally, that the largest single invasion of first class is recorded when, on a certain Fourth of July, no fewer than five hundred from tourist, fired with that intense patriotism of the temporarily expatriate, marched defiantly into the first-class lounge. But in most cases, it was a common challenge to have visited first class, if only for a look round. It was a habit that was tactfully and firmly discouraged, most particularly on French vessels. Pursers as well as first-class passengers reasoned quite logically that it made little sense to pay substantially higher fares for space that was available to anyone who chose to use it in defiance of regulations.

One could only wish that they had been as firm in enforcing the rule for first class who repeated the errors of their parents and felt it their privilege to visit inferior classes uninvited. Before the crossing was over, most young people in first had discovered that tourist and third lounges were far gayer than the stuffy respectability of their own public rooms. All the most attractive girls in the ship seemed to be there and westbound in late summer, the lower decks were filled almost exclusively with college students who

The *Majestic*'s main lounge in the early
thirties. Interlopers from other classes
needed, besides nerve, a dinner jacket.
(*Radio Times Hulton Picture Library*)

created and sustained a week-long party from port to port. A woman who traveled third class reported with distaste that every lifeboat, ventilator and steamer rug concealed a necking couple and that chaperones ostensibly enjoined with maintaining sexual decorum often had less of it than their charges. As a result, curfews in third class had a faintly institutional ring about them, even as late as 1936 on the *Bremen:* lights were extinguished in the social hall promptly at one in the morning and after that time, passengers were forbidden to be on the promenade decks until dawn.

One irrevocable step beyond those who momentarily violated class barriers were the ultimate interlopers, stowaways. To contemplate and carry off a free passage takes a certain kind of bravado that I admire. It is an admiration not shared by line officials, to whom stowaways have always been time-consuming nuisances. Sailing as uninvited guest of the company is tempting on any form of transportation. But whereas illicit passengers can be flung off a train at the next station, a stowaway apprehended after the pilot's departure from the ship has already achieved his or her goal.

In the days of unlimited immigration, large numbers of unpaid passengers used to stow away communally with the connivance of crew members, who were paid heavily for their assistance. Twenty-seven Italians were once discovered cooped up in the claustrophobic hell of an unused water tank. Another crewman once hid eight Poles behind the *Republic*'s paneling, only to have a cracked paint seam and chink of light give the game away to a vigilant inspector at Quarantine. Twenty-five illegal entrants once hid in a coal cave that collapsed on them in a storm; only three of them emerged from the bunker alive. One of seventeen stowaways discovered on an Italian vessel proved to be infected with smallpox, necessitating vaccination and internment for the entire ship's company at Hoffman's Island for twelve days.

This kind of group subterfuge ended in the face of quota restrictions in the early twenties; typical stowaways thereafter proved to be solo efforts. A few tried their luck in the holds of transatlantic ships with varying degrees of success. One man crept aboard a freighter sailing from Panama to London. In the holds was a cargo of melons, on which he subsisted for thirty days before surrendering to the captain suffering from acute malnutrition. Seven men who concealed themselves in a ship's hold had the misfortune to hide there just prior to a routine fumigation that drove them choking and gagging into the sunlight. Perhaps the most nightmarish story concerns the stowaway who shared a hold with a cargo of wild animals destined for zoos in the Western Hemisphere. During a severe storm, the cages were so tossed about that some of them were sprung open and the man was clawed to death by a terrified lioness before her keeper could intervene.

Engine spaces were usually too well patrolled to offer good hiding places. But frequently, when ships were between voyages in the Depression, Southampton derelicts used to slip on board for a night's warm sleep on top of the boilers. One failed to wake the following morning—indeed, he never woke up again. It was sailing day and his dehydrated remains were discovered many voyages later by an astonished officer of the watch.

The unfortunate man who was broiled on top of the boiler experienced a different agony from the Halifax girl who jumped into a ship's lifeboat in midwinter, determined to get to England for free. Following lifeboat drill five hours out, the covers were lashed firmly into place and two frigid days passed before the half-frozen girl could attract the attention of a passing sailor. She lost several toes from frostbite, which the authorities evidently considered adequate punishment, for she limped ashore at Southampton without further penalty. But she was the exception—apprehended stowaways were customarily returned to the port of embarkation and sent before a magistrate. Another man had himself nailed into a crate addressed to Lord & Taylor; he was removed protesting before the ship left Le Havre. The most popular stowaways in history were two Liverpool tarts who managed to board a troopship before it sailed in 1917. They were discovered in mid-ocean somewhere among the five thousand men on board and locked in an empty cabin with a round-the-clock detachment of marines on guard outside.

The classic stowaway is one who brazens it out, hiding like a tree in the forest and masquerading as a *bona fide* passenger. I am convinced that the best stories remain untold, that for every stowaway flushed out by the master-at-arms, another escapes detection. A storage room behind the *Queen Elizabeth* movie screen proved an ideal hideaway for several who crossed successfully after the war. One had iron rations which he supplemented by gorging himself at teatime when, faultlessly attired, he took a regular seat in the lounge, clapping distractedly as the orchestra completed each suite. He shaved and washed in third-class public lavatories and was prepared even to the extent of having earplugs to muffle the roar of the sound-track speakers that bracketed his lair. Once in New York, he "borrowed" a steward's jacket and walked ashore.

Ships were magnetic to adventurous children. One nine-year-old, the daughter of a stevedore, slipped on board the *Majestic* in New York. She was discovered before Ambrose Light and returned in the pilot boat. On the ship's next eastbound crossing, she tried again and escaped detection

Below, horse racing at sea. Seamen move the wooden mounts in the *Queen Mary*'s main lounge less than three weeks before World War II was declared. (*Radio Times Hulton Picture Library*)

until well out at sea. She was then put in the care of the third-class matron and returned on the *Homeric*. Her ship was met at Quarantine by a host of ship's reporters, who neglected the film stars on board in an effort to interview the celebrated stowaway. But White Star sensibly gave out no details of her escapade, *pour décourager les autres*. One distraught father in New York first learned that his missing children were in mid-Atlantic upon receipt of the following radiogram: YOUR CHILDREN ARE SAFE BUT UNPAID FOR PLEASE CABLE TWO ROUNDTRIP FARES INSTANTER. He did and there was a painful reunion on the docks ten days later.

The *Aquitania* seemed to attract the most arrogant stowaways. One young man brushed against some fresh paint the first day out and complained with such vehemence that he was exposed. He then compounded his unwelcome by confessing that he had wanted to stow away on the *Ile de France* because the food was better. Another was a girl for whom free ocean passage was evidently a hobby. Once the *Aquitania* had cleared Cherbourg, she was discovered passing out cards billing her as the world's champion stowaway. New York authorities returned her to Southampton where she was given a month's hard labor. She was contemptuous throughout her trial, her only delight seeming to be that she could add the *Aquitania* to an impressive list of credits.

Undisputed king of the Atlantic stowaways was Prince Mike Romanoff, the bogus Russian aristocrat who made several illicit crossings before he achieved the West Coast and respectability. His passage on the *Ile de France,* although unsuccessful, was an outrageous masterpiece. He befriended a sympathetic couple on the boat train and boarded with them. Once clear of Southampton, Romanoff eschewed the stowaway's traditional self-effacement and set out to establish himself as the social lion of the ship. If this insatiable thirst for adulation proved his undoing, it is hard not to admire the man's sheer, cold-blooded effrontery. So wide a swath did he cut that Captain Blancart was anxious to meet him, a master whom the "Prince" grandly acknowledged as "my favorite skipper." The Frenchman had his opportunity shortly thereafter, when Romanoff was included with Treasury Secretary Mellon's party at a captain's dinner and reception. Pursers who made out the guest list later confessed that the man had seemed so popular a colleague of the American's that they naturally included his name.

But Romanoff's need to be the center of attention tipped his hand. A passenger anxious to extend him a written invitation inquired of Henri Villar his cabin number. The famous Transat purser investigated and could find none. When queried on the grand staircase, the debonair stowaway announced that "the entire ship is my cabin" and waltzed down to dinner. It is probable that Villar had never been so nonplussed during his extensive career. After dinner, he confronted the man in his office and put him in custody. Exhibiting his customary *noblesse,* Romanoff never divulged his accomplices. There were bound to have been others in addition to the couple who helped him embark, for he was a persuasive and charming man. He was also incorrigible; detained and finally released from Ellis Island, he managed to stow away on the ferry to Manhattan.

The transgressions of the spurious Russian nobleman can be forgiven in one sense. His fellow passengers were lawbreakers as well—they were nearly all smugglers. In fact, there were very few on board Atlantic liners that didn't attempt to sneak something past customs. Short of thwarting the Eighteenth Amendment, flouting the Customs Regulations of the United States was one of the most popular sports between the wars, a tradition that continues to this day. One or two days out of New York, those with an indigestible amount of dutiable items agonized in public and private, weighing the odds against disclosure and payment as opposed to burying the goods somewhere in one of a dozen suitcases.

Women who assumed the recesses of their lingerie cases to be sacrosanct were in for as rude an awakening as those who took the time to sew old labels into new dresses. They usually did no more than duplicate the elaborately careless job done by the original seamstress but seldom bothered to use the same needle holes. Other female passengers intent on deception used to appear in a succession of stunning costumes during the course of westbound crossings so that they could declare in good conscience that their new clothes were both worn and old.

The mistake these naïve women made was to assume that grizzled old customs inspectors would be unfamiliar with things feminine. This was a common error and one they would have done well to remedy. The amateur smuggler was just that, an amateur pitted once or twice a year against a professional who spent his life scrutinizing passengers and their luggage. To their practiced eyes, a new dress was a new dress and likely as not, they could estimate its price to within a few francs. Furthermore, they were quite incorruptible. In the 1890s, there were passengers who used to scatter twenty-dollar bills through their most sensitive trunks. The supposition was that these were palmed without a word before the luggage was cleared. But that practice had ceased long since and instances of bribery on New York piers were few and far between.

Passengers who moved into the big league by not declaring expensive pieces of jewelry were also sadly uninformed. It never occurred to them, for instance, that Cartier's Paris and London shops had spotters who, as a matter of course, informed U.S. authorities about any large purchases by Americans. Acting on behalf of these and any other informants was a New York organization called the American Jewelers' Protective Association; part of their highly respected function was to assist tipsters in collecting a reward from the Treasury Department for exposing jewel smugglers. The passenger who offered a steward ten pounds to help smuggle a ten-thousand-dollar pendant was unaware that he could make fifty times that amount simply by cabling the Association.

But of course, jewelry did get through. Professional smugglers had methods far cleverer than their amateur shipmates. One man confessed, following his retirement, that he had used the same system for years on the *Ile de France*. After boarding at Le Havre, he drilled a small hole on top of his bathroom door. In it, he would drop a cache of precious stones, sealing the opening with a blob of chewing gum. They remained in hiding for the entire crossing, as well as most of the turnaround in New York. The smuggler went ashore without them but returned early the following day as a visitor, carrying an enormous box of flowers. He went immediately to his old cabin, located the steward whom he had tipped heavily the day previously and confided that he had a friend sailing in the same cabin whom he wished to surprise with a *bon voyage* bouquet. The steward would unlock the cabin and depart in search of a large vase. Within thirty seconds, the smuggler had the gems in his pocket. He then arranged the flowers, tipped the steward again and walked ashore carrying thousands of dollars' worth of diamonds into the country, duty free; visitors were never searched. The mystified occupants who arrived an hour later spent most of the crossing trying to guess which anonymous admirer had sent such an elaborate tribute.

Another staple of high-risk contraband was narcotics, although traffic in the thirties was far smaller than today's. Informants were invaluable here too but detection sometimes came about by fortuitous accident. There was a false panel beautifully worked into the *Mauretania*'s famous woodwork that had been used successfully many times. But it was in a narrow passageway, and one crowded sailing day a sleeve brushed against it and was torn by a slightly loosened screwhead. The sleeve in question belonged to a treasury agent and within moments, he had found a shipboard drop containing several pounds of hashish.

Perhaps the most colorful gang of smugglers were those who literally banded together before the First World War, as an amateur musical organization christened the Foo-Foo Band. They formed a raggle-taggle marching band and their impromptu displays became a traditional feature of sailing days. Crews in the midst of turnaround as well as boarding passengers hung over the railings when a hideous cacophony signaled the approach of the Foo-Foo Band. Down to the end of the pier they came, countermarching back and forth. Then, still playing, they paraded up the gangplank of the ship, around the embarkation hall and back to shore again. It was an off-duty agent with a musical ear who noticed one day that the tuba had flatted slightly on its return down the gangplank. He brooded about this and the next time the musicians appeared, the tuba player was stopped and searched following completion of the display. He was clean, but nestled in the coils at the base of his flaring instrument were several small packets of drugs, flung there by a confederate among the ship's crew. This disclosure terminated the run of the Foo-Foo Band and New York embarkations to follow were that much less colorful.

Some contraband was yellow with black stripes and alive. Perhaps the smallest and seemingly most insignificant illicit passenger ever discovered was a Colorado potato beetle on the *Aquitania* in July of 1948. A knowledgeable passenger had spotted the creature and preserved his remains in a jar. Experts from the Ministry of Agriculture met the ship at Cherbourg and during the Channel crossing, crew and passengers scoured the ship for additional pests. None was found, but sailors swabbed down the decks that turnaround with a reeking pesticide that stayed on board for months.

British concern about landing certain quadrupeds was legendary among dog lovers. Although they were the most common transatlantic animal passengers, few of them remained on board after a call at Cherbourg. Dogs admitted to Great Britain had to submit to six months in quarantine, which some did not survive. Personally, I have always felt this a small price to pay for the virtual elimination of rabies within the United Kingdom. The U.S. in turn has had an identical success with hoof-and-mouth disease, in large part due to the vigilance of Customs men.

In the old days, the butcher took complete care of passengers' dogs. This was appropriate and it is quite likely that no other crew member could have ensured that his charges would dine as well as their masters. But by the twenties, permanent quarters for dogs were fixtures on the sports deck of most vessels and a kennel man was employed to oversee things. It cost twenty dollars to ticket a dog across the Atlantic in the thirties and the owner of a bitch that produced seven stateless puppies in midocean was only spared a surcharge following intervention by the captain. Exercise was a problem; there is extant a Cunard rule from 1876 forbidding dogs on or off the leash abaft of the mainmast. Gertrude Lawrence was a habitual offender in this regard, forever sneaking her pet onto virgin decks from

The *Normandie*'s pool. Swimmers and spectators posed in a fashionable mélange. It was, incidentally, a moment of curiously inverted propriety in the evolution of bathing attire. Most men still had their chests covered although women were already wearing two-piece suits. (*Roger Schall*)

Terrier owners on the *Aquitania* in 1932 organize a show. (*Cunard*)

Although the *Normandie* had a proper theater, passengers on the *Aquitania*, below, made do. A room that had served both as lounge and hospital ward became a cinema each afternoon. (*Radio Times Hulton Picture Library*)

which she had been barred the day previous. (Why Captain Hambleton of the *Adriatic* ever allowed my mother on the promenade deck with an Italian burro quite escapes me.)

However, the extraordinary thing about dogs afloat is that they exhibit a curious reticence to perform their bodily functions, no doubt confused by the alien surroundings and the total absence of familiar smells. It was not just scatological chic that saw installation on both the *Normandie* and *United States* of a bogus hydrant in the midst of their elegant kennels. Helen Hayes' new poodle made an early wartime crossing on the *Champlain* and the dog's bowels became a matter of shipwide distraction. It wasn't until several days had passed that the concerned gallery that assembled for each exercise period had their vigilance rewarded.

Horses have always been the most reluctant quadruped passengers, with good reason: they are terrible sailors. Unable to vomit, they exhibited the extent of their suffering by an attack of what handlers called the "gapes." American and Canadian cavalry mounts transported across the ocean en masse during World War I were quite miserable. One of the hazards aggravated by rough weather was a phenomenon known as a horse storm, when the ship's roll was amplified by hundreds of animals trampling in frightened unison back and forth in their abbreviated stalls.

An English race horse called Papyrus was shipped to America on the *Aquitania* in 1923. There was a regulation in the Merchant Shipping Act which forbade accommodation of a horse above any space used by a passenger. This entailed special construction of two stalls deep within the bowels of the ship. The owners had sensibly decided to travel a companion horse with Papyrus and the lower deck stable was complete with a wooden floor and sides padded with air cushions. Both creatures were loaded on board at Southampton via a brow or equine gangplank, retained in port after heavy use during both Boer and First World Wars.

The crossing passed without incident but, as with many of their human fellow passengers, debarking in New York proved less pleasant. The horses having boarded on the port side, pier availability in New York necessitated a starboard disembarkation. To effect this, both animals had to negotiate a two-foot sill amidships, during which delicate maneuver Papyrus struck his head on the steel ceiling. Passengers boarding the *Caronia* on the opposite side of the pier grew so anxious watching the animals being coaxed off the ship that they broke into wild cheering when they were finally led down the gangplank. Papyrus reared and plunged in fright and it is not surprising at all that the English thoroughbred did poorly at Belmont the following month. Tom Mix's horse Tony was a consistently sophisticated traveler on the *Aquitania*. He was equipped with a special set of rubber shoes to prevent sliding on the decks. Needless to say, he was a great favorite at children's concerts.

Pets kept permanently on board were the exception rather than the rule. The Dolly Sisters once presented the *Aquitania* with a pair of white kittens that stayed on for years, named after their famous donors. Captain Hambledon, the White Star skipper who had sent the lady passenger flying up the Jacob's ladder, kept a pet canary loose in his cabin on the *Olympic*. It had been found abandoned by the crew on board the *Adriatic* during a strike. Some animals seemed determined to become ship's mascots. A monkey that lived aboard an oil barge in New York harbor jumped ship one day and clambered up the side of the *Majestic*. Before anyone could stop him, he had gone to ground in the labyrinthine ventilation trunks that connected every part of the vessel. He was finally routed out by stewards thundering on cabin walls with their fists, and was cornered in the captain's dayroom devouring the contents of a fruit bowl. The gym instructor was alerted and brought along fencing masks and gauntlets; even so, the men who finally captured the enraged simian were severely bitten through the heavy leather.

This all happened the morning of sailing day and is the only occasion I know of when a monkey delayed departure of the world's largest ship. But to have left the creature somewhere on board, to be discovered at sea by a passenger, was unthinkable. There had been a frightful brouhaha not too many years earlier on board another vessel of the same line when a large, although nonpoisonous, snake called Bronx had been sharing a cabin with its owner. He had brought his pet on board in a large valise discreetly perforated with air holes. When a passenger in an adjacent cabin was apprised of the serpent's existence, noisy hysterics necessitated removal of the offending creature to less elegant accommodations. The ship's butchers looked after Bronx for the remainder of the crossing and his owner was charged a full dog's fare, although the snake ate nothing except one dead mouse.

The *Laurentic*'s captain had a particular reason to despise canine supercargo on one crossing. After three days of fog, he spent a nerve-racking morning trying without success to locate the source of a mysterious foghorn that blew off to port, echoing the *Laurentic*'s signals. A subordinate finally reported that the noise came from a cabin just below the bridge. A Pekingese crooned mournfully through an open porthole in response to each blast of the foghorn. But the animal horror story of all times befell the Italian liner *Rex*. A woman traveling first class reported to the ship's surgeon two days out from New York with ugly red blotches covering her back. A salve was administered and she was lightheartedly admonished for eating too much caviar. The following day, however, when other passengers appeared with identical rashes, the surgeon reported to his commandant in frantic privacy that first class was overrun with fleas. They were presumably descendants of forebears reported in third class on the previous westbound crossing. The ship was withdrawn from service and fumigated. By some miracle, the scandal of the "*Rex* hives" never reached the press.

Ships sailing from northern Europe in midsummer traveled in a south-westerly direction to New York. Two days out, ship's officers appeared in tropical whites instead of their customary blue serge. It was an infallible sign that New York was imminent. There were other indications, too: the same preoccupation that marked landfall on the other side, most pronounced among the Americans. For travelers of choice, the New World lacked the mystique that it had had earlier in the century for travelers of necessity. Americans nearing the end of their voyage had little in common with those spurred west by economic hardship, buoyed by anticipation of a new life.

New York Harbor, one of the world's greatest, is also one of the fog-giest. It was suddenly there, one morning, heralded by a rocklike stability of the ship. At Quarantine, officials and ship's newsmen came on board, cynical members of the fourth estate. If there was someone of note on board, their ranks were swollen with newsreel cameramen; if there was not, the regulars had an hour, after accepting the purser's traditional liquid hos-pitality, to find something or someone on board they could make into news before disembarking with passengers at the pier.

Basil Woon wrote in *The Frantic Atlantic* of 1927 that Americans went to Europe in search of "drinks, divorces and dresses." My own feeling is that Americans found a kind of peace abroad, particularly in those pre-Vespa years. The leisurely pace they learned to savor over the summer was disrupted somewhere just south of the Battery. Like some infectious plague over the water came a compelling urge for haste. The familiar tempo was there, the race of traffic that swarmed and buzzed through fissures in Man-hattan's concrete bluffs. Assembled aimlessly in shore suits and faces, none could resist that frenetic call.

Passengers had risen early, finished packing and taken a needlessly hasty breakfast in a dining room packed as never before. Now they waited for immigration, for docking, for debarkation. They were laden with cam-eras, raincoats, hand luggage and, more often than not, guilt for their part in the encounter to come on the piers. Restlessly, they crossed from railing to railing, roamed through deserted public rooms filled with alien faces or returned, stateless refugees in the ship's domain, to the security they'd known in their cabins. But these were empty and impersonal now, made up for passengers due to sail east the following day. Stewards suffered with ill-concealed anguish any debarking clients who lingered too long. (They had been tipped by that time and a certain refreshing honesty colored their attitude.) So it was a deck chair on a stuffy promenade deck, angularly uncomfortable without its rug. This had been placed under lock and key by deck stewards wary of souvenir hunters. All was impatience and a longing to be off.

Fulfillment was not imminent. Off the ship was easy, once the lines had been made fast. But off the piers was not, save for passengers of immense international prestige completing a press conference in their suite. They were greeted by functionaries with magic eyes who passed officials and barriers with deceptive ease. Descent from those luxurious and well-kept quarters to the primitive wasteland of the piers was one of the ironies of Atlantic travel. In midwinter there was a chill that nipped the ears and penetrated shoe soles with a deathly numbness. In high summer they were caverns of fetid humidity, inhabited by Customs inspectors and longshoremen who, consigned there year-round, can hardly be blamed, respectively, for hostility and avarice.

Overhead, in admirable simplicity, were arranged large individual letters under which baggage was to be assembled as it came off the ship, either by hand from the cabins or by mechanical conveyor from the hold. Yet the supreme qualification for longshoremen assigned to accomplish this seemed both ignorance of the alphabet and severe color blindness. First-class overhead letters were red, tourist and third blue. It was inevitable that one or more suitcases would be found, after a depressing hour or more, dutifully buried under the wrong letter or color or both, in spite of large initials plastered all over them in primary colors.

The passenger's shipboard impatience to disembark was replaced by a maniacal anxiety to get off the pier. But there was an inexorable ritual to perform, tinged with frustration: assemble all thirty-eight pieces of luggage, find and seduce a genial Customs inspector and then, most agonizing of all, bribe a longshoreman to trundle the stuff grudgingly down to the street. There was no more effective purgatory in the world than a North River pier in early September. Americans were resigned to it but vulnerable Europeans experiencing it for the first time were quite stunned.

A *commissaire* on the *France* once murmured *"Bon débarquement"* as he came upon me about to leave the ship with my family; I have never had as courteous and sympathetic a farewell. (In point of fact, the French

Buzzing the *Normandie* in Southampton, this Royal Naval Air Arm plane caught one wing on a crane cable and landed, freakishly, on the prow. When told that his plane would have to be taken to Le Havre, the pilot, fearful of his commanding officer, asked to go too. (*Compagnie Générale Transatlantique*)

Below, the passenger's ultimate indignity: Customs inspection in New York, photographed on the North German Lloyd piers in 1909. To the left, implacable though headless inspectors wait patiently as a passenger gropes through his trunk; an amused wife is no help. (*Library of Congress*)

Line relieves parents on board of much madness by screening an endless parade of cartoons from breakfast on.) Although this book is not intended as a travel guide, I find it hard to resist the impulse to proffer advice to that dwindling band who stick with the liners. Once on the pier, I reduce the potential misery to near zero by sending my family, empty-handed, to find their own way home while I devote the remainder of the day to bringing up the rear with what the Romans accurately called *impedimenta*. I make no appointments for that day save with Customs men and recommend the same scheme to my fellow travelers. Spared the frustration of haste, I dawdle quite happily until the pier has emptied and inspectors look for passengers rather than the reverse. I have also cultivated the acquaintance of a pair of rascally longshoremen whom I have christened the forty thieves. They appear at my side like magic whenever I set foot on the pier and are tipped outrageously for locating and collecting missing items of baggage. Yet however effective the distribution of largesse, there is no substitute for patience.

Thirties passengers were just as extravagant as those in the twenties. Yet if the woman who requested and obtained exclusive use of the *Normandie*'s swimming pool for two hours was at least a genuine eccentric, she was not typical of the millions of Americans who crossed in those golden prewar years. Perhaps the most telling picture of a voyage comes from a meticulous scrapbook that a correspondent of mine was kind enough to send me. She and three college friends made a round trip on the *Bremen* in the summer of 1939. They booked third class in a four-berth cabin with no porthole and a defective ventilator, which meant leaving the door open for long periods of time.

Included in the scrapbook were pen-and-ink sketches and some photographs, including one double-exposed to combine a view of the *Bremen* taken from the Southampton tender superimposed bizarrely over a study of Winchester Cathedral. That the print was retained despite its improbable value best typifies the anxiety of the diarist to preserve any fragment of that memorable summer. There were jokes and games, forays into first class and a series of innocent liaisons with fellow passengers. Eastbound photographs show a tentative quartet, cheerful but naïve, a late thirties collage of broom-stick skirts, peasant blouses and saddle shoes. Near summer's end, later snapshots indicate a browner and wiser look, betraying a sophistication absent in June.

One of their great amusements was to ape the German crew who heiled and saluted the swastika that flew from the after halyards. They arrived in New York in late August, among the last passengers ever to sail on that record-breaking ship. A few days later, she was gone, racing north of her accustomed lanes, blacked out and carrying only her crew.

Yet in terms of Atlantic travel, the most significant event of that year occurred in June. A Pan American clipper flew from Long Island to Portugal via the Azores. It was by no means the first aircraft to span the Western Ocean but it was the first to do so on a regular schedule carrying passengers. The monopoly of the ship, reestablished after the *Hindenburg* crash, was broken and from that moment on, the aircraft was in the ascendancy. After June of 1939, there was an alternate link, another way to cross that doomed those magnificent vessels. Haltingly, the air age had begun across the Atlantic.

—FLAG SIGNAL FROM A SHORE STATION AS
THE AQUITANIA SAILED TO BE SCRAPPED

12.
Parade to the Block

War gave ships of any description an almost incalculable value. Winston Churchill, foreseeing the inevitability of another German conflict, suggested in Parliament that the *Berengaria,* bound for Scotland and oblivion, be retained for the duration of an international crisis. His remarks were made as late as December of 1938 and were ignored by his fellow Honorable Members. Scarcely a year later, the proud old ship would have been worth a good percentage of her weight in gold. The cost of maintaining superannuated express liners, prohibitive in the thirties, would have seemed insignificant in the decade to follow.

Within two years of their merger, Cunard White Star wrote off as redundant the *Majestic, Olympic, Mauretania, Homeric, Adriatic, Albertic,*

Doric and *Calgaric*—eight ships to be replaced by one, the *Queen Mary*. Across the Channel, the elegant *France* went to the Dunkirk breakers and the *Paris* was lost, victim of a pierside fire. French Line officials suspected arson but never proved it. The ship was swamped with water by Le Havre firemen and capsized away from her pier. In so doing, she effectively blocked the *Normandie*'s departure from the dry dock directly behind her, necessitating masts and funnels being cut off underwater before the French flagship could emerge.

First to go was the venerable *Mauretania*. During her final years she had been painted white as a West Indian cruise ship, starved out of service on the North Atlantic. She also suffered the indignity of weekend voyages to nowhere—"booze cruises," as they were called. Originating from New York in the early thirties, these combined Depression escapism with the tail end of prohibition. Somehow, those rowdy outings seemed inappropriate for gracious old ships, but in the lean years, any and all passenger revenues were essential; whether or not they were offensive to a vessel's earlier image was of little interest to management.

A ship deteriorates in funny cumulative ways, more rapidly if taken out of service. The engines last longest because they receive the most exacting care. But boilers are susceptible, as are plumbing and electrical wiring. As early as 1911, after only four years in service, end-of-voyage reports on the *Lusitania* included mention of fires caused by short circuits behind the paneling, started by rats that gnawed rubber insulation from the wires; intelligence of this kind was naturally withheld from passengers. Both the *Berengaria* and *Majestic* had continual wiring failures that caused a rash of small fires in unlikely recesses. Although seldom serious, they were embarrassing for the Company and frightening for passengers. There was one on the *Berengaria* in the late twenties: passengers dressing for dinner in mid-ocean were summoned to boat stations and the ugly stink of burning insulation lay throughout the ship. The fire was quickly extinguished but was followed by others on subsequent voyages. The *Leviathan,* despite all her other woes, avoided this particular German weakness. At the time of her American conversion, Gibbs, America's foremost naval architect and a fire fanatic to boot, had ordered completely new wiring.

The *Mauretania* had had her own near-fatal fire in July of 1921, while tied up at Southampton during a routine turnaround. A man cleaning carpets on E-deck with inflammable fluid worked with a cigarette in his mouth. There was a flash fire that took hold at once, sending clouds of impenetrable black smoke throughout the ship. Municipal fire fighters poured on gallons of water and the *Mauretania* leaned ominously away from her pier,

Sudden death. Victim of a mysterious fire, the
Transat liner *Paris* burns at Le Havre. Tons of
hose water, collected on upper decks, have initiated a fatal list. (*Topix, London*)

The *Mauretania* (left) and *Olympic* tied up at Southampton's Berth 108, a kind of maritime death row. (*Frank Braynard Collection*)

A quarter of a century old, R.M.S. *Olympic* ready for a final sailing from Southampton, victim of the Depression and Cunard's merger. (*Frank Braynard Collection*)

seemingly determined to complete the inevitable ritual of pierside fire. But Bisset, then a junior officer, worked with a desperate gang of men under nine feet of water, struggling to release the catches on a starboard entry port. They finally got it open and tons of excess water, collected on the low side of the ship, drained into the harbor. The *Mauretania* was saved from capsizing. E-deck was entirely gutted and Cunard took the opportunity of combining fire repairs with conversion to oil burning.

By the mid thirties, the *Mauretania* was getting on, showing decrepitude as well as age. Some additional bathrooms had been worked into her hull in the twenties. For cruises, temporary canvas swimming pools were installed on deck. But her malaise necessitated the kind of massive renovation that her owners were in no position to undertake. There were stubborn patches of rust all over the hull and superstructure that even another layer of gleaming white paint could do no more than forestall.

A landmark's destruction is predictably a matter of public emotional regret. In the case of the *Mauretania,* the urge for universal commiseration was particularly strong. Whether it represented the passing of an institution, a subtle reminder of the fragility of human endeavor or literally the death of a living thing is difficult to say. Traditional use of feminine pronouns in reference to a ship makes this latter affectation contagious.

Certainly, it was understandable among the crew. They were close to the ship and attributed very real emotions to their steel home. Her affectionate nickname was the "Mary," just as her unfortunate sister had been called the "Lucy." In his memoirs, Captain Sir Arthur Rostron recalled once in the Dardanelles that the *Mauretania* gave "a shudder of delight." This tendency to personify vessels was as old as the sea, and Cunard encouraged it in the *Mauretania*'s later years. Gallantry was an effective substitute for fashionableness after she lost the Blue Riband. There was plenty of sales mileage in the poignant image of a champion done in by an arrogant German usurper, living out the remainder of her life with quiet courage. Near the end, as she was about to disappear forever, this sentimental outpouring spread not only to habitual passengers quite literally deprived by her loss but also to landlocked millions who had never been near her.

In point of fact, the truth was tribute enough. The *Mauretania* was a finely built vessel whose owners skillfully amassed a reputation for fast reliable service in war as well as peace. She was known in the twenties as the Rostron Express because her crossings from Ambrose to Bishop's were often consistent within minutes; her captain was also able to catch the three-thirteen train to Liverpool. By the time she was withdrawn from service, her career had lasted one month short of twenty-seven years and she had steamed two million miles on the North Atlantic alone. In September of 1934, the same day that she left New York for the last time, a new and grander *Mary* thundered down the ways in Scotland.

Death row for British ships was Southampton's Berth 108. Vessels whose future was in jeopardy tied up there, a quiet backwater in an otherwise busy port. It was on this pier that a sale of the *Mauretania*'s interior fittings was held. Furniture made for the White Star's *Britannic* had been sold by auction in 1919, items designed for the ship prewar but never installed. The sale was listless and had no particular appeal, for the vessel lay at the bottom of the Aegean and had carried no civilian passengers before she was lost. She had no image.

But news of the *Mauretania*'s auction attracted hundreds of buyers who bid spiritedly for everything that could be wrenched from the hull before it went north to the breakers. The brass letters that spelled her name and port of registry across the stern went as one lot for sixty pounds, while the larger ones on the starboard bow were sold as separate souvenirs, eleven pounds the letter. Some items were enormous: lot number 237 was "A white marble mantelpiece from the Library, complete with marble kerb and hearth." The next day, lot number 371, "the enamelled barrel-vaulted ceiling to centre of smoking room," was disposed of, together with "panelling of polished harewood, sold in two portions, port and starboard." All the lifeboats were sold, including the original sixteen Tyne-built ones as well as those added later after the *Titanic* went down.

A man from the Channel Islands bought the bulk of the paneling from the *grand salon,* staircase and dining room with the intention of reselling it as the basis of a projected Hotel Mauretania in New York. But neither the plan nor the assistance of an American millionaire, that favorite character in English fiction, ever materialized. The choicest part of the *grand salon*'s boiserie decorates the dining room of a Bristol pub and the balance is still in storage. The following year, some of the *Olympic*'s dining room was snapped up at her auction and incorporated into a hotel bar in Northumberland. The same publican took a fancy to one of the ship's parlor suites and used its paneling to line the walls of his best bedroom. Scores of northern drummers have occupied the same room as did the Prince of Wales eastbound in 1924.

Preservation of architectural entities is both ambitious and laudable. American philanthropical giants delight in the wholesale purchase, transshipment and reassemblage of chapels, suites or castles. These expensive transmigrations serve as invaluable academic tools and a means of satisfying those unable to visit the original locales. But as a means of recapturing the

The first of a thirties phenomenon: Auctioning the furnishings and fittings of a retired express liner. Bidders crowd the *Mauretania*'s main lounge in Southampton. (*Frank Braynard Collection*)

The *Mauretania*'s arrival at Rosyth. Within an hour, engine room telegraphs on the bridge rang down "Finished With Engines" for the last time. (*Frank Braynard Collection*)

past, these recreations are only partially effective. The Blumenthal Patio, the sixteenth-century courtyard of Velez Blanco that stands miraculously intact in New York's Metropolitan Museum of Art, is incomplete, through no fault of its donor or curator. Although stone and mortar have been meticulously reassembled, other intangibles have not. Overhead, wired glass panels obstruct what should be a Spanish sky, either the cobalt glare at midday or the infinite pale vault of dusk. Would that some electrical legerdemain could produce a ray of sun to throw a cornice into startling relief. But there is no warmth locked in the stone, no fragrance in the air, not even a blood-red banner flung over an upper balcony. In the northwest corner, a Florentine fountain, penny-choked, dribbles bravely, a poor substitute for the constant plash of water without which no Moorish dwelling was ever complete.

By the same token, one would have thought that the faultless duplication of a ship's cabin in Britain's Maritime Museum might have some evocative viability. Unfortunately, there is none, even though curators there were dealing almost solely with an interior. But the space is no more than a shell, devoid of reality. So too is Bristol's Mauretania Pub. Although the handsome mahogany paneling encloses a dining room in constant use, it has very little relationship to the vessel from which it was taken. The subtle breathing and creaking of the ship, the sea light from the promenade deck, the smell of beeswax and cigar smoke, the solicitous stewards and the genteel scraping of a string orchestra are all gone. I think those who collect souvenirs, whether pocketing a restaurant's coffee spoon or bidding wildly at an auction of memorabilia, suffer similar disillusionment. A gilt cherub rescued before wreckers demolished the Metropolitan Opera House is only a mute, curiously inadequate fragment of a glorious past. Authenticity is no substitute for ambience; there is more to the memory of a football game than a splinter of the goal post.

When the *Mauretania* sailed for Scotland and the breakers, crowds lined either shore, just as they had done twenty-eight years earlier when, brand new, the ship had passed down the Tyne so full of promise. Now she was like a ghost, white, stained and gutted. Among those who waved from the pier was Cunard's Commodore Sir Arthur Rostron; he had refused to board her. All along Southampton Water, people stood silent or, like Cowes residents, whose cellars had once been flooded by the wash of her wake, sang "Auld Lang Syne." Near Bembridge, a bugler sounded "The Last Post." There were even a few passengers on board, including one couple who had crossed on their honeymoon nearly three decades earlier. All were fed indifferently in the third-class dining room, the only public room that remained furnished.

The trip north was uneventful, the great turbines producing an effortless eighteen knots. Her masts had been cut down for passage beneath the Firth of Forth Bridge. From the stump of her abbreviated mainmast flew a veritable Blue Ribband, emblazoned "1907–1929," her reign as Atlantic champion. As she was warped in to Admiralty Dock, a piper in full dress played a lament, "The Flowers of the Forest." Her steam whistles sounded for the last time, on board at any rate. They had been sold with her fittings and were later installed on the roof of a factory at Rugby, signaling the end of the work week and, during the war, the approach of German aircraft.

Other items from those doomed ships of the thirties had some practicality for their new owners. The *Olympic*'s auction was held in Jarrow, a Tyneside town whose Member of Parliament had bought the ship to provide employment for his severely depressed constituency. The ship's canvas padded cell went to a South Shields fun fair. The ice-cream room was dismantled and put to work ashore. Even the mortuary was snapped up by a shrewd Northumbrian undertaker. And in Newcastle to this day, there is a butcher shop where joints hang suspended from hooks that once were in the *Olympic*'s cold-storage room.

But most of the stuff had little real value; there was, rather, lot after lot of pure nostalgia. Chart tables, megaphones, the carpet from the captain's cabin, the ship's bell, the dinner gong. There were ten framed notices ("The White Star Company is not responsible for valuables kept in the cabin . . ."), a bottle opener marked *Café Parisien,* a patent egg timer from the first-class pantry, the mahogany fittings of the chief sauce steward's cabin. The contents of the gymnasium, all those massive cast-iron German mechanisms, went intact, as did all the elevators, gilt balustrades and inlaid divans from the Turkish baths.

Arthur Knight, from the firm Knight, Frank & Rutley charged with the sale, dropped his conventional auctioneer's bonhomie on the first day of business. He stood on a platform of smoking-room tables lashed together, addressing the crowd assembled in the gloom of the *Olympic*'s lounge. It was November and the sale was held too far north to attract buyers from London. "I have in my time," he announced, his breath visible in the unpleasant chill, "broken up many a noble and historic home, and today, I have the unhappy task of performing the last rites for this magnificent ship which has been for many years the home of the gallant crews sailing in her. It is impossible to be unmoved by helping to destroy such a monument to man's achievement, and I feel that I owe the *Olympic* my apologies before starting my undignified labors." Moments later, lot number 1 was sold, seven pounds for two settees from the engineers' smoking room.

Right, scrapping the *Leviathan:* The cruel
desolation of the boat deck at Rosyth.
Near the end, breakers have removed so
much of the hull, far right, that remaining
buoyancy thrusts the propellers conveniently above the surface. (*Frank Braynard
Collection*)

Left, Ballin's second and third great ships at Rosyth. In the foreground, H.M.S. *Caledonia* (ex-*Majestic*, ex-*Bismarck*) has only one of three funnels left intact. Just beyond lies the hulk of the *Leviathan* (ex-*Vaterland*). (*National Maritime Museum, Greenwich*)

Following an auction of her fittings in January of 1939, the *Berengaria* followed the *Olympic* to Jarrow. Wreckers subsequently found a cache of four hundred pounds concealed behind paneling in the glory hole. It was either the savings of a crew member or, more probably, profits from smuggling, hidden on board because they could not be spent ashore without arousing suspicion. The *Majestic* survived as H.M.S. *Caledonia,* a Royal Navy training vessel. Her masts were cut down like the *Mauretania*'s to fit under the Forth Bridge and she was converted to a floating barracks for naval cadets. The central rotunda at the head of the winter garden staircase, designed by the Germans as a restaurant and converted by White Star to a ballroom, saw its third and final incarnation as a gymnasium, complete with boxing ring. Promenade deck walls were lined with exercise bars and cabin partitions below decks were torn down to create dormitories. When she left Southampton's Berth 108 for the journey north, oily smoke from her disused funnels obscured the sky.

A similar smoke screen lay over much of Manhattan when the *Leviathan* sailed east for the last time in January 1938. She was so badly silted up that fueling was accomplished off Staten Island, leaving her as light as possible to leave her Hoboken berth. The ship had spent so many years tied up in New Jersey: as the captive *Vaterland,* then again as a retired trooper and finally as an expensive white elephant following the Depression. Her masts and funnels were topped and she sailed from New York flying the red duster of the British Merchant Marine. Captain Binks, the master in command of the *Olympic* when she rammed the Nantucket Lightship, came out of retirement to sail the ship east with a prize British crew. She began the crossing firing thirty-six boilers and had only two thirds that number in operation when she arrived. Somewhere aft, there was a stubborn leak that the pumps could not contain, and only careful reballasting with fuel and water enabled trim to be maintained. Perhaps most bizarre of all, the wire controlling operation of the steam whistle contracted from the cold in midocean and triggered a series of ghostly blasts, reminiscent of her behavior as a trooper years earlier.

So those grand old ships sailed to the breakers in the waning peace of the thirties. Almost mystically, many of them returned to die in the same northern waters that had given them birth. Most were gone by the time hostilities broke out. The "Lucy" had been sunk in another war, the "Mary," the "Berry," the "Magic Stick" and the "Levi Nathan," as their crews called them, were no more than scrap or weathered relics, memories of happier years. Only the *Aquitania,* "Old Irrepressible," survived, the last of her breed to serve in both World Wars.

13.
War Again

Just two decades after the First World War had ended, the Second began. Events on the North Atlantic conveyed a sense of familiar repetition. The links between Europe and North America were severed or restricted: telephone service ceased, cables underwent rigid censorship and the Western Ocean ships steamed desperately for home or neutrality, as their elder sisters had done in high summer twenty-five years before.

Germany's *Europa* lay in Bremerhaven, from which port she would never sail again flying the German flag. Her sister ship *Bremen* made a vast northern detour from New York, passing north of Iceland and the British Isles to appear in Murmansk; from the security of that neutral port, she later slipped back down to Germany. Eastbound in midocean, the *De Grasse* turned tail and fled to Halifax but the *Aquitania,* blacked out and zigzagging, completed her voyage to Southampton. Spared the tonnage pogrom of the thirties, she performed invaluably in the years that followed. The *Mary,* westbound to America, raced into New York and tied up at Pier 90. Across the slip to the south lay her French rival the *Normandie,* whose owners had signaled her from Paris to remain indefinitely in New York. These two huge vessels, paradoxically less vulnerable to underwater attack than any of their smaller and slower sisters, were considered too precious to expose to the slightest risk and endured months of inactivity in the safety of the Hudson.

For Americans abroad, the languid summer games were over. Once again, they besieged their embassies, stranded by canceled sailings on a hostile continent with distinctive maroon passports that had assumed a new significance. Ambassador Kennedy cabled from London for American ships to come and gather up peacetime tourists who were a nuisance to the belligerents and a drain on his embassy's resources.

When it was announced that the *Aquitania* would make a crossing despite the outbreak of war, anxious passengers stampeded the pier at Southampton. American passports were collected at the gangplank and their owners asked to assemble in the lounge. There, a tight-lipped consular official read a statement that included the caveat: "American citizens are hereby advised that they are taking passage on a belligerent ship and are subject to sinking without notice." (The wording might have been lifted almost verbatim from the ominous notice that appeared in American shipping pages the morning the *Lusitania* sailed on her final voyage twenty-two years earlier.)

Following this bleak announcement, there was some panic among the Americans that spread to the crew; elements of both left the ship forthwith. The handful of British passengers, however, exhibiting a curiously resilient phlegm, appeared in the gloom of a smoking room with painted-out windows even before the buzz of excitement had dissipated from the neighboring lounge; they were clad in dinner jackets and chatted in detached tones about the war news. At dinner that night, crewmen lashed a ladder to the dining-room balcony. Ventilators all over the vessel were covered with paper, a precaution taken to render the *Aquitania* immune to a gas attack. Those Americans who disembarked opted to wait for the rescue fleet promised from New York. It was on its way, including the *Manhattan, Washington* and *President Roosevelt,* all with large American flags painted on their sides.

Passengers were quite naturally hesitant to commit to British vessels.

Twelve days after war was declared, the *Queen Mary* was already gray; her neighboring rival, the *Normandie,* lay untouched for months. Apart from its historical significance, this photograph serves to accentuate the French ship's rakish image in contrast to the *Mary*'s conventional hauteur. (*Prints and Photographs Division, Library of Congress*)

One man who overcame this reluctance was a young Viennese doctor named Lustig who, with his bride, booked on the *Athenia* sailing from Glasgow. She carried nearly three hundred Americans as well as refugees anxious to get to America. On the evening of the very day that war was declared, the *Athenia* was sunk off the north coast of Ireland. As if to set the tone of German intentions against unarmed merchant vessels, U-boat 30, under the command of Fritz Lemp, sent a pair of torpedoes into the hull of the thirteen-thousand-ton Cunarder.

Most of the passengers were at dinner but the Austrian couple remained on deck in the bright light of a northern summer's eve. While his wife lay on the hatch cover next to him, Dr. Lustig started a duplicate letter to both their parents, letting them know that they were safely away. He had just typed *"Lieber Vater, liebe Mutter"* when there was a sudden rushing sound. It was not an explosion, he remembered thirty years later, only a mighty exhalation that obliterated the hatch cover and everything on it. He was unharmed but his wife had disappeared. Looking over the edge of the hatch moments later, directly above one torpedo's point of entry, he saw only her purse amidst a tangle of wreckage. Other ships raced to the rescue of the stricken *Athenia*'s passengers, including a trio of Royal Navy destroyers. Their efforts were complicated by a school of whales that sported among the lifeboats.

The ship had left Scotland with a maximum of security precautions. Company agents in Montreal, her destination, had neither a passenger list nor estimated date of arrival. But news of her sinking spread across the Atlantic like wildfire. As one result, the *Aquitania* made straight down Channel, aborting her customary Cherbourg call. Passengers who held tickets there raced overland to Le Havre in the hopes of finding a French ship. But the harbor was empty save for the desolate *Paris* which still lay capsized at her pier, gutted the summer before. The *Normandie* and *Ile de France* were in New York, the *De Grasse* Halifax-bound and the *Champlain* about to arrive at the south side of Hudson River Pier 88, overloaded with nerve-racked passengers.

The *Champlain* had crossed in a week and a half, eleven days that spanned both peace and war. On board there had been an atmosphere of misery that contrasted ironically with the traditional gaieties of shipboard life. Cot beds were everywhere. The smoking room was once again exclusively a gentlemen's preserve, this time as a dormitory; carpenters had cut an additional doorway giving private access to one of the public bathrooms outside. Another man shared the children's playroom with four Polish rabbis who periodically rent the air in vociferous lamentation. A few husbands and wives were able to share cabins but most were separated and called the most pathetic domestic trivia back and forth each morning. All portholes had been sealed shut and doors were left open to improve circulation. News of the *Athenia*'s fate was foolishly released to the already nervous passengers in midocean. It was confirmation that what later became known as the Phoney War did not include the Atlantic.

In March of 1940, the brand-new *Queen Elizabeth* arrived in New York following the most discreet maiden voyage in history. The eighty-thousand-ton express liner had been launched just a year before the war began. She was not, strictly speaking, the *Queen Mary*'s sister ship; her looks were quite different. She had only two funnels and cleaner topsides, closer in feeling to the *Normandie*. There was no well deck forward and three rather than two anchors. Placement of this third and central bower meant the *Elizabeth*'s stem had a sharper rake to allow a clear fall to the water. But despite these variations, the new *Queen* gave much the same impression as the *Mary* and was certainly a sister ship in intent if not in actuality. She was christened by and after the new Queen, and the monstrous hull began inching its way toward the Clyde before Her Majesty had actually pressed the launch button.

The second ship's interiors were done in a style similar to the *Mary*'s, although Cunard White Star's design ambitions were a little more restrained. However, the same use of exotic veneers obtained. Although most of her decorative components were completed ashore before the war, the second *Queen*'s interiors were not finally installed for seven more years. One unpublished difference between the two *Queens* emerged in postwar years when crewmen had an opportunity to serve on both vessels. Their preference was overwhelmingly in favor of the *Queen Mary* despite her greater age. In their experience, she was an easier ship to work and, consequently, a happier ship. Throughout her long career, crews on the *Elizabeth* never established the same operational harmony that the *Mary* knew all her life.

I have always felt that the chaos of her early years contributed to this phenomenon, that the *Queen Elizabeth* was bound to have suffered somewhere in transition. It is a subtle thing, this ease of working a ship, seldom affecting passengers directly. It can involve nothing more trivial than the awkward placement of a deck-pantry counter, the cupboard where stewards' vacuum cleaners are stored or the particular slope of the engine room ladders. Yet trifling little imperfections of this kind, perhaps borne initially out of wartime expediency, permeated the *Elizabeth*. She was made ready for sea in haste, when no one had the time or authorization to put things right. I can only assume that it was for this reason that the *Mary,* with three years

Completed in time for war. Workers at
John Brown labor on the *Queen Elizabeth*. (*Cunard*)

of superlative peacetime service behind her before conversion to trooping, was the better working of the two.

Navy ships are traditionally assigned a shakedown cruise. This extended voyage, under the corrective scrutiny of company personnel, hones down the minor imperfections of design seldom fully eliminated on the drawing boards. Once permitted to remain, these flaws insinuate themselves as permanent inconveniences of a ship's working spaces to which a crew will grudgingly resign itself. Passenger liners would do well to submit to this same procedure, as was the case with the *QE2*. Were it not for turbine troubles, Cunard had planned to offer large numbers of shore staff and their families a free cruise on the new *Queen,* using them as guinea pigs to test every conceivable passenger facility. But in the old days this was unheard of, and maiden voyages never attained the smooth perfection that came after a series of crossings.

In the first winter of the war, it became imperative to move the *Queen Elizabeth* from her fitting-out berth—before completion if necessary. She was a tempting target to any German pilot who might penetrate that far north. She was also of secondary importance, by then, to Royal Navy ships badly in need of the repair facilities she occupied. It was decided that she should go to America and that essential work allowing her to sail be accomplished by late February. This was imperative—the depth of water necessary to float her down the Clyde would not recur for six months. There would be two consecutive maximum flood tides, one of which would take the *Queen Elizabeth* down to the sea, the other bring the battleship *Duke of York* upstream to take her place. It was a piece of inverted wartime protocol: His Grace displacing Her Majesty.

Sending the world's largest vessel across the Atlantic in absolute secrecy was perhaps a simple decision to make but astonishingly difficult to implement. Tight security was paramount. The four hundred crewmen handling the empty ship, most of them recruited from the *Aquitania,* were advised that the *Elizabeth* was sailing for Southampton and dry-docking. This was traditionally routine procedure following trials. But officials in the southern port heard of this and tartly reminded the Company that they had no docking plan. Faked documents were hastily sent to assuage suspicion. A carefully worded signal was dispatched to New York, requesting Cunard's Marine Superintendent to clear the north side of Pier 90. The new *Mauretania* was tied up there and had to be moved.

Once down river, the *Elizabeth* was repainted, latest and largest addition to the anonymous gray fleet of wartime. Engine and compass trials were carried out in one day and the ship formally handed over after a desultory ceremony in the third-class dining room. Captain Townley had no definite confirmation of his destination until the arrival of a King's messenger, dispatched by First Lord of the Admiralty Winston Churchill on March 2. Later that day, the *Queen Elizabeth* set a course for New York. Still affixed to the hull were portions of the launch gear. A record-breaking trip was quite clearly out of the question. The Southampton cover plan was evidently successful: Luftwaffe formations quartered the Channel on the day of her supposed arrival.

Manned by one third of her normal complement and carrying almost no passengers, the *Elizabeth*'s maiden voyage was quite bizarre. On board were only a handful of technical advisers and Company officials, all but lost in the empty splendors of the ship. The catering staff looked after them admirably. Indeed, their remarkable crossing was achieved in comfort identical to that of those elegant hundreds who, war notwithstanding, would have sailed on the maiden voyage the following month. Most striking of all was the ship's emptiness.

I spent a night on board the same vessel thirty years later in the humidity of Fort Lauderdale with only the fire watch for company. A deserted liner under any circumstances has a haunting quality—miles of echoing passageways, the moribund silence of the lounge and dining room, the desolation of splintering, weathered decks. But to have been one of a handful of passengers on board the same vessel, in March 1940, racing empty through a hostile Atlantic, must have had a surreal distinction reminiscent of the play *Outward Bound*. Once anxiety about a German attack had passed, there was little enough to do. They dined in one corner of the eight-hundred-seat dining room, strolled about on acres of deck and retired each night to their splendid quarters. To help pass the time pleasantly, Purser Charles Johnson founded a seriocomic club known as the Unruffled Elizabethans. It came as instinctively to him as organizing a treasure hunt for a group of shy children.

One day out of New York, radio broadcasts received on board indicated that the ship's departure and destination were common knowledge on both sides of the Atlantic. A Trans World airliner first spotted the *Elizabeth* forty miles south of Fire Island, its passengers unsurprised by that pale ship steaming west. Her subsequent unheralded appearance in New York harbor had a kind of panache nevertheless. To the *New York Post,* the ship appeared like "an Empress incognito, gray-veiled for her desperate exploit." She remained at Quarantine for four hours. By the time she reached her berth in late afternoon, thousands of office and shorefront workers thronged the West Side to cheer in the newest *Queen.* If she was scarcely dressed for

The *Queen Elizabeth* approaches New York, having completed her secretive maiden voyage. The decks are deserted, her windows painted over and some of the davits empty. (*The Mariners Museum, Newport News, Virginia*)

Assembled in one harbor for the first and last time. The three prewar giants tied up in New York at the start of the war. From left to right: *Normandie, Queen Mary,* and *Queen Elizabeth.* (*The Mariners Museum, Newport News, Virginia*)

the occasion, the brilliance of her escape from the Germans gave the moment a particular drama all its own. That vast, somber ship, nudged delicately into the slip just north of her sister, gave symbolic presence to the war that America was yet to enter.

For a fortnight, the three largest vessels in the world were tied up at the Hudson piers in somnolent camaraderie, as though mourning a departed era. Longshoremen christened them The Monsters. Then, two weeks after the *Elizabeth* arrived from Scotland, the *Queen Mary* sailed from New York. In November, six months later, the *Elizabeth* sailed too, leaving only the *Normandie*.

Still in her peacetime colors, the French ship was manned by a nucleus of a hundred and fifteen crewmen, the balance—nearly a thousand men—having departed for Montreal and home in the first month of the war. Life on board for the next two years was a monotonous round of preventative maintenance that eroded the fiber of crew and ship alike. Four tons of moth crystals, shipped from France, were brushed into miles of blue carpeting. Canvas runners were laid as walkways across the deserted public rooms. Furniture in these rooms had special dust covers kept on board for use while drydocking; now they remained in place, together with shrouds on the lacquered walls. In the cabins, bedding from each bunk was put in the closets and doors left ajar, as a fire precaution as well as an attempt to dispel mustiness. Each morning and evening, there was a simple ceremony at the stern as the tricolor was raised and lowered.

Morale was hard to maintain, even though New York was the ship's second home and, under normal circumstances, a good liberty port. But the enforced inactivity, the worry about families left in France and the unending routine made life intensely frustrating. Inactivity is the curse of ships as well as of the men who sail them. There was little to do on board and English lessons by record player palled after a few months.

The officer in charge was Captain Zanger—Captain Thoreux, Chief Engineer Hazard and Commissaire Villar, the famous first string, had returned to France. There was scarcely any need for a purser except to take care of the reduced payroll. Brightwork was greased and painting continued in an endless progression around the superstructure. It was like the Golden Gate Bridge—when it had been completely painted, it was time to start all over again. Canvas funnel covers were rigged across the three stacks.

One detachment which had been left on board intact was the fire brigade, an elite corps of Paris-trained firemen, a score of whom patrolled ceaselessly up and down the sleeping corridors. These *veilleurs* were kept in a state of superb readiness, as was their central fire station. Admission to the ship, even before the fall of France, was by photographic pass only. Having negotiated the security of the pier, rare visitors crossing the gangplank were scrutinized in front of a white wooden door built into the main embarkation port, with a sliding peephole reminiscent of speakeasies.

Captain Zanger acquired a dog which his crew, in ironic salutation to their port of internment, called "Yankee Doodle." Like the crew of the *Vaterland,* tied up across the river for two years in another war, the French seamen on board the *Normandie* felt more like captives than allies. In May 1940, when France fell to the Germans, the ship was placed in "protective custody." Ship's personnel were augmented by armed Coast Guardsmen who remained on board. One of their missions was to assume equal responsibility with their shipmates in the matter of fire patrols.

Meanwhile, both *Queens* were in service in the Far East, having been transformed into troopships in Singapore and fitted out in Sydney. There was a kind of North Atlantic reunion in those alien blue waters—the *Queen Mary,* the *Queen Elizabeth,* the *Ile,* the *Aquitania* and the new *Mauretania* were all in Sydney at one time that year, an astonishing change of venue that only war could have provided. But in New York, the *Normandie* lingered on. Gold leaf in the *grand salon* began to flake off and French wine ran out, replaced by suspicious stuff from California.

After Pearl Harbor, events moved with a swiftness that was in ironic contrast to the years of idleness that preceded them. By Executive Order, the vessel was seized and her owners promised compensation. The Company's New York officials were delighted to be rid of their thousand-dollar-a-day responsibility. The Navy put out bids for the conversion contract; it was subsequently won by a subsidiary of Todd Shipyards called the Robins Dry Dock and Repair Company, Incorporated. There was no dry dock in New York capable of taking the ship at that time and it was decided to implement the work at Pier 88 where she lay. The pier became an "extension" of the dockyard. First call of the new troopship following her conversion would be Boston and the same dry dock in which both the *Majestic* and *Leviathan* had begun peacetime service in the twenties.

At two in the afternoon on December 16, 1941, the French flag was lowered at the stern for the last time and the S.S. *Normandie* became the U.S.S. *Lafayette.* She was officially known by this name for the remainder of her short life. When she burned, press, public and the Navy referred to her by her original name: not surprisingly, when she was salvaged, the Navy reverted to the new one. To me she was the *Normandie* throughout her ordeal, and will be referred to as such during the account that follows.

In point of fact, the seeds of the vessel's destruction were sown quietly

Messboys on the *Queen Mary* prepare for
a sitting of two thousand troops, two and
a half times the dining room's peacetime
capacity. The animated models of the two
*Queen*s that used to inch across the mural
are gone, as are, curiously, the hands of
the clock. (*Cunard*)

in the months preceding the disaster. The first American Coast Guardsmen who came on board in mid-1940 were there to assist the skeleton Transat crew in protecting the *Normandie* from fire. Their patrols were patterned on the French system but there was a startling discrepancy in numbers. Duty rosters specified eight instead of twenty men on rounds at a time. By the time she was completely manned by Coast Guard after Pearl Harbor, this reduction in strength had become standard operating procedure. Furthermore all switches, directions and instructions on board were in French and, even though translations of critical material were made, effective vigilance was further reduced by this lingual barrier. Then too, most astonishingly, it turned out that the remainder of the Coast Guard detachment placed on board in December 1941 had neither assignment nor fire stations in the event of general alarm.

In January, the Navy authorized a private firm to make a survey of the ship's fire-fighting equipment. Information gleaned from this study was not reassuring. It was reported that only ten percent of the fire extinguishers on board were built "according to American design." (The wording is taken from the text of a subsequent report made to the House Naval Affairs Committee and seems hardly surprising in the light of the *Normandie's* French origins.) The firm went on to remark that extinguishers lacked operating instructions and that only fifty percent of them were in good condition. This conclusion was reached on the basis of having tested no more than four of the over six hundred instruments kept on board. The report closed with a recommendation that all foreign fire extinguishers be replaced with American equipment, a not unusual suggestion for U.S. Navy ships. However, in the light of subsequent events, it gave popular credence to the notion that, prior to the American takeover, there was little effective fire-control equipment on board. Such an assumption is both prejudiced and inaccurate. It would be safe to say that the *Normandie,* fully manned and operating under French service conditions, was as carefully protected from fire as any ship of her era.

But at the time of the fire, no new extinguishers had been placed on board. One aspect of conversion to American specifications had been implemented. Workers were in the process of replacing French with American hose couplings. However, it became apparent that an oral directive, issued at the same time, recommending retention of compatible couplings throughout the schedule of changeover, had been ignored. This was just one indiscriminate error, a tessera in the mosaic of disaster that ensued. There were others as well.

Article 11(a) of the Robins Company contract read as follows: "The contractor shall exercise the highest possible degree of care to protect the vessel from fire. To this end the contractor shall maintain an adequate system of inspection over the activities of welders, burners, riveters, painters, plumbers and similar workers. . . ." In discharging this obligation, it is apparent that the force of fifty civilian fire watchers employed by the Company was hopelessly inadequate. Untrained and unskilled, they were largely senior men awarded the post as a kind of sinecure. Their qualifications had little relationship to their employment. Furthermore, their authority was minimal. It was also understandable that careful supervision of each welding and cutting operation throughout a vessel swarming with workmen under wartime pressure was little more than a theoretical precaution. It was quite a different task from the orderly patrols made on a deserted ship. As the pace of work accelerated, as more and more men were taken on, the number of fire watchers remained the same. During the first week in February, there were often eighty jobs requiring the services of fifty men; it was a physical impossibility for each to be supervised, however ineffectually.

The attempted rate of conversion can only be described as catastrophic. A complicated job at best was made even more so as administrative realignments in a novice Washington war machine sent reverberations through American military establishments all over the world. The following two paragraphs from the *Summary of Findings of the United States Navy Court of Inquiry* give an inkling of the problems faced by the Third Naval District's Matériel Officer. Captain Clayton Simmers, the Navy's man on the spot, was evidently an officer among whose primary qualifications must have been the patience of a saint:

> When the conversion work began about December 24, 1941, the tentative date of completion was February 1, 1942. On January 15, 1942, the District Matériel Officer was informed that the *Lafayette* would be operated by the War Department which required modification of the conversion work. On January 27, 1942, the District Matériel Officer was informed that the Navy Department would operate the vessel. This indecision caused a delay in the progress of the conversion in certain areas of the vessel which made it impossible to complete the work by February 1, 1942, and the completion date was extended to the latter part of February 1942.
>
> On the evening of February 6, 1942, the Chief of Naval Operations by telephone informed the Commandant of the Third Naval District that the *Lafayette* was to be made ready for loading on February 28, 1942. On February 7, 1942, the Bureau of Ships informed the District Matériel Officer that it was desired that the *Lafayette* leave

New York on February 14, 1942 for docking at Boston, Massachusetts
on February 15, 1942.

Between the lines of this terse documentation, it is not hard to envision the desperation of Captain Simmers and his subordinates, deluged with contradicting directives that came relentlessly up from Washington.

Navies all over the world delight in doing the impossible. Resourceful accomplishment of insuperable tasks is encouraged and even expected under conditions of stress. But the transformation of the passenger liner *Normandie* into the troopship *Lafayette* was more than a coat of gray paint and a few thousand bunks. The Navy had certain requirements of its ships, specifications that Yourkevitch had not included in the *Normandie*'s original plans. There were longitudinal torpedo bulkheads to be installed, transverse bulkheads that had to extend upwards, gun tubs, paravanes, cranes, searchlights, ammunition hoists and lockers—a host of bewildering wartime necessities that might never be put to use in combat but that Washington, in its wisdom, felt would be necessary adjuncts to a troop-carrying auxiliary. At one point in the early conversion discussion, there had been some grand talk of turning the *Normandie* into an aircraft carrier; elements of this original bravado remained in the cloud of new specifications that poured into Simmers' office. They helped the confusion. In retrospect, I would hazard that U.S. Navy planners were still locked in the mythology of fighting auxiliaries that the British and Germans had relinquished in 1915. Neither *Queen* ever submitted to the intensive restructuring that Americans felt essential before the *Lafayette* could sail.

It is tempting, therefore, to suppose that the original ship was somehow structurally deficient. As a warship, she certainly was. But as a means of transporting large numbers of passengers across the seas at high speed, she had only two near competitors, both of which were already providing invaluable service of this kind in the Far East. Furthermore, she had proved herself in four years of exceptional peacetime employment. Yet the Navy felt that drastic refitting was essential and pressed for the kind of miraculous completion that wins Presidential as well as public commendation.

As it was, the magnitude of the task, the changes in specifications, the limited facilities at Pier 88 and the scheduling of impossible deadlines led to a kind of logistical chaos on board. Decisions taken in the rarified detachment of a Washington bureaucracy came down the ladder of rank, to be implemented *in situ* by officers whose frustrating mission it was to transmit the urgency they felt to civilians. They dealt with a work force whose stake in the matter was scarcely more than financial, whose careers did not depend on the commissioning date of the U.S.S. *Lafayette*. Completion of the work in two months, even without the barrage of countermands from Washington, would have been one of the minor production miracles of the war. But the folly of instilling a panicky haste into this kind of undertaking led of necessity to a breakdown in supervision, judgment and common sense. All over the giant, semifunctioning vessel there was a tempo of desperate naval ambition juxtaposed against civilian apathy. Disparate and incompatible elements of the fitting out had to be effected in hazardous combination that would have been forbidden under less harried circumstances.

The situation in the main lounge on the morning of February 9, 1942, provides a classic example of this scheduling turmoil. Outside, it was only a few degrees above zero, clear and sunny, with a chill wind blowing across from the Jersey shore. Barges delivering stores to open cargo ports on the ship's side away from the pier nosed through a mush of salt-water ice that filled the slip. Overhead, suspended in pipe scaffolding, painters bundled against the bitter cold completed a scheme of camouflage to cover the streaked black plates. Working alongside them were welding parties fitting steel blanks over portholes. (How many were covered at the time their work was interrupted later that day was a matter of some contention; a Robins vice-president assured the Navy that all portholes but one below B-deck were sealed but divers who explored the wreck later would dispute this.) Rows of oblong life rafts were hoisted in place above them, covering windows that were already painted out. Both promenade decks and connecting winter garden had been converted into berthing compartments, filled with standee bunks. The writing room was now an enormous washroom, its walls lined with steel shower stalls.

In the vast public rooms amidships, work scheduled for that day included the removal of all carpeting as well as subsequent installation of linoleum. There was also a steel cutting job to be done. Both *grand salon* and *fumoir* had been permanently combined into one enormous chamber by removal of the motorized fireproof wall that the French designed to separate them. Even if it had still been in place, it would have been impossible to operate. In its path lay a jumble of carpet and linoleum rolls, as well as nearly the entire troop allotment of life preservers.

These latter were filled with kapok, an oil-impregnated silk-cotton fiber that is ideal for flotation although highly inflammable. Thousands of them had been delivered prematurely from Brooklyn and been dumped in the *grand salon,* the only space on board large enough to stow them temporarily. They were in their original factory wrapping, ten to a bundle that was double layered, tarred paper inside and burlap covered with a fuzzy nap on the outside. These bales, eleven hundred of them, were stacked in gargantuan heaps all along the port side of the lounge, waiting to be unpacked, stenciled and distributed to cabins below.

Appropriately, Navy planners had designated the space as the main troop recreational area. Part of the resulting modifications involved removal of the quartet of lamp standards that had provided illumination as well as thirties chic to the center of the room. The glass cascades were gone and only the structural elements remained, heavy steel tripods, eight feet high, on top of circular bases. These bases would remain as table supports but the steel above them had to go.

The method of removing the four light stanchions was for a cutter armed with an oxyacetylene torch to burn through one of three legs. Then other workers, dubbed a "chain gang," would bend the tripod on its side to allow the remaining two legs to be cut. Both starboard fixtures were removed in the morning and after lunch, the port forward one was taken down. The fourth and last was almost concealed by baled life preservers and work was suspended as the cutting crew shifted some of them to obtain access to it. They didn't remove enough. As it was, the cutter and his mates knelt on a convenient, burlap-carpeted layer of bales surrounding the base while the torch did its work. The characteristic flying sparks were contained, as before, by a steel shield and asbestos sheet held by the chain gang. There were two buckets of water nearby but, contrary to explicit regulations, there were no extinguishers, no hoses run out and no fire watchers present at any time.

In the schedule of work priorities at the time, it is probable that removal of these four stanchions was little more than a nuisance job, insignificant in comparison with the rush of complicated steelwork progressing elsewhere on board. The first leg was burned through and the standard pulled over on its side. The top rested on a roll of carpeting. As literally the final cut was being made, the chain gang prematurely removed the asbestos sheet and white hot steel fragments showered down onto the burlap fuzz. In a moment, it was alight.

Reaction was swift but ludicrously ineffectual, a kind of Marx Brothers comedy turn. A worker running over with the two water pails tripped and fell. The foreman who ran instantly onto the promenade deck for a hose got no more than a gallon from its nozzle before pressure dropped to nothing. Another workman raced in with an extinguisher which he was then unable to operate. Others tried beating out the flames with their hands and coats. Some tossed burning bales to a cleared space amidships in an attempt to extinguish them and only succeeded in igniting others. Unhindered, the flames roared up and started licking against the port wall of the lounge.

The tragicomedy of errors was not confined to the lounge. The central fire station had been moved to a different section of the ship and was yet to be equipped with a telephone. One member of the fire brigade stood by in the original space, ready to relay incoming messages on foot to the new headquarters. A direct telegraph line from the bridge to the New York Fire Department had been disconnected in mid-January and never replaced. The man on the bridge who received a telephone alert called in from the theater below him dutifully operated the dead switch. No signal went out.

It was later determined the fire had started at two thirty-seven; the New York City Fire Department responded to a call turned in from 12th Avenue and 49th Street twelve minutes later. It was the first alarm, a "special building" call followed within an hour by five successive full alarms which sent a total of forty-three pieces of equipment to the pier. Every Fire Department vehicle in Manhattan moved that day, either in direct response to the fire or to take up covering positions in empty West Side stations.

In point of fact, the first equipment came by water, the fireboat *James Duane* up from 35th Street. Moments after it came into the slip, smoke which had traveled down to the *Normandie*'s engine rooms through ventilation trunks and elevator shafts forced engineers to evacuate. Furnaces were shut down and a quarter of an hour later, steam pressure was down to zero. The giant ship was without power for either pumps or illumination. She was a dead ship, totally incapacitated only half an hour after the first spark had ignited in the lounge, neither *Normandie* nor *Lafayette* but somewhere in between, her vital systems unmanned or inoperable.

As the first plumes of water arced up over the port railings, newly installed loudspeakers crackled into life despite the power blackout and a gravelly voice intoned monotonously "Get off the ship, get off the ship." There were more than three thousand men on board at the time the fire started, half of them Robins Company employees, the balance a mixture of Navy crew, Coast Guardsmen and civilian subcontractors. Most of them did not know the ship at all and had to feel their way through the hysterical confusion of smoke-filled passageways in total darkness. Over two hundred were injured but, incredibly, only one man was killed. He was mortally wounded, blown down a ladder as a steel feeder tank caught in the flames blew up.

Choking and gagging, men poured down gangplanks connecting the ship to the pier, obstructing city firemen struggling with hoses in the opposite direction. One lot of workers trapped on the port side lowered a lifeboat down to the water and rowed ashore. Another man followed, sliding down the falls. Two others dove into the water through broken promenade deck windows and were fished out by fireboat crews before they froze to death.

Events surrounding the fire must be put into emotional as well as historical context. The date is important, only shortly after the Japanese attack on Pearl Harbor. During those first weeks of war, the United States had suffered a succession of reverses. Much of the Pacific Fleet had been destroyed or crippled at the outset and the enemy overran a series of island outposts with apparently effortless inevitability. Guam, Bataan and Wake were national humiliations fresh in the public consciousness. Hong Kong had fallen and Singapore was about to capitulate. Confidence in allied armed capability was badly shaken and, to a nation hungry for revenge, there was precious little good news coming out of the Pacific. Any kind of restorative to wounded pride was essential.

Conversion of the *Normandie* to a troopship seemed to fit the bill, a positive move against the dark forces of the Axis. Currently, we are not used to the heady euphoria of what has been called, almost nostalgically, a just war. In the early forties, committal to the struggle was total and public enthusiasm for battle an instrument to be played assiduously. Americans craved a focus. The term "Arsenal of Democracy," coined by a valiant President, had a pugnacious ring and seemed to encompass traditional as well as ideological weapons. Rapid and methodical production of planes, tanks, guns and ships was a question of survival as well as enormous pride.

The vital war work starting at Pier 88 on Christmas Eve of 1941 offered concrete proof that something was being done to settle the score. The ship had lain inactive while her British rivals had sailed from neighboring berths on the urgent business of war. The image of girding the *Normandie* for battle, in full public view, was immensely satisfying, particularly for New Yorkers, who have always felt that they owned the great ships for which their port is a second home. In addition, fusing new life into the sleeping giant was a symbolic gesture to a fallen comrade; there was a strong emotional aspect of Franco-American cordiality, dating back to the eighteenth century, that reemerged in times of crisis.

Now word spread rapidly that the *Normandie* was on fire. Disaster threatened an old and valued friend and New Yorkers swarmed impulsively westward to the piers. Thirty thousand of them were held back at 11th Avenue by two companies of soldiers. Gossip of sabotage raced through the crowd with the same rapidity as the flames that had leaped from bale to bale in the lounge only a short time earlier. A block away was the giant

February 9, 1942: The *Normandie* on fire. Sub-freezing temperatures and a brisk wind from across the river hampered firemen's efforts. (*United States Coast Guard, National Archives*)

Seen from 12th Avenue in late afternoon, the *Normandie* lists perilously to port. Notice the open cargo port just above the fireboat's bow, one of several that was not closed prior to capsize. (*The Mariners Museum, Newport News, Virginia*) prow, wreathed in smoke. This same smoke drifted inland, a noxious pall that blotted out Manhattan's winter sun and reached the far boundary of Nassau County by dusk.

Fanned by the wind from over the port quarter, the fire swept relentlessly forward, devouring hundreds of canvas bunks on the promenade deck, searing and curling the Babar murals in the children's playroom, roaring through the florist's shop and servants' dining room and gutting the bridge. Handwoven carpeting, rolls of linoleum, acres of rubber tiling and cork insulation and thousands of kapok life preservers blazed amidships. There were few flames to be seen from the shore, only occasional glares of angry red that darted through the black fumes from that colossal chemical stewpot. Half a dozen coats of heavy marine paint blistered, bubbled and fell away; the third funnel directly over the smoking room was restored momentarily to peacetime colors before that skin too peeled and dropped.

On the pier, evacuation proceeded as men rallying from the initial pandemonium went back on board to rescue fellow workers from below. Firemen extended a perilous swaying ladder from atop the West Side Highway to the bow and over two hundred workmen clustered forward on the whaleback clambered gratefully ashore. On the forepeak stood a Navy signalman, eyes streaming from the smoke, wigwagging vital messages to a man below on the stringpiece. For a critical hour or more, this was the sole means of communication between the burning ship and those on shore.

Only some of the watertight doors, triggered from the bridge with the first alarm, had closed. It was an operative inconsistency combining lifesaving and fatal effects. Scaffolding in the way of many lower deck doors mercifully prevented their closure. Many who might otherwise have perished in tombs of vertical hull segments capped by fire could thus escape forward and aft. Fully closed doors on the upper decks hindered the rapid march of the flames. Incredibly, the theater was untouched; the original fireproofing held. That this wall resisted that awful siege of heat speaks well for its construction.

But preventing the explosive radiation from that great central inferno, buttressed by raging stacks of kapok, was futile elsewhere. Containment was impossible. Firemen later recalled that they had never experienced such heat. One man was severely scalded by clouds of steam that fired back from ice water hosed against a glowing bulkhead. Even a momentary dousing with water in that awful cold meant severe exposure and frostbite minutes later. It was the fireman's nightmare—an inaccessible fire of severe intensity, goaded by winds, situated high above ground level in a monstrous, unlit devastation of a ship. Their only weapon was water, tons of it. With a disabled ship, essentially crewless, its internal systems totally ineffectual, there was nothing else to fight with. Their determination to drown the fire at any cost was strengthened by the sight of burned and asphyxiated comrades and the knowledge that the pier and possibly other ships were threatened if they failed.

Watertight doors along the upper burning decks did close, creating efficient water catchments along their length. Glistening rivulets of molten lead, liquefied electrical conduits, ran down hot bulkheads, hissing into pools of collected water. Chilled into immobility just below the surface, the lead created a stubborn subaqueous stratum that securely plugged drainage scuppers on the low side of the vessel. The inexorable ritual of shipboard fire within reach of land-based companies began. There occurred the same disastrous flooding that had threatened the *Imperator, Europa* and *Mauretania* and capsized the *Paris*. When Captain Simmers arrived at the pier at three twenty-five, he noted an appreciable list to port. An hour after the first alarm it had reached fifteen degrees, and straining hawsers had plucked a pair of immense iron bollards like molars from the cement of the pier.

Gaining access to the scene of the fire was, by this time, almost impossible. Surrounding the clutter of essential fire equipment was an incredible assortment of vehicles in chaotic profusion. New Yorkers, like the rest of America, had flocked to enroll in volunteer organizations, connected, however remotely, to successful prosecution of the war. Now suddenly, only weeks after their inception, here was a real-life, honest-to-God emergency, located conveniently in midtown Manhattan, within easy reach of any enthusiastic lunatic with an armband or steel helmet. It was as though a class of first-year medical students was miraculously offered a heart transplant to play with.

From all five boroughs and New Jersey they came, air-raid wardens from Queens, trucks filled with doughnuts, ladders, ropes and rulebooks, Women's Auxiliaries in modish uniforms of every shape and color, volunteer firemen from a dozen suburban communities. Kept from assisting, these zealots assumed the role of guardians, independently directing emergency traffic and demanding credentials of any who sought entrance to the pier. It was a field day for those well-meaning incompetents, vaulted giddily into the midst of crisis. Patriots, volunteers, visionaries and fire buffs, including Mayor La Guardia, spiritual leader of them all, arrived in their hundreds before the day was out. They joined with police, firemen, reporters, ambulance drivers and personnel from all four services in creating a belt of hyperconfusion about the burning ship. Among the hundreds denied admission through their lines was an excitable Russian who wept in frustration when refused entry. He was Vladimir Yourkevitch, the man who had designed the *Normandie* and whose invaluable knowledge might just possibly have saved her from destruction.

For whatever glories, real or imagined, these determined amateurs lived out on 12th Avenue, efforts inside were scarcely better handled. Following a series of hasty conferences on the pier, a predictable rift developed between Navy men and Fire Department officials. The latter argued with understandable urgency that the fire must be extinguished at all costs while their nautically minded opponents were vehemently opposed to increasing the critical top weight any further. Even as they argued, scores of pulsing hoses continued their fatal inundation. Already, sheets of water poured down the port side from overflowing promenade-deck windows, indicating a substantial depth of water on that deck alone. But those cascades flowing into the harbor were insignificant compared to the deluge that had flooded down into a series of vertical catchments on board. Several gaping cargo ports along D-deck were held open by scaffolding and as the list increased, the water level crept up to these vulnerable entries. Somewhere in the midst of the cavernous dining room was an unseen vertical span connecting two hypothetical points in space. Had it been plotted, it would still have indicated a small, though positive, metacentric height. But for each gallon that came on board, that slender margin of stability was reduced.

Carl Vinson, then a member of the House of Representatives, remarked caustically during a later investigation that he was "unable to find out who was the boss on the *Normandie*." His confusion was understandable. Tradition had it that the senior fireman, be he chief, marshal or even commissioner, takes charge at the scene of a fire. The owner of a burning warehouse ashore might offer advice to the firemen combatting the blaze but it would be unthinkable for him to assume command. This tradition of total departmental authority makes sense on land but its validity is blurred in transition to a vessel tied up at a pier. The Navy's dilemma increased in that none of their officers seemed willing, in retrospect at least, to assume command of the ravaged vessel. The commandant of the Third Naval District, his matériel officer, the prospective master of the ship, the captain of the port, the officer commanding the detachment of Coast Guardsmen, all denied authority, performing an elaborate ritual of deference to each other in negating ultimate responsibility. This reluctance of an individual officer to assume control doomed naval prosecution of any forceful counterproposal to the Fire Department's single-track solution.

Captain Simmers did what he could. He tried cutting holes in the upper port side plating but due to the confusion on the pier, neither men nor torches could be gotten in position. He was able to flood four tanks low in the starboard side through openings burned in the shell plating. This counterflooding appeared to arrest the list. But my suspicion is that what actually stopped the *Normandie's* rotation to port was a combination of low tide and the rock ledge left in the slip by engineers when lengthening the pier inland in the thirties. When the fire started, it was the thrust of the ebbing tide on the ship's exposed flank that instigated a fractional list to port rather than starboard.

At low water, there was normally only five feet between keel and bottom. Any inclination of the hull automatically exceeded this clearance. By early evening, then, the *Normandie's* port bilge keel rested on the edge of a rocky shelf marking the harbor engineers' original cut made a decade earlier. Before the flooding tide returned, the ship lay thus effectively aground while firemen, who had the flames under control, continued mopping up smoldering pockets of fire.

It was, incidentally, this condition of grounding that the Navy sought to effect completely, pressing the Fire Department to let them scuttle the ship. This expedient had saved the *Europa* in 1929 when she burned at her fitting-out pier. But New York's Fire Department demurred, fearful that a layer of burning oil might spread the fire to other parts of the harbor. Even with the Department's compliance, I doubt that any but the original French crew could have located the seacocks in those lifeless black catacombs below, let alone opened them in the delicate sequence that would have set the ship upright on the bottom of the slip.

After the fire was out at six o'clock P.M., there was a three-hour hiatus. The monumental traffic jam dissolved and fire hoses frozen to the 12th Avenue cobbles were taken up. The ship's list during this time was a "safe" sixteen degrees. But by nine o'clock, water which had come in through submerged openings increased the list to twenty degrees; at eleven thirty, it was nearer forty.

All personnel were ordered off the ship an hour later and tugs and fireboats backed out of the slip. There were only two sounds—the relentless drumming of emergency lighting generators and the sporadic *creak-pop* of hawsers along the starboard side parting under frightful stress. Three separate gangplanks, their offshore ends still secured to the deserted hull, were pulled off the pier's edge to fall with a crash against the plating; the last one dropped at one-forty. Then watchers on shore heard the same death rattle that occupants of the *Titanic's* lifeboats had remembered when their ship upended for the final plunge. But the *Normandie's* agony was longer, extending for over an hour: loose gear, cranes,

Between fire and water. The burned-out shell of the *Normandie*'s smoking room staircase photographed before she capsized. Below, the same staircase six years before, with Baudry's *La Normandie*, now a poolside feature at Miami's Fontainebleau Hotel. (*Top: Navy Department, bottom: Avery Library*)

The morning after the fire, the *Normandie* lies canted grotesquely across the slip between Piers 88 and 90 on Manhattan's west side. A fireboat hoses down a stubborn pocket of fire on the starboard sports deck. (*Navy Department*)

life rafts, tools, tanks and nameless thousands of items clattered down to the port side or slid off the decks into the water.

At quarter to three in the morning, almost apologetically, the scarred gray hull finally rolled over on its side. There was astonishingly little commotion and the ice in the slip was hardly disturbed. The funnel stopped three feet above water and the top of the mainmast extended to within ten yards of Cunard's pier to the north. In its final collapse, the ship's bow plunged away from its mooring, sending the rudder up under the corner of the pier and destroying five piles. Near dawn, flames in some dislodged combustibles broke out anew and a fireboat nosed cautiously back between funnels one and two, spattering the sloping decks with icy water.

The ship lay thus for eighteen months. She had passed from passenger liner to naval auxiliary to hulk within the space of seven weeks. Investigations into the disaster by Congress, the Navy and New York's Fire Department reached similarly bleak conclusions—that gross carelessness rather than sabotage had been responsible. In 1946, an accused German murderer interrogated in Hamburg by American Military Police claimed to have set the *Normandie* fire. However, his subsequent confusion as to specific details exposed his "confession" as mere sensation seeking.

The Navy's particular disgrace was compounded by having the result of their neglect on permanent display. Had the ship been lost at sea or sustained irrevocable damage within the sanctity of a naval dockyard, the passage of time as well as the press of wartime events would have quickly displaced its topicality. But to have the *Normandie* canted across a Manhattan slip like a discarded bathtub toy, visible for all to see, seemed an extraordinarily galling reminder of official ineptitude. That the Navy chose to conceal the pier and its approaches by a twelve-foot plywood wall along 12th Avenue is hardly surprising.

Two and a half months after the fire, Secretary of the Navy Frank Knox appointed a preponderantly civilian committee to determine whether the vessel should be raised or broken up where she lay. They were also asked to decide whether it was worth restoring her as a naval auxiliary. Besides civilian experts and a trio of admirals, the committee included William Francis Gibbs, dean of American naval architects. Present also was Commander Sullivan from the Bureau of Ships, the Navy's salvage officer already in charge at Pier 88. They met for the first time on the nineteenth floor of 17 Battery Place, an orange building overlooking the Lower Bay, southernmost sentinel of the downtown cluster of skyscrapers.

Sullivan's testimony, given freely in closed session, indicated that the

The capsized *Normandie*. Immediately
following the disaster, barge-mounted
cranes moved into the slip and removed
the naval ordnance from the afterdecks. (*Navy Department, Courtesy of
Murphy-Pacific Salvage*)

Normandie continued to be a monstrous fire hazard. To clear away the tons of assorted internal debris, to get at anything in the vessel, was monumentally difficult due to the extreme flammability of insulating materials. There were layers of granulated cork everywhere, between every deck and partition, so that any attempt to burn through steel carried the risk of fire. According to Sullivan, there was at least one conflagration each working day. Additionally, city equipment had responded to a three-alarm blaze only the week previous, following an abortive effort to cut into a starboard cold-storage room. Two weeks' worth of Navy provisions were on board at the time of the fire and a carrion reek had prompted workers to open the compartment and clear out tons of putrid meat. Despite their precautions, flames had spread via an unknown ventilation trunk, igniting cork insulation en route. It burned stubbornly for hours before it could be put out. One way to circumvent this difficulty would have been to implement a scorched-earth policy, controlled burning that would have gutted the ship of all combustibles before attempting any further cutting.

But this expedient was part of a larger option that the committee ultimately rejected. The slip had to be cleared. Failure to refloat the vessel meant scrapping it in place. Surrounding the ship with a cofferdam so that this work could be done above water was rejected as impractical on two counts: there was a national shortage of the necessary structural steel, and disruption of supporting silt might weaken adjacent piers. Breaking up the hull, too, would mean substantial blasting which, whether above or below water, might transmit dangerous tremors inland via the rock ledge. If the *Normandie* was to be cut up under water, it was proposed that wreckage remaining fifty feet below low water be left in place and covered with sand and gravel.

However, an absent but powerful voice was quite specifically opposed to anything but flotation. When advised by Chairman J. Barstow Smull of the alternatives being explored by his committee, Mayor Fiorello La Guardia's response was swift and clear. Nothing could remain in the slip that would deny effective use of two of the city's largest piers. Wreckage buried under gravel could foul anchors and dredges indefinitely. As for the committee's proposal of "controlled burning," the Mayor wrote:

> Please, please don't press this request. It will take our country years to live down the original fire. I can see now ambulance chasers running up and down Manhattan, getting retainers to sue the city and the government and perhaps even you, personally, for damages caused by smoke, soot and other nuisances created by the fire.

Smull had been right in his original estimate of La Guardia's probable reaction when he opined to his fellow members that the Mayor was "a funny little fellow who might go up in the air."

So salvage was inevitable. Gibbs' advice was also to the point. He felt strongly that the Navy should, in effect, save the ship, to clear not only the slip but also its own good name. It would be, he argued, good public relations. Gibbs also felt that the ship, if recommissioned, could be an invaluable contribution to the prosecution of the war. There were, to be sure, certain tactical deficiencies built into the *Normandie*'s hull: he particularly disliked the inclusion of all four alternators in one open compartment. But he argued that the hull and propulsion machinery were sound and worth protecting, to be raised intact if possible. Genius that he was, he always saw the larger picture. At one point, when witnesses disputed the cost of scrapping either in place or after flotation, he interjected: "Most of the things in the war effort are not dollars-and-cents value. They are questions of time and the importance of the particular thing at the time—the cost is not so vital as the result."

Knox got his decision. The *Normandie* should be raised; what became of her after that was left in abeyance. The giant task was entrusted to New York's Merritt-Chapman & Scott, the largest marine salvage concern in the world. Their wreck master was Captain John Tooker, who was assigned to supervise the work in conjunction with Commander Sullivan.

Tooker was a man of vast experience who had worked under his father, Captain Izzy Tooker, when he was wreck master on the salvage of the *St. Paul* in 1918. She had also burned and capsized at a Manhattan pier. In her case, a row of vertical girders had been erected along her exposed flank. After the hull was sealed and pumped out, she was pulled upright, intact with all of her superstructure. But she had been half the length and a quarter displacement of the *Normandie*; trying to effect the same righting moment on such a vast bulk was quite clearly impossible.

Reassuringly, other enthusiasts than those who had rushed the pier on February 9 now came forward with schemes of salvage. No less than five thousand earnest Americans responded unbidden to the Navy's dilemma, bombarding Commander Sullivan with suggestions. Their motives ranged from the mercenary to the bizarre: WHAT COMPENSATION FOR ERECTING SS LAFAYETTE AS IS IN 72 HOURS wired one. Another zealot invoked divine witness to his credentials:

> Sir I solemnly swear before God the Almighty that given the materials and tools and all the specialized skilled men I should want that

I can set the *Normandie* on even keel and floating and will stake my life on this oath.

There were preposterous schemes involving air bags, ping-pong balls, ice cubes and cables suspended from blimps. A Chicagoan wrote that his half-million-dollar solution would complete the job:

> After all, I'm too old to go to war, but if I can be of any help in raising the *Normandie,* I feel it would further our war effort and make the day closer when the madman Hitler is dangling on the end of a rope. After all, I am a busy man and cannot come east unless I have my expenses paid. Would appreciate an early reply.

A dentist from Philadelphia sketched a series of towers erected atop Pier 88, equipped with tackles attached to the convenient starboard railing; a row of spectacular dynamite charges was to be exploded propitiously underneath the port flank at the *moment critique.* A mystical zany who could see the vessel from his New Jersey window was craftier:

> Your boat the *Normandie* can be refloated within twenty days. Are you interested?

In a postscript, he requested no publicity. Sullivan's favorite was from a woman who wrote at great length, proposing that the water filling the slip be frozen, imprisoning the hulk in ice. Then, the enormous glacial block would be towed to a position beneath the George Washington Bridge, to which it would be attached by taut cables at flood water. The ebbing tide would exert a vertical strain, righting the vessel as the ice melted.

Once again it was an opportunity for patriotic Americans, chafing at inactivity, to indulge their most persistent fantasies. Each cherished, I suppose, the role of dealing fate a devastating counterstroke, of offering Tom Swiftean inspiration that would pluck the *Normandie* from the North River muck to fight again. A few made sense but for every one remotely helpful, there were dozens quite obviously from children or benign lunatics. Sullivan assembled the letters on the pier in a drawer labeled Nut File and his reaction is quite readily understandable. But those above him were more cautious and treated the affair with kid gloves. Letters were answered on handsome Navy Department stationery, advising each correspondent that his suggestion was being taken under consideration.

In point of fact, the Navy's own solution was simple, in concept if not in execution: remove the superstructure, clear out the debris, subdivide into watertight compartments, pump them dry and let the ship's natural stability do the rest. From occupied Paris, an anonymous engineer who was also a director of the French Merchant Marine smuggled a message to New York via the American Embassy at Vichy.

> The *Normandie* is a ship of considerable stability and has a much greater righting arm than other ships of the French Line. She is a stiff, snappy roller.

Confirmation of the vessel's superior self-righting ability was in refreshing contrast to New York gossip following the disaster, which had branded her as a tender ship. This was nonsense; a tender ship suffering similar abuse by six thousand tons of crippling top weight would have been on her beam ends long before the *Normandie*.

Yet to salvage men, each aspect of the Navy's plan presented incredible complications. The question of accessibility alone was formidable: a vessel frozen at the terminal point of a seventy-nine-degree roll offers hazards within seldom encountered ashore. Miles of interior deck were transformed into a giant, diabolical fun house. One man who stepped inadvertently on a painted promenade deck window fell through it thirty feet. Starboard was overhead, port was below and longitudinal passageways had to be negotiated on all fours. Fragile bulkheads separating staterooms from passageways made inadequate decking and it was not unusual for workers crawling along passageways to disappear suddenly through a splintered plywood panel into an inside cabin. Existing ship's ladders and staircases were useless novelties and athwartship alleyways only gave vertical access down to the water. Elevator shafts and funnel casings became horizontal tunnels into the wreck, once their entrances had been achieved via ladder from barges moored alongside the sharply angled boat deck. A fellow officer from the Bureau of Ships scribbled a personal postscript at the bottom of an official document addressed to Sullivan: "You have got a tough job. I don't envy you."

Removing that portion of the superstructure above water was comparatively easy. Funnels, davits, railings, the bridge, machinery and deck plating were ruthlessly cut away and loaded onto waiting scows below. This time, fire precautions were rigid. In command was a New York Fire Department battalion chief and a minimum duty roster of twenty-five newly retired firemen toured the ship around the clock. Smoking anywhere on board was grounds for instant dismissal. Among the settlement of maintenance shacks that sprouted along the upturned flank of the ship was a huge collection of carbon dioxide tanks piped to every corner of the vessel. An eight-inch fire main ran along the starboard rail.

"A stiff, snappy roller": The *Normandie* in a
heavy sea, photographed from the starboard
wing of the bridge by her master. (*Courtesy of
Pierre Thoreux*)

Cutting away the *Normandie*'s superstructure. This photograph was taken from the top of Pier 90 to the north. Number one funnel has already gone, exposing its starboard uptake, the giant honeycomb right of center. It is apparent that workmen had converted the writing room (slightly higher and to the left) into a series of shower stalls. At lower left, on the barge, is the *Normandie*'s wheel, shortly before it disappeared. (*Navy Department, Courtesy Murphy-Pacific Salvage*)

Once the boat deck was pierced, the shadowy cavern of the *grand salon* lay exposed, a vast blackened grotto where oily waters lapped over piles of charred kapok. From the top of Pier 90, it was as though a full-scale, animated rendering of the original plans had been set in motion. Incongruous peacetime frills appeared under the cutters' relentless assault. The silver-gray theater was revealed, half of its three hundred seats hanging untouched above the water. A white line of rubber tiling came to light along the promenade deck, ending in a graceful flourish at the midships entrance to the public rooms. Inside remained the ghostly profile of a dance floor and orchestra platform that had survived the elements like some ancient cave painting.

After all superstructure above the promenade deck had been sliced off, the hull was cleared of debris. The *Normandie* was filled with the discarded clutter of disaster. Jagged shards of glass, lines, hoses, piping, tools, furniture, paneling, bunks and carpeting lay in impossible tangles on the port side of every compartment. Some interior spaces were booby-trapped as though with fiendish cunning: the purser's safe was found balanced on an electric light cord. In their first forays into the interior, divers worked in trios, one worker tended by two assistants who did nothing but guide lines past hazardous obstructions. There were seventy-five divers working simultaneously during the latter stages of salvage and two separate schools to train them in operation on the pier. No fewer than three sons of Captain Tooker were employed under water.

Diving conditions in the slip were appalling. Visibility was reduced to zero a few feet below the surface by a permanent suspension of industrial wastes, clotted oil, mud and sewage that even powerful electric lamps could not penetrate. All work on the wreck had to be accomplished by touch in total darkness. Divers worked blindly, feeling their way with hands that in winter, at least, were numb with cold moments after immersion.

As each bargeload of rubble was towed up to Riker's Island as fill, its estimated weight was recorded to assist in determining the ship's new center of gravity. Once the hull had been cleared of man-made litter, there remained a horrendous accumulation of silt. Through every opening on the port side, harbor mud had oozed obscenely, filling outside compartments to a depth of more than ten feet. Suction hoses cleared these spaces until the offending port was exposed. Then water jets drilled a hole in the mud beneath and an ingenious device, called a Tooker patch after its inventor, was used to seal the opening. It was a heavy wooden disc, constructed so that it could be bent in half. In folded position, it could be inserted through the porthole; then it was opened and drawn back, complete with rubber gasket, against the brass rim and secured internally with a strongback. No matter how strong the water pressure, it could only seal the patch more tightly. When possible, divers worked only in one section of the hull, to capitalize on their familiarity with underwater landmarks; but one patient man affixed all three hundred and fifty-six of the *Normandie*'s Tooker patches.

Salvage is a brutal job at best. Those who righted the *Normandie* at least worked in protected waters with effective logistical support close to hand. Yet the patience and skill of those men was quite extraordinary. The thought of working fifty feet down, separated from surface assistance by a labyrinth of steel corridors, sounds like a live nightmare to the uninitiated. Descent into that icy black slime must have required a kind of hard-bitten professionalism that almost defies comprehension. There was also the constant painful irritation of minute particles of spun glass insulation, which penetrated the exposed skin of the hands and were only removed by letting them grow out. In summer, those working above the surface were exposed to another occupational hazard of harbor salvage. Raw sewage emptying directly into the slip from two city mains created pockets of toxic fumes within certain compartments which, if not necessarily fatal, combined with heat and humidity to make conditions nearly intolerable.

Miraculously, there were no deaths and few injuries. Morale was astonishingly high, even among Navy divers, whose pay of five dollars a day over base pay was one fifth the amount Merritt-Chapman's men received for identical work. However, it is probable that their ultimate take-home pay approached parity with that of their civilian colleagues due to the inevitable gambling that flourished during off-duty hours. A service barge moored parallel to the wreck was used both as a lunchroom and a literally floating crap game; it was christened *Monte Carlo* by the men. Thousands of dollars changed hands there daily.

The very hugeness of the *Normandie,* the same vast scale that awed passengers and dismayed firemen, created a monumentality peculiar to the job. Everything about it was vast. Statistics quoted liberally by Navy Public Information officers were larded with zeroes: eight thousand pounds of glass removed, ten thousand cubic yards of mud pumped out, quarter of a million board feet of lumber installed as shoring and bulkheads. Incapacitated as she was, like some great gray whale washed up on a beach, the sheer bulk of the ship perpetually amazed. Refloating her is still the single most ambitious piece of salvage ever attempted.

In midsummer of 1943, New York's hottest ticket was a seat in the grandstand erected by the Navy across the stringpiece at Pier 88, complete with blue-jacketed ushers and an illustrated program. It was a giant spectacular designed quite simply to refute any lingering doubts about naval competence. The show at the foot of West 48th Street boasted a cast of thousands as well as the largest piece of movable scenery in the world. Special lighting had been installed that turned night into day, allowing the performance to continue around the clock. It was the finale of a veritable Manhattan Passion Play, the suffering, resurrection and ascension of a martyr. Its single ultimate flaw was its interminable length, a drama whose duration could be blamed more on circumstance rather than on any fault of the producers.

At one o'clock on the morning of August 4, 1943, full-scale pumping operations began. From a row of portholes along the starboard side rose nearly a hundred noxious diesel exhausts. Their concerted roar would continue in varying orchestration for more than a month. Down the steep slope of the promenade deck poured a steady white cataract as the first of thousands of tons of water thundered back into New York Harbor.

Rigid control of rotation was essential. Raising the ship too hastily could violate a complex balance of port-side weight, hydrostatic head and righting moment. Those who packed the grandstand those first days in expectation of seeing the *Normandie* bob gaily upright were soon disillusioned. Movement, by design, was tantalizingly slow and measured in fractions of inches. Special valves had been installed in underwater cargo-port patches through which compressed air was jetted to dispel mud suction. As each hour passed, telltale numerals on the forepeak indicator were slowly revealed, indicating that the *Normandie*'s hibernation was ending.

The *Log of Pumping and Righting Operations* maintained by the Navy through August and into September offers terse insight into the finesse and patience required during those critical weeks. Levels and weights of water in individual compartments were reduced by feet or sometimes inches. Just before midnight on August 6, pumping was retarded to slow movement of the hull; an hour later, the entry reads "Began pumping to keep vessel moving." That day too, divers cleared tons of silt from vestigial remnants of superstructure emerging from the mud. At the same time, protective guy wires were attached to minimize lateral stress across the promenade deck. A fracture anywhere along its length could have jeopardized the entire operation.

In the designation of compartments requiring particular attention, number 16 appears with relentless frequency. At two-fifteen on the morning of August 11, a diver pinpointed a split plate directly beneath it. (It is only momentarily extraordinary to imagine a diver finding anything at that hour under water, until one recalls that it was always the middle of the night in those inky depths.) That leak was patched but the following day's entry indicates that the trouble was just beginning: "Pumps operating continuously in Compartment 16 and divers searching for leaks." Hundreds of pounds of waste rags, oakum, sawdust and even mattresses were dumped overboard next to the leak. Divers with long sticks poked them under the plating in the hope that inrushing water would carry debris with it and choke off the flow. But it was quite apparent that the fractures were not only numerous but extended inboard to include the complex of wing and bottom tanks.

On August 13, an entry reads: "Built Tooker patch for hole, frame 237." Its subsequent placement seems to have had little effect for at six o'clock that evening, two more ten-inch pumps were wrestled into Compartment 16 in aid of the seven already straining to keep the level down. There followed a three-day attempt to seal the leakage from within. Through the night of the seventeenth, a hundred-and-five-cubic-yard cement patch was laid in the turn of the bilge. For two days, it held; but by the evening of the eighteenth, divers were once again searching for leaks. "Water in Compartment 16 gaining with all pumps going." Two hours later, a diver groping through the impenetrable murk of number 2 fire room located yet another series of ruptures. These were almost completely inaccessible from within due to a jumble of dislodged boilers and from outside because of the rock pinnacles thrust up tightly against the crumpled steel.

It was this inability to prevent leakage in Compartment 16 that extended the final weeks of salvage and cramped the Navy's showmanship. But rushing the process merely to effect a successful denouement would have been gross stupidity. Retaining a vertical column of water amidships could have endangered the bulkheads separating it from drained compartments on either side. It was, ultimately, the application of hundreds more tons of cement from within, together with the buttressing of adjacent bulkheads, that overcame the delay.

On September 12, over a month after the pumping began, the *Normandie* finally assumed an angle of forty-five degrees. Beach gear winches took up the strain and two days later had inched the hull sixteen feet up river. The move was doubly fortunate because it placed the holed compartment directly over an underwater junk heap of mattresses and rags. By the next evening, all the pumps in Compartment 16 (there were now thirteen) managed to retain an eleven-foot head.

At eight the following morning, there was a cautious but triumphant

The wreck of the *Normandie* in the midst of her epic self-righting, an agonizing process that consumed six frustrating weeks in the summer of 1943, climaxing the single greatest work of salvage ever attempted. (*Navy Department, Courtesy Murphy-Pacific Salvage*)

entry: "Ship apparently afloat at this time." This was at high water, however. It wasn't until two more days had passed that she remained buoyant following the ebb. There is a significant final entry for the last day's operations: "Pumping continues in Compartment 16."

The rest was routinely anticlimactic. Merritt-Chapman & Scott handed the vessel over on October 27 which was, appropriately, Navy Day. On the third of November, the empty hulk, devoid of all shoring now, was towed by fifteen tugs from the slip she had occupied for more than four years. A two-degree artificial list was maintained to keep water that still flowed into Compartment 16 collected in a convenient pocket for pumps to handle. Except for a series of bizarre stripes along her low port side, oily growth rings marking her ascent from the depths, she looked very much as she had when launched nearly eleven years previously to the day. She had a wooden platform built over her whaleback and a bridge of sorts amidships. There was a Navy captain in command, a brace of docking pilots at his side and two hundred dockyard workers who ate picnic lunches on the vast promenade deck as what was left of the *Normandie* passed slowly down the harbor.

The move down to Brooklyn's Navy Yard had been planned specifically against an incoming tide to simplify the tow. The giant rudder was locked amidships. Firemen, medical personnel and a diving team were carried on board. Extra diesels had been laid on as stand-bys for the vital pumps and the generating plant was hooked up to emergency riding lights in the event some extraordinary delay necessitated navigation after dark. But there was no flag and, pathetically, no means of answering the myriad harbor craft which saluted joyfully as she passed.

Most anticlimactic of all, she languished in Brooklyn's Erie Basin for three more years, ravaged by her salvation. Having cleared the slip and discharged its debt, the Navy apparently had no further use for her. Neither time, money nor materials could be spared to put her back to sea. In September of 1945, she was declared surplus and turned over to the Maritime Commission for disposition. They sold her, in turn, to the Lipsett Corporation for scrapping.

She was the first ship that Lipsett had ever demolished and they got a bargain. The *Normandie* had cost the Navy in excess of eleven million dollars since taking her over. As scrap, the ship realized a hundred and sixty thousand for the government and a million-dollar profit for the wreckers. The final journey of her short life was made from Brooklyn to Port Newark under still another name: LIPSETT was daubed in monstrous white letters along each flank. On October 6, 1947, all that remained was an ungainly steel raft floating next to a Jersey pier. It was a seventy-ton fragment of tank tops from under a boiler room. A crane hauled it onto the pier, where it was cut apart and loaded in open cars of a final freight headed for a Pennsylvania steel mill. The *Normandie* was gone. Until the very last, even after she had been sold to Lipsett, Yourkevitch still talked of restoring her to civilian passenger service as a two-stacker.

The Compagnie Générale Transatlantique got a replacement of sorts. Deprived of choice maritime spoils in 1918, the French were awarded the *Europa*. She had survived hostilities intact, although her sister ship, the *Bremen,* had been bombed and sunk at her berth by the Royal Air Force. Following initial postwar use by the United States as a troopship for homebound GI's, the ex-German was delivered to Le Havre in 1946.

Like most Channel towns, the port was still a scene of utter devastation. Before departing, the Germans had wreaked terrible vengeance. The sea wall was broached in several places, docks had been systematically blown up and there were four hundred wrecks scattered about the harbor. The handsome Gare Maritime was a shambles and the railway leading to it a tangle of twisted steel. Shortly after the *Europa*'s arrival, a violent storm broke her loose from her moorings. She was swept across the harbor where she collided with the wreck of the capsized *Paris*. Holed on the starboard bow, the *Europa* sank upright for the second time in her life, with scarcely more than her superstructure remaining above water. It was a bitter blow to French maritime recovery as well as Le Havre's hard-pressed Port Autonome, already coping with more wrecks than it could handle. But salvage crews raised her and she emerged from St. Nazaire two years later as the *Liberté*. She joined with the *Ile de France* and the *De Grasse* in French postwar service on the Atlantic. Once again, German tonnage inadvertently served the cause of her rivals.

Cunard did better. The two *Queens* and the *Aquitania* survived the war as invaluable transports. Millions of soldiers were carried all over the world—Anzacs to and from the Far East, German and Italian prisoners to North America and, predictably, division after division of Americans to European battlefields. The Germans never managed a crack at any of the three. The closest call involved the *Queen Mary*'s collision with the Royal Navy cruiser *Curaçao* in October of 1942. With the same curious inevitability that had marked the *Hawke–Olympic* debacle years earlier, both ships converged in full daylight twenty-four hours from Scotland. For reasons never clearly established, the escort vessel cut directly across the bows of her monstrous charge. It was a tragic error—the cruiser was sliced clean in half and over three hundred of her crew were drowned. Act-

The *Europa*'s second sinking. Wrenched
from her Le Havre moorings by a storm,
the ex-German is sunk by the wreck of the
Paris. She was salvaged and sailed as the
Liberté. (*Frank Braynard Collection*)

ing under standing orders, the *Mary*'s Captain steamed on without stopping. To have picked up survivors and risked a German torpedo was expressly forbidden. The Cunarder's stem was buckled under water but she made port with ease.

It is probable that the most extensive damage sustained by the *Queens* was from their millions of involuntary wartime clients, particularly the American ones. During the D-day buildup, when both ships were pressed exclusively into North Atlantic service, the accumulation of discarded chewing gum on their decks was so overwhelming that its sale was ultimately barred in ship's canteens. Railings suffered too, carved with so many initials that most of them had to be replaced after the war.

The hard lessons learned in the North Atlantic during the First World War were used to good effect in the Second. Organization of blacked-out convoys and air and naval escorts was instituted immediately war broke out. Following the sinking of the *Athenia,* there were no illusions about German U-boat intentions. But traveling at thirty knots, the *Queens* sailed alone. No convoy or escort could keep up with them, and safety lay in speed. Masters got their sailing orders from a combined operations headquarters in New York City at 17 Battery Place, the same building in which the German Consulate, at least until December 1941, was located. Each crossing was assigned a different course and the rapid loading of troops became a fine art. Approximately fifteen thousand were carried at a time, and in summer weather entire regiments slept on deck.

In August of 1945, the *Queen Mary* reentered her home port for the first time since before the war. For six long years, she had put in regularly at Gourock on the Clyde estuary. Still giddy from V-J Day celebration, Southampton accorded their beloved three-stacker a boisterous reception. Between them, the *Queens* carried more than two million servicemen. Churchill's estimate that the two vessels shortened the war by a year had obvious validity; had the *Normandie* been spared, it is probable that her contribution might have shortened it even more. But she was gone, victim of a war that ended in its sixth summer. It seemed that peace had returned.

A prize that eluded the Germans. R.M.S. *Queen
Elizabeth* arrives at Gourock, her wartime
Scottish port. (*Cunard*)

*Blessed are the meek, for they shall inherit
the earth—if they're nimble!*
                    —WILLIAM FRANCIS GIBBS

14.
Columbia, the Gem

Within two years, the *Queen Mary* and *Queen Elizabeth* were back
in peaceful tandem, fulfilling for the first time the unique task for which
they had originally been designed. Samuel Cunard's essential weekly service was finally maintained by a pair of complementary vessels. That
enormously comfortable, year-round passage between Southampton, Cherbourg and New York was a welcome constant in a world trying to return
to prewar. Incredibly enough, Britons subsisting at home on worse rations
than at any time during the war were able to field a luxurious Atlantic
team. The two *Queens* were rushed into their original finery in time to
catch the first waves of eastbound Americans. Also cashing in on the postwar boom was the Holland-America Line's *Nieuw Amsterdam,* completed

One of the rarely photographed encounters between the two giant consorts: The *Elizabeth* outbound from New York as the *Mary* arrives. The two Cunarders dominated the postwar decade on the North Atlantic. (*Cunard*)

just prior to hostilities and converted instantly to trooping. She is still running to this day, last surviving Atlantic liner from before the war, her proud foursquare profile a regular feature at the most sensible passenger terminal in Manhattan.

Despite a glittering century to its credit, the postwar decade was the most profitable in Cunard's history. It is quite probable that Cunard's singular success prompted American enthusiasm to enter the Atlantic lists once more. Congress evidently felt that a superliner that could double as a naval auxiliary was a worthwhile investment. It is only to be regretted that they didn't authorize funds enough for a pair of them. There was something of the *Leviathan*'s pathetic isolation inbred into the *United States*—her sole disadvantage the absence of a competent running mate.

However, incorporated into the ship was every possible refinement of naval architecture. Although her design phase occupied five years, from 1943 to 1948, she had been on a mental drawing board for thirty. William Francis Gibbs finally had his chance. Into that sleek racing hull, he packed every technological advance that he and the Navy could afford. She was to be, in effect, a seventy-nine-million-dollar wonder, a red, white and blue retaliatory weapon whose image Gibbs had cherished since his youth.

To know the ship, one must know her designer. Besides being a perfectionist, Gibbs had a basic antagonism for Europeans and their accomplishments. The truth was that it galled him, privately, that preeminence in his chosen field seemed a traditional European prerogative, that American shipping interests were unable to overcome the economic pitfalls of building and operating superliners. This foreign domination of the giant Atlantic merchant fleets offended Gibbs' old-fashioned, ingrained patriotism. He was a firm believer in American know-how and methods and had been balked for most of his career by the inability of the United States to implement that know-how and those methods for maritime supremacy.

Yet he wasn't above borrowing from overseas competitors when it suited him. Within a day of the *Normandie*'s first arrival in America, Gibbs and a male secretary joined anonymously with thousands of fellow New Yorkers lining up for a visit on board. In mid tour, Gibbs suddenly signaled to his companion and they ducked through a doorway marked CREW ONLY. For the next two hours, America's foremost naval architect burrowed through engine spaces on the *Normandie,* poking, peering and somehow evading the duty engineers. Then the two men retired to a corner of the smoking room where Gibbs poured out for immediate dictation a dizzying compendium of facts and figures, almost total recall of the controversial turbo-electric drive he had just absorbed. When the *United States* was afloat, it was more than routine naval security that kept her technical data under wraps; it was Gibbs' own sense of jealous secrecy. He was well aware that others could and would duplicate his own piracy. But then again, there were vital national issues at stake. In building his dream ship, he was not merely fulfilling a commission; he was accepting a self-imposed mandate to sweep the Atlantic forever.

He had three great passions in life—ships, theater and fire engines. It is hardly surprising that two of his epic legacies were the world's fastest passenger vessel and the most powerful fire pumper in existence. On board the *United States,* he elevated fire precaution to a religion hitherto unknown. An effective publicity gimmick for the new ship claimed that the only wood on board was contained in the butcher's chopping block and the pianos. In fact, Gibbs was anxious to eliminate these latter, and badgered Theodore Steinway for months to provide him with an instrument encased in aluminum. But Steinway refused and won his point only after promising to ignite a fireproof mahogany piano doused with gasoline at his own expense, to prove that it would not burn. (Gibbs neglected to publicize the fact that balsa wood filled each bilge keel and that propeller bossings were lined with traditional lignum vitae; in rebuttal, he would probably have argued that neither area was part of passenger spaces.)

But his reluctant musical compromise seemed only to increase his phobia elsewhere on board. Prior to final acceptance, fire-retardant paints and fabrics were subjected to brutal testing. On abandoned piers near Newport News, completely decorated steel cabin mock-ups were put to the torch. Their contents included a typical collection of passenger belongings—clothes, luggage, a Sunday *New York Times,* cleaning fluid and, inexplicably, a case of whiskey. During fitting out, the ship's captain was presented with a handsome reclining chair for his day cabin. Unfortunately it had a wooden frame, and Gibbs personally ordered it removed from the vessel. Similarly, a score of handsome radios presented to the ship's officers were banished because of their mahogany cabinets. Some years later, Gibbs came across a short wooden shelf that one of the bakers had installed for his own convenience. The next time the *United States* came into her home port, a perfect facsimile of the offending item, reproduced in aluminum, was presented to the astonished baker.

The amusing aspect of Gibbs' anti-inflammable edict was that he violated it himself every time he stepped on board: incredibly superstitious, he carried in his pocket at all times a small piece of wood on which to knock should the occasion arise. (He would not sign a letter with thirteen paragraphs.) But elsewhere, he was quite ruthless. The *United States* was

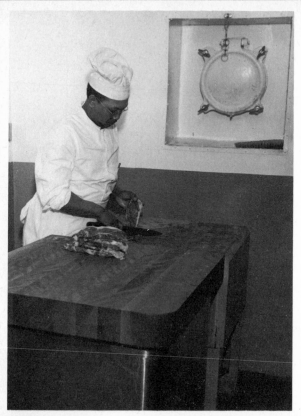

One acknowledged use of wood on board the *United States;* the other was for pianos. Purists might carp at the knife handle as well as the scrubbing brush parked on the porthole ledge. (*Newport News Shipbuilding and Drydock Company*)

The hull of the *United States* under construction at Newport News in June of 1951. Photographs of this kind were highly confidential at the time and were not released by the Navy for a decade after the maiden voyage. (*Newport News Shipbuilding and Drydock Company*)

lavishly decorated with etchings, lithographs and, of course, watercolors but no oil paintings. The oars in the aluminum lifeboats were hollow aluminum as well. In fact, there had never been, anywhere or at any time, such an assemblage of aluminum as rose in Graving Dock number 10 at Newport News during 1950 and 1951.

Gibbs had eschewed the conventional wooden ways, not for reasons of inflammability but because no ways long enough existed. Furthermore, by building the *United States* on perfectly horizontal keel blocks, he not only spared his ship the rigors of a traditional launch but was able also to facilitate the loading-on of prefabricated components. Those invited to watch Mrs. Tom Connally christen the ship on June 23, 1951, saw a vessel that was two thirds complete; engines, boilers, bridge and funnels were already in place, an advantage permitted by dry-dock construction.

Rather than slide his ship into the water, Gibbs brought water to the ship. The morning of the twenty-second, workmen opened sluice valves and let the James River flood into the dock. By four-fifteen the following afternoon, the *United States* floated off her keel blocks on cue. Coincidentally, her underwater hull was concealed from the public. Details of its configuration were top secret. New Yorkers who came to admire the builder's model on display at the United States Lines office found everything below the boot topping encased in plywood, completely masked from view. Gibbs' mania for secrecy was happily buttressed, in this instance, by the severe security consciousness of the United States Navy.

The *United States* had a brace of sampan-topped funnels together with a silhouette that seemed at first reminiscent of Gibbs' last passenger vessel, the prewar *America.* Yet even when the tugs pulled her out into the river, her broadside perspective betrayed a definite preoccupation with speed. Even at rest, the ship seemed to strain at the leash. There was a raked clipper stem and a hull that seemed as glassy smooth as an almost complete absence of rivets could make it. Her funnels, the largest ever installed on any boat deck, had not only a purposeful rake but a massive, no-nonsense strength about them. She looked a champion, all along the sweep of her nine hundred and ninety feet. Gibbs had created a mid-twentieth century throwback to the esthetics of the German racers that had defied the British fifty years earlier. There wasn't an ounce of superfluous flesh on her, only a lean frame that hinted strongly at the Blue Ribband.

Inside, she was impeccable if slightly cold. Flotation reserve requirements forbade vast open spaces and there was little monumental luxury in the traditional sense. All was metal and synthetics, low key and understated. Glass panels were used to good effect, as on the *Normandie;*

but the profusion of patriotic emblems adhering to the walls gave some portions of the ship the look of a cookie-cutter display. With none of the opulence commonly associated with Atlantic travel, she had a clean, ascetic look that was occasionally carried into the sterile.

Gibbs' touch was everywhere—every fireproof door had a hinged corner flap that enabled a hose to pass through it even when closed. There was no vista along any of the ship's corridors; a succession of interruptive jogs added structural muscle to the hull. The first-class dining room boasted an unusual number of stanchions, further concessions to Navy standards of strength and safety. Open decks throughout the *United States* were covered with a composition called Neotex. This was a fireproof teak substitute, approved by Gibbs only after he had tested its durability by surfacing the shipyard's main truck route with it during the construction phase. There was one refreshing touch of humor—hidden somewhere on board and found only by a handful of persistent passengers was a gloriously buxom mermaid, etched into a glass panel in the smoking room.

The ship's real glory lay below, in the forbidden sanctity of the engine spaces. There were only eight boilers, six of which were in operation at any one time. The steam generated within them packed an enormous wallop, particularly when compared with America's first Atlantic steam venture a hundred and thirty-three years earlier: the *Savannah*'s boiler pressure of one pound per square inch had been increased a thousandfold on the *United States* and boosted to a superheated nine hundred and eighty degrees Fahrenheit. These figures, highly confidential at the time of her maiden voyage, were not released to the public until the midsixties. Her designers are still reluctant to discuss the matter of shaft horsepower. Extreme measures were taken to restrict performance details. During trials, Chief Engineer William Kaiser ordered canvas covers lashed over the engine room revolution counters, barring even those privileged souls on board the satisfaction of knowing just how well Gibbs' incredible ship could do. Her power plant was a miracle of marine engineering, sophisticated alloys wrought into the world's most powerful turbines. The ship's evaporators, christened Kaiser's Waterworks, could distill two hundred thousand gallons of water daily, a high output designed to reduce the weight of drinking water carried with a shipload of troops.

American liners sail east on the first leg of their maiden voyage. In the case of the *United States,* the gala reception that greeted her at New York in the summer of 1952 prior to departure seemed prophetic if premature. Rumors brought ashore by those on board for acceptance trials off the Virginia coast had already snowballed into a contagious optimism.

Despite rough weather on the day of her trials, the *United States* lived up to Gibbs' expectations. An accurate record of her incredible rate of progress through the water was plotted by a special radar buoy. A fine mist at the waterline betrays the vessel's speed. (*William T. Radcliffe Collection, The Mariners Museum, Newport News, Virginia*)

The first American challenger in a hundred years. The *United States* points her bow toward fog-shrouded Manhattan for the first time, in June of 1952. (*Newport News Shipbuilding and Drydock Company*)

The new American flagship sailed under an aura of vast expectation, perhaps best symbolized by the halo of mist that cloaked her forepeak at high speed. The tumult in New York Harbor was, happily, an anticipatory celebration that events four days later proved perfectly justifiable. Surely there was significance, too, in the coincidence that her inaugural crossing should encompass as patriotic an observance as Independence Day.

Gibbs, William Francis, was on the passenger list, curiously enough the only time he completed a transatlantic voyage on his beloved ship. He and his fellow passengers sailed for the first time in a totally airconditioned ship. Portholes were sealed shut and there were no fans hung traditionally on cabin walls. But one passenger prevailed upon a crew member to open her cabin porthole in midocean. She was Margaret Truman, now Mrs. Clifton Daniel, crossing as guest of honor. Leaning far out over the glistening flank, Mrs. Daniel remembers first looking down at the white sea boiling and hissing forty feet below. Then for a last instant, she turned her head forward, directly in the slip stream; it was like a blow in the face.

On that memorable voyage to Europe and back, the *United States* raced at a unique speed, faster than she would ever sail again yet, according to her delighted owners, not as fast as she could do when pushed. She *averaged* thirty-five-and-a-half knots, completing the eastbound crossing in three days, ten hours and forty minutes. It was ten hours better than the *Queen Mary*'s fastest time. The two ships passed each other at sea, the *Mary* westbound for New York, her passengers lining the rails for a look at the American challenger.

There was a sixty-mile-an-hour gale blowing as the *United States* approached the finish line at Bishop Rock the morning of the fourth day. In fact, conditions were hardly auspicious for a record-breaking passage. But as always, one of the prime requirements of transatlantic vessels was a reserve of power, a capacity to maintain schedule despite adverse weather. In this case, the reserves were fantastic, and the schedule has never been duplicated. Most of the passengers stayed up until dawn; the President's daughter remembers sitting wearily in a corner of the bridge, only a few feet from where Gibbs huddled with the ship's officers. The gleam from Bishop Rock was almost totally obscured by a rain squall but the moment it passed abeam of the bridge, even before the triumphant bellow of the ship's whistle, a hysterical celebration began two decks below. Americans had been denied the prestige of a Blue Ribband since the Collins liner *Arctic* a hundred years earlier and the event was observed with the same compulsive gaiety that infects Times Square on New Year's Eve. The

The new champion at Le Havre. Lines go ashore as the *United States* touches Europe for the first time. Flaked paint on the forward shell plating is characteristic of a record-breaker. (*Radio Times Hulton Picture Library*)

To the end of her active life the *United States* was impeccably maintained. After sixteen years, she looks nearly new, barring some inevitable weathering along the hull. Here, she is about to enter drydock at Newport News for her annual overhaul. A year later, she was abruptly withdrawn from service. (*Newport News Shipbuilding and Drydock Company*)

ship's orchestra's rendition of the national anthem evoked an emotional ovation and the musicians were kept busy well into daylight pursuing conga lines up and down the promenade decks. Nondancers tried to drink the bar dry.

The reception that greeted the superliner in Europe was quite the equal of the one that had awaited it in New York. Southampton, home port of the deposed Cunarder, stifled any regret and gave the ship an extravagant welcome. Even *The Shipbuilder,* as solidly British as Big Ben, wrote a glowing account of the *United States'* triumph, only querying politely if spontaneous electrolysis might not occur where aluminum superstructure met steel hull. For the shipload of passengers, for her owners in New York and most of all, for a deeply moved naval architect, it was a moment of supreme joy. After a century of mediocrity, disinterest and noncommitment, a superb American liner had swept the Atlantic of all possible contenders, probably forever. It is extremely doubtful that any but a radically new hull form will surpass her incredible four-knot margin over the *Queen Mary.*

True to form, as holder of the Blue Ribband, the *United States* prospered. She was, like the *Ile de France,* an instant hit, the first postwar ship and sea miles ahead of her competition. The ship received no higher accolade than the near continuous patronage of the Windsors, who transferred their affection from the *Queens* to their new American rival. To say that Gibbs was besotted with his creation would not be overstating things. "Grandfather," as he was known privately by a devoted staff, telephoned the ship every day she was at sea, following performance and fuel consumption figures closely. Whenever the *United States* sailed past the windows of Gibbs & Cox in lower Manhattan, he would grin with pleasure as she boomed a special triple salute.

I have quoted the following paragraph from the last page of Frank Braynard's excellent biography of Gibbs. It gives some indication of the incredible closeness that existed between the man, his ship and the crew that sailed her:

> The *United States* was in New York the day William Francis Gibbs died, Wednesday, September 6th. She sailed the next day and when she passed 21 West Street her flag was at half-mast. Her master, Commodore L. J. Alexanderson, walked from the pilothouse out onto the sleek port flying bridge. It was noon and the ultra-modern aluminum radar-mast just atop the chartroom cast no shadow. The mammoth red, white and blue forward stack glistened in the sun. Below him, nearly 2,500 passengers and crew busied themselves about their

several pleasures, happy to have the leavetakings and farewell parties over at last and ignorant of the drama of the moment on the wing of the bridge. Commodore Alexanderson, third regular master of the superliner, raised his right arm and saluted the vacant office of William Francis Gibbs. Behind him the great ship's whistle blasted three deep-throated salutes to honor the man for whom the ship had been a life-long dream come true.

The new QE2 *will not merely ferry
passengers glamorously back and forth
across the Atlantic. Instead, she will
operate as a self-contained sea-going resort,
offering vacationers unmatched variety of
facilities for fun and relaxation.*
　　　　　　—CUNARD PUBLICITY RELEASE

15.
The End of the Line

In 1969, two years after William Francis Gibbs died, his ship died too. The *United States* was condemned to death in early middle age, victim of a familiar American malaise: prohibitive union scales and dwindling passenger revenues. She was withdrawn from service indefinitely and lies today in a quiet backwater of the same river that saw her birth.

The real villain of the piece was, quite simply, the airplane. Over the postwar fleets that sailed the North Atlantic flew aircraft that would cripple the ships as no storm ever had. Five years after the *United States'* maiden voyage, a sinister milestone was passed: in summer of that boom year, as many crossed by air as by sea. The ancient route was busy as ever but the cream of the traffic preferred to fly. From that moment on, the margin of air passengers increased ominously and shipping began a fatal decline. The same obsession with speed that had spurred Atlantic shipbuilders for decades now served as the instrument of their defeat.

At first, steamship companies were reluctant to face realities. "There is no freedom to fly the air," concluded a *Cunard Report and Accounts* in April of 1955, "as there is freedom to sail the seas, and it is very doubtful if there ever will be such freedom in view of the way in which air traffic has grown up as a political pawn of the Government of every country." Later on, when passenger figures plummetted, they took things more seriously.

Cunard's slogan for those twilight years on board the *Queens* tells the story—"Getting there is half the fun." It was apparent that the liners' only salvation was the glorification of shipboard life, making a passage into something it had never had to be before, a holiday and respite. Preoccupation shifted to cruising and, near the end of her life, the giant *Queen Elizabeth* was given an overhaul that included lido decks for outdoor swimming and air-conditioning to give her some competitive edge in the Caribbean. Yet despite an apparently endless demand for space on winter cruises, a peculiarly obstinate Company policy prevailed: obsessed with an outdated need to "show the flag," Cunard pulled the *Elizabeth* north four times each winter throughout the lucrative cruise season, so that she could make expensive North Atlantic crossings carrying only a handful of clients.

By the mid sixties, fueling the *Queens* was an expensive proposition and the Company sought revenue wherever it could. The midships lobby blossomed with the same kind of slick commercial displays that have effectively destroyed the ambience of Grand Central Station. Unannounced, the servant ratio dropped alarmingly and habitual passengers noted that things were a little slower coming on both ships. Menus and choices were trimmed. The days were over when a request for breakfast bacon would be countered by a polite interjection: "Which kind, sir?" (There were originally three.) Evenings in the lounge revolved around marathon variety shows as Cunard sought desperate means to liven their image.

But the truth was that the two grand old ships were just that—too grand and too old. Younger rivals were in New York Harbor, bent on wooing the residue of transatlantic passengers who preferred ships to jets. In addition to the *United States,* the Holland-America's *Rotterdam* appeared, a sleek gray vessel boasting the Atlantic's first after stack, far ahead of the *QE2*. In the early sixties, the Compagnie Générale Transatlantique's vast *France* was put into service, a successor to the *Normandie*

Funny Hat Competition on the *Queen
Elizabeth*. The last vestige of prewar
Fancy Dress Parades remained as a fixture
on both *Queen*s. (*Cunard*)

Götterdämmerung: An awesome quintet of vessels tied up at Luxury Liner Row in November of 1966. From top to bottom: the *Constitution,* moth-balled in Baltimore; the *United States,* permanently laid up at Norfolk's International Terminal; the *France,* the grandest ship in the world, now in service as the *Norway*; the *Rafaello,* an anchored barrack for the Iranian Army; the *Queen Elizabeth,* a gutted hulk in Hong Kong Harbor being cut up for scrap. (*The Port of New York Authority*)

but with none of her structural daring. She too had an eye-catching profile, each of two funnels sprouting futuristic if ineffectual ailerons. From Genoa came a new generation of Italian ships to lure Americans to the Mediterranean, just as Mussolini's *Rex* and *Conte di Savoia* had done in the thirties.

Whether designed for it or not, these liners led a double life—summers on the North Atlantic and winters in the Caribbean. They spent as much time cruising as crossing. The layout of the passenger spaces, the firm commitment to two classes that could painlessly unite into one and the vibrant palette of their interiors were cruise oriented—sun drenched, fog free and irresponsible. The polished brass, glistening veneers and understated elegance of the North Atlantic's past seemed quaintly at odds with the new barbarians, whose decor revolved about maintenance-free aluminum, vinyl and nylon. There was no mileage left in period revival, floating Leicester Square cinema palaces or even the strangely muted stridency of the *Ile de France*.

By 1970, both *Queens* were retired, gone to rest quietly in American waters. First to go was the *Mary*. She sailed from New York for the last time in September 1967 and public regret at her departure evoked the same intense nostalgia as the *Mauretania*'s farewell three decades earlier. She had completed just over a thousand crossings and flew from her mast three hundred and ten feet of paying-off pennant, ten feet for each of thirty-one years of service. Treasure Jones, her last master, presided over a lugubrious ceremony in the main lounge the last night out from Cherbourg, offering a toast to the ship that was echoed by the assembled passengers.

Unlike her elder sisters, the *Mary* never went to tne ship breakers. Her final passage was a thirty-nine-day marathon to California. She had been bought earlier that year by the City of Long Beach for nearly three and a half million dollars, as was. Her new owners turned a tidy profit by booking over a thousand passengers for a "Last Great Cruise." Too broad to fit through the Panama Canal, her route lay round the Horn. It was a pathetic travesty of her former existence. Staff and crew were drastically reduced and only two of her four propellers drove her at twenty knots.

The ship passed through tropical latitudes for which she had never been designed. The same brutal 'tween-deck heat that had killed scores of prisoners in the Red Sea during World War II now drove aggrieved senior citizens to the questionable relief of open decks. Scandal erupted on board —a swarthy Latin-American beauty was put ashore at Rio, surrounded by shocked whispers of prostitution.

Port calls were shortened as engineers on board realized that the drag from two inactive propellers might retard the date of arrival at Long Beach. Disenchanted passengers left the ship at succeeding stops, in final objection to this compressed scheduling, the heat and indifferent food and service. At Tierra del Fuego, a curious squabble developed on the after end of A-deck where a pair of London buses were parked; passengers fought for the privilege of sitting inside them, thus affording themselves the unique if dubious distinction of having rounded the Horn in a bus *on* a liner. An end-of-term prankishness infected staff and clients alike. On more than one occasion, lunch was disrupted as stewards and passengers hurled rolls at each other across the vast reaches of the main dining room.

Somewhere off the coast of Chile, it was reported that a dead albatross had been placed on the Captain's bunk. It was a piece of intelligence later proved false, but rumors of that kind reflected the ugly mood on board.

Off the West Coast, an airplane bombed the *Queen Mary* with thousands of carnations, most of which unfortunately fell into the sea. Thus was recreated a salute to the Cunarder first offered in June of 1936, when Rickenbacker led a trio of DC-3's on the same mission as the ship approached New York for the first time. Outside Long Beach, an armada of five thousand boats had assembled to escort the *Mary* into harbor. From those pleasure craft directly beneath the railings came the cry: "Throw us a souvenir!" Disgruntled passengers only too happy to comply precipitated a rain of ashtrays, glasses, rugs and even deck chairs, anything that could be hurled from the decks down to the hungry fleet below. Through a dining room porthole came a brimming soup tureen, spattering the shell plating on its way down, symbolically anointing the hull with the last *Crème Sévignée* to be produced on board. The *Queen Mary* had arrived in California.

Restoration is now complete, a multimillion-dollar face-lift financed by Long Beach's share of the oil pumped from offshore wells. Large sections of the machinery spaces have been gutted to permit the installation of shops, galleries and museums. The trio of funnels was replaced by aluminum facsimiles. For a time, incredulous tourists willing to part with a dollar were allowed to drive their cars through one of the rusted originals as it lay on its side next to the vessel. It was a fitting full circle, reminiscent of the same privilege extended for the first time to motorloads of Northumbrian gentry en route to the *Mauretania*'s launch so many years before. Only there was a difference—the *Mary*'s funnels were discarded and would never see use again.

Maiden arrival of the *France* in New York
harbor in the early sixties. Right, fueling
at her pier as the *Queen Elizabeth*,
twenty years her senior, arrives upstream.
(*Compagnie Générale Transatlantique*)
(*Barney Stein*)

Left, on September 16, 1967, the *Queen Mary* sails from Southampton on her last westbound crossing to New York. A year later, the *Elizabeth,* below left, departs her home port too, bound for Florida and ultimate destruction. (*Cunard*)

Below, immortality of a sort: R.M S. *Queen Mary* at her permanent berth in Long Beach. Gutted, aluminized and impotent, the Cunarder has become the world's largest floating exhibit. (*William Batchelder*)

Following the second *Queen Elizabeth* auction in September of 1970, C. Y. Tung ordered the new name painted on her bow. (*Fort Lauderdale News*)

The morning after it began, fire rages on board the *Seawise University,* ex-*Queen Elizabeth*. Within hours, she lay on her starboard side. Salvage men all over the world refer to the ship only as "the Hong Kong job." (*Island Navigation Corporation, Ltd.*)

Almost every fitting or furnishing taken from the old Cunarder has turned a profit for the enterprising. Chips of her ancient paint, sandblasted off the superstructure as a fire hazard, have been sold mounted as cufflinks and tie pins; some carry a minute historical reminder in the form of a gray striation sandwiched between layers of peacetime white.

Every weekend, hundreds of tourists jam the ship as faithfully as they used to each sailing day, suntanned, gumchewing and curious. At eight-minute intervals, lifeboat number 23 creaks down the falls in an Abandon Ship drill. One can stroll throughout the vessel in air-conditioned comfort. The dining room is now a convention hall and Long Beach Rotarians have hung their plaque within. In the last remaining engine room, taped engine noises are broadcast perpetually and a visit there is climaxed by entrance into a plate-glass chamber welded onto the outside of the after shell plating. From this California appendage, the *Queen Mary*'s last remaining propeller can be seen rotating in futile slow motion.

The *Queen Elizabeth* was less lucky. First sold to Florida promoters as a hotel, she was tied up in Fort Lauderdale, looming over acres of unreal green and baking in the sun, the scarred old Cunarder looked ludicrously out of place. It turned out that she was; those who hoped she might emulate the *Mary*'s Long Beach potential reckoned with neither the vast sums necessary nor the political infighting that her arrival precipitated.

After two years of negligible activity, the ship went on the block for the second time and was purchased by C. Y. Tung, a millionaire shipowner from Hong Kong. Having bought the world's largest express liner, he decided to change its name to his: the R.M.S. *Queen Elizabeth* was rechristened *Seawise University*, an acronym suggested by Mr. Tung's first two initials. Even braver than buying the vessel was his decision to sail her to Hong Kong for conversion to a kind of cruising university. Two years of neglect on top of thirty years' hard service had wreaked havoc with the boilers. Prophetically, a water main had burst on B-deck during her Florida residency and the engine room, once the pride of Cunard engineers, had the look of an abandoned warehouse.

The ship sailed from Fort Lauderdale in February of 1971. Before the pilot was off the ship, one of her six boilers went out. Two days later, other boilers blew twenty miles off Haiti, leaving the thousand-foot liner adrift. She was taken in tow by a pair of tugs to Aruba, where Chinese technicians and spare parts were flown in from Hong Kong. It was reminiscent of the *Rex*'s three-day layover in Gibraltar in the thirties, only this time there were no testy passengers to placate.

The *Seawise University* lay off Aruba for two months. Adding to the

In February of 1950, the last four-stacker was de-commissioned. Left, the *Aquitania*'s double house flags are hauled down after thirty-five years of service. (*Southern Newspapers Ltd.*)

In all probability the last giant hull to be launched onto the Clyde, *Queen Elizabeth 2* enters the water, launched by Queen Elizabeth II. Her Majesty cut the launch cord with the same pair of gold scissors used by her grandmother and mother when christening the two previous *Queens*. (*Cunard*)

The *France* and *Queen Elizabeth 2*, below, tied up at
their respective home ports, Le Havre and Southampton. The *France* was laid up suddenly in the fall
of 1974 and the *QE2* remains in solitary splendor on
the Western Ocean run. (*Top: Compagnie Générale
Transatlantique, bottom: Cunard*)

ignominy of her arrival was the spectacle of gravity-activated latrines suspended over the side of the ship; an acute water shortage necessitated the embarrassing installation. It was another three months before the ship limped into Hong Kong.

By early 1972, after six million dollars worth of refitting, the *Seawise University* was ready to sail for Japan and dry-docking. With no stewards yet on board, the Company hired a local catering firm to assist with a farewell cocktail party for dock workers and their families. On the afternoon of January 9, a fire broke out in the kitchen and roared unchecked throughout the vessel. Two hundred workers and three hundred guests were evacuated and the great ex-Cunarder burned like a torch all through the night. Firemen augmented a pair of fireboats with land engines mounted on ferry boats but they were ineffective. The following morning, the gutted hulk rolled onto its starboard side, its nearest geographical feature named, appropriately, Junk Bay. It was exactly thirty years less a month since the *Normandie* had suffered a similar fate in New York Harbor.

So two of the most famous ships in the world are gone, ironically ending their days in the Pacific rather than the ocean that gave them their raison d'être. Steamship service to Europe will be severely curtailed. From Genoa comes the distressing news that by the mid seventies, all four of the Italian Line ships will have succumbed to the airplane. The thrifty and dependable Dutch will withdraw from the ferry service even sooner; by 1972, there will be no transatlantic service available on ships of the Holland-America Line except for those crossings made to and from drydocking in Rotterdam.

The New York Port Authority's plan to modernize the superpiers seems an idea whose time has not only come but gone as well. The great terminal of the Western Ocean mailboats has already lost its preeminence to Miami as America's major passenger-handling port. There seems no end to the demand for Caribbean cruise space, summer as well as winter, and embarking passengers from Florida makes economic sense. It takes a lot of valuable fuel to position the ships from New York to the tropics and back; moreover, impatient sunworshipers see no reason to endure thirty-six hours of discomfort en route to their cruise. It is not too remote a possibility that boat trains, long unheard of in the United States, may someday take passengers south to Florida.

What is left on the North Atlantic? Only one traditional giant, Cunard's *Queen Elizabeth 2*, still plies between Europe and America during the warm months. She and the Holland-America Lines' *Rotterdam* circle the globe every January, sensible winter employment for these Western Ocean dowagers. The *France*, laid up for half a dozen years at the *Quai de l'Oubli* in Le Havre, has been rescued from oblivion by the Florida-based Norwegian Caribbean Line. Refitted at vast expense in Bremerhaven's Hapag-Lloyd yard over the winter of 1980–1981, she made a second maiden voyage the following spring, calling at New York before disappearing south, presumably forever, to accommodate 2,000 passengers each week out of Miami. She towers over everything else at Miami's busy Dodge Island terminal and her vast interiors—brought lavishly up-to-date by New York designer Angelo Donghia—attract brisk bookings.

The renaissance of this beloved ship is something of a shipping miracle. With her demise, in 1974, the Compagnie Générale Transatlantique ended not only the life of a beautiful liner but, even more tragically, over a century of impeccable service between Le Havre and New York. That, regrettably, will never return, but the great Transat flagship, stunningly metamorphosed into the *Norway*, continues in service elsewhere.

Samuel Cunard started it all in 1840 with his immortal *Britannia* and it seems he will end it all as well: his company remains in sole contention on that ancient Western Ocean route. I only hope that this last great *Queen* sails forever. Shipboard isn't the same but familiar things remain. If the creaking woodwork has been replaced by the rattle of aluminum, those synthetic interiors smell precisely the same as they did half a century ago. There is still music in the main lounge at teatime, although there isn't a violin to be found on the *QE2*. Devoted and attentive service continues, as always, the key to a pleasant crossing.

On sailing days in high summer, there is the same quickening of the pulse as the whistle thunders overhead. Once clear of the port, the same brilliant sea light dances on the cabin ceiling; in midocean, there is a delightful insouciance, for both Europe and America are still happily two days away.

If you would like a rolled, uncreased version of the Ship Chart printed on the reverse of this book's dust-jacket, suitable for framing and inscribed and autographed by the author, please send an international money order to the value of US $10.00 to: John Maxtone-Graham, 117 West 78th Street, New York, New York 10024, USA.

Bibliography

ANDERSON, ROY, *White Star*, T. Stephenson & Sons Ltd., Prescot, Lancashire, 1964.

ANGAS, COMMANDER W. MACK, *Rivalry on the Atlantic, 1833–1939*, Lee Furman, New York, 1939.

APPLEYARD, ROLLO, *Charles Parsons: His Life and Work*, Constable & Co. Ltd., London, 1933.

ARMSTRONG, WARREN, *Atlantic Highway*, John Day Company, New York, 1962.

AYLMER, GERALD, *R.M.S. Mauretania; The Ship and Her Record*, P. Marshall & Co. Ltd., London, 1934.

BABCOCK, F. LAWRENCE, *Spanning the Atlantic*, Alfred A. Knopf, New York, 1931.

BAKER, GEORGE S., *Ship Form, Resistance and Screw Propulsion*, D. Van Nostrand Co., New York, 1915.

BARBANCE, MARTHE, *Histoire de la Compagnie Générale Transatlantique*, Arts et Métiers Graphiques, Paris, 1955.

BEAUDÉAN, RAOUL DE, *Captain of the Ile*, translated by Salvator Attanasio, McGraw-Hill Book Company, New York, 1960.

———, and ARMAND DE NIEUWENHOVE, *Un Diplomate en bleu marin*, R. Julliard, Paris, 1961.

BECK, STUART, *The Ship—How She Works*, Adlard Coles Ltd., Southampton, 1955.

BEESLEY, LAWRENCE, *The Loss of the S.S. Titanic*, Houghton Mifflin Co., Boston, 1912.

BEMELMANS, LUDWIG, *I Love You, I Love You, I Love You*, Viking Press, New York, 1942.

BENSTEAD, C. R., *Atlantic Ferry*, Methuen & Co. Ltd., London, 1936.

BISSET, SIR JAMES, *Commodore*, Criterion Books, New York, 1961.

———, *Ship Ahoy!!*, Charles Birchall Ltd., Liverpool, 1924.

BONSOR, N. P., *North Atlantic Seaway*, Prescot, Lancashire, 1955.

BOWEN, FRANK, *A Century of Atlantic Travel, 1830–1930*, Little, Brown and Company, Boston, 1930.

BRADY, EDWARD MICHAEL, *Marine Salvage Operations*, Cornell Maritime Press, New York, 1960.

BRAYNARD, FRANK O., *By Their Works Ye Shall Know Them*, Gibbs & Cox, New York, 1968.

———, *Lives of the Liners*, Cornell Maritime Press, New York, 1947.

————, *S.S. Savannah,* University of Georgia Press, Athens, 1963.

BRINNIN, JOHN MALCOLM, *The Sway of the Grand Saloon,* Delacorte Press, New York, 1971.

BROOK, RUPERT, *Letters from America,* Charles Scribner's Sons, New York, 1916.

CANGARDEL, HENRI, *De J.-B Colbert au Paquebot Normandie,* Nouvelles Editions Latines, Paris, 1957.

CECIL, LAMAR, *Albert Ballin,* Princeton University Press, Princeton, 1967.

CHADWICK, F. E. et al., *Ocean Steamships,* Charles Scribner's Sons, New York, 1891.

COEN, MARTIN J., *Ship Welding Handbook,* Cornell Maritime Press, New York, 1943.

COOPER, DUFF, *Old Men Forget,* Rupert Hart-Davis, London, 1953.

CORSI, EDWARD, *In the Shadow of Liberty,* Macmillan, New York, 1935.

CORSON, F. REID, *The Atlantic Ferry in the Twentieth Century,* S. Low, Marston & Co. Ltd., London, 1930.

CRONICAN, FRANK and EDWARD A. MUELLER, *The Stateliest Ship,* The Steamship Historical Society of America, New York, n.d.

DIGGLE, E. G., *The Romance of a Modern Liner,* S. Low, Marston & Co. Ltd., London, 1930.

DUGAN, JAMES, *The Great Iron Ship,* Harper & Brothers, New York, 1953.

DUNN, LAURENCE, *North Atlantic Liners 1899–1913,* H. Evelyn, London, 1961.

————, *Passenger Liners,* Adlard Coles, Southampton, 1961.

ELLSBERG, EDWARD, *The Far Shore,* Dodd, Mead, New York, 1960.

FLEMING, The Reverend John, *The Last Voyage of His Majesty's Hospital Ship Britannic,* n.d.

FLETCHER, R. A., *Travelling Palaces,* Sir Isaac Pitman and Sons, Ltd., London, 1913.

FLEXNER, J. T., *Steamboats Come True,* Viking Press, New York, 1944.

FORWOOD, WILLIAM B., *Reminiscences of a Liverpool Shipowner,* H. Young & Sons, Ltd., Liverpool, 1920.

GIBBS, C. R. VERNON, *Passenger Liners of the Western Ocean,* Staples Press Ltd., London, 1952.

GOLDING, HARRY, ed., *The Wonder Book of Ships,* Ward Locke & Co., London, 14th ed., n.d.

GRACIE, ARCHIBALD, *The Truth about the Titanic,* M. Kennerley, New York, 1913.

GRATTIDGE, HARVEY, *Captain of the Queens,* E. P. Dutton & Co., New York, 1956.

HARTLEY, HERBERT, *Home is the Sailor,* as told to Clint Bonner, Vulcan Press, Birmingham, 1955.

HAYES, SIR BERTRAM, *Hull Down,* E. P. Dutton & Co., New York, 1925.

HOEHLING, ADOLPH and MARY, *The Last Voyage of the Lusitania,* Henry Holt and Company, New York, 1956.

HOFF, RHODA, *America's Immigrants,* Henry Z. Walch, New York, 1967.

HOLMES, CAMPBELL, *Practical Shipbuilding,* Longman Green & Co., London, 1904.

HULDERMANN, BERNHARD, *Albert Ballin,* translated by W. J. Eggers, Cassell & Co., London, 1922.

HURD, SIR ARCHIBALD, *The Merchant Navy,* volumes I, II & III, John Murray, London, 1921–1929.

ISHERWOOD, J. H., *Steamers of the Past,* Sea Breezes, Liverpool, 1966.

JACKSON, GEORGE GIBBARD, *Steamships: Their History and Their Deeds,* "The Boy's Own Paper" office, London, n.d.

——, *The Story of the Liner,* The Sheldon Press, London, 1931.

JORDAN, HUMPHREY, *Mauretania,* Hodder & Stoughton, London, 1936.

KELLEY, J. D. JERROLD, *The Ship's Company,* Harper & Brothers Publishers, New York, 1897.

LaDAGE, JOHN H., *Modern Ships,* Cornell Maritime Press, New York, 1953.

LANIER, EDMOND, *Compagnie Générale Transatlantique,* Plon, Paris, 1962.

LAURIAT, CHARLES E., *The Lusitania's Last Voyage,* Houghton Mifflin Company, Boston and New York, 1915.

LAWRENCE, JACK, *When the Ships Came In,* Farrar & Rinehart Inc., New York, 1940.

LEDOUX, KATHERINE R., *Ocean Notes for Ladies,* G. P. Putnam's Sons, New York, 1877.

LEE, CHARLES E., *The Blue Riband,* S. Low, Marston & Co., Ltd., London, 1930.

LIGHTOLLER, CHARLES E., *Titanic and Other Ships,* I. Nicholson and Watson, Limited, London, 1935.

LOBLEY, DOUGLAS, ed., *The Cunarders 1840–1969,* Peter Barker Publishing Limited, London, 1969.

LORD, WALTER, *A Night to Remember,* Holt, Rinehart and Winston, New York, 1955.

MACDOUGAL, MICHAEL, *Gamblers Don't Gamble,* as told to J. C. Furnas, The Greystone Press, New York, 1939.

MAGINNIS, ARTHUR J., *The Atlantic Ferry,* Whittaker & Co., 1892.

MARCUS, GEOFFREY, *The Maiden Voyage,* George Allen and Unwin Ltd., London, 1969.

MASTERS, DAVID, *Epics of Salvage,* Cassell & Company Ltd., London, 1953.

McNEIL, SAMUEL, *In Great Waters,* Faber & Faber, Ltd., London, 1932.

MEIER, FRANK, *Fathoms Below,* E. P. Dutton & Co., New York, 1943.

MORRIS, JAMES, *The Great Port,* a Helen and Kurt Wolff Book, Harcourt, Brace & World, Inc., New York, 1969.

MOSCOW, ALVIN, *Collision Course,* G. P. Putnam's Sons, New York, 1959.

NEWELL, GORDON, *Ocean Liners of the 20th Century,* Superior Publishing Co., Seattle, 1963.

NIEZYCHOUSKI, ALFRED VON, *The Cruise of the Kronprinz Wilhelm,* Doubleday, Doran E. Company, Inc., Garden City, N.Y., 1929.

NOVOTNY, ANN, *Strangers at the Door,* Chatham Press, Riverside, 1971.

OLDHAM, WILTON J., *The Ismay Line,* Charles Birchall and Sons Ltd., Liverpool, 1961.

OWEN, H., *Ship Economics,* G. Phillip & Son, London, 1911.

PADFIELD, PETER, *An Agony of Collisions,* Hodder and Stoughton, London, 1966.

——, *The Titanic and the Californian,* Hodder and Stoughton, London, 1965.

POTTER, NEIL and JACK FROST, *The Elizabeth,* George G. Harrap & Co. Ltd., London 1965.

——, *The Mary,* George G. Harrap & Co. Ltd., London, 1961.

——, *Queen Elizabeth 2,* George G. Harrap & Co. Ltd., London, 1969.

RIMINGTON, CRITCHELL, *The Bon Voyage Book,* John Day Company, New York, 1931.

ROSSELL, HENRY E. and LAWRENCE B. CHAPMAN, eds., *Principles of Naval Architecture,* The Society of Naval Architects and Marine Engineers, New York, 1941.

SASSOON, SIEGFRIED, *Siegfried's Journey,* Viking Press, New York, 1946.

SIMPSON, GEORGE, *The Naval Constructor,* D. Van Nostrand Co., New York, 1914.

SPEDDING, CHARLES T., *Reminiscences of Transatlantic Travelers,* J. B. Lippincott Co., Philadelphia, 1926.

SPRATT, H. P., *Outline History of Transatlantic Steam Navigation,* The Science Museum, London, 1950.

——, *The Merchant Steamers and Motor Ships,* The Science Museum, London, 1950.

SPURGEON, SIR ARTHUR, *The Burning of the Volturno,* Cassell & Company Ltd., London, 1913.

STANFORD, DON, *Ile de France,* Appleton-Century-Crofts, Inc., New York, 1960.

STEVENS, LEONARD A., *The Elizabeth: Passage of a Queen,* Alfred A. Knopf, New York, 1968.

STEVENSON, ROBERT LOUIS, *The Amateur Emigrant,* Charles Scribner's Sons, New York, 1911.

STREET, JULIAN, *Ship-Bored,* Dodd Mead & Co., New York, 1924.

TALBOT, FREDERICK A., *Steamship Conquest of the World,* J. B. Lippincott, Philadelphia, 1912.

TAYLOR, DAVID B., *Steam Conquers the Atlantic,* Appleton-Century Company, New York and London, 1939.

THAYER, JOHN B., *The Sinking of the S.S. Titanic April 14th–15th, 1912,* Philadelphia, 1940.

THOMPSON, FRANK E., *Diving, Cutting and Welding in Underwater Salvage Operations,* Cornell Maritime Press, New York, 1944.

THOREUX, PIERRE, *J'ai commandé Normandie,* Presses de la Cité, Paris, 1957.

TURC, C., *Le navire pour passagers,* E. Bernard & Cie., Paris, 1903.

TUTE, WARREN, *Atlantic Conquest,* Little, Brown and Company, Boston, 1962.

VILLIERS, ALAN, *The Western Ocean,* Museum Press, London, 1957.

WHEELER, GEORGE JAMES, *Ship Salvage,* E. W. Sweetman, New York, 1958.

WHITE, E. B., *Here Is New York,* Harper & Brothers, New York, 1949.

WILSON, R. M., *The Big Ships,* Cassell & Company Ltd., London, 1956.

WILSON, V. S. FELLOWES, *The Largest Ships in the World,* Crosby Lockwood & Son, London, 1926.

WOON, BASIL, *The Frantic Atlantic,* Alfred Knopf, New York, 1927.

YOUNG, FILSON, *Titanic,* G. Richards, London, 1912.

Index

Figures in italic indicate illustrations.

429